GEORGIAN
LINCOLN

Detail from the South-west prospect of the City of Lincoln by
Samuel and Nathaniel Buck, 1743

GEORGIAN
LINCOLN

BY

SIR FRANCIS HILL

C.B.E., LL.M., LITT.D., F.S.A.

CAMBRIDGE

AT THE UNIVERSITY PRESS

1966

PUBLISHED BY
THE SYNDICS OF THE CAMBRIDGE UNIVERSITY PRESS

Bentley House, 200 Euston Road, London, N.W. 1
American Branch: 32 East 57th Street, New York, N.Y. 10022
West African Office: P.M.B. 5181, Ibadan, Nigeria

©

CAMBRIDGE UNIVERSITY PRESS
1966

Printed in Great Britain at the University Printing House, Cambridge
(Brooke Crutchley, University Printer)

LIBRARY OF CONGRESS CATALOGUE
CARD NUMBER: 65–18925

CONTENTS

LIST OF ILLUSTRATIONS

PLATES

FIGURES

MAPS

TO THE
LINCOLN CIVIC TRUST

PREFACE

I T is pleasant to turn, in this third instalment of my history of Lincoln, from a community in decay to the growing community of the eighteenth and early nineteenth centuries. Though other work continues to make my progress slow and spasmodic, I still hope to go on to the study of the Victorian period, and so to complete the task to which I set myself some forty years ago.

In this period, as in the previous one, the principal thread has been provided by the minutes of the common council of the city, but as the common council declines, the record becomes more formal and less valuable. Many decisions, no doubt, were left to the mayor and his brethren the aldermen, or were taken informally. Some such decisions, missing from the minutes, have left their mark in the mayors' and chamberlains' rolls, which cover most of the years of the eighteenth century, though the rolls for some years are lost. There are various supplementary volumes in the city archives, details of which are contained in Dr de Grey Birch's *Catalogue*, published in 1906. These records are now in the Lincolnshire Archives Office. I have not generally included references to these sources in the footnotes as they would have been too numerous. Students will readily identify the evidence taken from them.

The records of the Bishop of Lincoln and the Dean and Chapter are also in the custody of the County Archivist. The city parishes have their registers, and some have vestry minutes and accounts; some parishes have placed their records in the Archives Office, and some still keep them in the vestry. Enough of such evidence has survived to illustrate the working of the parish as a unit of civil administration. It was only in writing this book that I came fully to realise that in the emergence of the civil parish is to be found one of the secrets of the decline of the common council. The parish registers and the bishops' transcripts have provided the statistics of baptisms, marriages and burials. All that now remain of the minutes of the Lincoln House of Industry are in the Archives Office.

For the history of the city parliamentary elections the richest single source is the Monson papers, some at South Carlton and some in the Archives Office. I am grateful to Lord Monson, as I was to his father and grandfather, for giving me easy access to them. Among other collections in the Archives Office which have been of value are those of the families of Ancaster, Whichcote, Massingberd and Massingberd Mundy, Tyrwhitt Drake, and some of Sibthorp. The Lincoln County Hospital papers are also there.

At the Lincoln City Library are the records of Lincoln Christ's Hospital, Lincoln School and the Subscription Library, and a few more Sibthorp papers; but the letters used in Canon Maddison's *The Sibthorp Family*, privately printed in 1896, have not been found. The minutes of the Witham General Commissioners at the Lincolnshire Rivers Board Office, the Lincoln Court of Sewers at the Upper Witham Internal Drainage Board Office, Lincoln West Drainage at the Archives Office, the Aire and Calder Navigation and other canal papers at the British Transport Commission Record Office, have all been used. Mr J. Ellis Flack, formerly Nottingham University Librarian, searched the Hatfield Chase papers in the University Library for me; in the quest for the Ellison family origins the Town Clerk of York, the Borough Librarian of Doncaster and Mr J. E. Day gave help; the Ellison Fossdyke papers are part of the Burton Scorers deposit at the Archives Office; Mr L. A. Baker of the National Provincial Bank produced the Smith Ellison letters, and Mr J. E. Wadsworth of the Midland Bank and Mr D. Robson of the Westminster Bank helped, the former with the beginnings of the Lincoln and Lindsey Bank, and the latter on the Ellison banking connections.

The Earl of Scarbrough kindly allowed me to use his papers at Sandbeck, and Mrs Tennyson d'Eyncourt lent me the Bayons Manor papers, which I read at leisure before she placed them in the Archives Office. The Delaval papers then in the Newcastle Public Library, the Vyner papers in the Leeds Public Library, and various navigation papers in the Sheffield Public Library, have all yielded something of value. The Spalding Gentlemen's Society has a rich and varied collection, including the Banks Stanhope papers, and the Society's officers made it easy for me to consult them.

Mrs Dorothy Owen brought to my notice the diary of Bishop Wake which has lately come into the Lambeth Palace Library. Dr Richard Hunt told me of the letters of Sir Charles Anderson among the papers of Bishop Samuel Wilberforce in the Bodleian Library, and he not only introduced me to the Dashwood Collection there, but obtained permission of Sir John Dashwood Bart. to deposit the Lincolnshire part of the collection in Lincoln for my use. The Gainsborough Bridge records are at the Lindsey County Offices, and the Dunham Bridge records at the offices of Messrs Danby Eptons and Griffith of Lincoln.

Lieutenant-Colonel Sir Benjamin Bromhead Bart. kindly allowed me to visit Thurlby Hall constantly a few years ago to study the bound volumes (some 81 in number) of family letters, notably those addressed to his collateral ancestor Sir Edward French Bromhead, which include a long series from the redoubtable Dr Charlesworth. These proved to be a rich source of evidence for the early years of the nineteenth century. Unfortunately the collection of printed works made by Sir Edward Bromhead has been dispersed by an intermediate generation. Some of his bound volumes of tracts passed into the collection of the late Captain Cragg of Threekingham, part of whose collection has now been bought by the Lincolnshire Archives Committee, other parts unfortunately having been dispersed. Dr Charlesworth had himself made a local collection, but no trace of it has been found.

The known collections of Sir Joseph Banks's papers still in this country, and chief among them the Dawson Turner transcripts at the British Museum (Natural History), have been calendared by Mr Warren Dawson in his monumental volume *The Banks Letters*, published by the Museum in 1958. With great generosity Mr Dawson lent me his own Banks papers, and sent me copies of passages likely to be of use to me from letters at the British Museum, the Royal Society and the National Library of Wales. Miss Mander Jones of the Mitchell Library in Sydney sent photographs of some Banks papers there, and Mr H. B. Carter of Edinburgh and the late Mr A. C. Townsend of the Natural History Museum introduced me to the riches of the Sutro Library now in the University of San Francisco. Mr Townsend kindly lent me a large number of photographs of papers in this collection; and the Sutro Librarian, Mr Richard H. Dillon, to whom I was introduced by Dr A. L. Rowse and Mr Huntington Holliday, sent microfilms of more. Mr H. B. Carter sent me proofs of his book *His Majesty's Spanish Flock* (1964), which I was able to use at a late stage. Other Banks letters, calendared by Mr Dawson, are in the Lindsey and Holland County Library, the Spalding Gentlemen's Society Library, and my own collection. According to Hamer, *Guide to Archives and MSS in the United States*, there are 10,000 pieces of Banks in the Sutro Library, 3,500 at Yale, and 140 in the University of Wisconsin; and though many of them relate to subjects other than Lincolnshire, there must surely be many as yet unused that do relate to it.

The letters of Mary Yorke were first brought to my notice by the late Mr E. A. B. Barnard, who wrote a series of articles on them in the *Tewkesbury Register*, the Lincoln section beginning on 10 May 1952. The originals are now in the Bedford Record Office, and by the kindness of the Bedford County Archivist, Miss Joyce Godber, I have been supplied with photocopies of the relevant letters.

At a late stage I learnt of the Massingberd Mundy papers given to the Society of Genealogists, and had the opportunity of making a hurried search of them. The Society had not then had time to complete a calendar of the papers. Some of the letters were used by Canon Maddison in the *Associated Architectural Societies Reports and Papers*, XXIII (1896), at p. 296.

To the owners and keepers of all the collections referred to I wish to express my warm thanks for all they have done to help me.

The unpublished collections of the Lincolnshire historians whom I have mentioned in my earlier prefaces have continued to benefit their successor. The first is that of Thomas Sympson, in the Bodleian Library: he died in 1750. The Willson Collection has been the richest for this period. The collection was advertised for sale in 1879; it was repeatedly offered to the Cambridge University Library, as Mr A. E. B. Owen of that Library has informed me, before it was acquired by the Society of Antiquaries, to whom it now belongs. The Society kindly deposited it in Lincoln for my use some years ago. The collections of John Ross, now in the Lincoln City Library, have continued to be of use; they are now supplemented by the Ross Correspondence, in my possession. I bought the letter books from a bookseller in Rye, who could throw no light on their provenance. There deserves to be mentioned in the same category a book of family reminiscences and journal, based on recollections and old diaries, compiled by Sir Charles Henry John Anderson, last baronet of Lea, which unfortunately ends at 1844. This and other of Anderson's remains are much used in this book.

The Lincoln City Library has a large collection of books, pamphlets and broadsheets relating to the city and county, and also a series of volumes of the *Lincoln Rutland and Stamford Mercury*, almost complete from 1793.

It is impossible for a busy amateur to keep up with the results of historical research; and when even expert local historians prudently specialise it is obviously dangerous for an amateur to try to write the history of a city, in some aspects of which he must necessarily be less at home than in others. But to follow the fashion would be to abandon my purpose, and I would rather attempt it and fail than not attempt it at all. For the most part I have tried to limit my liabilities by avoiding generalisations for which I have neither the knowledge nor the inclination.

I am fortunate, however, in friends who have guided me in their special fields. The late Sir Lewis Namier sent me copies of his biographies of members of parliament, gave me advice, and approved an early draft of chapter IV. Professor J. D. Chambers of Nottingham University was a most stimulating critic of chapters V–VIII, and helped me to avoid many pitfalls. Mr E. Maxwell Howard, the Director of the Lincolnshire Agricultural Society, has out of his great practical knowledge answered questions about crops and livestock and corrected mistakes. For those that remain I am of course solely responsible.

My greatest debt is owing to the County Archivist, Mrs Joan Varley. She has been untiring in tracking down evidence and giving helpful advice.

Not only Mrs Varley, but her former colleagues Mrs Dorothy Owen and Dr Mary Finch, and her present colleagues Mr Michael Lloyd and Mrs Pamela Nightingale, have all read my typescript, and have supplied references in instances where I read through collections of papers before they were catalogued.

It would be wrong not to refer to the Lincolnshire Archives Committee —and their constituent authorities the administrative counties of Lindsey, Kesteven and Holland and the city of Lincoln—under whose auspices a splendid collection of records relating to the history of the county and diocese has been built up, making available to students material on a scale which has never been possible before. Under the leadership of Her Majesty's Lieutenant, the Earl of Ancaster, much has been done in a relatively short time, and the long disused county gaol at Lincoln Castle put at last to a worthy use.

At the Lincoln City Library I have always been able to turn to Mr F. T. Baker, who fills so many roles in Lincoln, all of them generously and well. To all the members of his staff, and especially to Miss Elfrida Jahn and Mr Laurence Elvin, whom I have plagued so often, I am grateful for their friendly patience and help.

Thanks are due also to Canon Jones, the Rev. E. R. Milton and Canon Riches for providing access to parish records still in their vestries. Mr and Mrs Burden compiled for me the population statistics from the registers, and Mr Alan Lyons helped in their presentation. Many years ago I began to search the State Papers Domestic at the Public Record Office, a task which Miss Flower has completed for me. My secretary Miss W. O. Hunt has been the indispensable auxiliary throughout, and has cheerfully borne a heavy burden of work.

To the Syndics and officers of the Cambridge University Press and their adviser I am grateful for friendly guidance and help.

It had been my intention to associate with the dedication of this book the name of Arthur Malcolm Cook, sometime subdean of Lincoln and first chairman of the Lincoln Civic Trust. It is now too late. He was a great figure in the city and county and diocese: incisive in mind, crisp in speech, prompt in action, utterly honest with himself as with others, modest and kind in heart; a preserver of the past for the sake of the future; at an advanced age still eagerly looking forward; a good citizen indeed. His memory and influence grow as time passes by.

J. W. F. HILL

Lincoln

Easter 1965

ACKNOWLEDGEMENTS

The author's thanks are due to the following for permission to reproduce illustrations: the Trustees of the British Museum for Plates 3, 4(a) and (b), 5(a) and (b), 6(a) and (b), 7(a); the Mayor, Aldermen and Citizens of Lincoln for Plates 2, 7(b), 8, 9, 10(a) and (b), 11(a) and (b); Lord Monson for Plate 16; the Dean of Lincoln for Plate 17; the Hon. Mrs Dudley Pelham for Plates 18, 19; and the Trustees of the National Portrait Gallery for Plate 20; and to the Lincoln City Libraries Museum and Art Gallery for photographs.

LIST OF ABBREVIATIONS

A.A.S.R.	*Reports and Papers of the Associated Architectural Societies*
Adversaria	'Collections for an history of the city of Lincoln. Indigesta Moles. March 1737'. Bodleian Library, MS Gough, Lincoln 1
Banks Corr.	Dawson Turner transcripts of Sir Joseph Banks's Correspondence in the British Museum (Natural History)
B.M.	British Museum
Bromhead MSS	Correspondence in the possession of Lieutenant-Colonel Sir Benjamin Bromhead, Bart., Thurlby Hall, Lincoln
C.J.	*Commons Journal*
D.N.B.	*Dictionary of National Biography*
E.H.R.	*English Historical Review*
Hill, Banks	Papers of the Banks family of Revesby in the possession of J. W. F. Hill
H.M.C.	*Historical Manuscripts Commission Reports*
L.A.O.	Lincolnshire Archives Office
L.A.S.R.	*Lincolnshire Architectural Society Reports*
L.D.B.	*Lincoln Date Book*
Lincs. N. & Q.	*Lincolnshire Notes and Queries*
Lindsey C.L.	Lindsey and Holland County Library
L.J.	*Lords Journals*
L.P.L.	Lincoln Public Library
L.R.S.	Publications of Lincoln Record Society
L.R. & S.M.	*Lincoln Rutland and Stamford Mercury*
M.L.	*Medieval Lincoln*, by J. W. F. Hill
Monson	Papers in possession of Lord Monson
P.R.O.	Public Record Office
Ross Corr.	Correspondence of John Ross in the possession of J. W. F. Hill
Sutro Coll.	Banks MSS in Sutro Library, University of San Francisco
T. & S.L.	*Tudor and Stuart Lincoln*, by J. W. F. Hill
V.C.H.	*Victoria County History*
Wilberforce MSS	Papers of Bishop Samuel Wilberforce in Bodleian Library
Willson	E. J. Willson Collection in the Library of the Society of Antiquaries

CHAPTER I

COUNTY CAPITAL

THE first known attempt at a picture of the city of Lincoln seems to have been that of the engraver Samuel Buck about 1725, when he was at the beginning of his career; being a Lincolnshire man, he began near home. In 1743, out of a greater experience, he and his brother Nathaniel produced their better known view of Lincoln from the south-west. It shows the Minster and the castle on the hilltop, a cluster of houses about them and on the hillside, a long ribbon of houses punctuated by church towers across the valley, and Brayford pool to the west of it.[1] The hill comes as a surprise to those who think of Lincolnshire as a duckpool, and indeed the explanation of it is not obvious from a glance at a map of England. A long limestone ridge running north and south is interrupted by a gap through which the river Witham, after flowing north along the western side of the ridge, passes on its way south-eastwards to the Wash. The old walled city stood on and below the crest of the hill on the north side of the gap. The hilltop is about 200 feet above the valley, and in its steepest part the hill has a gradient of 1 in 4.

When Horace Walpole approached the city from the south he looked across the valley to the cathedral, noting how high it stood; and he noted also the rich vale, watered as he thought by the branches of the river, and the Swanpool to the west. The limestone ridge, which falls away sharply to the west, he described as a natural and regular terrace commanding for some miles a rich and beautiful view.[2] The view from the west was described by Robert Southey, who had crossed the river Trent by Dunham ferry:

The nearer we approached the more dreary was the country—it was one wide fen—but the more beautiful the city, and the more majestic the

[1] See Plate 1. 'Nathaniel and Samuel Buck were really meritorious artists; and we must be grateful to them for many memorials of fine buildings that would otherwise have been totally lost. The earlier drawings were rude and wretchedly deficient in accuracy of detail. They began in Lincolnshire, their native county, and so we have the poorest specimens of their works. Their latter works, of 1740 and after that time, were very superior in skill and accuracy to the former ones. I want to pick up a large print of the Bucks, dated, I think, in 1724....It is a coarse engraving...' (E. J. Willson to John Ross, 21 June 1849. Ross, Corr. 1). There is a copy of the large print in the Usher Art Gallery, Lincoln. Samuel Buck was working in Lincoln with his 'valuable friend Dr Stukeley' in July 1725 (Bodl. Gough Maps 16, f.18, ex. inf. Miss Molly Barratt). The views of particular buildings in the county by Samuel were mostly published in 1726. Charles Dibdin said that Buck, 'a learned antiquarian', was a native of Lincolnshire (*Observations on a Tour* (1801), I, 378).

[2] *Journals of Visits to Country Seats* (Walpole Society XVI), 71.

cathedral: Never was an edifice more happily placed; it overtops a city built on the acclivity of a steep hill—its houses intermingled with gardens and orchards. To see it in full perfection, it should be in the red sunshine of an autumnal evening, when the red roofs and red brick houses would harmonise with the sky and with the fading foliage.[1]

But Southey was a poet; other witnesses said more of the general air of dilapidation and decay which the city wore.[2] It had been decaying for a very long time, and having changed hands several times during the Civil War, had suffered much damage to houses and churches. Its powers of recovery were small, and it was to be several generations before the damage was made good.

Daniel Defoe, an experienced journalist who seldom fails the local historian of his period, was chiefly interested in social and economic conditions, and he gave a brisk and scathing account of the city: only the cathedral moved him. He thought it a very noble structure, its situation being more to advantage than that of any other cathedral in England. He noticed that the steepest part of the ascent of the hill was the best part of the city for trade and business, although the street between the upper and lower town was so steep and strait that coaches and horses were obliged to fetch a compass another way, as well on one hand as on the other. The only part of Lincoln he thought it tolerable to call a city was the part between the castle and the cathedral; here he found some very good buildings and a great deal of very good company, several families of gentlemen having houses there, besides those of the cathedral clergy.[3]

The importance of the hill in the history of the city can hardly be exaggerated. It is Lincoln's principal physical feature. It had been scaled boldly by the Romans, whose Ermine Street became the north–south axis first of their *colonia* on the crest of the hill, then of a southward Roman extension of the walled area, enclosing the hillside, and later of the suburb of Wigford across the valley; it is known in part as the High Street and in part by the modern names of the Strait, Steep Hill and Bailgate.[4] The hill has generally been regarded as impracticable for wheeled traffic, and after Colonel Sibthorp had driven down it in a four-in-hand for a wager, the

---

[1] *Letters from England*, ed. J. Simmons (1951), pp. 266–7. His visit was in the period 1803–7.

[2] See Abraham de la Pryme's *Diary* (Surtees Society, 1869), pp. 19, 87; Lord Harley's comments in *H.M.C. Portland*, vi, 86; and for other references, *T. & S.L.* p. 201.

[3] *Tour through England and Wales* (Everyman edn), ii, 91–4. See below, p. 138. The *Tour* was first published in 1724–6, but the material for it was no doubt gathered over a lengthy period. Defoe was in Lincoln as a government agent in 1712 (*H.M.C. Portland*, v, 224).

[4] Some of the street names ending in *gate*, in spite of their deceptive air, were invented in the nineteenth century (see *M.L.* p. 33).

city council placed a rail across it to prevent similar pranks in the future. As Defoe noticed, roads slightly less steep made detours to the east and west, both within the walls, of which the western one, the present Michael-gate (also a modern name) and Hungate, was known as the old coach road, because up it were dragged the coaches, with all hands pushing behind. It was difficult to maintain a surface on such a gradient: the middle of the coach road was from time to time worn almost into a ditch by the washing of heavy rains, and the parish had then to fill it with a few loads of stones. They were soon washed away.[1] To the east of the town wall an oblique road—shown by Buck—ran north-eastwards from the lower city and entered one of the gateways of the cathedral close at a sharp angle. The road in parts was so steep that many accidents happened to heavy loads passing along it.[2] The obstacle of the hill meant that visitors from the north put up their horses and carriages in the upper city and those from the south in the lower city, and so there were many inns both above and below the hill.

Defoe had noticed the social distinction; with it the hill also marked an administrative one. At the Norman Conquest the upper Roman enclosure had been annexed to the castle, which stands in its south-west quarter, as an outer bailey: it was and is still called the Bail. With the castle it became parcel of the duchy of Lancaster, whose steward held a great court leet and court baron in the shire hall of the castle, and received castle guard rents from houses in the Bail, and tolls from the fish and vegetable markets on Castle Hill. The castle was the centre of the county administration: the judges held assize and the sheriff his court in the shire hall there, and there also was the county gaol. On the east side of the Bail, and partly carved out of it, is the cathedral close, walled in the fourteenth century, once owned and governed by the dean and chapter. Until 1835 the Bail and Close were part of the county at large and not of the city, and together they formed a petty sessional division of the parts of Lindsey.[3] They were surrounded by lands which were part of the municipal borough, but the phrase 'abovehill' was normally used especially to describe these areas which were the headquarters of diocese and county. Here, within mouldering Roman defences and medieval walls and gateways[4] lived a

---

[1] Willson, v, 41.

[2] *Ibid.* v, 56. In Thomas Sympson's time (*c.* 1737) there lay on the brow of the hill several huge pieces of rock and part of the foundations of the Close wall, cemented together as hard and solid as the rock itself, and said to have been thrown down by an earthquake ('Adversaria', p. 272). For later improvements to the road, see below, p. 146.

[3] See *M.L.* chapters v and vi.

[4] Much of the Roman wall was standing in the early nineteenth century: Stukeley had shown the northern half of the Bail with wall and ditch, making his plan by pacing as he

tiny society of clergy and gentry of whom much must be said later. As the century went on there grew up a social adjunct to the Close in the parish of St Peter in Eastgate. North of the Bail was the suburb of Newport, a remote and neglected part of the city where there lived labourers in the city fields, and south of it, on the top of Steep Hill, was the poor parish of St Michael. A later writer, having excepted the central part of the upper city, said that the rest consisted of a number of ugly inconvenient narrow streets, or rather lanes, formed by houses mean and disgusting in the extreme, and he added that the abode of poverty and wretchedness in and about Fishmarket Hill (in St Michael's parish) could only be considered as a disgrace to the city, and called loudly for removal.[1] So closely did the gentry and the poorest class jostle each other.

The first moves towards improvement of a worn-out and war-damaged medieval city were taken in the abovehill area as the gentry and clergy slowly recovered from the war. In 1688 an attempt (not, perhaps, successful) was set on foot to build a new shire house in the castle.[2] St Mary Magdalene's church was rebuilt by the parishioners in 1695, and the chancel of St Paul's in 1700. New houses—the red brick and tile that Southey saw—followed. Part of the ruins of the bishop's palace was leased in 1727 with a view to its being made habitable, occupation being reserved to the bishop during visitations.[3] In 1736 John Disney, of a puritan family of gentry, was buying land in Eastgate, just beyond the Close, and clearing part of an old inn, the White Bull.[4] He employed Abraham Hayward, a Lincoln builder, to build him a house there: and Disney Place still stands, its back to the road. Sir Cecil Wray, the eleventh baronet of Glentworth, built Eastgate Court across the Roman foss; it was drawn by Buck in his sketch book.[5] The Archdeaconry house (now become flats) was built by the Reynolds family soon after 1764. Other houses were being repaired and improved, and in 1734 the dean and chapter allowed their tenant at the White Hart to take down part of the Close wall for improvements.[6] It was noted in 1764 that there were many good houses in the modern taste in Lincoln towards the top, though the buildings were generally old.[7]

walked about the city (see Plate 12). The plan is inaccurate in some details, but gives a good general impression. The Close wall was maintained and its gates closed at night until the making of the turnpike road through the Close under an Act of 1756 (see below, p. 123).

[1] *Lincoln and Lincolnshire Cabinet* (1827), p. 5.

[2] *Cal. Treasury Books*, VIII (1685–9), p. 2006.

[3] L.A.O. Bishop's Possns, leases, 55.

[4] L.A.O. Chapter Acts 1731–61, f.29r; *Archivists' Report*, 10, p. 21.

[5] In the Bodleian Library: Gough MS Linc. 15. Deeds of part of the site now in L.A.O., Misc. Dep. 110.

[6] Chapter Acts 1731–61, f.21r.   [7] *England Illustrated*, I, 404.

The gentry came and went; they were often in their manor houses, and the richer or more fashionable of them in London for the season; and the cathedral dignitaries resided only by turns, moving on to their other preferments. There were a few doctors and lawyers, and persons of independent means, and one or two private schools. In the periods between the excitements of assizes, quarter sessions, visitations, races, elections and musters, life was slow and dull. Apart from bringing up their families and attending to domestic affairs, the ladies could only look backward to the last ball or rout or forward to the next one, and gossip in their small circle about neighbours or visitors, and about births, marriages and deaths, especially in their financial effects. The fortunate habit of the Banks family at Revesby of keeping their letters has preserved a few glimpses of this society. Mrs Chaplin of Blankney wrote to Mrs Banks that she knew Miss Hales wrote so often that there was no need to tell any Lincoln news, though there was subject enough to employ many pens; and she went on:

poor Lady Delorain has suffered much, and daily suffers more. They pull her to peices, and I think have been exceeding rude to her, but I hope she has spirit enough not to regard 'em, and those that marry into the town of Lincoln had nead have a large share to be able to stand the shock.

Miss Hales lived up to her reputation. She wrote that she had a thousand things to tell about the Deloraines when they met; and she had some news of an impending marriage which she was only willing to trade in exchange for news about whom Mrs Banks's father was hoping to marry:

Miss Ball had discarded Mr Beck, Miss Molly Cunington has for sertain refused my cousin Nevill. I am quite angry at our Ladys over rateing themselves. It spoils the market for the rest.

And again:

Mr Jo. Banks I hear has made his proposeall to Miss Cassia. Lady Wray tells it so, they will be in town in a fortnight. Ten thousand down he desires, and twenty more at his death, which I think will just fetch him. We do nothing but marry and stuf ourselves with the turkey diet.[1]

It is satisfactory to add that Miss Hales at last was married herself, though outside her own social circle: she wed a London grocer, said to have been the natural son of Sir Cecil Wray.

Mrs Massingberd, who wrote a little later, was not such a rattle. She wrote of the kindness of Lady Dunmore, who was described as 'very high and stately in her carriage'. Lord Dunmore had been convicted of high treason in the jacobite rising of 1745, but pardoned and confined to the

[1] 6–7 May 1733, 19 Jan. 1736, *Banks Family Letters*, ed. J. W. F. Hill (L.R.S.), pp. 147, 148, 176.

city for life.[1] He had ensured that his heir was brought up in loyalty
to the reigning royal family, and to this end had sent him to the new
university in Hanover. Mrs Massingberd said of an impending festivity
that the duke of Ancaster for some disgust did not promote it, but

Lady Monson will doubtless shine away and the Familys of Whichcott and
Maddison be in high felicity whatever others are, indeed I don't lament being
absent, for as I don't partake in any diversions, 'tis duller than other times.[2]

On 13 January 1753 she mentioned that the town had been quite full of
gentlemen on account of the drainage from Lincoln to Boston, and the
previous week there had been a great cocking between Lord Monson and
Lord Vere Bertie. She added an account of the visit of the young Lord
Scarbrough and his bride to Lincoln on the way to his house at Glentworth.
The wedding party were met near Lincoln by the mayor and aldermen.
Scarbrough and his brother-in-law Sir George Savile alighted from the
first coach and mounted their horses, which like themselves were adorned
with gold and silver. Attended by Mr Chaplin, his friends and the mob,
they proceeded slowly through the town, the bride in an open landau, and
others in coaches and post chaises. They went without stopping to Glentworth, but later visited the below town assembly, where they were met by
the families of Lord Vere Bertie, Lord George Manners, Sir Francis Dashwood and others, including many of the Lincoln ladies that had the convenience of coaches. Thereafter they kept open house at Glentworth in the
most magnificent manner. Miss Whichcot described the entertainment
there: two courses and dessert at dinner, the raspberries and cream being full
of ice—no great rarity in January—with sweetmeats in brandy. They danced
until supper, the second course of which was served on gilt plate, a present
from the Prince of Wales and bearing his arms.[3] Everything was as elegant
as French cooks and confectioners from London could make it, the attendants
being numerous and dressed in laced clothes and white silk stockings.[4]

Here was food for gossip for a long time. Mrs Massingberd had commented earlier that the Lincoln races did not answer her expectations.
There was not half as much company as she had seen at Nottingham, but
she remembered that she was growing older:

[1] He was probably tried at Lincoln; the trials of rebels were held there and at Carlisle
and York (*H.M.C. Carlisle*, p. 202).
[2] Mrs Maddison was the mother of the new Lady Monson and the sister of Thomas
Whichcot, the member for the county. She lived in Lincoln.
[3] Scarbrough's father, the third earl, who died in 1752, had been treasurer to
Frederick, Prince of Wales, 1738–51.
[4] 'Massingberd Family Letters' in *A.A.S.R.* xxiii (1896), 300, 303, 311; L.A.O.
Anderson, 5/1/20. During the latter part of her life Mrs Massingberd lived at the
Cantilupe Chantry in Minster Yard, where she died in 1762.

I confess I was only indifferent to the entertainments, and went with the crowd to ill-acted plays, a foolish medley and a dusty assembly with great tranquillity of spirit, and passed through the whole round of fatigue with as little delight or disgust as anyone in the company.[1]

It was a small society. The qualification for membership could hardly have been defined, but its members could be listed without much difficulty.[2] Even within this small society there were gradations of rank, and the most select circle was reserved for the nobility and some of the more fashionable families who had a place in London society and who brought London manners back into the country; between them and the rustic gentry who never aspired beyond the high sheriff's ball there was a great gulf fixed. A dean's wife might seek to enter the smaller circle; if she were the daughter of a bishop and the daughter-in-law of a lord chancellor there could be no doubt of her acceptance. Mary Yorke was the only daughter and heir of Dr Isaac Maddox, bishop of Worcester, and brought a great fortune to her husband James Yorke, the youngest son of Lord Hardwicke.[3] They regularly travelled between Lincoln, the dean's living at Reading, and her estate at Forthampton in Gloucestershire; and they had the entry to the highest whig circles. She was a good letter writer, and happily many of her letters have survived. With her knowledge of a wider world she was able to see the abovehill society in Lincoln from the outside as well as from within. She remarked that she was so used to travelling that her clothes and things almost jumped into their proper places; exile she accepted with good humour, but writing from Lincoln she did once confess that she would be glad when her husband's residence was out and she was once again within tolerable reach of her friends.

[1] L.A.O. Massingberd, 13/32.

[2] The list of subscribers to *Poems on Several Occasions* by the Rev. John Langhorne, vicar of Hackthorn (1760), would be a good starting point. The most exclusive circle is given in Mrs Hobart's list of guests at a masquerade at Nocton in 1767 (Sir Charles Anderson, *Lincoln Pocket Guide* (1892 edn), p. 54).

[3] Lord Hardwicke wrote to the duke of Newcastle on 17 June 1762: 'I am going to marry my youngest son, the Dean; and perhaps you may be a little surprized when I tell you to whom. It is to Bishop Maddox's daughter and only child. Her mother is a very worthy lady, and the daughter a very deserving girl; and tho she has no money portion, is a great fortune. She has a real estate of £1500 per annum, £1200 per annum in Gloucestershire, which the Bishop purchased of the Dowdeswell family, and a fee simple house in Arlington Street of £300 per annum. All this is settled to my satisfaction, and I hope in God it will succeed well, and think it may be completed in a very short time' (P. C. Yorke, *Life and Correspondence of Philip Yorke, Earl of Hardwicke* (1913), II, 597). The Rev. William Cole (*Blecheley Diary* (1931), p. 37) described the Yorkes as a family 'remarkable to a proverb for foresight in their matches; all the brothers who are married having taken prudential caution that the ladies they attached themselves to should be able to maintain themselves'.

31 December 1764. Lincoln is *never* remarkable for furnishing anecdotes, and at this season of the year less than in summer, as the distance of the neighbouring families prevent their coming to the Town now the roads are bad and the days short....The weather here has been remarkably mild during this winter till within this fortnight...therefore we must think ourselves particularly fortunate in having taken up our abode here in so good a season. We have spent our Christmas not unpleasantly considering all things. Lord Hardwicke from his kind attention to us has inabled us to bear our part in the hospitality of the season. We have received the two does from Wimpole in consequence of his orders, and desire he would accept of our thanks for them. We were so lucky as to entertain General Parslow upon a haunch of one of them. He was in his way to Mr Secretary Weston's with his daughter. There have been many balls in our neighbourhood, but as my dancing days are over, and my resolution not good to encounter bad roads by night I declined them all. My amusements therefore have been confined to cards and musick within the purlieus of Lincoln. Of this kind is our history....Our house here is large, warm and airy, and therefore we shall be unwilling to part with it till we can find some comfortable abode [in London].

16 October 1766. Mr and Mrs Cox spent ten days with us, and we sent them home again fully convinced that Lincoln is the gayest place in the world, for in the course of that time I carried them to two Assemblys and two or three plays, indeed we were obliged to his Royal Highness the Duke of York for some of the splendour of our entertainments, and he in return seemed perfectly pleased with the reception he met with, but his curiosity not tempting him to see the Minster, the Dean had the good fortune to be excused from all ceremonys on his part.

The duke was fresh from Doncaster races; and the Minster could not compete with a ball in the Assembly Rooms.

She has an interesting comment on the isolation of places at a distance from London, and the little stir that great events there made:

22 April 1769. Perhaps your Ladyship will hardly believe that tho we have been at Lincoln three weeks we have scarcely heard the names of Wilks, Lutterell &c. three times since we came; for my own part I am convinced in general that the spirit is confined within a circle of 50 miles round London; they say a few of the lower people begin to be a little infected with it here, so we had by way of precaution an excellent sermon upon the subject last Sunday. I will not say who preached, for fear I should be suspected of partiality. I called it reading the Riot Act in the church (as it seems they have done in the Assembly Rooms at Bath). I am told the people of this place intend to *call* for it again when wanted, as it did a great deal of good. You see the spirit cannot be very violent that is silenced by a sermon.

May 1769. In this place I never hear a word upon the subject,[1] and indeed to say the truth the people in general of Lincoln have the least curiosity for anything out of their own circle that ever I met with, there ideas in general being cheifly confined to three things, eating, going to Church, and card playing, but there are some exceptions, and some few very agreeable people.

---

[1] I.e. Wilkes's *North Briton.*

I would not have this account of them transpire for the world, but it puts me in mind that I must immediately relieve your Ladyship from this dull scrawl by getting myself dressed for dinner, as Lady Vere Bertie &c. &c. dine with us to-day; we have I think since we came had above *three score* gentlemen and ladies to eat their mutton with us, as they call it, but our country neighbours are many of them not come down.

12 June 1769. I must do the Inhabitants of this place the justice to say, that they are good natured enough to be pleased with our living amongst them, and will I don't doubt regret our departure next week, at least till we are succeeded by another residentiary. Last Wednesday we had a dinner, *pour faire le bon bouche*, for a dozen militia officers, and an assembly at night for all my acquaintance in general, but the most agreeable part of the entertainment was conducted by the Dean without my knowledge, which was a little concert consisting of a French horn and four or five other instruments below stairs for the amusement of the sitters by. Perhaps a *rout* in *June* may sound quite as ridiculous as *hot rolls and butter* in July. I believe it even appeared so to my daughter Peggy, for she collected a vast nosegay together of honey suckle &c. and laid them in the drawing room that morning, for she told me I had invited such a number of people she was afraid the room would be *fusty*. Lincoln ideas however differ in these points, and to them we conform in everything but playing cards ourselves. P.S. The Dean dines out to-day, and this is the only evening I have not been engaged for this last fortnight. We expect the same amusement next week.

11 April 1770. Little Polly is very much amused with the circle of ladies that she sees every afternoon placed in the drawing rooms. She will stay there two hours together observing their dress and admiring their fans &c. with the true taste of a London fine lady.

19 January 1771. I resigned myself to the common ideas of this place, such as bells ringing, clocks striking, men drinking, women talking, and children dancing eternally....We have had extream sharp weather here for these last ten days, frost and snow a foot deep, but I do not at all regret it, as I believe it is a very happy change for this Town and neighbourhood, which were both becoming unhealthy and liable to putrid disorders for want of frost...the Dean escapes cold amazingly considering what whirlwinds and storms he encounters in his way to Church. With Mr Stewards leave I must dignify Lincoln Minster with the Title of the Temple of the Winds, for it really deserves it. I am just come from thence myself and believe I shan't get the use of my fingers again this two hours. It is an observation by the inhabitants of this place that the air upon the top of this hill is much keener than upon the hills in our neighbourhood which are still more northerly. The reasons for it I don't know, except for being a point surrounded on three sides by a deep valley, alias fen, which I suppose collects the wind.

23 November 1771. The Dean is seldom without a slight cold in this situation, and I have just got one in my head which makes me very stupid and affects my eyes a little; but we are not at present at leisure to nurse ourselves, being obliged to go out to dinners &c. almost every day. After all it is a sad thing to spend one's time in a manner that one cannot look back upon with the least satisfaction of mind; to sacrifice day after day and nobody be the better for it. In the course of this week we have been asked to four dinners, two assemblys, a play and a concert, not to mention company we have had at our own house; and we must not refuse these more public diversions of assemblys &c. as they are generally set on foot and countenanced by some particular person whose name they bear. The common subscription ones I never go to, nor do I ever play at cards, or admit them into my drawing room, so that I hope by degrees to secure some hours of an evening to myself and children. This however is a distant prospect, being already engaged for five days in the next week. The moonlight nights favour our present excursions into the country, where our dining visits would be very uncomfortable if it were not for the fine weather and the bright moon to come home by. . . . this situation like many others upon the tops of high hills is most remarkably damp; and what is particularly unfortunate at that time, all the houses on the north side the Minster (except our own) smoaked, nay even the Deanery is not allways quite free from this inconvenience, tho thanks to our stoves we are much better off than our neighbours. I wish I could find any method for the Dean's sake of drying the Church as easily as I can our old house; for on a foggy day, and a south west wind, I have seen water stand upon the pavement in the Church just as if it had been mopped.

At the end of 1773 came the prospect of an offer of the bishopric of St Davids, which filled Mary with dismay, for Lincoln deanery had produced nearly £1000 a year, whilst St Davids, which would be more expensive, would bring in only £700 or £800. The dean was however able to ensure that he could continue to hold his deanery with the bishopric.

12 November 1775. With respect to ourselves we have hitherto proceeded in our residence with admirable success, made visits, in Town and out, and received near five dozen of our dining Company, which I look upon as having got through a material part of the duty of a residence; so that if the Bishop should be called to London (which some people have imagined might be the case during the present Session of Parliament) we shall not be very much in debt to our neighbours here. The country ones I have seen the most of are Lady Vere Bertie and Mrs Hubbart, the former (poor woman) seems to be going very fast with the dropsy, the latter, whom I spent a day with last week, is all spirits as usual; and preparing a long gallery at Nockton for a play (the *Journey to London*) which is to be acted in the Christmas holidays; the theatre is plain and neat, indeed very little more than benches set across a long galery, and a little stage raised at one end; no change of scenes, but only two neat ones let down at the end. . . . Nobody goes but by invitation (about sixty people generally) and no list is published of the Company. The actors are chiefly their own family and Lord George Sutton's. None but people of fashion are admitted to any part of the performance *on* or *off* the stage; now the thing is, my Bishop says it will not be proper for him to be a spectator. Mrs Hubbart is of a different opinion (and I am of her side). She says she shall be quite disappointed if he does not come. I wanted him to promise if another Bishop (whom she expects) should not disappoint her, whether that would not prevail upon *him*. Pray, dear Madam, determine this point between us; I will promise for him he shall sit quiet, and still, upon a back bench, and never once jump upon the stage whatever blunders may be made. I forgot to mention the farce is the *Guardian*. . . .

In the end the bishop went; whatever he may have thought of Vanbrugh and Colley Cibber's play *The Provoked Husband, or a Journey to London,* he cannot have felt particularly cordial towards his hostess. Mrs Hobart was an inveterate gambler, she and some kindred spirits being known as 'Faro's daughters'. She gambled away the fortune of her father Lord Vere Bertie.[1]

28 December 1775. Last night I was at the first of Mrs Hubbart's plays, tonight I attend my young folks to a ball, tomorrow sally forth again to Nockton, and so proceed through a course of balls, concerts, and dinners and tea drinkings till the whole will end in one fine squeeze by way of rout at my own house on the Queen's Birthday, when I shall rout the Bishop out of his study, convert the green table (now labouring under the weight of learned authors and musty folios) into a loo table, in short take possession of the house and, according to the old phrase, turn it out of window. But perhaps your Ladyship may be impatient for the detail of our last night amusement; it has occupied the thoughts and conversation of this place for three weeks past and will no doubt for three weeks to come. The weather was fortunately extreamly fine, and the Bishop with myself and another lady sallied forth with a moon lanthorn in our budget, at 4 o'clock. We lead all the carriages from this Town, in number about seven, and made a fine trail across the Heath, reaching Nockton ten minutes before the play began.

After supper and dancing they set out for home about 2 o'clock.

30 December 1775...we have performed all this *night-errantry* without either cold or fatigue...the last night's performance (*The Way to keep Him*) exceeded the former....The Ball and supper as before, and we arrived home safe without making use of our moon lanthorn, or rather Lord Monson's, which we have made bold to borrow...not time to think of politics.

Lord Hardwicke, she reported, was not sanguine about affairs in America, which is not surprising. Earlier she had written much about the war with the American colonies, and gives a glimpse of Sir Francis Bernard,[2] who as Governor of Massachusetts had contributed to the exacerbation of feeling among the colonists, talking as might be expected of a returned proconsul,

---

[1] *The Albinia Book,* compiled by A. L. Cust (1929), pp. 71, 81. Her husband became the third earl of Buckinghamshire in 1793. The Hobarts came into possession of Nocton in 1776 when Lady Dashwood surrendered her life interest in the estate for an annual rent of £3100 and other payments (Bodl. MSS DD. Dashwood (Bucks), B19/2/17). Many of their guests might well have agreed with the judgement of the Dashwood agent upon Mrs Hobart: 'But the woman is the Duce and all. I am afraid he can't keep her in any bounds. It would have been more prudent to have been satisfied with the house for some little time, and done things by degrees, whilst his income had been larger, and not to run on at this rate. I foresee the rate he now lives at is greatly more than what his income can allow, therefore must be running out' (B19/5/24). Lord Vere Bertie had proposed a house in Lincoln for Mr Hobart, 'but his Lady has too great a contempt for Lincolners ever to come to it' (Massingberd Mundy MSS, Society of Genealogists).

[2] See below, p. 82. Bernard took a lease of College House in the Close in 1771.

and favouring strong measures: 'he was hot, and talked much about what ought to have been done four years ago.'[1]

She thought the cathedral colder than Westminster Abbey: and as for the deanery:

7 February 1776. I had the curiosity to try the experiment one Sunday morning of seeing how long boiling water would be before it froze, and accordingly poured some into the slop basin, and found it *ice* in less than thirty minutes, and yet we had a good fire in the room, but I had better have left my experiment alone, for I really believe I was the colder for it (or at least fancied myself so) all Church time. . . .

She turns then to gossip about the young Lord Monson:

The match you mention for Lord Monson has, it seems, long been the idea of Sir G. Warren, *his Lady*, and Lady Monson. No doubt the bait has been thrown in the gentleman's way since his return, but by what I can find he does not *bite*, however, he has condescended to observe that she is a *good fine girl*, and *much grown*. I suppose his taking a trip to Bath with his brother when she was there gave rise to this fresh report. His Mother (who we must allow to be a little partial) always speaks of him as a most aimiable dutiful son, and that he constantly visits her every day, and is continually making presents to his sisters, but from *other* accounts of him I do not think it impossible that before the winter is out he may exhibit a *tropic feather* in his hat as well as Lady Jersey in his head.

The question was soon settled. He married Elizabeth, the daughter of the fourth earl of Essex.

20 October 1777. I find my new neighbour Lady Monson very civil, good humoured and sensible, and as little *fine* as one out of that school could be expected. That, however, is rather too much to allow her to pay any civilities to the gentry of this Town or to attend any of their amusements. The only time she has at all appeared here (except at the Races) was to hear the Infirmary Sermon, when I let her into my own private pew with a key, unseen; an unfortunate fear in a coach deprives her distant neighbours likewise of much of her company, but I really believe she returns everybody's visits. With respect to ourselves they came to us first. . . . Lord Monson is pretty well for him: Lady Vere Bertie and Mrs Hobart both ill, and Lady Priscilla Bertie is in a bad state of health of a hectic kind and a pain in her side, the Duchess[2] is uneasy about her. . . our neighbour Mr Dowdeswell who seems to be very sanguine as to our success in America. . . .

Presently, after recording that Monson had commenced foxhunter, and Mrs Hobart recovered and busy about her play, she sent a copy of

---

[1] John Bourne, an estate agent, wrote from Croft to Mr Drake that his young brother in America had lately been dispossessed of his property in West Florida by a party from the American army: the area was in such a convulsed state that cultivation was impossible; and he was trying to get a commission in His Majesty's service (L.A.O. Tyrwhitt Drake, 4/84).   [2] Of Ancaster.

Governor Pownall's epitaph upon his wife Lady Faulkner, now to be seen in the north lobby at the west end of the cathedral:[1]

24 November 1777.... these lines, dictated no doubt by the bleeding heart of her enamoured husband are ingraved upon it in *red letters*, so that it really is hardly legible. It has been, you will easily believe, much talked of and criticised, but I think the best reflection that has been made upon it was by Mrs Abington, the actress, who upon hearing Mrs Hobart read it, only asked with a grave face, Has he no friends?

When the Yorkes were in Lincoln again at the beginning of 1780, Mary wrote that she expected the usual round of festivities, adding

2 January 1780. Our new acquaintance indeed, Lady Clarges, is so fond of dancing, she would tempt our young folks out continually (but we shall endeavour to be moderate). Lord and Lady Monson likewise are prevailed upon to be much *gayer* than usual. I want to know a little of the history of Sir Thomas Clarges[2] and his Lady. I only just know her father's name &c. She is said to be much accomplished, and certainly sings with great taste and sweetness, but so low that it is difficult to hear all her notes.

James Yorke became bishop of Gloucester in 1779 and was translated to Ely in 1781, when he resigned the deanery of Lincoln. It is fitting that the last of Mary's Lincoln letters should relate to a visit to Lincoln Minster after the bishop had carried out a confirmation near Peterborough:

...we could not resist the inclination we have long felt of taking a peep at Lincoln cathedral, whose gradual progress we had watched (through a course of years) from the depth of dirt, damp and green mold to its present state (all *but the pavement*) of exquisite beauty; this last ornament has completed its elegance; and I believe now it is allowed to be the first Gothic building in

[1] Thomas Pownall was born in Lincoln and attended Lincoln Grammar School. He became governor successively of New Jersey, Massachusetts and South Carolina. After his retirement he lived in Lincoln for some years. His biographer, C. A. W. Pownall, claimed that he was the author of the *Letters of Junius*. The epitaph on his wife reads: 'Here is entombed Dame Harriot daughter of Lieu: General Churchill: wife in her first marriage to Sr Everard Fawkener Kt: in her second to Governour Pownall. She dyed Feb:6:1777 aged 51. Her person was that of animated animating beauty, with a complexion of the most exquisite brilliancy, unfaded when she fell. Her understanding was of such quickness, & reach of thought, that her knowledge, although she had learning, was instant and original. Her heart, warm'd with universal benevolence to the highest degree of sensibility, had a ready tear for pity: and glowed with friendship as with a sacred & inviolate fire. Her love to those who were blest with it, was happiness. Her sentiments were correct, refined, elevated: her manners so chearfull, elegant and winning, aimiable, that while she was admired, she was beloved: and while she enlightened and enlivend, she was the delight of the world in which she lived. She was formed for life: she was prepared for death, which being "a gentle wafting to immortality", she lives, where life is real.' It was originally placed in Bishop Fleming's chantry chapel; it was claimed that the inscription was composed by Pownall's friend Horace Walpole.
[2] See below, p. 93. He married Miss Skrine (Burke, *Extinct and Dormant Baronetcies*, p. 117). He had a house in the Close in 1780, where he had three male servants.

England. I left it with regret, more impressed by the fine proportions and elegant dignity of the whole than ever I had been when I lived there, but if I had been mistaken in my ideas of the Church, I had not been less so in those of the old Deanery, which we walked over. I once thought it a comfortable habitation. What was my surprise to find it one of the most wretched, dismal unwholesome places I had often seen.

And she was glad to return to their excellent house at Ely.[1]

No apology is needed for such extensive quotation of shrewd, patient and kindly Mary Yorke. She evokes more vividly than any descriptive summary could do the spirit and atmosphere of Lincoln abovehill in the eighteenth century. In spite of their high connections and their affluence the Yorkes's sense of the obligations of residence made them enter fully into social life against their personal inclinations; although they had the entry to the most exclusive circle they did not cut themselves off as the nobility did from a rather wider society. She was welcome everywhere, and as she was resident for only a few months in each year she must be secured when she could, and so the give and take of hospitality had to be severely compressed in time, with the results that she bewailed but accepted. It must not be supposed that the other residents of the Close had so continuously gay a round. There were lengthy intervals of tedium for the ladies while their husbands engaged in sport and to a much less extent in public business.

Even casual visitors provided a welcome diversion. When Scrope Bernard (son of Sir Francis) and his wife visited his sister and her husband Charles White, a barrister living in the Close:

10 August 1785.. . .we had not been in Mr White's house many minutes before our arrival was discovered, and the Minster bells struck up, to the great danger of the steeple, which is out of repair, insomuch that the Dean sent the ringers word after half an hour's ringing, that they had done enough for a compliment, and that he was sure the newcomers would be sorry to occasion any harm to the Cathedral.

At dinner the city waits attended them, and played their whole store of airs and marches. There was an assembly that evening, which was more fully attended than usual in the hope of seeing the visitors, but they were too tired to go. On Sunday they went to the City Church belowhill, and sat among the aldermen and aldresses; and in the afternoon to the Minster, where the chantor, Dr Gordon, was so good as to interest himself that they should have a good anthem. In the evening they took a short walk on the Minster Green, 'which is the Mall of this place'. One evening Mr White had a party for dinner and cards, and another evening the dean favoured them with a grand dinner, to which they sat down nineteen in number.[2]

[1] Bedford Record Office, L30/9.
[2] Mrs Napier Higgins, *The Bernards of Abington and Nether Winchendon*, III (1904), 82–3.

The principal county assemblies were held in the great room at the Angel in the Bail. It was no doubt on a dark night, in an ill-lit highway, that Parson Dymoke, coming in liquor from the Angel, stumbled into the Chequer well and was drowned: he might have been saved if the neighbourhood would have given him any assistance.[1] Although a visitor in 1733 remarked that the assembly house was a very fair building,[2] it was generally thought not to be good enough; and at a meeting of gentlemen assembled for the races in September 1742 it was resolved to build an assembly room, and to open a subscription for the purpose. Two years later, a fund having been raised, it was decided to proceed, and the lord lieutenant, the third duke of Ancaster, entered into a contract to build.[3] Here was the 'county' as a social entity in action. In order to raise more money the invitation to subscribe was extended more widely, but only to those whose quality and relation to the county should make it proper: the limits were narrow and defined. Money was raised on mortgage, and it was said that on one occasion when the interest was in arrear, Mr Vyner the mortgagee seized the rooms and stopped the assembly. Francis Bernard acted in Lincoln for the duke, whom he consulted in 1756 on several momentous questions: whether, if there were five assemblies at the races, the price of tickets should be raised; whether there should be an assembly or a concert on Saturday night; whether ladies' names should be placed on their tickets as gentlemen's were, or whether they should continue to be transferable.[4]

Then there came into the history of the Assembly Rooms, as into so much else, the great Sir Joseph Banks of Revesby. The young Joseph had sailed with Captain Cook in the *Endeavour* in 1768 at the age of 25. Three years later they returned, and Banks at once became a famous man. Although a great variety of work kept him away from the county for most of the year, he normally went to Revesby for the autumn: for the harvest, for Revesby feast, for Lincoln races, and for public and estate business. In his later years, with his fame and his growing imperiousness, he dominated the county, where no business could safely be undertaken without him.[5]

In 1787, on Banks's initiative, subscribers to the Rooms surrendered their right to free admission in order to raise a better income: William Lumby drew a plan for an addition to the scalding room—where tea was scalded—to provide for gentlemen taking wine or a glass of punch, but the

[1] *Banks Family Letters*, ed. J. W. F. Hill (L.R.S.), p. 177.
[2] *H.M.C. Hare* (14th Rep.), p. 235.
[3] L. P. L. Ross Scrap Books, Lincoln vol. i. Hayward was the builder.
[4] L.A.O. 2 Ancaster, 10/6/3.
[5] See Plate 20 and J. C. Beaglehole, *The Endeavour Journal of Joseph Banks 1768–71* (Sydney, 1962). See the chapter 'The Young Banks'.

work was not carried out.[1] The Stuff Ball or Color Ball had been inaugurated at Alford in 1785 to encourage the local manufacture of woollens, the lady patroness choosing the colour of dress for the year. It was transferred to the Assembly Rooms in 1789, Lady Banks being patroness: Sir Joseph, who never did things by halves, went in a full suit of stuff, coat, waistcoat and breeches. The Stuff Ball at once took its place as the chief and most exclusive occasion of the year.

There were theatrical performances in private houses, but shortly before 1732 a small playhouse—later described as 22 yards by 8 yards—was built in a lane under the castle which came to be called Drury Lane.[2] Ladies went to it in sedan chairs, as the lane was too narrow to admit carriages. The boys of the cathedral choir in their surplices were allowed to perform the chorus in *Romeo and Juliet*, and Lady Deloraine is said to have seen a puppet play there. The earliest surviving playbill is dated 1750, and the latest 1763, after which the manager William Herbert, who was esteemed a good actor, migrated to the lower city.[3]

Apart perhaps from the cathedral library the more serious-minded gentlemen had to rely for books and newspapers on their own purchases and private borrowings; but they felt the need for something more, and at last in 1786 the county newsroom was opened, with twenty-one gentlemen of the county and thirty gentlemen of the town as members. Gentry and clergy were prominent, with some doctors; there were two members of the Ellison family, of commercial origins; and one, Robert Obbinson, who still savoured of belowhill society. The great William Paley was soon to become a member. Here were newspapers and a book club, and glimpses occur occasionally of evenings of whist and the periodical distribution of books.[4]

In all these social activities the citizens belowhill had almost no part. Generally speaking they accepted their social inferiority as part of the natural order, and they copied their betters by providing an assembly room for themselves: subversive ideas only began to creep in after the French Revolution. Tradesmen relied on the custom and the patronage of the gentry, and no charity could flourish belowhill without a noble or at least a gentle president. A like relationship existed in the popular sports of horse-racing and cock-fighting, which the gentry did not attempt to carry on alone but which the citizens would never have thought of trying to manage without most deferential reference to them. In 1711 the common

---

[1] Willson, VII, 99, 104.

[2] A. R. Maddison, 'A Ramble through St Mary Magdalene's Parish', *A.A.S.R.* XXI (1891), 43.

[3] Willson, V, 55; J. B. King in L.P.L. U.P. 1911. The playhouse was later converted into two cottages. Herbert's company offered to perform for the County Hospital in 1777 (*L.A.O. Archivists' Report*, 7, p. 34).   [4] *Lincs. N. & Q.* III (1892–3), 79.

council of the city voted money for a plate to be run at such time and in such manner as the city and the gentlemen they consulted agreed, and thereafter money for plate was regularly voted. The king gave a 100 guineas to be run for in 1716.[1] In the first racing calendar, published in 1727, flat racing and steeplechasing at Lincoln were mentioned. For several years races were run on courses both to the north and to the south of the city, until the one to the south, a round course of four miles on Waddington heath, became the accepted one. There was a famous race in 1744: a six-year-old horse belonging to Southcote Parker of Blyborough and one aged 21 belonging to Gilbert Caldecote of Lincoln ran 14 miles round the course in 39 minutes for 100 guineas, which were won by the former by a horse's length. There were great wagers, and the greatest concourse of people ever seen there on such an occasion.[2]

The inclosure of the heath drove the races off; in 1770 the mayor and his brethren viewed Canwick common, but this, being on the hillside, was clearly unsuitable, and for several years the races were held on Welton heath until, again, inclosure drove them off. In 1773 the mayor and others waited on his grace of Ancaster at his lodgings abovehill to give the city's consent to a scheme for marking out a course and building a stand on the Carholme and Long and Short Leys, and expressed the hope that the noblemen and gentlemen subscribers to the race would find it agreeable to form the ground and pay for the stand at their own expense. The course their patrons may have had to pay for: the stand was not built until 1806. The races had once lasted five days, but they dwindled to two.[3]

There were cockpits in the yards of the King's Arms and the Reindeer downhill, and nearly every public house had a cock-fighting on Shrove Tuesday and at Christmas. Lord Vere Bertie, who lived at Branston, was a patron of the sport, and when he died the Rev. Peregrine Curtois, the rector of Branston, succeeded to the breed, and preserved it for many years. It is said that the Heneage family were great cock-fighters about 1740, and that the squire of the period bid so high as to endanger his estate.[4]

Hunting and coursing were more exclusive sports. Gentlemen with parks kept deer for ornament, for venison and for sport. The young Joseph Banks (Sir Joseph's grandfather) had his own parks at Revesby and

---

[1] *Stamford Mercury*, 6 Sept. 1716.

[2] *Horse Racing: its History* (1865), p. 244, quoting *Westminster Journal*, 23 June 1744. Mrs Massingberd wrote in 1758 that Caldecote was walking lame, having put out his ankle joint and broken the little bone in his leg with wrestling with some countryman, having just won three guineas with hopping: 'did ever you know such a great boy?' (Massingberd Mundy MSS, Society of Genealogists).   [3] Willson, VI, 60.

[4] *Ibid.* VI, 65. Hogarth depicted the blind Lord Albemarle Bertie presiding over the cockpit at Westminster.

Tumby, with his own hounds: the duke of Bedford sent him twelve bucks in 1733, and in 1739 Lewis Dymoke wrote to confess that he had killed a buck in Banks's park.[1] There were deer at Nocton in Dashwood's time, and at Skellingthorpe. Deer at Scampton park were bought by Sir Thomas Hussey and put in his woods at Doddington. They used to stray to other woods, such as Whisby. Hussey, who kept a pack of buckhounds, would send them to drive the deer home or kill them, as he thought fit. At Skellingthorpe Henry Stone, the lord of the manor, preserved his own deer. After Hussey died in 1706 there was no resident family at Doddington, and the hounds were disposed of. When timber was being felled and sold there and at Skellingthorpe the noise of carts and workmen made the deer stray more. The lords of other manors gave deputation authorising killing, and no doubt poachers found their opportunities.[2]

The coursing of hares was a popular sport, especially about Ancaster heath.[3] When the steward at Dunston on the heath called Dr Willis's attention to his defective fences there, the doctor replied that the hole in the wall was a great preservative to the hares against coursers, but that he would repair it.[4]

But coursing gradually gave way to fox-hunting, and it did not survive the inclosures. By 1731 Lord Monson had a pack of hounds in the old kennels at Burton. The boundaries of the Burton hunt came to extend on the north to Gainsborough and Hainton, and on the south to Bloxholme and Newark.[5] In 1741 a clubroom was added to the Green Man, a small inn on the heath in Blankney parish, by Thomas Chaplin, adorned with plaster busts of the principal members of the club.[6] The concourse of riders, with large establishments of horses and servants, meant much in patronage of inns and stables in the city; and the exploits of the day provided conversation in the bar parlours as well as among members of the hunt.

[1] *Banks Family Letters* (L.R.S.), *passim*. The map of Lincolnshire, published in 1779 by Andrew Armstrong (4 feet 9 inches by 6 feet 9½ inches in 8 sheets), shows parks at Fillingham, Belton, Syston, Aswarby, Brocklesby, Grimsthorpe, and Revesby (amongst others); other places where there was ornamental planting, though not given the conventional sign for parks, include Burton, Hackthorn, Caenby, Norton Place, Glentworth, Doddington, Thorney, Skellingthorpe, Branston and Dunston Pillar. A drawing in the corner shows hunters and hounds passing in front of Dunston Pillar. Armstrong was denied the approval of Banks (*Banks Letters*, ed. Warren Dawson (1958), p. 22). For an extract from Armstrong's map, see Plate 14.

[2] Bodl. MSS DD. Dashwood (Bucks), B19/5/12; L.A.O. Lindsey Deposit 71 (Christ's Hospital). Kip's engraving of Doddington shows deer in the park.

[3] Cox, *Magna Britannia*, p. 1456; *H.M.C. Portland*, VI, 84.

[4] Bodl. MSS DD. Dashwood (Bucks), B19/6/7.

[5] The Blankney country was carved out of it in 1871 for the convenience of Henry Chaplin.

[6] *Gentleman's Magazine*, vol. 56 (2), p. 837; and see *Lincs. N. & Q.* XXII (1933), 69.

The masters of the hunt and their leading supporters had great social influence, and political influence also, when they chose to exercise it, as the Monsons did.

The second Lord Monson[1] was so much addicted to the sport that his mother complained that 'he spends too much of his time hunting with his hounds down in Lincolnshire'. A verse of an old hunting song depicts the scene:

> In seventeen hundred and sixty and three,
> The third of December I think we agree,
> At eight in the morning by most of the clocks
> We rode out of Lincoln in search of a fox.
> There was jolly Ned Wills and Hobart so keen,
> And Lawrence in scarlet with capes that were green,
> With Penney and Raley, those huntsmen so stout,
> Lords Bertie and Monson, and so we set out.[2]

In 1769 Burton Hall was enlarged, partly to increase the space for hunt breakfasts, and new kennels were built in 1771. Mary Yorke wrote in 1773 that Lord Thanet kept a very good pack of hounds in the town, though he himself was confined by gout:[3] it seems that he was in charge of the Monson pack. The third Lord Monson hunted the Burton for twenty years. In 1791, when the Spilsby neighbourhood was hunted by a Mr Leigh, Monson thought he could hunt it better than a stranger from 200 miles off, and wrote to Sir Joseph Banks that if Leigh did not fulfil his engagement—he had made only a short stay in the previous season—he would like to hunt about Revesby and Tower moor (at Woodhall). Banks diplomatically replied that if thereafter he was adjudged to have recovered the fox-hunting jurisdiction over his property in the neighbourhood of the fen and Tower moor he would transfer it: he excused Leigh's conduct by suggesting that foxes were not well preserved in the Spilsby country, where there was more interest in the preservation of game than in foxes, adding that Leigh had explained his short stay by the distemper among his horses. Banks's neighbour Thomas Coltman approved of this reply, describing Monson's attempt as ill-judged.[4]

The fourth Lord Monson, who died in 1809, was also a fox-hunter: in compiling his history of the family the sixth lord could only find to say of the fourth that he was a good rider, fox-hunter and a hard liver and died at the age of 24.[5] The pack was then sold to Squire Osbaldeston.[6]

---

[1] Thomas Pownall wrote to him in 1754 wishing him 'plenty of foxes, good scenting days, no lame horses, and the devil take the hindmost' (L.A.O. Monson, 25/1/46).

[2] *V.C.H. Lincoln*, II, 500.

[3] Bedford Record Office, L 30/9.   [4] Hill, Banks 2/38, 3/10.

[5] Ross Corr. v, 11 Sept. 1862.   [6] Below, p. 267.

But even the most ardent rider to hounds must turn to business sometimes. Quarter sessions brought the squires to Lincoln to transact the
business of the county, and at assizes they served upon the grand jury and
occasionally passed resolutions on matters of public moment.[1] There were
several very large pieces of business to engage their attention. The old shire
hall was in poor condition, and a new hall was built in the castle yard in
1776. At the same time the activities of John Howard were calling attention
to the state of prisons in this country and abroad. He visited Lincoln in
1774 and 1776, and described what he found. The debtors' rooms in the
gaol had floors of tarras (or plaster) which could not be kept clean, and the
windows were close glazed. The free ward for debtors—for those who
could not afford to pay for better accommodation—was a room at the
end of the building, paved with small stones, which was a thoroughfare to
sundry places. A trap-door in the pavement led down ten steps to two
vaulted dungeons, one the pit, the other the condemned cell. There was
a little straw on the floor, and both dungeons were offensive. For the
felons there was no water and no sewer. Those felons who could pay for a
bed had other rooms. There was no chapel, service being performed in the
shire hall, and no infirmary.[2]

[1] A special piece of business for three of the justices occurs in 1724. Sir Cecil Wray,
Edward Beresford and Joseph Banks II were appointed by the judge of assize to attend
to the transportation of eighteen felons to the plantations. They made a contract with a
Fenchurch Street merchant, who sent a sloop to the Humber to take the felons; statements
taken led the justices to believe that the gaoler and others connived at their escape on the
Essex shore. The justices asked the Secretary of State to issue an advertisement inviting
any of the escaped felons to turn king's evidence and discover the roguery: 'for the
country is very uneasy to be at so great a charge and to have such rogues loose again,
especially on account of two considerable robberies that have been since committed
in this county' (P.R.O. State Papers Domestic, George I, 53/16).
  In 1756 the lord lieutenant was ordered to instruct the justices of the peace to cause
all 'straggling seamen' to serve in the king's forces (Lindsey C.L. Banks, 13/3/1).
[2] John Howard, *State of the Prisons in England and Wales* (1st edn 1777), pp. 296–7.
Carr may even have been in advance of Howard, for on 1 June 1774 Charles Amcotts
wrote to W. B. Massingberd: 'Mr Carr called here last October, and also took the
trouble to follow me to Harrowgate the day after I had left that place to offer my
services to my worthy friends at Boston. He therefore yesterday sent me a very sensible
genteel letter, with a design for a county gaole, which I propose to deliver to you at
Ormesby, and I think you will approve, for it appears to me to be elegant, altho plain
and neat, also convenient, but whether it will be carried into execution by our wise and
frugal Lincolnshire gentry is more than I will promise. If it is, I shall attribute it to the
fortunate alteration that was made at the last county election' (Massingberd Mundy
MSS, Society of Genealogists). By her will, proved in 1715, Rebecca Hussey bequeathed
the interest of £1,000 for the release of poor debtors from Lincoln castle; but no debtors
had received the benefit for many years. Thomas Hazledine left to the prisoners in the
county gaol £3 or £4 a year from the rent of a house in Lincoln. Some frightful traditions
were current later about the state of the dungeons and pits of the old building (Brooke,
Guide through the Streets of Lincoln, p. 11).

Howard's impetus to public opinion was felt at once by the county magistrates—he tactfully remarked that the prison was out of repair, perhaps because the county designed to build a new one—and the building of a new gaol (which had to await the passing of an act of parliament in 1784) was begun in 1786: first designs by Carr of York were abandoned, and it was designed and built by William Lumby in accordance with Howard's plan. Its management 'under the humane and religious attention of the county magistrates' was warmly commended a few years later.[1]

At times of assize not only the inns but the private houses and indeed every corner of the upper city and perhaps of the lower were filled with learned counsel, jurors, parties and witnesses.[2] Once in his life each of the gentlemen served as high sheriff, an onerous and costly office to be avoided as long as possible and accepted with a good grace when the time had clearly come. His under-sheriff had to find him lodgings; and the problem is illustrated by a report on arrangements when Banks was sheriff in 1794. The under-sheriff said that Banks could not go to Mrs Weatherall's lodgings as they were engaged by counsel. The best he could do would be at Mrs Weekes's, a house lately used as a boarding school. He could have the large schoolroom, which would be desirable in hot weather, and have another sitting-room, two bedchambers with a dressing closet, and a bedroom for a female servant. The house was in Eastgate: it sounds like Atton Place. Mrs Weekes was afraid that her sheets would not be good enough, and he suggests that Banks should bring his own. Banks approved. In reply to an inquiry from the sheriff of another county Banks wrote:

The business of high sheriff is conducted here in as economical manner I believe as in any county of large extent in England. The judge requires 20 javelin men, 6 footmen and 2 pages in the high sheriff's livery, the bailiffs and trumpeters are all the attendance usual.

He added that by the custom of the county the sheriff was not permitted to entertain any gentlemen when the grand jury dined at the high sheriff's table; every man paid his own shott.[3]

The judge also, of course, required lodgings, and he was provided for in various houses—College House or Atton Place—until (under an Act of 1809) the white brick lodgings were built for him on Castle Hill about 1812.[4]

---

[1] L.R.O. Co.C. 3/1, Grand Jury Minute Book, pp. 156–90; quarter sessions minutes for Lindsey, Kesteven, Holland; *Gentleman's Magazine*, vol. 75 (1) (1805), p. 195.
[2] A new brick house was advertised for sale or to let in 1716: the chance of letting lodgings for assizes and races was pointed out.
[3] Banks Collection in the Mitchell Library, Sydney.
[4] L.R.O. Co.C. 3/8. College House formerly stood on the green near the chapter house. For many years it belonged (no doubt on lease for lives from the dean and chapter)

The high sheriff presided over the shire court held in the shire hall. One piece of business was occasionally transacted there which now has more interest than the rest, for there the freeholders chose the knights of the shire who would represent them in the House of Commons; or perhaps it would be more accurate to say that they sealed by formal election the choice already made by the gentry in their social gatherings, and, so far as the greater among them were concerned, at meetings of the lieutenancy or of the Lincolnshire Club held at Pontacks or the Globe or the Thatched House in London. But the deliberations of the magnates, carried on in their absence, were watched with suspicion by the squires, who were capable of asserting themselves when they saw fit.[1]

At the beginning of the eighteenth century the dominating figure in county affairs, the lord lieutenant, was Robert Bertie, fourth earl of Lindsey. The Berties were descended from the ancient line of Willoughby, and had transferred their chief seat from Eresby by Spilsby to Grimsthorpe. They had been ardent royalists, the first earl having died of wounds received at Edgehill. The third earl, whose sister had married Danby, Charles II's minister, supported the Revolution, and by 1705 his son, the fourth earl, was joining the whigs. In 1706 he received a marquisate, and he was named by George I as one of the lords justices pending the royal arrival from Hanover. In 1715 he was created duke of Ancaster and Kesteven.[2]

The great man considered himself entitled to nominate one of the knights of the shire. In 1705 he secured the election of his brother Albemarle Bertie along with Colonel Whichcot of Harpswell,[3] and in the three later parliaments of Anne his son, Lord Willoughby de Eresby.

The prospect of the accession of the House of Hanover to the throne was not universally approved, and hints of the dislike of the Act of Settlement

to Benjamin Bromhead. The dining-room had no carpet, and sand was sifted on the boards on special occasions. Then the judges moved to Mrs Weekes's house, Atton Place, in Eastgate, then to Mrs Fisher's house on the south side of Castle Hill, and later to a house in Minster Yard facing the east end of the Minster. The county used to allow a hogshead of ale for the use of the servants and others at each assize, but the allowance was discontinued about 1836 (Willson, v, 108).

[1] In 1720 Stukeley attended the Lincolnshire feast at the Ship Tavern, Temple Bar, with Sir Isaac Newton in the chair (*Diaries and Letters* (Surtees Society), p. 59).

[2] *H.M.C. Rutland*, II, 182; IV, 231; *T. & S.L.* p. 195.

[3] *H.M.C. Marquis of Bath*, I, 70: Samuel Wesley took part against Whichcot and Bertie, and was presently arrested for debt by some of their partisans and imprisoned in Lincoln Castle. In 1720 Sir John Meres wrote to the younger Whichcot that his father's elections had incumbered the estate, but he hoped the son had lived prudently since he gave up standing for the county (L.A.O. Aswarby, 10/26/19). In the same year Albemarle Bertie wrote that the members of parliament had got so much by the civility paid them in the South Sea subscriptions—in bribes from the company—as was sufficient to carry their elections (L.A.O. 3 Ancaster, 8/2/13).

occur in the diary of Bishop Wake. In 1706 his visitation address met with dissent from the Reverend Samuel Wesley, the rector of Epworth, and others. Several declined to subscribe the address to the queen at Horncastle, and there was opposition at Boston:

the minister of the town, an honest but warm man, preached: seven or eight refused to subscribe. Mr Kelsey the vicar complied. One Mr Francis, a rich clergyman in the neighbourhood, keeps up the party: yet there are several of a better temper hereabouts.

At the end of his tour he noted that not above thirty declined to subscribe in the whole county. At his visitation of 1712 Mr Wesley preached at Epworth. It was a party sermon; after dinner the bishop went to see his own house, in place of the rectory which was burnt.[1]

Whatever backward glances there may have been at the death of Queen Anne, there was little overt movement at the time of the jacobite rebellion in 1715.[2] The under-sheriff of the county reported that only the Widdringtons of Blankney had been out with the rebels.[3] The steward at Glentworth told Lady Mary Saunderson that

we have not had the least disturbance anywhere, only a while ago 3 drunken fellows proclaimed the Pretender at Horncastle, 2 of 'em, 'tis said, were immediately taken up; the 3rd made his escape...2 expresses sent to my Lord

[1] Wake's Diary, Lambeth Palace Library. It was in 1716–17 that there were the mysterious 'noises' at Epworth rectory which figure in books about the Wesley family. Much has been written about them. When the Rev. Charles Garvey was taking temporary duty for the rector of Epworth in 1847, he wrote that the enthusiastic disciples of John Wesley still obtruded themselves on the rectory premises, which was the spot, though not the building, of John Wesley's birth: 'yet still the present one was the house where he was bred, and in which his father was sadly tormented and vexed with substantial proofs, in the shape of knocks and blows, of the unsubstantial spirits of the air. With regard to which I have been informed here, that his daughter, like Giles Sharp, "the good devil of Woodstock", was the prime mover, and that she administered to her father those anything but filial knocks, which the old gentleman, drawing largely on his own credulity, full believed as evidence of the existence of a spiritual world. I fancy myself there was a Jesuit or someone of a kindred character, at work in the family, for the whole matter as an historical fact resolves itself into a matter of politics, the noises and blows only commencing when the prayers for the Hanoverian line commenced' (Ross Corr. I, 13 June 1847). For the activities of Francis, Wesley and others, see Norman Sykes, *William Wake, Archbishop of Canterbury 1657–1737* (1957), I, 152–4.

[2] An Irish Catholic who proclaimed King James at Boston was put in the pillory at Lincoln and sentenced to seven years' imprisonment (C. Petrie, *The Jacobite Movement: The First Phase 1688–1716* (1948), p. 154, quoting *The Flying Post*).

[3] He went to Blankney to secure their goods, to be told that all but a few had been sold (*Records of the English Catholics of 1715*, ed. J. O. Payne (1889), p. 117). It was long believed that Widdrington had hidden a large chest of plate in a vault under the great staircase, but when at last it was opened it was found only to contain a salt cellar of white metal and an iron ladle (G. Oliver, *History of the Holy Trinity Guild at Sleaford* (1837), pp. 38, 39).

yester night at Gainsborough which brought the joyfull news of the utter defeat of the Rebells, and that it was thought scarce one would escape...the designs of the Pretender and all his adherents will be in vain for the future, as I sincerely pray they may, so that the Crown may sit easy and safe upon the head of the best of kings, who left his own ease to make us a happy people, if it be not our own fault.[1]

The steward's betters were not likely to show such devotion to the person of the new king. The rising raised new suspicions of Roman Catholics, who were subjected to penal legislation: among them were the Heneages of Hainton, Fitzwilliam of Lincoln, Thorold of Little Ponton, Thimelby of Irnham and one of the Bertie family.[2]

At the election of that year Ancaster was displeased by the return of Sir John Brownlow, who had sat for Grantham and was to do so again for many years, and Sir Willoughby Hickman of Thonock near Gainsborough. When Hickman died in 1720 Ancaster put up Albemarle Bertie; he was decisively defeated by Sir William Massingberd of Ormsby, who said he stood at the request of the Champion Dymoke and others.[3] The Champion had the reputation of being a tory and a jacobite, and at heart Massingberd was also.[4] As another general election approached, Brownlow, a whig whose support of the government was rewarded by his being created an Irish peer as Viscount Tyrconnel—by which name he appears as a patron in Dr Johnson's *Life of Mr Richard Savage* and in Boswell—wrote to Mrs Whichcot to say that he was standing with Sir William Monson, and asking for her interest.[5] Dymoke announced that he would stand: Massingberd was in the field again, and Henry Heron of Stubton. It was thought Mr Monson might stand on Sir William's interest, and perhaps Sir George Thorold, though they were all of the same party, and they were in no way daunted by the knowledge that the duke was dissatisfied because the last time his family had not named one member.[6] In the end Massingberd and

[1] Monson, I, 100.

[2] *The English Catholic Non-Jurors of 1715* (1885, ed. Escourt and Payne), pp. 160–67. In March 1719 Joseph Banks the elder received a report from Yorkshire of jacobite activities that he evidently forwarded to the Secretary of State. It was said that jacobites at York boasted openly of impending invasion. 'One lately said publicly he hoped shortly to make the streets flow with protestant blood. The Pretender's health, I'm told, is drunk every night at a Club of 'em where some of our clergy are present very often.' There were reports of the delivery of firearms and other weapons. 'The King's interest daily lessens here by reason of these partizans of the Devil' (P.R.O. State Papers Domestic, Geo. I, vol. 15, no. 78).

[3] W. O. Massingberd, *History of Ormsby* (n.d.), p. 153. The Dymokes of Scrivelsby, in succession to the Marmions, were hereditary King's Champions. The voting was, Massingberd 2,603, Bertie 1,683.

[4] See below, p. 29.

[5] L.A.O. Aswarby, 10/35/4.

[6] *Ibid.* 10/28/3.

Heron were returned without a contest; the gentry did not yield to the duke, and perhaps the spate of offers to stand was prompted by a desire to exclude the ducal family.

Massingberd died in December 1723, and there burst forth a simmering jacobitism which had been too slow to find expression in 1715. Robert Vyner, of the family of London goldsmiths, sent out letters to the freeholders in opposition to the young Sir Nevile Hickman, a pronounced tory. Vyner was the purchaser of Gautby and a newcomer to the county.[1] He had once sat for Grimsby, but failed there in 1721. His recent arrival must have given his opponent, whose family's London origins were decently concealed by several generations of residence in the county, a decided advantage. The Whichcot steward at Harpswell wrote of Hickman to his mistress that 'what interest sets him up I don't know, it must be a very good one, and a deal of gold that will get him in'.[2] Knowing that Mr Whichcot had a great interest in the Isle of Axholme—the part of north-west Lincolnshire lying west of the Trent—Vyner asked his steward to accompany him there. The steward did so, and reported that they had the freeholders entire in Epworth, Belton, Crowle, Luddington and Althorpe, but some in Haxey and Owston, who were committed to Hickman, would be canvassed.

The gentleman that has made this interest for Sir Nevil is Mr Hooke the Minister of Haxey, who was bred a Presbyterian, and was the last election a very great friend of Mr Bertie, but this county very much abounds with such Reverend Gentlemen.

Vyner and his friends were mobbed in Gainsborough, the Hickman strong-hold. The steward also went to Sir John Meres's estates at Kirton and

---

[1] He must have settled there by 1713, when he acquired a one-third interest in the pack of hounds of Charles Pelham and Sir John Tyrwhitt. Vyner (*Notitia Venatica* (ed. 1892), p. 185).

[2] L.A.O. Aswarby, 10/35/6. Among the few local items in the early numbers of the *Lincoln Rutland and Stamford Mercury* are two of this election period. The paper quotes a letter 'from a gentleman of Lincoln to a gentleman of Stamford' commending Hickman as a gentleman hearty in the true interest of his church, the king, and his country. Matthew Boucherett of North Willingham, a leading whig squire of Huguenot descent, published an indignant reply to a letter he had received signed 'Gregory Mejo': he said he was the son of a divine of the Church of England, and educated in its most excellent doctrine and discipline; always ready to sacrifice his life and fortune in defence of it, King George and the Protestant interest, against all opposers: 'and I disdain to fear the threats of being chained in the middle, or be forced to leave these kingdoms and my estates, or be hanged, as is therein expressed, for being in the Protestant interest' (Press cuttings in the Ross Scrap Books, L.P.L.). In 1716 the grand jury of Lincolnshire presented the printer of the *Stamford Mercury* for false and scandalous reflections on the government (G. A. Cranfield, *Development of the English Newspaper 1700–1760* (1962), p. 141; see also pp. 121, 161–2). The paper no doubt took its tory tone from the local gentry.

Algarkirk in the parts of Holland; he forecast victory for Vyner.[1] When Hickman visited Stamford he had the support of Lord Exeter and Lord Cardigan: the latter wrote that 'Sir Nevill scarce met with any denial; I hear the other side brag much, but I can't find where their interest lies'.[2]

In the later stages of the campaign the whigs circulated prints of an affidavit made on 3 February 1724 by Francis Anderson of Lea that some months earlier Hickman had, in his own house, drunk the health of the duke of Ormonde and of the Pretender, by the name of James the Third. Anderson had told him that his father was a wiser man than to be guilty of such things, and that his town deserved a troop of horse; to which Hickman replied that if Anderson would head them he would head his. Anderson had of course to explain his delay in making his affidavit; he said it was due to his compassion for Hickman's youth (it seems he was not yet 23),[3] and to a family relationship. He added that he had told several gentlemen of the incident within a few days. Hickman's friends issued a denial, but the election day was too close for counter affidavits to be made and circulated.

The whig version of Hickman's candidature is given in a ballad:

> Two Fox-hunting Peers and a Champion most brave
> Their names but for Scandalum mag:[4] you should have
> With a Bird both for drinking and cowardice known
> Swore none should be chose but a Fool of their own.

They were joined by two parsons, T(hom)ps(o)n and Wh(i)te, of popish inclination, and set themselves to find a candidate.

> This brought to remembrance an hot headed Fool
> Who married a wife before he left School
> Who fear'd not to toast the Pretender or Pope
> And in him (contra Spem) they placed their whole Hope.

The news spread about the county, and they made for Lincoln.

> Now flushed with vain hopes secure of the day
> Their Tagg Ragg and Bobtail they mount and away,
> But when to the city of Lincoln they came
> In each honest man's face they soon read their doom.

Their badge was the white rose; for a motto the ballad proposed 'veritas vino'. Burrell Massingberd wrote that the (second) duke of Ancaster had been commissioned to go down and bring in Vyner right or wrong: 'all

---

[1] L.A.O. Aswarby, 10/27/11, 12.

[2] *H.M.C. 5th Rep.* (Duke of Sutherland), p. 189.

[3] He was baptised at Gainsborough, 13 May 1701, succeeded to the baronetcy in 1720, married about 1722, and died in 1733 (*Complete Baronetage*, II, 217).

[4] *Scandalum Magnatum*, the defaming of great personages.

agree the baronet has a great majority, but Mr W(alpo)le lays the matter so much to heart that I doubt he will be made a young man of'.[1]

Although Hickman polled heavily, he was defeated by 2,584 votes to 2,406; a result which is remarkable evidence of the strength of the tory cause and of jacobite sympathy in the county.[2] The ballad goes on:

> So homewards they sneak but laughed at and scorned
> And may live to be hanged but never be mourned.

Henry Pacey, M.P. for Boston, supported Hickman, and so also most of the parsons (including Parson Bird) in the Boston neighbourhood; the movement emanated from the parts of Holland. Young Joseph Banks was in Lincoln at the time, and he wrote to his father in London that their enemies had brought vast numbers of white roses made of ribbons, badges of attachment to a popish pretender, and would have carried a victory with a high hand; the whig gentry saw to it that the whig mob did not incommode the tories.[3]

After the event the Whichcot steward wrote of the whigs that 'they believe it is now out of the power of the tories ever to choose another member for our county'. The Gainsborough people were subdued, but he believed that for their former insolence they would have some soldiers quartered among them.[4]

After such excitement feelings must have continued to simmer for a long time, and Bishop Reynolds was probably right in thinking that the riots that broke out in 1726, though they were expressed as a protest against the proposal of the dean and chapter to remove the spires from the western towers of the Minster, were really an expression of disaffection to the

---

[1] L.A.O. Massingberd Mundy, 11/1/65. Massingberd found himself in hot water as a tory in London 'except in our old club' (11/1/67). His son William met Prince Charles Edward, the Young Pretender, at Derby, in 1745, but was sent home bearing with him a miniature of the prince (*History of Ormsby*, p. 179).

[2] The sheriff's return, 12 Feb. 1724 (Leeds Public Library, Newby Hall MSS, no. 2498).

[3] The ballad, which was dedicated to V(incent) A(mcotts), C(harles) H(all) and M(atthe)w L(iste)r, leading whig gentry, the affidavit and other papers, are among the Banks Stanhope papers in the Spalding Gentlemen's Society library, 6/3. The affidavit is printed in *Lincs. N. & Q.* I, 15. The more dramatic story, recorded in the *Lincoln Date Book* (*sub* 1716), that Hickman, overcome by enthusiasm and liquor, rushed into the yard of the Angel in the Bail of Lincoln, knelt on his bare knees and drank the health of King James, is not supported by evidence.

[4] L.A.O. Aswarby, 10/27/13, 14. A poll book was printed after the election. Boston was fairly divided between the candidates, but much of the Holland division was heavily in favour of Hickman, as were Stamford, Horncastle and of course Gainsborough. In Samuel Wesley's Epworth, Vyner polled 58 votes and Hickman 1. Wesley voted for Hickman as from Wroot. Voters living in the Bail and Close voted for Vyner in the proportion of 8 to 1; and most of those living in the city who voted in virtue of county freeholds voted for Vyner.

State.[1] His opinion is supported by a report made at the same time by William Pownall, an energetic county magistrate living in Minster Yard, to the duke of Newcastle, who was Secretary of State. In making specific complaints against Mrs Southcott of Blyborough, he says that

the Papists do really use their Protestant tenants with great severity, and I may say persecution, and then if they draw the execution of the laws upon themselves they make an outcry of persecution as if exercised towards their religion.

He knew no instance, he said, where the laws against recusants had been put in execution when they kept within reasonable bounds. He added that not only in the country but in the city and suburbs of Lincoln the priests had made a dozen converts to the Romish superstition since the king's accession,

in which practices they are much assisted by one Mrs Crane, daughter to the noted midwife concerned in the juggle of the Pretender's birth, for she takes upon her to satisfy weak people of the legitimacy of the Pretender's birth, and she having served Queen Katherine to her death has got a plentiful fortune, and being a single woman now settled in the city of Lincoln, with the encouragement she gives and the ill use she makes thereof does great prejudice to the Government, for besides those that are perverted in their religion, there are many that though they do not swallow the camel, yet by her relation of matters of great consequence are seduced from their duty and affection of his Majesty.[2]

The parties were exhausted by the election struggle, and it is significant that thereafter there was no contested election in the county until 1807: the contests took place in private in the colloquies of the squires, and those whose interest proved inferior to those of others withdrew, declaring that they would not disturb the peace of the county—this became the usual formula— and sometimes being rewarded for their complaisance by being chosen later.

The new knight of the shire, Robert Vyner, though a whig, seldom voted with the government: he appears in company with Pulteney, an opposition whig, and tories like Windham and Shippen, and amongst the tory country gentlemen in 1757.[3] The first Lord Egmont wrote of him in his diary, 5 February 1730:

...he speaks to figures in the House, and with spirit, and always divides with the Tories, and does not want for sense, nor words in private discourse, in which last he is a little redundant for he swears like a dragoon.

[1] Below, p. 40.

[2] P.R.O. State Papers Domestic, George I, 63/26. A search for a Jesuit at Blyborough failed, but his breviary and some 'other rituals' were found. The Southcotts were among the richest Roman Catholic families in the county (Cosins's *List of Catholics and Non-Jurors 1716* (1862 reprint), pp. 65, 66).

[3] *H.M.C. Carlisle*, p. 64; Sir Lewis Namier, *Personalities and Powers* (1955), p. 70. There is a 'whip' urging his attendance to vote on the Hanoverian troops, sent to him in the names of Pitt, the Grenvilles, Waller, Dodington and others, 10 Nov. 1743 (Leeds Public Library, Newby Hall MSS, 2504). They were opposed to Carteret's policy of taking Hanoverian troops into British pay.

So perhaps the Lincolnshire tories began to think that he was not so bad after all. The second Lord Egmont, in a survey of *c.* 1730, described him as 'a whimsical man of projects of reformation, especially about the Army and Militia'.[1]

Meanwhile there had occurred the rebellion of 1745. In October a subscription was raised for the payment of forces for the security of the king and government, from which the names of Massingberd, Dymoke and Hickman were missing. Local events are more conveniently dealt with below.[2]

Vyner sat until the parliament of 1754, being joined in 1727 by Sir Thomas Lumley Saunderson, who had inherited the Lincolnshire estates of Lord Castleton in 1723, and built a house at Glentworth, apparently intending to make it his principal seat.[3] When in 1740 Saunderson went to the Upper House as third earl of Scarbrough, Thomas Whichcot was returned; he held the seat until the dissolution of the parliament of 1768. He and Vyner had been desired by the gentlemen assembled at the horse-races in Lincoln to stand, and they accordingly sent out their letters asking for support: setting aside the 'cant word' of the country interest, they stood for 'independency and incorruption'.[4] In 1747 there was a great appearance at the election, for it was expected that the third duke of Ancaster would revive his old family claim and nominate a candidate against Vyner and Whichcot.[5]

Whichcot first sided with the opposition, but in 1744 he joined the

[1] I am indebted to the late Sir Lewis Namier for these references.

[2] See below, p. 83; *H.M.C. Ancaster*, pp. 444–6. A story was preserved and repeated in 1848 of a visit to the county by Charles Edward. It was that he landed at Theddlethorpe and was conducted by a fisherman to Maidenwell, then in the tenancy of Michael Moseley, who was believed to be a Lancashire jacobite who escaped from prison after the fight at Preston in 1715, fled to France, and later settled at Maidenwell under an altered name. The prince is said to have attended a ball at Lincoln, which his friends in France considered a joke until he mentioned the breaking of a chandelier at the Lincoln ball, which on writing to Lincoln they found actually occurred (G. S. Gibbons in *Lincs. N. & Q.* XXIV (1936), p. 46, and for other references see *The Local Historian* (Lindsey Local History Society), no. 18, March 1938).

[3] He was already M.P. for Arundel. His Glentworth mansion is depicted in Paine's *Plans*. Byng wrote in 1791 that Scarbrough, with *special* taste, and folly of expense, added a new, flaring, red brick, back front; the old part had been turreted and inner-courted. The house was neglected and the furniture had been sold (*Torrington Diaries*, II (1935), 398).

[4] Spalding Gentlemen's Society, Banks Stanhope, 6/4.

[5] Monson, XXVI, 20. Coningsby Sibthorp told Dashwood that Lord Vere Bertie would decline Boston, and that the duke would nominate him in place of Whichcot (Bodl. MS DD. Dashwood, B10/1). When Newcastle sent out his circular letter of summons to attend the House in 1761 he summoned Whichcot directly, and also through Ancaster. Whichcot replied that he would try to be there (Sir Lewis Namier, *Crossroads of Power* (1962), p. 63).

government side and generally supported the duke of Newcastle. When the latter resigned, Whichcot wrote to him from Harpswell as one 'of the old Whigg-race, now almost extinct...I am not sure of the loyalty of the person that may succeed you...'.[1] Thereafter he was generally against the government. He withdrew before the election of 1774 on the grounds of age and infirmity. He held the family influence—and had great personal following—in the Isle of Axholme, which contained so many more free-holders than other parts of the county that it used to be said that whoever could get the Isle could get the county. His marriage to one of the Andersons of Manby strengthened his position. He had the reputation of standing up for the rights of the people: he annually drove a coach and four across the park made at Fillingham by Sir Cecil Wray, knocking down walls in his progress, by way of asserting a public right of way which Wray was trying to extinguish.[2] He was a decided protestant whig, hailing 'our glorious Deliverer, King William III', and hating the administration of Lord North, and especially the wicked Lord Bute, who bore the detestable name of Stewart. In 1770 he wrote to Sir William Anderson that he did not see the least appearance of much good at the opening of the parliamentary session, or he would be glad to attend 'to throw in my mite for the preservation of this poor Nation'. So many consciences would be sacrificed at the Whitehall Cockpit—the meeting of government supporters held on the eve of the opening of the session to hear the King's Speech read—to the Premier that he would not risk his health in cold weather to attend. The hiring statutes at Spital, in their confusion and the nature of their business—labourers selling themselves to employers for a year—reminded him of the meeting at the Cockpit.[3]

In 1760 there were signs that the gentlemen in the Lincolnshire militia would consult together about the county seats, an expression of independence which Whichcot, Newcastle and the whigs viewed with foreboding.[4] Ancaster was preparing to recover a seat for his family by putting up Lord Brownlow Bertie, whose papers show that Sir John Thorold was also preparing to stand: a correspondent wrote that he thought Thorold would be glad to make such a compromise as would be agreeable to Ancaster and to him, 'without which Mr Whichcot would hearken to nothing'. There had been a move to set up Vyner jointly with Thorold against Whichcot, and it was hoped that Ancaster would join it; but he had clearly come to

[1] Namier and Brooke, *The Commons 1754–1790*, III, 628.

[2] L.A.O. Anderson, 6/2, p. 209.

[3] *Ibid.* 5/1/11. The letter has been printed in full by Margaret Beel, *The Lincolnshire Historian*, II, no. 7, pp. 43–5.

[4] L.A.O. Aswarby, 10/51/2; dean of Lincoln (Green) to Hardwicke; Sir Lewis Namier, *England in the Age of the American Revolution* (1930), pp. 133–4.

terms with Whichcot, and Vyner withdrew, writing to the duke of New-castle that he was 'in no manner the cause' of the division in the county. Whichcot and Bertie were returned,[1] a result which cannot have given much satisfaction to the independent gentry.[2]

In the parliament of 1774 Whichcot's seat was taken by Charles Anderson Pelham of Brocklesby near Grimsby, who had also succeeded to his great influence in the Isle of Axholme, having already an immense territorial influence of his own in the north of the county. He seems to have supplanted the Ancaster family as the predominant voice in county elections; and he continued to hold that position, and his son after him, after he had received a peerage as Lord Yarborough.[3]

Although the gentry disliked attempts by the nobility to nominate members, they nevertheless looked to them for a lead not only in social but in political matters. When the House of Commons declared John Wilkes to be incapable of sitting in the House there was a movement among the whigs to petition the Crown against this invasion of the rights of freeholders. Sir Cecil Wray was said by Lord Rockingham (17 July 1769) to have asked the Lincolnshire grand jury to desire the sheriff to call a county meeting, but without success; later Thomas Whateley told Burke that he thought that the county would petition if Lord Monson and Lord Scarbrough countenanced it, and that Wray would eagerly take the lead.[4] Others thought that Wray was always ready to take the lead.[5] He found no followers.

Sir Cecil Wray, the thirteenth baronet of Glentworth, who had built the peccant park wall at Fillingham, can hardly have been a popular figure in the county. According to Wraxall he had no superior talents, but had a high moral character and was independent in mind as well as in fortune.[6] He had been returned for East Retford in 1768, and had spoken in favour of conciliation with America and he was a member of the Yorkshire and West-minster Associations for Parliamentary Reform.[7] In 1782 he was elected member for Westminster, his fellow member being Charles James Fox,

---

[1] L.A.O. 3 Ancaster, 8/3/3, 9, 10.

[2] Mrs Massingberd was on the side of the gentry, and canvassing for Vyner and Thorold; a Yorkshire correspondent wrote wishing success to them and 'to all true hearts and sound bottoms' (L.A.O. Massingberd Mundy, vii/1/D/33). Bertie entered Lincoln without a single soul to attend him (L.A.O. Aswarby, 10/51/4).

[3] See below, p. 218. His son's marriage to the heiress of Sir Richard Worsley in 1806 brought an accession of wealth.

[4] *Correspondence of Edmund Burke* ii, (ed. L. S. Sutherland), 47, 48, 60, 102.

[5] *Grenville Papers*, ed. W. J. Smith (1853), iv, 452–3.

[6] *Memoirs of Sir N. W. Wraxall* (ed. Wheatley) (1884), iii, 80, and see p. 341.

[7] C. Wyvill, *Political Papers chiefly respecting the Attempt of the County of York . . . to effect a Reformation of the Parliament of Great Britain*, iii, 161.

the great whig leader, and indeed he accepted nomination under pressure from Fox. They continued to be friends until Fox joined with his old enemy Lord North in a coalition government in 1783. He was one of the first to oppose Fox's India Bill. In the most famous of elections, that at Westminster in 1784, Lord Hood, Fox and Wray were the candidates, and the beautiful duchess of Devonshire canvassed for Fox. The poll lasted for six weeks and ended in the defeat of Wray; there followed a scrutiny which continued for eight months until Hood and Fox were declared elected. Wray never sat in parliament again, though he would have liked to do so.[1]

In 1779 Lord Brownlow Bertie became fifth and last duke of Ancaster, and there ensued a by-election. The nobility tried to move in. The duke of Rutland and Lord Monson each thought of proposing his own brother, though Rutland withdrew early. Monson sent out the usual circular letter canvassing support.[2]

There survives a report of the county meeting. Dr Gordon moved a subscription to strengthen the hands of government; but he was hissed by many of the middling classes, and Mr Harrison, a follower of Fox and soon to be M.P. for Grimsby, said it was extraordinary that private purses should be thus strongly called on when those who received the overgrown emoluments of government had subscribed so triflingly, and he would give when they did. Mr Monson was proposed for election by Sir Christopher Whichcote and seconded; Mr Phillips Glover objected to him on the ground of his youth and his being a soldier, and proposed Mr Vyner, who thanked him, declined, and proposed Glover. Mr Wood proposed his brother-in-law Sir John Thorold, who was seconded, and seemed to be approved by the king's friends there present. Sir Cecil Wray was proposed by Mr

[1] C. Dalton, *History of the Wrays of Glentworth* (1881), II, 187–214. It was said that he never raised his rents.

[2] Monson received promises of support from the dukes of Rutland and Newcastle, Lord Bristol, the duchess of Bedford who gave her grandson's interest, the Whichcotes and others. Sir Gilbert Heathcote begged to be excused because of his acquaintance with both Monsons and Chaplins; Lord Fortescue promised support as he had no application from his old and much respected friend Mr Vyner; Lord Fitzwilliam wrote that it was impossible that Mr Chaplin should stand without the support of his uncle Lord Exeter, Fitzwilliam's neighbour, whom he did not wish to offend, though his tenants in other parts of the county had their instructions; John Pownall wrote from the Excise Office that he had a letter from Lady Elizabeth Chaplin, but would support the Monson interest; Sir Joseph Banks begged to be excused till he had learnt the inclinations of the county at the general meeting; Sir William Anderson thought Chaplin not of age, having no chance, and in another letter said he thought Vyner would not think of it, and he imagined Thorold had tried the experiment; Lord George Sutton withdrew a promise of support in favour of his nephew Mr Chaplin; Charles Pelham, the other member, was non-committal (Monson, xcviii, 138–83). In 1780 a handbill was circulated that there had not even been a nomination meeting, and that the withdrawal of Mr Monson left the county with only two candidates, which was an insult (Lindsey C.L. Banks, 14/4).

Monck, who had been told by Wray that, if the county unanimously approved him, he would be ready to serve them faithfully and to the best of his ability. 'There this ended, though the man not objected to.' Monson then withdrew, and Thorold was returned.[1] He was a whig and a supporter of Charles Fox, and he voted against Lord North and the American war.[2] Three speeches of his in the parliament of 1784–90 (to which he was returned with Pelham) were concerned with the export of wool, a subject of burning importance in the county.[3]

Thorold told Banks that when he and Pelham were about to be proposed for re-election in 1790 he met Wray on Castle Hill. Wray said he hoped they would be opposed: he was referring to 'that old thing the India Bill'. However, Wray did not speak in the shire court, and he signed the return. Thorold added, 'I told him just that I should be more immediately his enemy, that I knew he was mine, if he did not stay dinner, to which he acquiesced'.[4]

After sitting for the county in four parliaments Thorold withdrew. The reason was that Sir Gilbert Heathcote, a much richer man, had emerged as a candidate, and only a very rich man could sustain a contest in so large a county. Oldfield remarked that Thorold 'had conducted himself with that integrity and independence which could never have given umbrage to his constituents, but upon the wealthiest man in the county becoming a candidate, it remained the only question with Sir John whether he would part with his seat or his fortune. He wisely preferred parting with the former'.[5] *The English Chronicle* thus pronounced judgement on him:

He is a sensible man, and sometimes speaks in the House, but he wants that brilliancy of elocution which gives effect and grace to reasoning, and is not therefore at all eminent in the present list of parliamentary orators.[6]

[1] *H.M.C. Savile Foljambe*, pp. 150–1.
[2] The town of Thorold in Ontario, a settlement of United Empire Loyalists, was named after him in view of his opinions on colonial matters (ex inf. the Rev. Hy Thorold).
[3] See below, p. 118.
[4] B.M. Add. 33979, pp. 44–5.
[5] *History of the Original Constitution of Parliaments* (1797), p. 280. The ostensible reason was disgust with the turn that public affairs had taken (*L.D.B.* p. 442).
[6] Per Sir Lewis Namier.

CHAPTER II

MINSTER AND CLOSE

SINCE the burning of the episcopal palace in Lincoln during the Civil War[1] the bishop had had no house in the city; which, as Bishop Wake told Archbishop Tenison, had no good effect upon the cathedral or his courts, which were kept there. After complaining of the impoverishment of the see at the time of Edward VI, he proposed that if it should be thought fit to restore the bishop's seat again to Lincoln, the deanery or three of the prebends should be annexed to it.[2] No such action was taken, and the bishop's principal seat remained at Buckden in Huntingdonshire on the Great North Road, where part of the palace is still to be seen.

Meanwhile the bishops kept in touch with affairs in varying degrees: by correspondence, by visits of their clergy to them in London or at Buckden, or by their own visitations, though these were not always held by the bishop in person. When they held their visitations personally the episcopal progress was punctuated by social gatherings. For example, in 1706 Wake dined with the chapter after visiting Lincoln Cathedral; he then visited part of the archdeaconry of Stow and returned to Lincoln to dine at the White Hart; the next day he was entertained by the corporation of Lincoln. He was received by Sir Willoughby Hickman at Gainsborough, but returned to Lincoln on the same day, and on the following day he entertained the mayor and corporation and the gentry to dinner.[3]

Though Wake's two immediate successors were conscientious men they played little part in the life of the city. Richard Reynolds, who was bishop from 1723 until his death in 1744, is chiefly remembered for his provision for his own family; he appointed his son George archdeacon of Lincoln in 1725 and his son Charles chancellor in 1728. He told Lord Monson in 1734 that he was inclined to rebuild the old episcopal manor house at Nettleham[4] to provide for a son who had a lease of Nettleham, though a year later he abandoned the scheme, having made other provision for the son.[5]

John Thomas was bishop from 1744 until his translation to Salisbury in 1761. It was said that he squinted and was very deaf, but that his humour and his knowledge of German commended him to George II, who brought

---

[1] *T. & S.L.* p. 162.   [2] Norman Sykes, *William Wake* (1957), I, 158.
[3] Lambeth Palace Library, Archbishop Wake's Diary: 'We went quietly into Stamford, none of the Corporation meeting us: yet in the evening they brought us a present of wine, and drank it all up when they had done.'
[4] *T. & S.L.* p. 123n.   [5] L.A.O. Monson, XXII, 48, 49.

him from a chaplaincy in Hamburg to England with a promise of promotion.[1] He was followed by John Green, who had been master of
Lichfield School, regius professor of divinity at Cambridge, became dean
of Lincoln in 1756, and was promoted bishop in 1761. He died in 1779.
The Rev. William Cole, whose living at Bletchley was in the diocese,
contrasted Green with his predecessor

whose gentlemanly behaviour had gained him the universal love and esteem of
his clergy: whereas the clownish carriage and want of behaviour and manners
in the present Bishop was so notorious at his last Visitation that everyone was
scandalized at it, and among all my acquaintances I never heard him mentioned
but with the utmost disrespect....Indeed the Bishop's ungain, splay-footed
carriage and Yorkshire dialect is a full indication of his humble education and
mean extraction; Mrs Dowbiggin's father, his Lordship's brother, being a miller
at Beverley. I do not mean this as being any reflection on his Lordship: if I did,
I should bespatter my own self, whose father was no more than a substantial
farmer: all I mean is, that a person of such extraction and accomplishments,
when they forget themselves and their former acquaintances in gaining titles
and preferments, are sure to be remembered for their forgetfulness. Bishop
Thomas was as low bred as Bishop Green: yet his behaviour as a gentleman was
such that I never heard anyone make that reproach to his character: whereas
the contrary carriage of his successor is continually the subject of ridicule in
whatever company his name is mentioned.

He described scathingly Green's visitation at Newport Pagnell, which was
done in such haste 'that it evidently appears that it is no small burthen to
attend at all'.[2]

[1] 'Bishop Thomas was a man of humour and drollery. At his visitation he gave his
clergy an account of his being married four times; "and", says he, cheerfully, "should
my present wife die, I will take another; and it is my opinion I shall survive her. Perhaps
you don't know the art of getting quit of your wives. I'll tell you how I do. I am called
a very good husband; and so I am; for I never contradict them. But don't you know
that the want of contradiction is fatal to women? If you contradict them, that circumstance alone is exercise and health, *et optima medicamenta*, to all women. But, give them
their own way, and they will languish and pine, become gross and lethargic for want of
their exercise." He squinted much. He was entertaining the company with a humorous
account of some man. In the midst of his story he stopped short, and said, "the fellow
squinted most hideously": and then turning his ugly face in all the squinting attitudes he
could, till the company were upon the full laugh, he added, "and I hate your squinting
fellows".'
This prelate suddenly diffused a glow of feeling over his auditory, when, at the annual
general meeting of charity children at Christ Church, in Newgate Street, he opened his
mouth to preach, and with great pathos read Matt. xvIII, 14, 'It is not the will of your
Father Who is in Heaven, that one of *these* little ones should perish' (Hone's *Year Book*
(1832), p. 825).
[2] *Blecheley Diary of the Rev. William Cole* (1931), pp. 22–3, 33–5. Green's father was a
tax collector; Thomas', a drayman. See Abbey, *English Church and its Bishops 1700–1800*
(1887), II, 75, 271. For their confirmation tours, see *Lincoln Diocesan Magazine*, v, 73–4,
144.

The distribution of preferment for family or political reasons, though bad in principle, was not always bad in its results. Archdeacon Reynolds, for example, entered fully into ecclesiastical affairs, and took a leading part in the Convocation of 1741, which was the last to meet for more than a century.[1] On the other hand, as might be expected, Cole took a poor view of Bishop Green's sudden loading of his niece's husband the Rev. Robert Dowbiggin with preferment:

and as such a total change came all at once upon him, with no great head to bear it, it was rather too much for him, and made him act, and say things, which, probably, at another time he would be ashamed of: but in short, the poor creature was overpowered with his good fortune, and could not help expressing it ridiculously before the company. He seems to have been told that he is to expect a Prebend: He is now Subdean of Lincoln...we may see him an archdeacon if not a chancellor.[2]

The calls upon members of the chapter were not very onerous. There was no collegiate life among them: each of the residentiary canons was expected to keep his residence of three months in the year; for the other months he was free, and could move to any other preferment he might hold in plurality with his dignity. The chapter had told Bishop Wake that they duly kept their turns of residence, and that the prebendaries generally kept their preaching turns; but that when they did not their turns were supplied by one of the residentiaries, or senior vicars, or neighbouring clergy, and they added drily that 'we think the church doth not suffer by this, though we ourselves sometimes do'.[3] Their return of 1724 said that the dean was chiefly at Westminster, being a canon and subdean there.[4] The precentor had been indisposed for upwards of a year, but the chancellor and subdean constantly kept their full residence in their respective houses. The services were performed either by those responsible or by their deputies.[5]

The letter of the statutes was no doubt observed, even though it was sometimes observed by proxy, but episcopal suggestions for more services were not received with enthusiasm. In 1735 Bishop Reynolds issued letters

[1] See *An Historical Essay upon the Government of the Church of England, from the Earliest to the present Times*, by George Reynolds LL.D., archdeacon of Lincoln (1743), pp. 241–4, in which he justified the part he took.

[2] *Blecheley Diary*, pp. 38–9.

[3] Sykes, *op. cit.* I, 231, quoting Lincoln Register, xxxvi, f. 119.

[4] They might later have added that when young Charles Reynolds became chancellor he at once raised the question whether the dean should participate in the chapter revenues when he had a royal dispensation from residence on account of age. For the correspondence with the duke of Newcastle see P.R.O. S.P. Dom. George II, xv, ff. 93–5, 102–3, 110–13, 144–5.

[5] L.A.O. Episcopal Register, 38, p. 43.

mandatory for more frequent communion services. The chapter called in the senior or priest vicars, who said they thought compliance would be burdensome to the residentiaries, but if the bishop insisted they would comply as far as they could. It was left to the dean to represent to the bishop the inconvenience that would ensue. Questions again arose upon their respective duties in 1746. The residentiaries agreed that they themselves would read divine service in the choir on Sundays so far as statute and custom obliged them: but they appointed two senior vicars as their paid deputies, and warned the other two that they were not excused from their general obligation to attend the choir, much less from their turns of duty every fourth Sunday to assist at communion service. From time immemorial it had been their duty to read morning prayers in the chapel at 6 o'clock in summer and 7 o'clock in winter, and they were required to be more diligent in the performance of their duty personally, and not by deputy, save by approval of the dean.[1]

The return of 1724 said that the choristers and boys duly attended services, and were not permitted on Sundays to play in the churchyard, or on any other days in time of divine service: the clergy often sent their officers out to stop children from playing games during service. There was no burden permitted to be carried through the church, or beggars to beg there, though sometimes idle and disaffected persons walked about in the aisles during service: they were stopped as far as possible.

The difficulty of keeping order in church and close seems to have been greater than the return suggests. In 1703 the chapter sought to have the precentor placed in the commission of the peace, as so many accidents happened wherein the church suffered for want of a magistrate among them.[2] There are frequent entries in the chapter acts about the indecencies and disorders daily committed in the Minster. The chapter seem to have been reluctant to interfere with a public custom of making a short cut through the church from one part of Minster Yard to another; but they gave notice in 1735 that unless the indecencies ceased they would close the church doors except in time of divine service. Whether this threat was carried out does not appear; perhaps it was, for in 1755 an officer specially appointed was only directed to inspect the many idle boys 'who frequent the Minster for mischief sake and break the windows, spouts and do other mischief', and endeavour to reclaim them, and have them punished 'for all disorders'. In 1767 the custom of opening the cathedral doors on all public occasions was discontinued.[3] By 1787 there was a more limited concern to protect the cathedral lamps and stop boys from breaking

---

[1] L.A.O. Chapter Acts, 1731–61, f. 75r. [2] L.A.O. Spital Deeds 3/3.
[3] *L.D.B.* p. 185.

windows. Evidently these measures proved inadequate, for in the following year it was ordered that the Minster be kept closed even on Sundays except an hour before morning and evening prayer.[1]

Even before the Civil War the state of the cathedral fabric had been a cause of anxiety.[2] During and after the war it suffered, not perhaps so much from direct assault upon it as from wind and weather owing to broken windows and roofs stripped of lead. In the years that followed there was so much to be done with so few resources to do it that the fabric grew worse. A new effort to raise money was stimulated in 1724 by an offer from Lady Thorold to give £500 towards repairing and adorning the church provided a like sum could be raised to complete the same. The cathedral clergy and the gentry at once responded; and the dean and chapter issued an appeal to the prebendaries not to be behind those who had no obligations to subscribe. They were asked to send their gifts to Mr Cunington.[3]

The chapter called in the architect James Gibbs to advise them; it was at this point that Lord Harley visited Lincoln, and he commented that it

has been a most magnificent pile, but is now in a very poor condition, and has all the tokens of entire ruin approaching. They told us Mr Gibbs had been lately there to view it in order to think of some method of securing it against an utter desolation, and that the first thing the Chapter designed to do was to pave it, which I thought but an odd conceit to prevent the tumbling down of the tottering roof and pillars.[4]

But they were not so stupid.

Gibbs reported that the whole Minster was very much out of repair. The two western towers had damaged the arches and split the piers beneath them. Some of these arches should be filled with a stone wall, and the wooden lead-covered spires on the towers should be taken down, as they made the towers more liable to be shaken by the winds. They were loose, as timber fixed to stone must be. Furthermore, the gutters were defective, and the roof generally was so bad that there was no walking in the church when it rained without being wet. The glass was out of repair, and the paving very bad all over. But the most urgent work was the securing of the western towers and the removal of the spires. The chapter took a second opinion from John James, who had followed Gibbs as Surveyor to the Commissioners for Building Fifty New Churches in London, and who concurred.[5]

[1] Chapter Acts, passim. By the time of Victorian protests against the Minster being closed to the public the reason had no doubt been forgotten.
[2] Calendar of State Papers Domestic 1637, p. 512; T. & S.L. p. 123.
[3] L.A.O. D. & C. A/4/10, no. 45.   [4] H.M.C. Portland, vi, 84.
[5] P.R.O. State Papers Domestic, George I, vol. 63, no. 51 (2) and (3).

In looking for stone for repair the chapter turned their eyes to the ruins of the bishop's palace, and permission was duly obtained from the Crown and the archbishop to take stone from it, Bishop Reynolds stipulating only for the retention of the apartment occupied by Mr Debia, a priest vicar, the stable belonging to it, the square tower (no doubt the Alnwick Tower) and two vaults.[1]

The beginning of the work of removing the spires was the signal for a riot. Mr Cunington, a priest vicar, had notice of the approach of a mob of about fifty people from the city, and he shut the Close gates. The mob broke the Pottergate open, but dispersed when Captain Pownall, a county magistrate, read the proclamation against riots: all night the Close gates were guarded by cathedral workmen and others with firearms. Representations were made to the mayor and aldermen, with explanations about the spires. The latter were not convinced, but they promised to suppress all tumult so far as they could.

'Still we heard from everybody,' wrote Mr Haseldine, a junior vicar, to the dean in London

that a great meeting both of Town and County on Fryday would certainly bemurder me, pull down my house and Mr Cunington's for being chiefly concern'd, and everybody was very apprehensive of doings from the next mobb, and Mr Subdean and Chancellor after long consultation about the matter agreed to send word down hill to Mr Mayor again in the evening on Tuesday to acquaint him (that he might prevent any further rioting) that the spires should stand till some further publick satisfaction could be given of the necessity of taking down &c.

Haseldine took the message to the mayor, but before he returned the streets were so full that he could hardly pass. He told the crowd of the message he had delivered to the mayor; nevertheless, some 500 of them came up hill to have some assurance from Cunington, which he gave them, with something to drink. Haseldine and the chancellor and subdean also bought them off.

They went down hill, broke some windows of several presbyterians, and then some went to bed, others to the alehouse with money they had rais'd, kept some of 'em up all night, and next day they took a civil round to ask money of several, since which time we have had no disturbance; but yesterday we were in great fear notwithstanding Mr Chancellor and Subdean had order'd the breach in the spire to be repair'd, which was actually begun, otherwise I certainly believe a great deale of mischief had been done, and I was told on Fryday by some country people they had notice to come in to assist in keeping up the Church and pulling down our houses. They had a notion soldiers were sent for to withstand them till the spires were down, but every where they were scowering up their guns and swords to face any force should be sent for that purpose.

[1] L.A.O. Episcopal Register, 38, p. 132; D. & C. Ciii/2/5a.

This was written on 24 September. On 17 October John Willis, another of the vicars, told the dean there was talk of rising again if St Hugh's bells were not constantly rung and the pinnacles on the middle tower set up.

The fifth of November is the day we are most apprehensive of; and if a regiment of foot souldiers could be sent by that time; or a report onely spread in the Evening Post (which is the only printed paper I think that comes to Lincoln) of souldiers to come; or if a smart letter were written to our Mayor and Aldermen to take better care to keep the peace than they have done of late, with some seasonable menaces to them if they did not, it might probably prevent a great deal of mischief.

The aged dean in London accordingly procured a letter from the Secretary of State, Lord Townshend, to the mayor, requiring that he and the other magistrates should not only make strict inquiry into the riots in order to bring the ringleaders to justice, but that they should take proper care for the preservation of the peace. The mayor and his brethren replied that the disturbance was made by some of the lowest rank of people, and caused, they believed, by the beginning to pull down the great spires of the cathedral. They were first dispersed by the mayor and then by Pownall. On the following day they assembled near the Close, but while they were in the city they appeared to be in small numbers and without noise, and a magistrate could not take action. The offenders were all of so low a condition that they were not known to the magistrates. Strict watch would be kept, especially on days of public rejoicing, and housekeepers and masters of families would be warned to keep a careful eye on their servants and apprentices. The mayor and his brethren could not learn that one word had been uttered disrespectful to his majesty and his government.

Bishop Reynolds, who though absent at Buckden was well informed, wrote a strong letter of reproof to the mayor, with a reminder that the cathedral work was directed by two of the greatest architects in the kingdom. To Townshend he wrote that he was confirmed in his first opinion

that 'twas not a Lincoln, but a Lincolnshire-Riot, incouraged by the successes of former riots (of those particularly that have been in the neighbouring fens) and managed by malecontents, seemingly to express zeal for the Church, but *really* and truely to make show of their disaffection to the State.

He had heard that Mr Kent, last year's mayor, had had the stoutness to say 'That the people could rise 20 miles round in defence of their spires, and that the Gentlemen of the County were for preserving their spires'. He had heard from the same agent that there had been an association of the rioters in writing.[1]

It seems that the mob really thought that the chapter intended to pull down the towers themselves. Loveday was told in 1732 that that had been the proposal that raised the riots.[2] Sir John Monson had evidently written in this sense to his uncle Sir William Monson, who commented that it was extraordinary that the masters were for pulling down the church and the mob for supporting it; he had thought of leaving something in his will for the repair of the Minster, but he was too good a churchman to give money that might be used in demolishing it; 'this puts me in mind of Lord Pelham's saying, that the Mob was always in the right'.[3] Clearly whiggish prejudice against the clergy had taken charge.

The spires were left, and the towers were underpinned by Gibbs's new arches and walls, forming lobbies within the west doors.[4] But if this danger was averted, much remained to be done. Loveday described the condition of the church: he found the windows broken and the building dirty; the choir had been not long since paved with squares of a white stone, the other parts of the floor having great numbers of tombstones from which the brass plates had been torn.[5]

The defence of the chapter to a charge of neglect would certainly have been lack of funds. They resolved in 1731 that in view of the poverty and need of the fabric, each of them should lend £12. 10s. to the fabric fund to discharge part of its debt, receiving repayment as income came in. They were opening one of their quarries, and beginning with urgent repair work. Their clerk of the works was a man who is entitled to a place of his own in a history of Lincoln.

Thomas Sympson, who was born at Great Salkeld in 1702, had settled in Lincoln by 1724. He was a schoolmaster, and twice churchwarden of St Michael, and it was by his efforts that his parish church was rebuilt. In 1728 he was appointed clerk of the works at the Minster, and he became librarian there and a proctor of the consistory court in 1743. He was also engaged in compiling a history of Lincoln, searching the city and other

[1] P.R.O. State Papers Domestic, George I, vol. 63, nos. 11, 34, 38, 41, 46, 51, 57. And see J. W. F. Hill, 'The Western Spires of Lincoln Minster', *L.A.S.R.* v (1954), 101–17. Willson recorded the memory of an old man who said that the mob forced the postern gate on Greestone Stairs, made a circle, and forced Cunington to dance to calls of 'High church or low, jump again, Cunington' (Willson, xiii, 58–9).

[2] *Diary of a Tour in 1732* (Roxburghe Club), p. 205.   [3] L.A.O. Monson, 25/1/36.

[4] Essex is said to have concluded in 1762 that the alarm for the towers was unfounded (Bodl. MS Gough, Lincoln, ii, 511). The grave of Bishop William Smith, founder of Brasenose College, Oxford, was moved nearer to the west door when the foundations of the new work was being laid (Sympson's MS referred to in note 2, p. 42 below).

[5] *Op. cit.* p. 205. Cf. *Archaeologia*, i, 26.

records, lamenting that Bishop Sanderson did not record epitaphs cut in stone as well as those in brass at the Minster,[1] and remedying the omission by doing it himself: he corresponded with Browne Willis and Stukeley, and he collected coins. From the city he received no encouragement:

as to the city I have no expectation of any thing from them. There are few or none in that Body, except one, that have any turn of head that way. If my work had been completed in his mayoralty, 'tis possible something might have been proposed by him: but that is past.

Sympson died in 1750, and is buried in the Consistory Court, where his tombstone is still to be seen.[2]

It was a good time for antiquaries in Lincoln. New building was bringing to light relics of the Roman and medieval periods, some of them recorded by Stukeley.[3] William Pownall, the vigorous magistrate, exhibited to the Society of Antiquaries a coin of Stephen and one of King David of Scotland, with the remark that he 'never knew 'em dig at Lincoln but they find coins'.[4] He was also a collector of manuscripts and a man of some learning. According to Loveday he was allowed to study in the Minster Library, and made so free with the books as to convey some of them first to his pocket and thence to his friend Sir Richard Ellis at Nocton: from whence they passed to Blickling. Two of the greatest treasures of the Blickling Collection were the Blickling Homilies and Psalter: these had belonged to the city of Lincoln, and were begged by Pownall from the corporation, which agreed to present them to him in 1725: 'two little books of ancient characters of no use to the city nor any ways do concern the city's affairs.'[5]

To return to Sympson. The first of his published letters to refer to the repair of the Minster is dated 1740, and addressed to Browne Willis. He said he had a tedious piece of work in hand, in repairing part of the roof, which had suffered more damage in the last winter's storms than would be

[1] For the Winchelsea Book of Monuments see *T. & S.L.* p. 175.

[2] His manuscript 'Adversaria. Collections for an history of the city of Lincoln. Indigesta Moles' is in the Bodleian Library, where it is MS Gough, Lincoln, 1. It has been used by all subsequent students of the history of Lincoln. Some of his letters from B.M. Add. MSS 5833, 5841, have been printed in *Lincs. N. & Q.* IX (1906–7), pp. 65–90, and see *M.L.* pp. xiii–xiv. His notebook containing copies of Minster inscriptions came into my possession from the library of the late Colonel E. L. Grange. His collections, or the most part of them, had passed to his son, the minor canon, who offered them to Bishop Green: the latter declined them, and encouraged Dr Pegge to pursue the subject (Nichols, *Literary Anecdotes of the Eighteenth Century* (1812), VI, part i, 36, 243–4).

[3] *Itinerarium Curiosum*, p. 86; *Diaries and Letters*, I, 310.

[4] *Numismatic Chronicle*, 6th ser. XVIII (1958), 90.

[5] N. R. Ker, *Cat. of MSS containing Anglo-Saxon* (Oxford, 1957), nos. 287, 382; R. W. Hunt, 'William Pownall: Antiquarian', *L.A.S.R.* IX (1962), 158. The *Blickling Homilies*, ed. Rudolph Willard, is now vol. X in the series 'Early English Manuscripts in Facsimile', Copenhagen, 1960.

made good for some time. In 1743 he wrote that he had taken down the ancient image of St Hugh from the summit of a pinnacle at the south corner of the west front, and pulled down 22 feet of the pinnacle itself, which was ready to fall into ruins. He had got it half-way up again, and hoped to have the saint fixed on a firmer basis before winter.

This has been the only thing of consequence done about the Minster this summer; and if it please God to give it as happy a conclusion as the great leaden spire had the last, I shall congratulate myself upon having done more in two years in my place than my predecessors did in an age before.[1]

After Sympson's death the chapter addressed themselves to repair on a larger scale. In 1755 a programme was drawn up by a person unnamed amounting to a total of £12,000 plus £3,000 for dressing, cleaning and polishing walls, columns and arches. Perhaps it was this huge sum which led Bishop Thomas and the dean and chapter to appropriate a tenth of their incomes, and the fines arising from their episcopal and capitular estates, to the repair fund; and with the prospect of larger resources they called in James Essex, of Cambridge, where he had done much work on the colleges, to advise. He reported in 1761 and again in 1764; and when some necessary outside work had been done he turned to the interior. He designed the altarpiece[2] and the bishop's throne, and he repaired the choir screen. In 1773 the dean put to him the idea of restoring the spire which had crowned the central tower until it blew down in a storm in 1548. To this Essex replied that the tower was not designed to bear a stone spire, and it could not support one. A spire of timber covered with lead, like the old one, could be built, but if it were to be in proper proportion to the tower it would be too high for so exposed a position. Instead he submitted a design for four corner spires and open battlements. His proposal was adopted—though a suggestion that the spires should be painted to look like lead was not—and posterity has adjudged his design a happy one. The remainder of the floor was paved about 1780. When he concluded his work in 1784 Essex was presented with a piece of plate by the dean and chapter.[3]

[1] *Lincs. N. & Q.* IX, 83.

[2] Described by Horace Walpole as 'very proper and handsome' (*Journals of Visits to Country Seats* in Walpole Society, XVI, 71).

[3] L.A.O. D. & C. A/4/13, 16; James Essex, 'Journal of a Tour through Part of Flanders and France in August 1773', *Cambridge Antiquarian Society*, XXIV, ed. W. M. Fawcett, pp. xiv–xxi. A local carver, James Pink, carved the altar and the arched doorways at the west end of the choir aisles. He never became master mason because he was a dissenter. The chapter house roof was repaired under Essex's direction by Thomas Lumby, the cathedral carpenter. His son William Lumby became master mason in 1775. The pulpit and reading desk put there after the Restoration stood in the middle of the choir until Dean Yorke's repairs (Willson, XIII, 59). It seems that the account of the cathedral printed by Essex in *Archaeologia*, IV, 149–59, was written by Dr Richardson (Nichols, *op. cit.* VIII, 610–11; and see Bodl. MS Gough, Lincoln, II, 505).

By 1788 the bishop and the chapter had paid towards the fabric fund, since 1755, the sum of £9,698; invested funds to bring in £68 per year, and were ready to invest another £1,000 at 5 per cent. The fabric revenue, thus augmented, was declared to be adequate, and the self-denying ordinance of 1755 suspended.[1]

During most of the time that Essex had been in charge of cathedral works James Yorke had been the dean. He was appointed in 1762, and retained the deanery while he was bishop of St Davids (1774-9) and bishop of Gloucester (1779-81). To him Essex addressed his reports, and it is evident that he took his duties seriously: he was a modest and conscientious man, and was later known as an excellent bishop. The greatest tribute was paid to him by William Paley when he dedicated to him as bishop of Ely his famous *Evidences of Christianity*:

When, five years ago, an important station in the University of Cambridge awaited your lordship's disposal, you were pleased to offer it to me. The circumstances under which this offer was made demand a public acknowledgement. I had never seen your lordship: I possessed no connection which could possibly recommend me to your favour: I was known to you only by my endeavours, in common with many others, to discharge my duty as a tutor in the University; and by some very imperfect, but certainly well intended, and, as you thought, useful publications since. In an age by no means wanting in examples of honourable patronage—although this deserves not to be mentioned in respect of the object of your lordship's choice—it is inferior to none in the purity and disinterestedness of the motives which suggested it.

For a scion of a great whig family to be commemorated in such a way, at such a time, and in such a place, is fame indeed.[2]

Essex's last reports were addressed to Precentor Gordon. John Gordon, described as a Scotsman,[3] was a fellow of Emmanuel College, whence, according to his enemy the Rev. William Cole, being held to be overbearing, insolent and troublesome, he betook himself to Peterhouse. He busied himself on behalf of Lord Hardwicke in his contest with Lord Sandwich for the High Stewardship of the university: on account of which he was commended to John Green and became one of his domestic chaplains, dedicating a tract to him as dean of Lincoln in 1760. When Green became bishop of Lincoln he rewarded Gordon with the archdeaconry of Buckingham. In 1769 Gordon became archdeacon of Lincoln, and in 1775 precentor. As Green was not noticeably devoted to his episcopal duties, he relied on Gordon, who was eager to deputise, appointing him

---

[1] L.A.O. Fac. 4/27.

[2] P. C. Yorke, *Life and Correspondence of Philip Yorke, Earl of Hardwicke* (1913), II, 577–8, 597; G. Harris, *Life of Lord Chancellor Hardwicke* (1847), III, 485.

[3] *H.M.C. Savile Foljambe*, p. 151.

(and others) to hold his visitation in 1778, and at other times making him his commissary. Cole watched his progress with contempt, recalling the time when he was a haranguer among the younger scholars in the profane style, ridiculing religion; yet he had become a solemn archdeacon. When he had preached before the university he had justified the murder of King Charles; presently he was to write against Rousseau, and to become a staunch opponent of change.[1] He had the honour of receiving James Boswell at Lincoln in 1778. Boswell wrote that he

first received me with great politeness as a stranger, and when I informed him who I was, entertained me at his house with the most flattering attention; I also expressed the pleasure with which I found that our worthy friend Langton was highly esteemed in his own county town.[2]

At Lincoln Gordon showed himself to be energetic and imperious, standing upon the old ways; and, moreover, he was seldom absent, apparently having little other preferment. He was soon involved in a chapter conflict. It appears that in 1778 some posts and rails had been erected on the north side of the Minster to prevent idle persons from wandering and boys from playing opposite the deanery windows.[3] The precentor objected on the ground that, if erected, the pale would in a few years be succeeded by a wall, and the public be prevented from using the east door of the cathedral, which had in the memory of man always been left open for their use.

Richard Cust, of the family of Belton near Grantham, became dean in 1782, and presently he directed Lumby the carpenter to add palisades to the rails. Evidently the dean thought so small a thing could be done on his sole authority: the precentor thought otherwise. He directed the receiver

[1] *Blecheley Diary of the Rev. William Cole* (1931), pp. 33–4, 233. See a series of articles on 'Gordons in Pulpit and Paddock' in the *Huntley Express*, 6 Sept.–18 Oct. 1917 by J. M. Bulloch. Gordon sought the public oratorship and the regius professorship of divinity at Cambridge without success. Anderson referred to Gordon's 'unbounded hospitality and dignified conduct that embalmed him in the grateful recollection of the people of Lincoln' (Notes to *L.D.B.* in L.P.L.).

[2] *Boswell's Life of Johnson*, ed. G. B. Hill, revised L. F. Powell, III, 359, 528. Boswell was also received by Thomas Sympson, a priest vicar and the son of Sympson the antiquary, whom Dr Johnson is said to have visited at his house in Vicars Court in 1764, when he went to stay with his friend Bennet Langton at Langton by Spilsby. It was of this visit that Langton told Henry Best that when Dr Johnson came to the top of a steep hill behind the house he said he was determined 'to take a roll down'. 'When we understood what he meant to do, we endeavoured to dissuade him; but he was resolute, saying, "he had not had a roll for a long time"; and taking out of his lesser pockets whatever might be in them—keys, pencil, purse or pen-knife—and laying himself parallel with the edge of the hill, he actually descended, turning himself over and over, till he came to the bottom' (Best, *Personal and Literary Memorials* (1829), p. 65).

[3] It was, of course, the old deanery, taken down in 1849.

not to pay for the work; and according to the dean he sawed down part of the palisades with his own hands, menaced the workmen, and 'insinuated to the populace' that the dean was stopping up an old way to the church. The dean was incensed, and brought before the chapter resolutions condemning Gordon's actions as irregular, presumptuous and indecent; and he moved that the constant keeping open of the north door leading from the deanery into the cathedral for boys and girls and apprentices to play there whenever they pleased was improper and ought not to be allowed, and that the door should be opened only for services.

The precentor protested that he had not been given notice of matters affecting his character and conduct, and moved an adjournment until after the audit, when the chancellor could attend. The subdean interrupted and said that he knew that what the precentor said would be nonsense, contradictious, and in character. The precentor gave notice of appeal and moved a vote of censure on the dean, which was negatived. Gordon withdrew, the dean's resolutions were carried by the dean and subdean, and, with the foregoing narrative, written into the chapter minutes. These amenities were brought to a close by the death of the dean five weeks later.

Cust was succeeded (in 1783) as dean by Sir Richard Kaye, who, it was reported, 'was pleased with the place and the people were pleased with him, he being a very polite and agreeable man'.[1] Under him the work of repaving the Minster went on, to the grief of Gordon, who urged that the monumental graves should be preserved, and only the intermediate parts repaved, and he referred the complaints of Sir Joseph Banks to Banks's friend the dean. Apart from the question of propriety he thought even quaint and uncouth memorials were more suitable than a spruce, modern, uniform pavement.[2]

When Gordon died in 1793[3] his mantle as the prophet of conservatism was assumed by Banks. He noted that before Gordon's death Dean Kaye had ordered the east door of the Minster to be generally shut, and 'probably in order to countenance the intended plan, the principal doors of the cathedral, which were always accustomed to be left open, were also occasionally shut'.

In 1794, while I am writing this, the plot seems to be nearly arrived at maturity. September is the race time: the foundation of a brick wall is laid, where the pales were, and either because workmen are not at the season to be procured, or because it is not prudent to begin such a work when the county are assembled on the spot, it is covered over with deal boards.[4]

---

[1] J. Foster to Dr Pegge, Bodl. MS Gough, Lincoln, v. 77. See Plate 17.

[2] Banks Corr. v, 80.

[3] He had just become a freeman of the city by purchase, intending, perhaps, to take some part in city elections.

[4] Banks Corr. IX, 148; L.A.O. Chapter Acts 1762–89, pp. 253–6.

But there is no sign that the county were roused. Kaye was a tactful man: he had not clashed with Gordon, and he remained a friend of Banks. It was probably as a concession to Gordon in his lifetime that the choir aisles were directed to be paved with old gravestones (1791), and as a tribute to him after his death that no material innovation should be made in the plan of Church and Choir, but that only the perishing parts should be repaired and the defective parts restored.

Banks had a universal curiosity. When on a visit to the races in 1782 he found that the tomb of Robert Grosseteste[1] had been opened for the antiquary Richard Gough he persuaded Gordon to open it again: and with characteristic thoroughness he took full details and recorded them, and had drawings made. Thus he commenced antiquary. Later he and Kaye opened the tomb of Little St Hugh—the subject of one of the ritual murder charges against the Jews found in a number of English and continental cities—and found a boy's skeleton in a kind of pickle, which Banks is said to have tasted.[2] When Kaye brought the Swiss artist Samuel Hieronymous Grimm to Lincoln to execute drawings of the Lincoln scene, Banks expected them at Revesby to make drawings of Tattershall, but they failed him and he inquired for another artist.[3]

Grimm was in Lincoln in 1784: his drawings have preserved details of many buildings in the city which have vanished since his time, a service for which Kaye must be remembered with gratitude.[4]

One of his drawings depicts the reredos and panelled sanctuary walls designed by Essex and carved by Pink in 1769. There is a communion rail round three sides, as first introduced by Archbishop Laud. Two clergy in surplice, scarf and hood, wearing bushy wigs, stand, one at the north end of the table, reading, and facing westwards, the other at the south end, facing north. The communion vessels are swathed in voluminous linen cloths. Two candlesticks and a large almsdish stand on a shelf behind. The communicants, males on the south, wearing knee breeches and white stockings, and females on the north, mostly in close-fitting caps but some in broad-brimmed hats, kneel on long low benches running north and south. Their youthful appearance suggests that this may be their first communion following confirmation.[5]

[1] Bishop of Lincoln, 1235–53.

[2] Gough, *Sepulchral Monuments in Great Britain* (1786), I, 47–8; Banks Corr. II, 234–40, reprinted as Appendix III in *Robert Grosseteste* (ed. D. A. Callus, 1955); *M.L.* p. 229.

[3] *Banks Letters*, ed. Warren Dawson (1958), pp. 57, 547.

[4] They are now B.M. Add. MSS 15541, 15542. See Rotha Mary Clay, *S. H. Grimm* (1941), pp. 92–3.

[5] Plate 3. E. V(enables) in *Lincoln Diocesan Magazine*, VIII, 83. For the description of the service by Henry Best, who was a convert to Roman Catholicism, see his *Four Years in France* (1826), pp. 7–8.

A few years later, in 1791, John Byng visited the Minster. He thought the service nobly performed; there was a choir of ten boys and five men, of whom one boy and two men appeared to have good voices; the litany was chanted by two lay-vicars with voices like bulls. The six o'clock morning prayers had been discontinued for about five years, which he found a sad proof of idleness and irreligion. On another occasion, at 9.30 a.m., he went to the service:

...this was a decent and honourable performance, but, unluckily for us, no anthem, as that is performed on Wednesdays and Fridays at evening service. How few people attend! Any attendance will soon cease: and I shall live to see when none will be present at a cathedral service, but a reader, a verger, and two singing-boys, who will gallop it over in a few minutes.

He was writing under the shadow of the French Revolution.

The cloisters he found in great disorder; the library had a great collection of old manuscripts soon to be arranged; the east window was of new stained glass, inferior to the old; the bishop's palace was a sight of caverns, sutteranes, doorways and ruins enough to serve an antiquary for a week, and in the dining-room the gardener was breeding rabbits. Byng's last comment was made upon a round of the Castle Hill, when he looked into the fine new gaol: 'what ornaments to a country! What succession houses to Botany Bay!'[1]

It is pleasanter to recall Mary Yorke's tribute to the cathedral, whose progress had been watched by her husband and herself from the depth of dirt, damp and green mould to a state of exquisite beauty.[2]

In the course of the century much was done to improve the surroundings of the cathedral. The sawpit and the 'nettleyard' lay somewhere near, and cannot have added to amenity. A blacksmith's shop and other mean buildings had faced the west front: they were cleared away by Precentor Trimnell (1717–56) who had been chaplain to Wake; in their place he built the seemly 'Number houses', so called because they were the first houses in Lincoln to be known by numbers. The Galilee Porch had been walled up—as Hollar's print shows—and used as a casting house, and the room above was used by a glazier. The porch was opened. The surviving Exchequer Gate was used as an alehouse under the name of 'Great Tom', and the outer gate, which was taken down about 1796, housed the Duke of Marlborough inn. By stages the close was becoming a residential enclave and acquiring its modern dignity.[3] On the other hand the advent of the turnpike, which must have improved the road through the close, entailed

---

[1] *Torrington Diaries* (1935), II, 346–7, 400.   [2] Above, p. 13.
[3] Below, p. 274.

the abandonment of the medieval practice of closing the gates at night, so that the chapter could no longer have withstood riots as they did in 1726. There is no reference to the repair of walls and gates, and they gradually fell into ruins, the walls no doubt being used as quarries as opportunity offered.

After the Civil War the dean and chapter had reasserted their civil rights within the Close to the exclusion of the sheriffs and justices of the city, and they resumed their 'View of Frankpledge and Court of Galilee', but the record of the court ceases in 1729.[1] Presumably it was not worth the trouble and expense of keeping up. At the bishop's visitation in 1724 the chapter were eager to disclaim any authority over the inhabitants of the Close other than those belonging to the Church: they said that the whole Close was divided into two parishes, the churchwardens whereof were to take notice and present such wicked persons as happened in each parish, and they supposed that the public houses duly licensed in the Close kept such order as the law required.

The parish churches abovehill were closely linked to the cathedral body. After the first post-war efforts[2] little was done for several generations. St Peter in Eastgate lay in ruins, St Margaret had not been used in the memory of man, and the parishioners of St Paul in the Bail declared that their church was so ruinous that it could not be repaired and must be rebuilt. In 1778, perhaps on the initiative of Gordon, a petition was presented to the bishop for the union of the parishes of St Peter and St Margaret. It declared that the population of these adjoining parishes was small, that a church for the two was needed, and the most convenient place was the churchyard of St Peter: sufficient money had been raised, with the old materials, to build a new church. The order for union was made, and pews were sold as freeholds, at £10. 10s. each. The new church was consecrated in 1781. It was a plain stone box without a chancel, the altar being inclosed with rails: and the pews being appropriated, there were benches for the poor in the worst part of the church. Nevertheless, it was a church, and at the time large enough.[3]

A move was also made in St Paul's parish. In 1785, at a vestry meeting

[1] L.A.O. D. & C. Bii/3/15; *M.L.* pp. 125–6. For exhibits from the court book see C. L. Exley in *Lincolnshire Historian*, I, 307.

[2] Above, p. 4.

[3] St Margaret's Parish Book; Episcopal Act Book, no. 39, p. 309. A first list of subscribers is in L.A.O. Fac. 4/3. Dr Gordon, who as precentor was rector of St Peter, presented communion plate in 1786. A small addition was made on the north side of the church in 1831 (L.A.O. Fac. 13/1). The present church was built in 1870. Venables, writing after the Oxford Movement, was scathing about the church of 1781. He called it a mean conventicle with stable windows (*Lincoln Diocesan Magazine*, I, 103–4). See Plate 6 (*a*).

HGL

at the George and Dragon, it was decided to accept the proposals of John Barnard to take down and rebuild the church for £54. 10s. A subscription was to be raised, and augmented if need be by a parish rate. The foundation stone of the new church was laid in 1786 by Dean Kaye. The new church was a plain rectangle with a semi-circular apse, and according to the petition for a faculty it was to have twenty long seats, and hold 120 persons and twelve in the chancel.[1]

[1] L.A.O. Fac. 4/19. See Plate 5 (a).

CHAPTER III

SOCIETY BELOWHILL

I⊤ is almost impossible today to imagine the isolation in which the citizens belowhill lived, without even the leaven enjoyed abovehill of a few who knew the wider world. Lincoln was remote; it was small; it was old and decayed; and life in it, apart from a few special occasions, must have seemed to a visitor hardly to move at all. The roads leading to it were always bad and sometimes impassable. It was three days' journey on horseback from London. The fens virtually closed some of the roads to the south in winter months, and even the old north road was liable to be cut at Huntingdon; and the Trent interposed a barrier to the west, for it was unbridged below Newark, and could only be crossed by ferry, an unpleasant and sometimes dangerous operation. It was cut off from the north by the Humber, and the north-east of the county was occupied by the wild country of the wolds. More immediately there were great open heaths to the north and south of the city, which must be crossed in order to get to Brigg, or Sleaford, or Grantham, and to the south-west, on the way to Newark, was wide open moorland. There was no other town nearer than 15 miles, and few would wish to walk so far and back in a day.[1]

There was no regular stage-coach until nearly the end of the century. Only the rich could afford to travel by private coach, and others must go on horseback or on foot. Three times a week the northern mail dropped the letters for Lincoln at Newark, whence they were fetched by the postboy. There was no local newspaper, and it could be said in 1726 that the only printed paper that came to Lincoln was the *London Evening Post*.[2] No printer had yet appeared, and announcements and advertisements could only be published by the aid of the common cryer and his bell. There was no place of public assembly, no theatre, no newsroom, so far as is known no coffee-house, no library save the cathedral library, and a few books in parish churches or vestries which were dignified by the name of parish libraries. Social gatherings were confined to private houses or the inns, some select and some otherwise.

The city was deeply embedded in the countryside, and the townsmen had not yet become a separate race. They lived amongst rural sights and smells. Children were within easy reach of wild flowers, for the fields came up to the houses, bringing the scent of blossom in spring and new mown hay in summer; and butterflies and bees haunted the streets. Social, like

---

[1] See *T. & S.L.* ch. I.　　　　　　　[2] Above, p. 40.

economic, life was governed by the annual cycle of seedtime, haytime and harvest. For the citizens as well as for the countryfolk, to whom they were often closely related, many small observances punctuated the year, and provided the variety which was a sufficient spice for life to those who were not accustomed to more.

There were special food dishes to mark the seasons, to which everyone, especially the children, looked forward. The end of the wheat sowing was celebrated with hopper cake, round cakes of plum bread over which hot spiced beer had been poured; at sheep shearing or harvest supper both workers and guests had frumenty, which was wheat well soaked in milk, with currants or sultanas, eggs, nutmeg, and perhaps brandy and cream. For rook shooting there were rook pies, only the breasts and wings being used, with hard boiled eggs added. At the spring fair there had been Grantham whetstones, crisp cakes, which were eclipsed by Grantham gingerbread, which was discovered by mistake in 1740: it was made from flour, sugar, ginger, lemon, milk, candied peel and butter. When finished it was round and white, with a hollow interior, which was shiny, and resembled a miniature stalactite cave.[1] At Easter there was tansy pudding: it was a batter pudding into which was squeezed juice compressed from the aromatic leaves of a herb called tansy. It was eaten with orange marmalade.

Pride of place among dishes belonged to the pig. After the killing there were first the scraps, which made sausages, pork pies, brawn, jellies and haselets; and the great dish for May day week was stuffed chine. This delicacy consisted of a neck chine of bacon stuffed with herbs, parsley, a little thyme and marjoram, and raspberry and black currant leaves, lettuce and spring onions. Flour and water were added to make a stiff paste. At Christmas there was all manner of 'pig cheer', and mince pies.[2]

The villages had their annual feasts, to which citizens so minded—especially the lads and lassies—could go. There were Washingborough and Branston feasts in January; Thorney feast in April. At Easter came Nettleham flaun, a rollicking week with nightly dancing in the square, much frequented by Lincoln folk; the flaun was said to be named from flat cakes made of curd of milk mixed with eggs and sugar.[3] In May there were feasts at Fenton and Martin; in June at Boultham, Torksey, Canwick and Saxilby; in August at Dunham, Navenby and Coleby; in September at Carlton le Moorland and Norton, and the fair at Wragby; in October (the harvest well over) there were feasts at the Hykehams, Thorpe on the hill, Bassingham, Dunston, Navenby, Metheringham, Thurlby, Eagle,

---

[1] *Lincs. N. & Q.* xx, 80; xxii, 109.
[2] *Lincolnshire Magazine*, ii, 92, 114, 123; iii, 85 (by Walter Johnson); *Recipes from Wrawby* (1937).   [3] L.P.L. U.P. 1683.

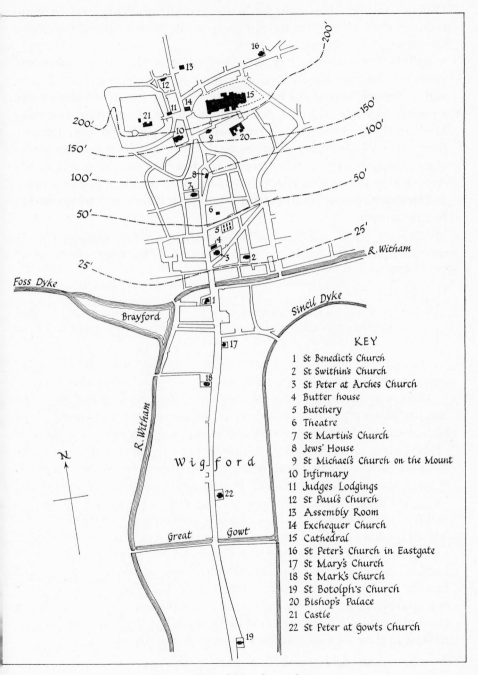

Fig. 1. Plan of Lincoln c. 1820.

KEY

1 St Benedict's Church
2 St Swithin's Church
3 St Peter at Arches Church
4 Butter house
5 Butchery
6 Theatre
7 St Martin's Church
8 Jews' House
9 St Michael's Church on the Mount
10 Infirmary
11 Judges' Lodgings
12 St Paul's Church
13 Assembly Room
14 Exchequer Church
15 Cathedral
16 St Peter's Church in Eastgate
17 St Mary's Church
18 St Mark's Church
19 St Botolph's Church
20 Bishop's Palace
21 Castle
22 St Peter at Gowts Church

Collingham and Harmston; in November at Swinderby and Skelling-thorpe.[1] Each village had its own maypole, its Plough Monday, its sheep shearing and harvest home suppers.

Willson later remarked of these festivals that their rude jollity and merriment had become less frequent; and that the refinement of manners, and a greater separation between the different ranks of masters and servants, together with the extending influence of sectarian (meaning Methodist) preachers, had repressed much of the old hospitality. Even so, there was no little drunkenness among the men, and often dancing parties were attended with a rude familiarity towards the other sex nearly approaching to licentiousness.[2] It is no surprise therefore to find farmers and stewards complaining of the effects of such festivities. The steward at Nocton wrote:

22 July 1765. These two feasts at (Potter) Hanworth and Dunston have so turned our labourers' heads from work that we have not been able to get all our hay mown last week.

He added a week later:

This last week has been our horse race, which has been another help to keep our heads turned from minding business, and this week is our Assizes. I hope when they are all over we shall fall to business again.

By 5 August he had finished haymaking, and had 'got shut' of a great number of idle haymakers who came for the money and to spend their time.[3]

There were also in the course of the year the Lincoln fairs and the races; and the assizes provided a state entry of the judges, and the panoply of the high sheriff and his javelin men and trumpeters abovehill, and the visit of the judges to the Guildhall to deliver the city gaol; and occasionally there was the excitement and the ghoulish pleasure of a public execution.

On a day in May proclaimed by the high constable there were the hiring statutes. All the farm servants engaged at a yearly wage took a holiday, which they spent in a round of amusement, sometimes in de-bauchery; and they often had their pockets picked or otherwise fell victims to rogues who lay in wait for the simple rustics. When after the usual bargaining the labourer came to terms with a new master, the latter handed him the 'fastening penny' as an earnest of the bargain, and the recipient spat gravely upon it before putting it in his pocket. In defiance of the usual superstition, the labourers wore peacocks' feathers, with rosettes or ribbons in their hats bought from hawkers in the streets.[4]

---

[1] These were the dates given in *Lincoln and Lincolnshire Cabinet* (1827). They may have varied occasionally.

[2] Willson, XIII, 62.   [3] Bodl. MSS DD. Dashwood (Bucks), B19/5/16–18.

[4] Gutch and Peacock, *Lincolnshire Folklore* (1908), pp. 10, 41.

Besides the great Christian festivals of Christmas, Easter and Whitsuntide, there were the observances added to the Prayer Book in 1662. On 29 May the Restoration was celebrated: the children thought of Charles II taking refuge in the oak tree, wore oak leaves and nettled those who had none, and chanted a demand for a holiday. In some parts of the county the ploughboy would adorn the head of his horses with oak leaves. The day marked the close of the birds' nesting season, and the boys considered it unlucky to take eggs later, and mostly did not.[1]

On that day the mayor and aldermen went to church in scarlet gowns to give thanks for the restoration of the king and the royal family. On 30 January, in black gowns, they observed the Martyrdom of the blessed King Charles I. On 5 November, in scarlet, they went to church to give thanks for the deliverance of King James and the three estates of England from (to quote the Prayer Book) 'the most traiterous and bloody intended massacre by gunpowder, and for the happy arrival of King William on that day, for the delivery of the Church and Nation'.

Guy Fawkes Day—gunpowder treason and plot—was a great event. It began with the ringing of bells. Bull-baiting was a favourite amusement, which was not suppressed until the nineteenth century. Vagabonds infested the streets for some nights before, making fires and breeding riots, and the mayor and his officers were kept busy in enforcing the peace. With the evening came the bonfires, each parish having its own, to which even the hard-faced parish officers were constrained to contribute.

The pomp and circumstance of civic life lent colour to this small confined society, and provided a spur to modest and worthy ambition. Any boy becoming a freeman might hope to be elected and installed mayor in the Guildhall, and invested with ring and sword; then to be played to his house by the waits, or municipal musicians, and attended by the council, whom he would entertain with cakes and wine, afterwards dining with them at the Reindeer. Then there were the days of attendance in state at divine service. On the king's birthday he might if he chose invite the aldermen to take wine with him at the Reindeer; and on the Sunday before he installed his successor the aldermen, sheriffs and chamberlains would take wine and fruit with him before accompanying him to church. Having attained the office of alderman he continued in office for life.

Within the confines of a small community the year was therefore full and diversified. Herein it was not markedly different from many other country towns, sharing with them institutions to which a village could not attain. It was however different from other country towns in being a county town and a cathedral city, and so in comprising two different but

[1] *Ibid.* pp. 205-6.

linked communities. The citizens belowhill never ceased to be conscious of the presence of their betters above the hill. Tradesmen were dependent upon their custom and that of the farmers, who were their tenants. Social functions needed the patronage of a nobleman or a gentleman; no charity could prosper without their blessing; no election could be fought without candidates from their ranks; and they took the lead in cock-fighting and horse-racing. Humanitarian impulses came from uphill; leadership and initiative were all too often absent below. New movements, such as Methodism, were difficult and slow to start; they were repressed by the domination of those at a higher social level who stood for the established order in Church and State. An element of deference and even servility was always present. Later there would be resentment at a calm assumption of superiority; if it existed earlier, it did not much appear.

For all these purposes the gentry came downhill, but there was no return traffic. Only occasionally did one who had made money by trade or banking, like Ellison or Brown, enter the uphill circle, or a tradesman's son, made sufficiently respectable by taking Holy Orders. The social differences were noted at the end of the century by a casual observer: Charles Dibdin, being a dramatist, put it in theatrical terms:

...this city is composed of a high and a low town, which are perpetually at variance with each other. I cannot explain this better than by saying that if there were a play-house at Lincoln, it must be in one of the following predicaments. If it was situated on the hill it would be all boxes; if under the hill all gallery, and if in the midway all pit; and, therefore, as a play-house cannot subsist but by the union of boxes, pit and gallery, I should apprehend fortunes are not acquired by theatrical performances at Lincoln.[1]

This is a very superficial account; there is a better and pleasanter variant of the theme by Charles Lamb. He tells of an aged gentleman who was found every Saturday at his father's table, and who had been a school-fellow of his father at Lincoln. They would sometimes talk about old days.

The houses of the ancient city of Lincoln are divided (as most of my readers know) between the dwellers on the hill and in the valley. This marked distinction formed an obvious division between the boys who lived above (however brought together in a common school) and the boys whose paternal residence was on the plain; a sufficient cause of hostility in the code of these young Grotiuses. My father had been a leading Mountaineer; and would still maintain the general superiority in skill and hardihood of the *Above Boys* (his own faction) over the *Below Boys* (so were they called), of which party his contemporary had been a chieftain. Many and hot were the skirmishes on this topic—the only one upon which the old gentleman was ever brought out—and bad blood bred; even

[1] *Observations on a Tour* (1801), I, 377.

sometimes almost to the recommencement (so I expected) of actual hostilities. But my father, who scorned to insist upon advantages, generally contrived to turn the conversation upon some adroit by-commendation of the old Minster; in the general preference of which, before all other cathedrals in the island, the dweller on the hill, and the plain-born, could meet on a conciliating level.[1]

Whether Lamb was romancing or writing with pedantic accuracy is uncertain; though there were many Lambs in the city then and earlier, neither his father John Lamb nor his family has been positively identified among them.[2] The story is broadly true.

The lower city had its own class distinctions. There were the old families, whose members had held civic office for generations; but their ranks were never closed, and there were others, comparative newcomers, who had prospered fairly fast and established themselves in the same circle. There were the lesser tradesmen, master craftsmen, the journeymen and the labourers. The Becke family are a good example of the old established family. They had taken a notable part in the city's affairs during the Civil War. Thomas Becke was born in 1690—in the year that his father John Becke was sheriff—and he was licensed to practise as an attorney in 1711, becoming chamberlain in 1720. Perhaps his professional avocations and his practice in the city court prevented his attaining higher civic office; but clearly he prospered, acquiring an estate at Cherry Willingham near Lincoln, becoming patron of the living, and building the church in the 'Augustan' style which houses his memorial. Herein his son John commemorated his professional ability and unparalleled industry, which 'enabled him to acquire a fortune (without the sordid means of avaricious Parsimony) in times to whose Extravagance few Patrimonys sufficed'. He died in 1757 at 67, 'an age to which Temperance alone can extend Vitality'.

His son John, who thought this a great age, did not long survive him. He reached the office of mayor in 1759, and died in 1763 aged 51. His daughter Mary married Joseph Dell, surgeon (mayor in 1768 and 1778), and their daughter Judith married Henry Hutton, a member of a family which lived on in Lincoln in affluence for several generations. One of John's sisters married Charles Newcomen, an attorney, and another married Gervase Gibson (mayor in 1749 and 1767), an apothecary.

It was the civic leaders who were gradually effecting improvements in social amenity. A few street lamps were set up at the city's charge in 1729; but the corporation preferred to remind the parishes that this was a job for them, offering that if the parishes would maintain the lamps, the city

---

[1] 'Poor Relations' in *Essays of Elia*.
[2] See E. V. Lucas, *Life of Charles Lamb* (1905), I, 3 n.

would light them. They did not amount to much, and the moon long continued to dictate the dates of the evening social occasions. In 1755 the city bought a fire engine, with buckets, ladders and firehooks, and combined pleasure with business by having it play on fair days, in horse-race week, and on Guy Fawkes Day.

There are more substantial evidences of a slowly rising standard of comfort and social life. For their own benefit the common council repaired and reseated the Guildhall, and so prompted the thought that the citizens might benefit by using it for social gatherings rather larger than was possible in private houses, and more genteel than in inn parlours. They had before them always the example of their betters abovehill, where the great room at the Angel was often the scene of festivity. In 1731, therefore, the gentlemen and ladies of the city applied to Mr Mayor for the use of the Guildhall and the inner hall for a fortnightly assembly. The application was granted. Then, as the gentry abovehill went one better and built the county assembly rooms, the citizens began in 1757 to raise a subscription for the building of an assembly room, card room, tea room, and other conveniences. By that time the new market house was built, and the promoters asked leave to build over it. The common council agreed to build at the cost of the subscribers, the market house being in no way prejudiced.[1] But it was not until 1797 that the council bought a sedan chair for the comfort of ladies.

The common council had already made provision for the social needs of themselves and their friends. They bought the Reindeer inn (formerly the George), in High Street, near to the Guildhall. It was a house the old part of which projected forward, the chambers being supported by a range of wooden pillars, forming a portico; and the council set about rebuilding and repairing it. Of course it cost more than they expected, and they had to borrow on bond. There was already a cockpit there, but it was not good enough for Lord Monson and Lord Vere Bertie, two of the patrons of the sport, who contributed to the interest charges on a new building. Presently the council resolved that all public dinners paid for by the city should be held at the Reindeer, and the number of guests who achieved admission had such a way of growing that occasional steps had to be taken to keep it down. The *London Gazette* and the official votes of the House of Commons were taken, and there the Aldermen's Club settled official and social business in comfort and seclusion.

Various male societies were coming into being or at least into sight. In 1730 a lodge of freemasons was meeting at the Saracen's Head. Clearly it owed its formation to Sir Cecil Wray, the eleventh baronet of Glentworth,

---

[1] See Plate 7 (*b*).

who was deputy grand master of England. The surviving minute book shows that he was master of the lodge in the period 1732–5, and no doubt it was his energy that brought together an unusual social mixture of clergy, gentry and citizens, including the host of the inn. Wray died in 1736, but he survives in a bust in Branston church, executed for him in his lifetime and therefore to be regarded as a likeness, in which, like Matthew Prior, he wears a turban. After 1735 only one meeting, in 1742, is recorded. Another lodge had been constituted abovehill, at the Angel in the Bail, in 1737, which seems to suggest that after Wray's death the social elements in the earlier lodge had flown apart.[1] The new lodge had vanished by 1754, and the old lodge was erased from the records of Grand Lodge in London in 1760. Single social gatherings could flourish in Lincoln, but apparently the social pulse beat so feebly that a continuous organisation could hardly be sustained.[2]

Joshua Peart wrote in 1751 of a club with printed articles, among whose members were John Becke, himself, and many other freemen who were friends of Mr Monson.[3] It was no doubt the centre of the 'red' or Monson election interest in Lincoln.

Friendly societies were being formed for the benefit of a poorer class, journeymen and labourers. They met at public houses, a fact which spoke ill for the prudent management of their funds. There was one formed at the Royal Oak in 1734; at the Peacock in 1737; at the Crown in 1766; at the old Crown in 1784, and others later.[4] The rules of the Peacock society, which are probably typical, provided that its members must be under forty years of age on admission, not disaffected to the government, nor troubled with any distemper. Members paid a shilling for any of the half-yearly feasts, there were sickness and funeral benefits, and the widow of a member received a lump sum. But it had to meet at a licensed house, and part of the monthly subscription had to be spent there.[5] For some years the curate at St Peter at Arches preached two sermons a year for the friendly societies.[6] These societies are not likely to have been better managed than those that came under criticism later.[7]

It was probably the better men among the poorest class who were members of the friendly societies. A picture of the dullest and stupidest

---

[1] Certainly two brethren of uphill society did not appear at the old lodge in 1742.

[2] W. Dixon in *Ars Quatuor Coronatorum*, IV (1891), 97, and his *History of Freemasonry in Lincolnshire* (1894), pp. 1–20. Thomas Becke was a brother of the old lodge. His church at Cherry Willingham owes something to his masonic interests.

[3] L.A.O. Monson 25/2/102.

[4] *Lincoln and Lincolnshire Cabinet* (1829), p. 57.

[5] They were printed by William Wood in 1759.

[6] *L.A.S.R.* VII (1958), 162.   [7] Below, p. 287.

was given at the end of the century, and was no doubt equally true at its beginning:

The amusements of the lower classes of Lincoln are by no means on a par with those of their neighbours. They have no happiness, no enjoyment but in an alehouse. When there they form no social club where 'the Catch, and the Glee and the Song go round'; but closing their mouths with a pipe or a cigar, they never move it from their lips except to drink their pot of ale: for each man, though the room be full, has his separate pot; he forms his own company, and has no connexion with the crowd around him, except to do his share in emptying *pots round* at the decision of a wager. Conversation is unknown, and unless some doubt arises of the time of suffering of some notorious malefactor; the winning of a plate by a certain horse; or the money made by the last election; a Lincoln man continues as taciturn as if Nature had not blessed him with a tongue.[1]

The author would not have quarrelled with a description of the inhabitants of the Gainsborough area in the early years of the century:

> The Goths were not so barb'rous a Race,
> As the grim Rusticks of this Motly Place;
> Of Reason void, and Thought; whom Interest rules
> Yet will be Knaves, tho' Nature made them *Fools*!
> A strange half Human and ungainly Brood,
> Their Speech uncouth, as are their Manners rude!
> When they would seem to *speak* the Mortals roar;
> As loud as Waves contending with the Shore!
> Their wided Mouth do in a Circle grow,
> For all their Vowels are but A and O!
> The Beasts have the same language, and the Cow,
> After the Owner's Voice, is taught to low![2]

They have their place in the economic scene, but little more is heard of them in the city as a social class.

It was to be long before a local newspaper secured a foothold in Lincoln. There was a shortlived *Stamford Post* about 1712; the *Stamford Mercury* appeared in 1713; and there was a Nottingham paper about 1710. Like other provincial papers, the *Mercury* did not print local news, and was

---

[1] *Lincoln and Lincolnshire Cabinet* (1827), pp. 11, 23.

[2] *T. & S.L.* p. 11, quoting *A Satyr on Lincolnshire, in a Letter in From a Gentleman in Lincoln(shire) to his friend in Wolverhampton, Staffordshire* (2nd ed. 1736). Burrell Massingberd tried to reproduce the dialect speech in a letter to Thomas Allam (23 June 1705): '...who can expect less than that an old woman should presently come, with an "And please you, zur, hearing you can cast a figure, I whopp you well tell ma whar my quey may be fund, that I loost th'uther day". In short, my dear Mr Allam, unless you help me to a fresh supply of conversation from London (tho it were bottled up I would not care) I shall loose my very English, as well as my witts, for here they talk naught but dagmaferish. You can't send for a carpenter to bore an auger hole but he'll tell you "Ha'l ramble hather hes womble, and wurl ye and wurl ye a whul" &c.' (Massingberd Mundy MSS, Society of Genealogists).

dependent on London newspapers and newsletters for its material. It had therefore no advantage in time over the London newspapers; its advantage was that it could print extracts from a number of newspapers, and so give different points of view. It can only have made headway in Lincoln slowly, and perhaps not until it began to give local news later in the century. In 1784 it became an eight-page paper of increasing size of page; and Richard Newcomb's long association with it began about 1786.

The first attempt at a Lincoln newspaper was made by William Wood, who was also the first printer. When in 1712 John Garmston's sermon on the martyrdom of Charles I was printed at the request of the mayor and corporation, it was printed in London for John Knight, bookseller in Lincoln; in 1718 the forms for Bishop Gibson's Visitation were printed in London. Wood appears in 1728 as printer of the *Lincoln Gazette or Weekly Intelligencer*, a half-sheet of paper, folded in four leaves, but it ceased in the following year. He printed the Visitation articles in 1729. He sought admission as a freeman of the city in 1728, and twice in 1729, but without success; other booksellers may have been afraid of his competition. He was at last elected in 1741. His *Lincoln Journal* appeared in 1744, but had no more success than his *Gazette*. What appears to be the first book printed in Lincoln is dated 1748: it is *The Atheist Converted, or The Unbeliever's Eyes open'd*, being an account of the conversion of a Guernsey gentleman by his little daughter.[1]

It may have been Wood's son, William Wood the younger, who printed and sold *An Historical Account of the Antiquities of the Cathedral Church of St Mary, Lincoln* in 1771. Being, according to Willson, a weak man, possessed of no learning, he employed one John Abbot to help him. Abbot was an insolvent coach painter, and when he was working for Wood he was in the debtors' prison at the castle. The quotations were inserted at random, with references to authorities whom the author had never consulted. Browne Willis—who was remembered by old men as an old-fashioned gentleman in strange dress, his servants in liveries trimmed with a great deal of yellow lace, and large shoulder knots with points and laces— had given a copy of his *Survey of the Cathedral* to Mr Cooper, the master of the choristers, who lent it to Abbot. From this and other unacknowledged sources the pamphlet was put together.[2] Such was the inauspicious beginning of published local history in Lincoln.

---

[1] *The Library*, 3rd ser. II (1911), 319.

[2] Willson, VII, 9; XIII, 54. Willson was given the information by James Bunch, then a singing boy in the choir where Abbot's son was. Wood gave up business in 1787, and retired to Langworth, where he died in 1804 (Nichols, *Literary Anecdotes* (1812), III, 689).

By 1785 there were several booksellers.[1] Among them was Drury, who printed a *Lincoln Gazetteer or General Advertiser* in 1784; it was merely the *Stamford Mercury* with some local additions. It ceased in 1785, and recommended its readers to the *Mercury*.[2]

Perhaps the proprietor of the theatre in Drury Lane had already discovered the truth of Dibdin's remark about the difficulty of supporting a house in Lincoln. About 1764 he tried his fortunes downhill, in the King's Arms Yard off the present Clasketgate. Little is known of it, and no doubt it was small. It was recorded however that the Duke of York saw *Midas* there in 1766. It was rebuilt in 1806, when its elegance and accommodation were much admired, and Mr Robertson the proprietor congratulated.[3]

But a far greater part was played in the life of the city by the Church of England than any secular bodies; and a relatively small part by Roman Catholic and Protestant dissenters. The number of parishes had been reduced from the medieval forty-five to nine in the city belowhill plus those uphill in 1550,[4] a number which still far exceeded the needs of the population. Most of the churches were small and mean and in disrepair, and, indeed, several had fallen victims of the Civil War. St Botolph had collapsed, and the tower and nave of St Benedict were so much damaged that they were taken down, the tower being rebuilt across the chancel arch. St Swithin had been burnt: in 1705 it was described as 'unfit', and by 1721 as 'none'. The clergy stipends were miserably poor, and at most of the churches there were services only monthly or quarterly and perhaps on the greater festivals.

It was no wonder therefore that Mr Reid, a priest vicar and master of the grammar school, could also take charge of St Mark, St Margaret, St Mary Magdalene, St Mary le Wigford, St Peter at Gowts and St Swithin, and that Mr James Debia, a prebendary, served St Botolph, St Martin, St Michael, St Paul and St Peter in Eastgate, holding as well the rectory of Boultham and the vicarage of Skellingthorpe, both near the city. Pluralists they were, but not wealthy pluralists, and not really absentees: their combined income from their preferments hardly exceeded £60, and the shrunken population could no doubt be accommodated in the churches

---

[1] *Earliest Directory of the Book Trade*, by John Pendred (Bibliographical Society, 1955), p. 30.

[2] For the earlier papers see G. A. Cranfield, 'Handlist of English Provincial Newspapers 1700–60', *Cambridge Bibliographical Society*, *Mon.* no. 2.

[3] Willson, VI, 60, 64, 65; J. B. King's notes in L.P.L. U.P. 1911; for an address spoken there in 1782 see *Poems on Several Occasions* by E. Samuel (Lincoln: S. Simmons, 1785). U.P. 1083).

[4] *T. & S.L.* pp. 56–8.

still in use.[1] It seems that the church authorities would have liked to overhaul the parish organisation, unite some of the benefices, and dispose of the fabrics and sites of the ruined churches, but that they were defeated by the conservatism of the parishioners.

The only churches belowhill at which there were services every Sunday were St Peter at Arches and St Mary le Wigford, both of them under the patronage of the mayor and corporation. At St Peter's Mr Gilbert Benet, who lived in his vicarage house at Reepham, five miles to the east of Lincoln, was rector, but he had a curate:[2] there were prayers on Sunday morning, and twice every day in the year. On Sunday afternoon there was a sermon, and a great concourse of people went to it, there being no other (Anglican) sermon belowhill. This was the corporation church, and it had long been the custom for the aldermen and common councilmen in their gowns to attend Mr Mayor to service there on Sunday afternoons and on other public days, and also at the sessions and courts leet. Penalties for non-attendance had been imposed, and in 1711 teeth were put into the rules by the provision that the shilling penalty might be levied by distress on the mayor's warrant. The corporation paid the curate for reading public prayers every afternoon, and occasionally a sermon on behalf of the Protestant succession to the throne was printed at its cost. There were civic pews there, as there were also at St Mary le Wigford, where in 1719 the minister was asked to preach every Sunday afternoon.[3]

Virtually nothing[4] is known about the old church of St Peter. It was probably small, and in disrepair. The need for a new church was generally accepted, and it may be suspected that the first move was made under ecclesiastical pressure from Minster Yard. Whether this be so or not, the application for the brief for rebuilding was made by the city in 1719. Thomas Sympson ascribes the initiative to alderman John Lobsey, then mayor. The common council, roused to action, rather lightheartedly agreed to take up £1,000 at interest to rebuild the church by such ways and means as should be agreed upon. After time for reflection, they resolved to limit

---

[1] *Speculum*, pp. xvii–xviii (see below, p. 309).

[2] For an account of one such curate, Rev. John Willen, see *L.A.S.R.* VII, part 2, pp. 157–74.

[3] Mr Booth, the usher at the grammar school, was desired to print a sermon he preached there against the anabaptists, and was given help in printing a rejoinder to their answer.

[4] Save a few carved fragments which were found when its successor was taken down in 1932. Harley said the old church was commonly supposed to have been older than the Minster; it had several ancient monuments in it, 'but I do not find that there has been any care taken to preserve them as they ought to be; several of them are laid down in the floor for common pavement and covered with pews' (*H.M.C. Portland*, VI, 84–5).

their liability to that sum, and to pay £100 a year out of the city stock for ten years. To save the money the mayor's allowance was limited to £40 plus the quit rents on city property, and £20 for the Michaelmas entertainment 'for the body of the city', that is, the freemen, 'laying down the feasts on New Years Day, Holyrood day and the sessions'; but it was agreed that the private sessions dinners to justices and grand jurors should continue, and £3 was allowed for Holyrood day 'for the body of the city', whose indignation at being deprived of their traditional right to refreshment at the charge of the common stock the city fathers were not willing to face. A large body of trustees, nobility, clergy, gentry and citizens was set up to administer the building fund.

The trustees evidently knew what they wanted, for they chose as architect either Francis or William Smith of Warwick, whose work was well known.[1] They knew that they would get a rectangular church with large round-headed windows, Tuscan arcades, a semi-circular apse and a noble western tower. It would be a preaching church, with a great three-decker pulpit obscuring the altar, well fitted for denunciations of pope and pretender. The Haywards were the builders. The old church was pulled down in 1721, and the new one is said to have cost £3,373.[2]

The common council soon found themselves committed to raising another £600, and Sir Thomas Saunderson, who was building up a political interest in city and county, was made a freeman of the city for setting up handsome iron gates and rails with pillars of Roche Abbey stone round the church.[3] The building was finished and consecrated in 1724, and soon afterwards the bishop was invited to an entertainment at the city's charge. Members of the council were ordered in future to attend service on Sunday afternoons whether the mayor was present or not. For adornments, the altarpiece, the clock and a chime of eight bells from Rudhall of Gloucester[4] the city paid, and for the bellringers too. When repainting was needed, the cost was borne equally by city and parish, so close was the union of Church and State.

Meanwhile, in 1721, a citation had been sent to the parishioners of St Botolph to acquaint them that the bishop had given their ruined church with other demolished churches to the rebuilding of St Peter's, and they

---

[1] H. M. Colvin, *Biographical Dictionary of English Architects 1660–1840* (1954), pp. 555–6. Mr Colvin says that the church was of Roche Abbey stone, which would mean that the stone came from Sir Thomas Saunderson's quarry there, or from the ruined abbey.

[2] L.P.L. MS. 4938. See Plate 7 (*b*).

[3] The main gates now stand outside the ruins of Nettleham Hall, and a small one with rails outside The Greestones on Greestone Stairs. The church has been rebuilt in brick at St Giles, the stone facings and pillars and the design having been preserved, though the nave has been lengthened by one bay (see *M.L.* p. 135n.).

[4] The bells cost £381.

were summoned to show cause why it should not be so applied. The vestry's reply was that for some years past they had designed to rebuild a place out of the ruins, and had a paper of subscriptions for the purpose, but had nobody to put them in a method to manage the affair. Accordingly the whole parish appeared at court, where there was a discourse to them to show the piety of applying their stones to such religious use rather than that they should lie in ruin and rubbish, there being no likelihood of their being put to better use. The reply that the parishioners would rebuild the church was looked on as a ridiculous fancy, the parish being inconsiderable, and the tithes only for the use of the prebendary, who was under no obligation to serve the cure save at the further charge of the parish. They were, however, given time to consider further. They were not daunted by the thought of the capital cost plus a curate's stipend, and they used the time to some purpose: they raised £66 and contracted with Henry Grix of New Sleaford to pull down the ruins and build a new church for £70. It was a hard struggle to raise all the money needed, and it is said that some of the parish officers were imprisoned for debt. John Stanley, church-warden and leading spirit, gave generously, and many subscriptions were collected and loans received. When he found that the parish was in earnest the good-natured Bishop Reynolds helped, and the city gave £200 towards the endowment in order to entitle the parish to a like sum from Queen Anne's Bounty.[1] A lay of 5s. in the £ was ordered by the vestry in 1731— to pay off part of the heavy debt on the church, on pain of proceedings in the spiritual court.[2]

Other church building was undertaken, though rather less is known about it. Thomas Sympson made a move to get St Michael, which had lately fallen, rebuilt, and succeeded in 1739. A faculty was granted to sell four bells which had lain unused for over fifty years. The city gave £20 towards the cost, and a year later gave £50 towards a new tower for St Martin, and, said Sympson, 'a very handsome one it is, and I daresay had never been rebuilt but through the resolution of an honest gardener that happened to be appointed churchwarden'.[3] A new St Mark was

---

[1] See the account in St Botolph's parish book; Willson, v, 15; H. M. Colvin, op. cit. p. 249. The church was much altered in the nineteenth century. John Stanley bought and started the new parish book in 1725, to replace one which had served the parish since 1584, which, he alleged, had been made away with in order to asperse the promoters of the rebuilding, and to make it possible to insinuate that the churchwarden himself had kept it back to prevent an audit of his accounts. He reflected with some satisfaction that 'not unfitly might that expression be applied to this place, that the glory of the latter house have exceeded the glory of the former, and from all the parish so earnest for it we might have expected thanks and peace'. See Plate 5 (b).

[2] L.A.O. Fac. 11/22. John Lamb, bricklayer, was one of the petitioners.

[3] Lincs. N. & Q. ix (1906–7), 80.

begun in 1740.[1] With the exception of St Peter, all the new churches were small, plain, and innocent of architectural pretension; simple rectangular boxes, though large enough for their parishioners. St Peter's has been removed, and St Botolph altered and enlarged, but all these other eighteenth-century churches have vanished. Happily they were recorded by Grimm.[2]

Church and State being simply different aspects of the established order of things, religious dissent was regarded as a species of public wrong; it is under this heading that Blackstone placed it in his *Commentaries on the Laws of England*, and it was so regarded by the clergy. It was not fully sanctioned, but since 1689 it was tolerated. Dissenters had inferior civil rights, for they were subject to various civil disabilities, being excluded from most public offices and from universities and many schools. There were, moreover, ways of persecuting them, though after the heats of the Protestant Revolution of 1688 had died down the feeling against them was not so fierce as it became in the war years at the end of the century. For political reasons the whigs were willing to placate the Protestant dissenters by civility if nothing else.

There was a small community of Roman Catholics. From 1580 until after the Restoration they had been served by Jesuit fathers who lived outside the city; they met in a chapel or private house in the Bail described as being 'not very spacious but neatly decorated and much frequented'. It was probably this building that was burnt by the mob at the time of the Revolution of 1688, whereafter another chapel was established between old St Swithin and the river: about 1750 it was transferred to a house in the modern Bank Street.[3] There were among them a few people of note like the Manbys, who had succeeded the Granthams at St Catherine's Priory outside Wigford: one of them had become a magistrate under James II's Declaration of Indulgence, which was soon swept away. Papists were subject to disabilities and to penal taxation, and when in 1737 one of the city waits or musicians confessed that he had forsaken the Protestant religion of the Church of England and embraced that of the Church of Rome he was at once dismissed. When rumours of a jacobite rising were current in 1744, the common council addressed the king, denouncing a bigoted pretender directed by popish counsels, and pledged themselves to enforce the laws against papists and nonjurors. Willson records that one year on Guy Fawkes Day Lady Deloraine went to the Cornhill and

---

[1] See Plate 6 (*b*).   [2] B.M. Add. MSS 15541, 15542.

[3] The congregation used to assemble in a long narrow garret at the top of the house, with the door carefully locked while Mass was celebrated (E. J. Willson's notes to Drury's *History of Lincoln*, B.M. 1430, h. 14).

broke the windows of a Catholic lady, thereby testifying that she was a good Protestant.[1]

In his memories of life as a pupil at the grammar school, Henry Best, who was born in 1768, recalls that as his home was at some distance from the school, whenever it rained between 9 and 10 o'clock in the morning, the time when the boys went to breakfast (school began at 6 o'clock in summer and 7 o'clock in winter), he took his bread and milk at the house of three elderly ladies, one of whom was kin to his mother, and who were Catholics. (He was not allowed to drink tea, but they put sugar in his milk.) One wet day he stayed to dine: it was an abstinence day, and he found the boiled eggs and hot cockles satisfactory. The priest, Mr Knight, came in after dinner. As it was then a great risk for priests to wear black coats, he was dressed in a grave suit of snuff colour, with a close neat wig of dark brown hair, a cocked hat, almost an equilateral triangle, worsted stockings, and little silver buckles. 'I believe', Best added, 'that I was the only protestant lad in England, of my age, at that time, who had made an abstinence dinner, and shaken hands with a Jesuit.' When he reported his doings at home, his father replied, 'These old women will make a papist of you, Harry'.[2] They did; and Best built a chapel for the congregation in 1799.[3]

Mr Knight was succeeded by a French exile, the Abbé Beaumont. He had been rector of the university of Caen, and appointed canon of Rouen, and was about to take possession of his canonry after the French Revolution had broken out, when the order was issued, on account of the approach of the duke of Brunswick, that every priest, who still refused to take the oath prescribed by the revolutionary civil constitution for the clergy, should be

---

[1] Willson, XIII, 67. Willson records as an example of prejudice against Roman Catholics an incident of about the year 1745. Mr Gwillim, steward to Mr Heneage of Hainton, was coming from Rasen after attending the market and met with a stranger on the road who said he was travelling in order to buy wool, and they rode a short distance together. Mr Gwillim asked his companion what was the news, and he told him something which he had heard respecting the public affairs of the day; on which Mr Gwillim observed that if that report was true, the price of wool would soon be lower. They parted soon afterwards, when the stranger stopped at North Willingham to look at Mr Matthew Boucherett's wool. Whilst endeavouring to make his bargain, the wool-buyer, it seems, told Mr Boucherett what he had heard, and how it was likely that the price of wool would fall, as Mr Gwillim had predicted. This he said as an inducement to Mr Boucherett to take the price which he offered for the wool; but Mr Boucherett, who was not on good terms with Mr Heneage, and much prejudiced against Catholics, prosecuted Mr Gwillim, and he was thrown into prison for 18 months or more for a misdemeanour in disheartening his majesty's subjects (Willson, XIII, 66). Boucherett deed in 1749.

[2] *Four Years in France* (1826), p. 12. Rev. William Hett, who hated Methodists, pays tribute to Knight (*Letters respecting restrictions laid upon Dissenting Teachers* (1810)).

[3] *Records of the English Province of the Society of Jesus*, v (1879), 619 *et seq.*

banished from France. Beaumont was brought to Lincoln by a gentleman of the neighbourhood to teach French to his children.[1]

The returns made by the parishes to the bishop record some families of Anabaptists, Presbyterians and Quakers. There were conventicles of Presbyterians and Anabaptists in St Benedict's parish, where the latter, needing a river for baptism, occupied the site still occupied by their successors; the Quaker conventicle in St Martin's built a meeting-house soon after the passing of the Toleration Act with an emergency exit into the yard at the back of the women's gallery for use in the event of a raid by the justices, and they still occupy it, though it seems to have been closed about 1770, and there were no Quakers there in 1786;[2] there was another Presbyterian conventicle in St Swithin's. There were independents in St Martin in 1782 and in St Swithin in 1776.[3] The Anabaptists, whose trust deed dated 1726 recites that the meeting-house was built about 1701, submitted a certificate under the Toleration Act to the bishop in 1765 and again in 1770.[4] Yet they had fallen so low in numbers in 1769 that they let their meeting-house to a body of Particular Baptists on condition that the latter kept it in repair and allowed General Baptists to preach in it when they could find opportunity.[5]

Rather more is known of the conventicle which met in St Peter at Gowts parish. The house of John Disney there had been licensed under the Declaration of Indulgence.[6] Disney had settled in Lincoln before 1670, and in his autobiography his son Gervase says 'thither the Lord in his providence sent Holy humble and worthy Mr Abdy to be pastor of that congregation, for which he had liberty by the King's Proclamation and Licence of Indulgence'.[7] After his death Mr Drake came over from Fulbeck every Saturday evening to preach; he was certainly a Presbyterian and a member of the Folkingham classis. After James II's Declaration he removed to Lincoln. A chapel was built about 1725, and the trust deed directs that the land be held on trust for 'that separate congregation or Church of

---

[1] Best, *op. cit.* p. 42. Paley had a poor opinion of Beaumont. When someone referred to him as the cause of his conversion, Paley replied: '*He* convert; he never converted anything but a rump of beef into steaks' (Henry Best, *Personal and Literary Memorials* (1829), p. 197).

[2] *The Friends Library*, ed. W. and T. Evans (Philadelphia, 1837–50), v, 415; x, 470. I am indebted to Mr E. H. Milligan for this reference.

[3] L.A.O. Dissenters, I, 1782/3, 1776/19.

[4] Where the building and vestry are said to abut upon Brayford (L.A.O. Dissenters, I, 1765/5, 1770/2, 1776/19). It is more remarkable to find a certificate for a body of independents in the Bail in 1780 (1781/4).

[5] A. C. Underwood, *History of the English Baptists* (1947), p. 152.

[6] *Calendar of State Papers Domestic, 1672*, p. 380; *T. & S.L.* p. 181.

[7] *Some Remarkable Passages in the Holy Life and Death of Gervase Disney Esq.* (1692), p. 49.

Christ in the said City of Lincoln...so long as such separate congregation shall by law be tolerated'. Daniel Disney endowed a chapel at Kirkstead: in his will, dated 1732, he left legacies to the Lincoln poor who dined with him on the Lord's day. The little congregation continued for half a century, and furnished a certificate to the bishop in 1774, describing itself as Independent.[1] It had been described as Presbyterian in 1719, when its congregation was said to consist of 207 hearers, 16 voters, 1 esquire, 5 gentlemen, 2 yeomen, 25 tradesmen and 4 labourers.[2] Yet by 1774 the congregation had dwindled, and the trustees had it in mind that the society should be dropped, though the minister at Kirkstead was asked to come on six Sundays in the year.[3]

It was at this moment, when all the older dissenting communities were at a low ebb, that a few followers of George Whitefield obtained leave to use the meeting-house, and applied to the Countess of Huntingdon to send them a minister. There arrived the Reverend Cradock Glascott, one of the most eminent ministers of her connexion, who preached in many parts of the country. Like John Wesley he never ceased to be an Anglican, and presently he took a living in Devonshire. As other ministers followed him in the borrowed meeting-house the congregation began to assume that the lapse of time had given them a title to the property. The trustees were alarmed, secured the keys, and locked them out.[4] The Whitefield Methodists presently built Zion Chapel in Silver Street, and the survivors of the old puritan community resumed worship in the meeting-house as Unitarians: there survives a special prayer book for the use of Unitarian dissenters in Lincoln.

As the century advanced John Wesley's own movement became established in various villages round the city, and it is a striking fact that Wesley, who was often in the county, seemed to avoid it. He came in 1780, at the age of 77, remarking that he had not set foot in the place for fifty years, though herein he was mistaken, for he passed through it in 1749:[5]

The city crier having been employed to announce his intention of preaching on the Castle Hill, a large crowd assembled at six in the evening, to whom, under the canopy of heaven, he preached the word of life. The day after, at ten in the

---

[1] L.A.O. Dissenters, I, 1774/4. There was also a body of Independents in St Mark's parish (1782/3).

[2] Dr Williams's Library, John Evans's List of Dissenting Congregations, 1715-29, MS 34.4.

[3] J. C. Warren, 'From Puritanism to Unitarianism in Lincoln', *Transactions of the Unitarian Historical Society*, II. Dr John Disney, the vicar of Swinderby, had gradually adapted his church services to suit his changing views, until he resigned his living, and became a Unitarian minister at Essex Street Chapel in London. He recorded his resignation in the parish register at Swinderby, adding *Liberavi animam meam* (*A.A.S.R.* XXVI (1901), 128).

[4] Warren, *op. cit.*   [5] *Journal* (standard edition), VI, 284.

girls there was needlework; the purpose of the schools was to fit the children for their humble role in the world. About 1719 there was an annual subscription of £73.[1] The subscribers held a triennial meeting, with a sermon at St Peter at Arches and a collection in aid of the funds. The sermon preached by Dean George in 1752 was published at the request of the corporation and the nobility gentry and clergy concerned in the charity; and it was printed by William Wood.

There were a few parish charities for the instruction of one or two poor children; and in 1720 John Wilkinson, mason, left four cottages in the Bail and other property at Middle Rasen to provide for eight poor children of St Paul's parish and eight of Newport to be taught to read and write, and for another school at Rasen. Penistan Booth, one of his executors, made up the endowment himself to £90, and the four cottages were pulled down and a school house built. It seems reasonable to infer that where there was any urge to learn, children, even of the poorest class, might get the beginnings of an education.

The most popular charitable institution in Lincoln was the Bluecoat School. The Lincoln Christ's Hospital—to give it its proper name—had been founded by Richard Smith, a native of Welton by Lincoln who had practised as a doctor in London, for twelve poor boys from city Bail and Close and the two nearby parishes of Welton and Potterhanworth. Of this latter place he had been lord of the manor, and he gave the manor as the endowment of his hospital. Smith died in 1602, and the hospital was incorporated in 1611.[2] Since that time it had attracted further endowments from a number of notable residents. Dr Peter Richier of the Bail (by codicil dated 1732) had provided for two more boys, one from an uphill parish (St Mary Magdalene) and one from a downhill parish (St Martin). Alderman John Lobsey, by will dated 1748, left £200 to provide for another boy from St Martin. Edward Holland (1749) did the like. Alderman John Hooton (1767) provided for another city boy. Richard Barker (1766) left £100, directing that at the end of seven years the interest should be paid to so many honest and industrious old scholars as the master and governors should think fit, the minimum payment being £5.

By 1786 there were seventeen poor boys in the school. Other gifts came in: in 1804 Samuel Lyon, sometime town clerk, left £500 to increase the number of boys. The greatest increase of income however came from the inclosure of the lordship of Potterhanworth, as a result of which the annual rental rose from £194 to £393; and when leases fell in and holdings were rearranged it reached £807. The Witham drainage works added 600 acres to the area of profitable cultivation.

[1] Cox, *Magna Britannia*, p. 1496; *T. & S.L.* p. 214.   [2] *T. & S.L.* p. 135.

As the hospital prospered the governors felt justified in building a new hospital house. William Lumby was commissioned to build it, and it was completed by 1785. By the end of the century the cost was paid off, and an annual surplus was being invested in Consolidated Stock.

The boys remained in the school to the age of 16, when they were put out as apprentices. They were well looked after. They must be in by 5 o'clock in winter and 8 in summer. They must not go to fairs, markets or races unaccompanied. They might visit relatives living in the town once a month, or in the country twice a year. They might bathe in the river twice a week at the proper seasons, and they might be employed in milking cows or upon the other business of the family as the rules prescribed. It was not until later that questions began to arise about the success of the hospital.[1]

In the administration of these charity schools no conflict arose between the dean and chapter and the corporation. The chapter however took a different view of the grammar school, which was not a matter of poor relief. This was a union of the cathedral school and the city grammar school, effected in 1584. By the deed of union the dean and chapter were to appoint the schoolmaster, who must be a Master of Arts, able to teach Greek and Latin learnedly and skilfully, who was to rule the upper school; and the mayor, recorder and five of the most ancient aldermen were to appoint the usher, who must have commendable knowledge of Greek and Latin and be able to versify and teach Greek grammar at the least, and who would have charge of the lower school. The master was to receive £20 yearly from the chapter and £6. 13s. 4d. from the city, and the usher £13. 6s. 8d. from the city. The school was a 'free' school, being virtually free to the sons of inhabitants; but it attracted the sons of gentry and clergy, who boarded with the master or went into lodgings, and the master made his own terms with them. The number of pupils rose and fell according to the reputation of the master.

When the school fell on a bad period it was the council that made the move. They declared in 1724 that it had gone much to decay, and there being no prospect of making it flourish without a good master at a minimum salary of £50 a year and a fit house for boarders, the council resolved to increase their contribution towards his salary to £20 a year and £10 for a house. It was the duty of the chapter to find a master educated at Westminster or Eton, and of the degree of M.A., but the quest failed, and the Reverend John Goodall, late of St John's College, Cambridge, was appointed. To help him to secure more in fees the council resolved that no persons not born within the city might have the freedom of the school.

[1] L.P.L. Christ's Hospital MSS; *Charity Commission Report* (1839), Lincoln, pp. 351–8.

In 1732 the dean and chapter and the mayor and aldermen held a visitation of the school as a result of the usher's complaints that the master was making two removals in the year from lower to upper school in order to increase his own income from fees, and that he interfered in the usher's province. Perhaps the complaint failed, for no new rules were made. Goodall stayed in office and sent a number of boys to Cambridge. When he died in 1742 the council visitors formally declared that no person having offered himself from the dean and chapter as duly elected upper master within three months of the vacancy having occurred (as the deed of union required) the right of election had lapsed to them, and they accordingly appointed the Reverend Mr Rolt of Caistor. They had a much more intimate interest in the well-being of the school than itinerant members of the chapter, for it was their sons and the sons of their neighbours who were the sufferers from neglect.

At a later visitation in 1757, old orders of 1684 were revised. Prohibition of an old custom of barring out the master at Christmas was no longer required; and a rule that the two parts of the school should be of equal size was omitted. An older rule that a visitation should be held twice a year was revived.

Mr Hewthwaite was master in 1765: he sent a boy to Cambridge in that year. In the next year, he having undertaken to teach geography free instead of as a fee-paying extra, the city gave him 20 guineas for globes and maps. He held a number of livings with the mastership, which he continued for many years; perhaps that was the cause of a later complaint that the school was again on the decline.

These are dry bones; fortunately some life is breathed into them by the recorded memories of Henry Best. One morning in 1776 his father, having finished his breakfast, put off his dressing-gown and slippers, put on his second wig, and taking up his triangular hat and gold-headed cane, took him to school. At the east end of the Greyfriars Chapel, which housed it, was a pulpit from which the head boy read collects, below it the master's chair, a table covered with a green cloth, and beyond the table a long bench on which the boys of the first two classes sat during their attempts to translate Homer and Horace into the Lincolnshire dialect. On each side of the room were desks or pews in which the hope of the country was thumbing dictionaries. The names of many generations of schoolboys were engraved on the walls; and within them the boys were supposed to work seven hours a day, though a liberal connivance allowed the masters to arrive half an hour late. The pride of the masters was that their scholars were well grounded. 'We were *grounded*', wrote Best, 'with a vengeance: we learned Latin and Greek for the sake of going to school; as Tom Paine says, that Government raises wars to carry on taxes.'[1] The almost exclusively classical curriculum was already being criticised, but there was to be a long battle before other subjects were admitted to an equality with Latin and Greek. At this time county and city families were almost equally represented in the class lists. In 1776 it is a fair guess from the names in the list that parents included Dr Willis, Precentor Gordon, Mr Chaplin of Blankney, and among citizens Wrigglesworth, Wetherall, Paddison and Bullen. In 1793 the master announced that he had entered upon a large house in Broadgate and was taking boarders.[2]

There can be no doubt that there were several private schools both above- and belowhill, some of them being little more than a handful of children taught in a single room. In the absence of census returns or a gazetteer they have left no trace save a casual reference in a newspaper. In 1776 Mrs Craster, probably the wife of the usher at the grammar school, had the chief ladies' boarding school, and it was later surmised that it was her school that was continued in Minster Yard by Mrs Packharneis.[3] 'The old Boarding school' abovehill was advertised in 1794 as suitable for a large family or for conversion into two tenements. The Reverend William Hett advertised in 1795 that he took a limited number of pupils into his house at 25 guineas a year. More humble establishments in the lower city no doubt recruited their pupils in more private ways and at more modest costs.

[1] *Personal and Literary Memorials* (1829), pp. 246–65. The master, Mr Hewthwaite, thought that there was too much Christianity in the Church of England. He said to a party of his friends, 'I always read the creed of St Athanasius on the days appointed: I am required to do so: and I have engaged to do so: but I take care to begin by saying out aloud "The creed of St Athanasius". I do not tell the congregation that it is *my* creed or that it need be their creed: I tell them it is the creed of St Athanasius.' See also Best, *Four Years in France* (1826), p. 12.

[2] L.P.L. Lincoln School MSS: *V.C.H. Lincoln*, II, 446.

[3] *L.R. & S.M.* 8 April 1870.

CHAPTER IV

PATRONAGE AND PARLIAMENTARY REPRESENTATION

THE elector of Brunswick was proclaimed king in Lincoln the day after Queen Anne's death. The mayor and aldermen attended the proclamation in state, though no loyal address is recorded to have been presented: church bells were rung, and rung again when the king arrived in London from Hanover, and the parishes had ale and bonfires for the coronation.[1] In the following year the common council presented an address congratulating the king on the defeat of the jacobites in 'the late unnatural rebellion'.

The new reign called for a general election. In Lincoln the greatest single influence in election matters was that of Monson. The family lived at Burton, on the north-western edge of the city, and usually, though not always, could command one of the two city seats in parliament. The other was often held by one of the other neighbouring gentry, a Tyrwhitt, a Sibthorp, or a Vyner. Lincoln, however, was not and never became a pocket borough. The freemen, in whom the franchise was vested, were independent, and had to be moved by the most tangible arguments. What they came to fear most of all was an understanding between the gentry to share the seats and avoid an election, and thereby destroy the market for votes. So it was that it became a tactical advantage to be the third candidate to take the field, for to the third man belonged the credit of making a contest necessary. This system was soon to be in full operation.

At the election of 1715 there was no Monson available. Richard Grantham, one of the Goltho family, who had been returned in 1710 but unseated in 1713, was returned with Sir John Tyrwhitt of Stainfield, of whom Sir Horace Pettus was later to write to his sister-in-law Mrs Whichcot of Harpswell with Crossgrove's character of him: Crossgrove 'took Sir Jo for an honest Torry, which is now dropt; the dispute now is betwixt a Walpole Whig or Country Whig, one will do more dirty work than the other'.[2]

---

[1] There is a portrait of George I in the Guildhall, though no record of its purchase or presentation has been found.

[2] L.A.O. Aswarby, 10/20/6. The Tyrwhitt house at Stainfield, with the family portraits, was burnt in 1855 (*Notices and Remains of the Family of Tyrwhitt* (1872), pp. 50–1). The house surrounded a court; three-fourths of it were pulled down about 1773 (Marrat, *History of Lincolnshire* (1814), VI, 62). Byng visited what was left in 1791; he found some tolerable apartments and bad family pictures. The gallery, the billiard room and the timber in the park had all gone (*Torrington Diaries*, II, 351). Crossgrove was the editor of the *Norwich Gazette*, which was publishing anti-ministerial propaganda (see J. H. Plumb, *Sir Robert Walpole*, II (1960), 320).

In this election there was no contest. Better times promised when the young John Monson, then aged 32, emerged as a candidate in 1722 and defeated Grantham, the other seat being retained by Tyrwhitt. In 1725 Monson married Margaret, daughter of Lewis, earl of Rockingham, a marriage which brought him into the great whig family circle; and when the Order of the Bath was reconstituted Monson became one of the knights. When another election approached in 1727 there was a third candidate in Charles Hall of Kettlethorpe, with whom Monson would have liked to join in order to save expense; but the duke of Newcastle wanted to have Tyrwhitt returned. Monson wrote to the duke from Lincoln:

26 August 1727. Your Grace is so well acquainted with the hurry and confusion of elections that I hope you will excuse me for not having sooner return'd your Grace my most humble thanks for the honour you have done me in answering for my son. I have delay'd it the longer in hopes I should be able to give some account how the election is like to go here, where we are in great confusion. I was at Grimsby when I received the honour of your Grace's letter, to assist my Brother George who is chosen there; when I went thither I thought I had made my own interest very good and safe here, but at my return found all was to begin again, for in my absence the two other candidates had given hard money, a thing before unknown in this town: which obliges me to do the same thing. Sir Thomas Saunderson acts very heartily for Sir John Tyrwhit, and spends his money very freely for him, but without designing to hurt me: the consequence is, I must give so much money to secure my own votes (who in these populous elections when money is stirring expect likewise to be gratify'd) that it will cost me nigh a thousand pound more than it needed to have done would I have joined with Mr Hall, but as your Grace exprest a desire to have Sir John chosen, let the consequence be what it will I will not join with him, but assist Sir John what I am able without openly joining him, tho' since money is given my assistance cannot be very great, for I can't now command the second votes of those that are the most obliged to me. In this situation your Grace will judge it is impossible to know the event.[1]

It had seemed likely that Sir Thomas Lumley Saunderson would be a candidate. He had been entertaining the citizens, and presented a pair of iron gates and pillars of Roche Abbey stone for the new church of St Peter at Arches, which made the freemen cry 'A Saunderson, A Saunderson'.[2] In the event he was returned for the county, and in the city acted for Tyrwhitt.

The Lincoln freemen resident in London had already established their own market for votes. Monson wrote to his brother Charles:

14 August 1727. I am much obliged to you for the trouble you take of my affair in London. If Mr Hall has secured forty pray secure for me what are left, but

[1] P.R.O. State Papers Domestic, George II, vol. 3, ff. 30–1.
[2] L.A.O. Aswarby, 10/24/16. Thomas Lumley took the name of Saunderson when he inherited the estates of his cousin the earl of Castleton in 1723. He became third earl of Scarbrough in 1740.

take care they be certainly freemen. Mr Mayor told me there would be a freemen's court or two before the election, but could not fix the day. I will endeavour to get him to do it by the next post, when I hope I shall hear you have secured some more freemen. You must take the best care you can that those that take the money come down, and that none take both of me and Mr Hall. I would not have you buy off any till you hear from me again. Does Mr Hall give £10? If any will return his money and take yours let them do it, but don't outbuy him as yet. We are in great confusion and know not how matters may turn out, tho I think I stand very well. I hope you are better. The post stays.[1]

Monson headed the poll with 541 votes, and Hall came second with 362. Tyrwhitt polled 329 and lost his seat.

In the following year Monson was created a baron,[2] and in 1737 became a privy counsellor and first commissioner of trade and plantations. As these preferments imply, he was a consistent supporter of Walpole, though he seems to have been specially intimate with the duke of Newcastle, who acknowledged his goodness and affection, and who made him a trustee of the Newcastle estates.[3] When he died in 1748 Newcastle and the duke of Bedford exchanged condolences on 'the loss of so valuable a man and so aimiable a friend'.[4]

Monson's summons to the Lords caused a by-election in Lincoln, and his brother Charles Monson, a lawyer who had lost his right arm in a shooting accident, intimated by the customary circular letter that he proposed to stand for election. He received a number of promises of support, though Tyrwhitt begged to be excused until he knew how the citizens stood affected, 'my interest being entirely linked with theirs'.[5] Perhaps he foresaw the course of events. Monson arrived in Lincoln on 27 May; he offered himself to the citizens on the 28th; the writ came down on the 29th, and on that day the election was proclaimed for one week hence. Haste favoured Monson, who was in the field; it was against any other candidate, and it alarmed the freemen, who saw that they might be baulked of a contest by these storm tactics. They therefore resolved to approach Tyrwhitt, and the mayor with several aldermen and other freemen to the number of 220 or more (there being resident in the city not more than 380 freemen)

mounted on horseback went to Stainfield to desire that worthy gentleman to be their representative, without the least application from him; who entertained

---

[1] Monson, III, 6. Henry Monson wrote to his brother Charles that their brother George was standing for Grimsby: 'The highest bidder is I believe most likely to stand there' (III, 71).

[2] It is odd to read that the barony was conferred in recognition of his forebears' services to Charles I.

[3] Monson, XXI, 42. [4] *D.N.B.* See Plate 16.

[5] Monson, XXII, 24–9. The bishop promised his support (XXI, 45).

them sumptuously and next morning was prevailed to come with them to Lincoln, where they were met coming into town by about 50 more of the citizens and a considerable number of other of the inhabitants with the greatest acclamations of joy.

The poll began at once, and Tyrwhitt was elected with 257 votes against 221 for Monson, the former still having some votes to poll. It was pointed out especially that no voter received a shilling from Tyrwhitt; and high claims were made for the integrity of the freemen and the value of their example to other boroughs.[1] But the motives of the freemen were not so disinterested; they were angry with Monson, and determined that Lincoln should not become his pocket borough; they intended to maintain the market which alone could give a value of the kind they most appreciated to their franchise.

Thus the Monsons knew that if they wanted to win they must play the game according to the freemen's rules. As the next election approached there were plenty of prospective players. Charles Monson was canvassing again, and was advised by his brother to stop at Buckden on the way from London to Lincoln to see what encouragement the bishop could give him.[2] There were rumours of another whig candidate in Joseph Banks, whose father had set him up at Revesby as a country gentleman. Coningsby Sibthorp was being mentioned. In two generations the Sibthorps, recent comers from Nottinghamshire, had climbed into the ranks of the lesser gentry, built and left a town house in Lincoln, and settled at Canwick on the city's southern border; they had begun a long series of prudent marriages on which, like the House of Austria, they were to found their fortunes.[3] It was thought also that Thomas Chaplin would be a candidate. He had secured Blankney, a few miles south of Lincoln, on the attainder of the jacobite Lord Widdrington; but his chances were not improved by the fact that his uncle Sir Robert Chaplin had been a director of the South Sea Company and expelled from the House of Commons, in which he had sat for Grimsby with Joseph Banks the elder.

Catherine Banks was told the news by two agreeable gossips, the Hales sisters, who lived in Minster Yard:

24 February 1734. I wonder Hall gave his interest for Sibthorp. Nowadays youth are very aspireing. They neither value money or quallity, but a good assureance to carry them through, or how can he contend with Lord Monson or Mr Banks.

---

[1] Aswarby, 10/20/6; *Stamford Mercury*, 13 June 1728.
[2] Monson, III, 15.
[3] Sibthorp was later to be identified as a tory (L. B. Namier, *England in the Age of the American Revolution* (1930), p. 488). See Plate 18.

She could not conceive why Chaplin should stand save to hear his own character. A few weeks later Chaplin had not appeared:

25 March 1734. At a month since at his very name the popolace cryed out they would have no S[outh] S[ea] money, but rather than not have a third man belive they will except of some of it. Mr Sibthorpe has a notion at present he shall meet with no opposition, so is not quite so generous. He has a vast interest, but it must be money that gives him the election.[1]

Speculation continued, and Monson's steward reported:

11 March 1734. As yet we don't hear when Mr Chaplin intends coming, what he has to propose about the navigation[2] I believe will have little effect. The freemen say 'tis in order to drain his own lands more than to serve them. The money which I have disburst since your Lordship left the county, have sent an account on the other side: what money Mr Cracroft, Mr Dobbs, Mr Peart and Mr Obbinson of Boston have spent, cannot tell, as soon as I hear will inform your Lordship of it: herein have inclosed the names of persons in different parishes who are to give small sums to freemen to drink in an evening (as they shall see occasion), believe they will be discreet in the affair. If your Lordship do not approve of this method, your Lordship's friends will act in any other manner you shall think more proper.[3]

Mr Peart, an attorney and one of the agents, told Charles Monson:

3 April 1734. Mr Chaplin has this day declared himself a candidate and has entered the city with a very grand retinue which has occasioned Mr Burslem, as I am truly informed, to write to Mr Hall by this post to engage what London voters he can for Mr Sibthorpe, wherefore I humbly apprehend the same caution is necessary on your part also, and as Mr Chaplin is fully determined, as the world says, to treat every week and spare no cost to gain the election, I should think the expense of a little money when necessary on your side could not be amiss. I have of late been frequently rallying for you, and I hope will prove with good success, for the people in general seem to shew a very great inclination to serve my Lord and you. I don't doubt 'twill all be right provided there is no mismanagement at the Helm. I could heartily wish for your company speedily, as at present it is much required, and when you do intend to do us the favour might I advise I would have all the freemen have notice of your coming, that they might meet you, and you might be attended in a public manner, for I really believe 'twould be of a great service....[4]

Charles arrived, and was satisfied with his reception. He was advised not to join with Chaplin; and Lord Monson commented:

23 April 1734. I wonder Mr Chaplin should persist in standing a poll if there be no probability of his success, for I hear he has taken no care of the London voters, and I believe a great many will go down and all or most vote for you,

---

[1] *Letters and Papers of the Banks Family of Revesby Abbey 1704–1760*, ed. J. W. F. Hill (L.R.S.), pp. 156, 161.   [2] See below, p. 127.

[3] Monson, 25/1/35. The disbursements amounted to £142. 8s. 10d.

[4] Monson, vii, 97.

but you need not mention this. I am very glad Mr Gilby[1] is convinced that it is not proper for you to join Mr Chaplin. It was always plain to me that though it might be an advantage to him it would be a great disadvantage to you. I suppose by your saying you lighted at Ald. Brown that you remain at Lincoln. I should really think you need not entertain much now your writs are come down, and I think Mr Sibthorpe may make himself liable to a petition by doing it.[2]

Charles Monson headed the poll with 509 votes, and Sibthorp won the second seat with 461, though, as Lord Monson expected, there was an election petition against him.[3] Chaplin polled only 216 votes. In 1737 Charles was appointed Deputy Paymaster to the Forces,[4] and it was no doubt in this capacity, and in anticipation of further favours to come, that he placed an order for 500 pairs of shoes with the Lincoln Cordwainers Company; the shoes were to be sent by sea from Gainsborough to Whitehall.[5]

In the election of 1741 Monson, Sibthorp and John Tyrwhitt junior were the candidates, Tyrwhitt qualifying by purchasing the freedom of the city for £50. The freemen liked to begin the campaign early, and on Christmas Day 1740 Lord Monson was already writing to his agent:

I am sorry to hear the freemen continue to come to Burton. I was in hopes after I had left the country you would not have given them any more ale, for as long as you do that you may be sure they will not let you be quiet. That I will not have any more ale brewed till I give orders for it. I thought my brother had ordered some coals to be given at Lincoln. I am sorry you have not done it in that way, which I think would have been much the best, for I do not like giving money so nigh the election....[6]

Several months later he wrote to his brother:

5 May 1741. I received your letter yesterday by which I was glad to find you had so great an appearance at your entering Lincoln, and I hope you will meet with no great difficulties, but if you have any doubt, such of the freemen as are willing to go from London I believe may be easily had. They begin to inquire whether you intend to carry them down, and some talk of going whether they be ingaged or no, but I believe many of them cannot afford it, and those that can will not go against you: I suppose you take some care of the country freemen, will they not expect another treat; but I know not what has been done for them, so cannot advise. I cannot actually engage any of these freemen till I hear from you again. Hird shall go amongst them now...I hear Mr Sibthorp was to walk the town as yesterday.[7]

---

[1] The recorder of Lincoln.   [2] Monson, VII, 40.   [3] *C.J.* XXII, 373.
[4] *Gentleman's Magazine*, VII, 316.
[5] L.P.L. Cordwainers MSS, 2 July 1739; Monson, XXIX, 90–2.
[6] Monson, XXIX, 62.   [7] Monson, IV, 62.

HGL

It appears that Charles replied that it would not be safe to ignore the London freemen and rely on those living in Lincoln and the country, for his brother wrote again, from Broxborne:

14 May 1741. I writ to you from hence on Monday, and sent Hird to London as soon as I received your letter to ingage the London freemen; and as I knew a great many of them were resolved to go tho not ingaged I thought it best to bid him offer a guinea apiece to those he found would go, to retain them, and bear their charges down; that I believe most of them will come to you as soon as they get to Lincoln, where you will manage them as you see occasion. I gave him the list that you sent me, but bid him not press anybody to go that was not desirous of it, for I fear you will have more come than you wish, and that they may be very troublesome. Hird is not yet come from London, that I know not what he has done, but I charged him to give you an account both by Tuesday and to-day's post. I am glad your trouble draws towards a conclusion. Seven called here yesterday, most of them want to take out their freedom, and I hear of five more that went the other road. Spooner I believe is gone down, I sent to him on Tuesday but he was not at home, he is in Lord Albemarl's troop, and I dare say will be for you, and may ingage his two brothers. You say you have wrote to the Commissioners of the Customs, which I believe was unnecessary, for Leach is no longer in their service. It is now the son who has no right to his freedom. I suppose the county election was yesterday and no trouble. I wish yours was over too, for I fear you are but badly provided for at Burton. I have had a letter from Mr Bathurst, who is so good as to say he has writ to Mr Fowler that all his tenants should be for you; you will take care accordingly. I find by Hird who is just now come from London that he has ingaged some of the freemen as far as giving them a guinea apiece, and that he has sent you an account of what he has done. There were several more that were very desirous to go, but as they had not wherewithall he has not sent them, thinking nobody else will carry them, tho Mr Sibthorp has spent some money upon them, and they have been told he will do as much for them as you shall do, but as no money is deposited they do not seem much to depend upon it.

Since I wrote this, two freemen, Pearson and Martin, have called here. They promise to serve you, but refused to take a guinea apiece that Hird offered them. If the other candidates do not give much money you may have the Londoners cheap if you manage well.[1]

Monson again headed the poll, the second seat going to Tyrwhitt. Sibthorp was defeated; perhaps, in spite of a rumour that he was making a moneyed push at last, he had been too careful of his money. The Monson agent reported that his expenses on election day were £550, and that Sibthorp's party were very angry.[2]

In the following year the common council elected Charles Monson recorder of the city. Francis Bernard, a barrister who had settled in Lincoln at the suggestion of the late recorder, Mr Gilby, and had picked up some small appointments, wished to be his deputy, but as he acted for

---

[1] Monson, IV, 63.   [2] Monson, V, 13; XXIX, 65, 78, 86.

the archdeacon of Lincoln and so was under the influence of the dean and chapter, it was thought that his appointment would not be agreeable. Thomas Vivian was elected.[1]

A greater matter soon emerged, upon which the common council had already expressed their attitude in an address to the king, denouncing the jacobite design to invade the realm and place on the throne a bigoted pretender directed by popish counsels; and directing the enforcement of the law against papists, nonjurors, and disaffected persons.[2] In July 1745 the Young Pretender landed on the west coast of Scotland and raised the standard of the Stuarts. On 14 September the duke of Ancaster, as lord lieutenant, reported to Newcastle, as Secretary of State, that he had summoned a meeting to take measures for the tranquillity of the county. He thought the militia had been so long laid aside that it would be incapable of service without the assistance of arms, ammunition, and a few disciplined men. Newcastle agreed, and offered to send him the royal authority to form troops or companies for the defence of the government. On 1 October a 'general and numerous meeting' was held at Lincoln Castle. It resolved to address the king, to form an association and to open a subscription, 'what remains at the ceasing of the present danger to be returned to the subscribers in due proportion'.[3]

Commissions were being sought and promised right and left. Lady Cust reported that Lord Monson's son was to have one, Sir Thomas Trollope's son and Mr Chaplin's, 'now if you thought it worth while, I fancy we could easily have Dicky made a captain'. Colonel Sir John Cust was given command of the southern battalion, with Coningsby Sibthorp as captain of the Lincoln company, and Lord Scarbrough the northern battalion; and the two units were soon in dispute about billets in Lincoln.[4]

Lord Monson, at Burton, kept his brother Charles in London informed of events:

11 October 1745. I have heard nothing yet from the Duke of Ancaster what is to be done and we cannot take any steps till we receive his orders. I wish you would enquire at the offices if his commission is past, and how the inferior officers are to have their commissions, for as they are to be signed by the king I know not who is to take the care of them. I suppose the Duke will, if you find anything is to be done for Lewis I beg you will take care of it. . . . If the Duke of Ancaster has given orders about the commissions let Lewis' go with the others, for I would be very cautious in meddling in anything his Grace may think belongs to him and perhaps he may like to deliver the commissions himself.

[1] Monson, xxvi, 5; 25/2/97, 98.   [2] 7 March 1745.
[3] H.M.C. Ancaster, pp. 443–4.
[4] Records of the Cust Family, iii (1927), 49–50, 52; ii (1909), 263.

21 October. I think it is quite right for you to subscribe to the Lincolnshire subscription, and as they are this day going about from house to house in the city, I have sent Haw with your compliments to Mr Mayor, and that you desire to subscribe 100 guineas to his collection.

28 October. Vyner has the militia strong in his head...we are exceedingly busy in raising our regiment, tho we have not yet got the commissions.

13 November. Lewis received orders to march immediately to Stamford with his company, which set forward this morning, and he himself goes thither to-morrow, tho he has not received his commission. Whither they are to go from Stamford I know not, but hope he will be ready to march wherever he is commanded, his company being complete. He is in great spirits.

By 24 November four companies had marched from Lincoln for Hull, and the whole regiment was to follow.

2 December. Perhaps you may have heard what an alarm was spread in Nottinghamshire on Saturday that the Rebels were entered Sheffield. It reached Lincoln on Sunday morning, and to it was added that they intended being at Tuxford at last night. This was so generally believed that the Mayor called a Common Council and sent over the Post Master to acquaint me. I was called out of Church, and tho from the informations I had received the night before where the rebels were I could not believe it, yet I immediately sent messengers into Nottinghamshire to enquire into the truth of it and went myself to Lincoln, where I found the whole city in the utmost confusion. I went to the Hall to the Mayor, when after much noise and talking it was resolved to send out messengers to enquire where the rebels were. I then proposed to get all the arms, powder and ball that was in town into the town house and that if the news should prove true I would go along with those that were willing to go down to the Trent and secure the ferries in the best manner we could. This something quieted them. Upon the return of the messenger at night we were convinced it was a false alarm, and to-day the city is pretty quiet. I left the whole Body at the Hall at twelve o'clock. I thank you for enquiring what things are necessary for Lewis to have. His regimentals he already has, sash &c. are bespoke by the Col!. that I think he will want nothing at present but a tent with the appurtenances, a bedstead and bedding, mattresses, a table and stool. I would have them good but as plain and cheap as may be tho it is uncertain when they may be wanted. I am glad you have bespoke them and beg you will hurry them as fast as possible and let me know when I may depend upon their being done. Pray enquire how these things are carried when the Regiment marches and whether it be not necessary to bespeak a baggage saddle. I would not have at present any camp kitchen nor kitchen tent &c. As neither the Duke of Ancaster nor Lord Scarborough are in the county I am unwilling to leave it till we see further what progress the rebels are like to make, but it will be very inconvenient for me to stay much longer upon many accounts besides that all my provisions are nigh exhausted.

7 December. We have been all this week under continual alarms from the rebels. Before we were well settled from the false report we received on Sunday, on Wednesday we had certain advice that they got to Derby, which prevented me writing to you by that post, being all the day at Lincoln. The people of Nottingham flocked thither, and assured us they were marching this way, and would be there that night or the next morning. We immediately despatched messengers all over the county, and found they were certainly at Derby, and made a show of coming this way, but we had last night certain intelligence that they were gone yesterday out of Derby, and had taken the road back to Ashburn. What they can mean by these marches and counter-marches does not easily appear.[1]

The Young Pretender was in retreat, and on 16 February 1746 his army was routed at Culloden.[2] The following day, and before the news could reach them, the Privy Council sent to Ancaster repeating a previous order that he should call on his deputy lieutenants to search for and take up straggling seamen, 'seeing that in the present hazardous state of affairs, when attempts may be made to invade the kingdom, it is absolutely necessary that His Majesty's fleet should be equipped immediately'. By 10 June the king was informing Ancaster that his regiment must rendezvous at Lincoln and be disbanded there, and that Major-General Churchill should attend the doing thereof.[3] So ended the rebellion and the steps taken to meet it.

When the election of 1747 was impending Lord Monson was annoyed to find that his brother Charles had decided not to stand. He wrote to urge him not to write to Lincoln to say so until there had been time to decide what to do to maintain the family interest.[4] Charles asked him to assure his Lincoln friends that he was honoured to have represented them in two Parliaments, and that if he had any intention of being in again he could have no thought of offering his services any where else.[5]

Meanwhile, however, events had moved, and parliament was suddenly dissolved. On 8 June Alderman Harvey wrote to Charles that his presence was necessary.

There were a great many freemen at Burton yesterday, and Mr Sibthorpe gives the freemen ale at Canwick, and it is given out he will keep open house there to-morrow, being the feast day. Most of this day hath been taken up with Sir Philip Honywood's reviewing Bland's soldiers quartered here, that I have

---

[1] Monson, III, 43, 65, 66, 70, 74, 75. There was a tradition in the Chaplin family that when news of the rebels at Derby reached Blankney they agreed to retreat to the fen, in which there was a kind of island, with a house upon it, to which they could get by jumping from hassock to hassock of quaking bog, as the gosherds did after their geese. The butler suggested poisoning the cellar, as the intruders would be most likely to turn first to the beer barrel (Sir C. Anderson, *Lincoln Pocket Guide* (1892 edn), pp. 33–4).

[2] In honour of Culloden Thomas Whichcot presented a clock to Harpswell church: the inscription recording the gift remains, though the clock has gone.

[3] *H.M.C. Ancaster*, p. 446. One Gravenor, an old inhabitant of St Botolph's parish in Lincoln, directed that he be buried in a grave seven feet deep without any memorial. It was thought that he was a prisoner on parole (Willson, v, 101).

[4] Monson, IV, 75.   [5] Monson, IV, 76, 77.

not had an opportunity of communicating your letter to Mr Haw and Mr Obbinson and such of your friends as they shall think proper, but shall do it to-morrow, and if anything material shall arise will acquaint you by the next post. Sir John Tyrwhitt's friends don't appear yet for him, nor do I hear anything of him. I see Mr Whichcott at the review, he then took no notice of the Parliament, that I believe he was not fully apprized thereof.

10 June 1747. I mentioned that Mr Sibthorpe would entertain the freemen at Canwick yesterday, which he did, and there were about 100 freemen who had as much ale as they could drink but no meat. I was this morning with some of Sir John Tyrwhitt's friends who inform me that they have not heard from him, nor is anything done on his account.[1]

Charles Monson's design went awry in a manner described in a letter to him from Lord Monson:

24 June 1747. I got here on Saturday, and immediately sent to Mr Mayor, Obbinson, Harvey, &c., to come to me the next morning, when I proposed to them to set up my Brother Harry, he having given me leave to make use of his name, which they readily consented to, and thought it would be agreeable to the city, upon which it was resolved Mr Mayor should call a common hall next morning, and that I should go thither and propose him. Accordingly I went to Lincoln by eight a clock, but found everything there in the utmost confusion. Mr Cracroft was come into the town the evening before, and had declared himself a candidate in the place of Sir John Tyrwhitt, upon which my friends told me they believed I might choose my brother Harry, but that the common people grumbled that I should impose a man upon them whom they did not know, who had never been among them, who had not taken his freedom, who they understood did not design to be at the election, and whom perhaps they might never see, and all advised me to name you for the candidate, which I have ventured to do, and hope you will excuse it. I entreat you to take no notice of this till I see you, when I doubt not I shall convince you of the necessity I was under to do it. Our election is on Monday. How it will go I cannot yet judge, but I hope well. The Duke of Ancaster seems resolved to have an opposition in the county, but we do not yet hear who is to stand, that I am in hopes it may end like his Grace's other schemes.[2]

Charles replied that he hoped it was not too late to set up his brother Harry, adding that Lord Scarbrough had gone down in a hurry, and that apparently he had declared in favour of Mr Sibthorp.[3] The same day the recorder Vivian wrote to Charles that the whole interest favoured his nomination, adding that Sibthorp 'will be your brother member if he is not too much tenacious of his purse, for Mr Cracroft is bailed by Dr Wilson of Newark and money flows freely, that it is but ask and have, excellent times indeed'.[4] Cracroft had married the niece of Dr Wilson, who was a formidable supporter: by the influence of the duke of Newcastle he had

---

[1] Monson, xxvi, 16, 18.
[3] Monson, iv, 79.
[2] Monson, iv, 78.
[4] Monson, xxvi, 57.

become vicar of Newark. He then quarrelled with the duke and, having built up a fortune by dubious means, set up a rival political interest.[1]

However, it was not sufficient, and Cracroft was left at the bottom of the poll with 358 votes, the unwilling Charles Monson being at its head with 493, followed by Sibthorp with 419. The contest was described as a severe and costly one.[2]

Lord Monson died in 1748, and when in 1752 a dissolution of parliament began to be discussed, Charles Monson, who had been in poor health for some time, once again determined to resign, and without waiting for the general election. He wrote to his nephew, the second lord, that Lord Scarbrough was resolved to support Mr Chaplin, and that others would do the same, and that it was said that Cracroft would try again. He thought there was no fear that one of the family would not be chosen. Monson decided to nominate his brother George at the by-election, and Charles wrote to the mayor to commend his nephew. George took up the matter with Lord Scarbrough, and reported to Charles:

3 January 1753. His answer did not amount to a denial; but refers me to Mr Chaplin, who would not give me a positive answer till I had Mr Cracroft and his friends' consent under their handwriting that they would not oppose me; and then he said he did not doubt that he should give me a satisfactory answer; all these things being considered and the great expense of a single election, with the uncertainty of pleasing the common people of Lincoln as well as the Londoners, makes Lord Monson think it will not be for his advantage to stand a single election. I hope this will be no great disappointment to you, as you seem'd averse to go into Ireland. Lord Monson writes by this post to Mr Pelham.[3]

Charles accordingly did not resign. It appears that Cracroft was the opponent; and that Sibthorps and Monsons were friendly, as is shown by letters from Humphrey Sibthorp, professor of botany at Oxford and brother of Coningsby Sibthorp, Monson's colleague in the representation of Lincoln. Sibthorp wrote that the professor of physic (whose chair he coveted) was ill, and asked for his interest with Mr Pelham, adding later that he had missed a post at Charterhouse, and 'had I in any instance acted contrary to your interest, it had been impertinent in me to have asked any favour'.[4]

---

[1] Brown, *Annals of Newark on Trent* (1879), pp. 219–21; A. C. Wood, 'An Eighteenth Century Portrait', *Transactions of the Thoroton Society*, LII (1948), 1–34.

[2] Seventy-two persons took up their freedom to enable them to vote; 25 freemen resident in the city did not vote; 39 came down from London (Lord Scarbrough MSS, M.P.M./1). [3] Monson, XXI, 62; XCVIII, 29.

[4] Monson, XXII, 103, 104. Charles Monson, who surrendered the recordership in 1760, died in 1764 in his 69th year. There is no known portrait. His personal servant, William Brummell, an ancestor of Beau Brummell, was admitted a freeman of Lincoln in 1753 in consideration of his master's signal favours to the city.

There was great electioneering activity, and Mrs Massingberd wrote:

22 November 1752. Mr Chaplin's money flies about so fast as if it were to disperse with as much speed as it was acquired, and some are surprised they begin so soon to make interest unless they have any secret intelligence of a new Parliament that is not yet known to the public.[1]

Lord Monson was preparing for action, and he asked his uncle Charles for a loan on account of the great cost of the impending contest.[2] In the course of the canvass George Monson and his friends called on Mrs Massingberd to desire her interest, but she had ordered her servant to deny them, to oblige both them and herself, by preventing a salute from each of them, 'which is the foolish custom of this Town'.[3] In August Mr Harvey reported that Sibthorp was not standing, and that Lord Scarbrough and others would support Mr Chaplin of Blankney: he had acquired the freedom of the city in time. There was still a rumour about Cracroft.[4] Mr Peart, another attorney engaged in the Monson interest, asked Charles Monson to come to Burton as soon as he could, as the 'Jew Bill' had done them harm, and both opponents were sparing neither money nor pains to defeat them.[5] The candidate was worried on the same score:

24 November 1753. I think it would be a great advantage to me if you would write to the Mayor and acquaint him concerning the Jews' Bill, and if you was to say that it was with pleasure you could acquaint him that the bill is or will be repealed, I think it would satisfy the town that you did not vote for it before, which will be a great satisfaction to the whole Corporation; things go on in a bad way and at a very great expense.[6]

The election came at last in April 1754, when Captain George Monson headed the poll with 635 votes, the second seat going to John Chaplin with 617, Robert Cracroft polling 430. It was described as the most corrupt election ever known in Lincoln, some electors getting 20 guineas for their votes. Only Alderman Davis took the oath against bribery and corruption. Afterwards Cracroft published a list of 222 persons who promised to vote for him but voted for his adversaries.[7] An account in the Scarbrough papers shows disbursements made, evidently on Chaplin's behalf, of

---

[1] *A.A.S.R.* xxiii (1896), 307. The rapid acquisition of money is a reference to the South Sea Bubble.

[2] Monson, xcviii, 74.   [3] L.A.O. Anderson, 5/1/20.

[4] Monson, xxvi, 33.   [5] Monson, xxvi, 54.

[6] Monson, xxi, 65. In 1753 Newcastle procured the passing of an Act allowing Jews to obtain naturalisation by special Acts, but it provoked such a clamour on the eve of the election that the Act was repealed in the same year (Basil Williams, *Whig Supremacy 1714–1760* (1939), p. 71). And see Lecky, *England in the Eighteenth Century* (1892 edn), I, 327–31.

[7] *L.D.B. sub anno.*

£5,316.[1] The cost of the campaign was due partly to the extraordinary time that it lasted, and Lord Monson thought himself entitled to ask the duke of Newcastle for this to be taken into account when, four years later, he was applying for a Mastership of Foxhounds:

22 May 1758. It is not in my power any longer to support or even maintain the interest I so dearly bought at the last general election at Lincoln (by the desire of Mr Pelham, more than my own inclination) if your Grace will not think of me; and that the spending £7,000 and upwards exclusive of my house being like a fair for two years should not have intitled me to some small favour before this I own I think hard....[2]

It is not easy to define the political affiliation of candidates outside the whig circle. The Sibthorps and the Tyrwhitts were independent country gentlemen, though at the moment Sibthorp was acting with the whig Lord Scarbrough. As Cracroft was the nominee of Dr Wilson, Newcastle's enemy at Newark, perhaps he may be accounted a tory. John Chaplin was sponsored by Scarbrough; Newcastle wrote to Lord Sondes in 1762, asking him to write to his brother Monson 'to speak to Mr Whichcote, Mr Chaplin and all Lincolnshire *friends* to be at the House the first day': an early example of a whip.[3] The gentry found a useful point of contact in the militia, revived by William Pitt and hated by the whigs; for example, Coningsby Sibthorp was colonel of the southern battalion of the Lincoln-shire militia. In 1760 John Green, the whig dean of Lincoln, wrote to Lord Hardwicke that letters had been sent to gentlemen serving in the county militia 'that as they were so considerable a body together, and had so large a share of property, they would do well to consult together about proper persons to represent the county'. Green thought a concerted scheme of this kind might spread to other counties; and Newcastle commented that 'this spirit of dictating from that species of gentlemen will spread, and we shall soon feel the effects of this militia in many shapes'.[4]

In the course of a correspondence on militia matters, Sibthorp mentioned to Sir John Cust on 1 October 1760, that 'hot work is begun at Boston; as yet we are silent at Lincoln, and I believe that at present will scarce have an opposition'.[5] With the support of Scarbrough[6] he was returning to the

---

[1] They were made through Harvey and Garmston, both Lincoln attorneys, Chaplin and Sibthorp (Scarbrough MSS, MPA/5). It appears that the first printed poll book for Lincoln relates to this election. Thereafter they regularly appeared until the Ballot Act 1872.

[2] L. B. Namier, *Structure of Politics* (1929), I, 132. George Monson was made Groom of the Bedchamber to the Prince of Wales in 1756, and in 1757 a major in the 64th Foot.

[3] L. B. Namier, *England in the Age of the American Revolution* (1930), p. 26n.; and see *E.H.R.* XLIV, 609n.

[4] *Ibid.* pp. 133–4.   [5] *Records of the Cust Family*, III, 305.

[6] *H.M.C. Rutland*, II, 239.

fray. Perhaps it was already known that Chaplin would not stand: his brother-in-law Lord Exeter was to return him for Stamford. George Monson was abroad. When Draper's Regiment was raised in 1757 he was gazetted to it as a major for service in India, and sailed in 1758: he wanted to go abroad anywhere, and it seems that he went to get out of a scrape.[1] He was, however, nominated in his absence. A contest was ensured by the appearance in the field of Thomas Scrope who had offered himself, unsuccessfully, for New Romney in 1756.[2] He was one of the Scropes of Cockerington, though he lived at Coleby near Lincoln, having inherited the Lister estates there. He was to achieve still greater notoriety. On one occasion he declared that he had shot a highwayman who attacked him; on another he visited the House of Commons and, being a militia officer (in which capacity he was always creating trouble), greeted his colonel (Sir John Cust) who had become Mr Speaker. He was accused of drawing his sword, though he denied it, and he was carried away by the Serjeant-at-Arms. In his apology he wrote, 'I have behaved like a fool and I have been treated like a madman'. Later he took up the cudgels on behalf of John Wilkes; and, when Wilkes was expelled from the House in 1764, Scrope declared himself a candidate for his seat at Aylesbury, emblazoning his banners with the motto 'Wilkes and Liberty'. He was declared of unsound mind, and was for a few months in the custody of his brother, though he recovered his freedom.[3]

Sibthorp's circular letter of application for support said:

16 March 1761....the friends of Colonel Monson and myself have offered the lower sort to give something in case there is no opposition, *and as much as any person should there be one*....[4]

Lord Monson wrote to Newcastle:

28 March 1761. We had no thought of Mr Scrope's offering himself a candidate till the day before the election, when he came to Lincoln attended by a great many people, many not freemen, and giving out that he came to support the liberties of the free and independent voters, occasioned a great riot, and the mob broke into the Town Hall and drove everybody out, broke all the windows and did other mischief, but on the magistrates of the city ordering the constables to attend and giving proper orders everything went very well.[5]

---

[1] Namier and Brooke, *The Commons 1754–1790*, III, 151; MS Memoirs of the Monson Family at South Carlton. Monson fought at Pondicherry and Manila, and in 1773 became one of the Supreme Council of Bengal.

[2] *General Evening Post*, 30 Sept. 1756, per Sir Lewis Namier.

[3] *Records of the Cust Family*, III, 72, 207, 214; *Notes on the Visitation of Lincolnshire, 1634*, ed. A. Gibbons (1898), pp. 134–5. It seems that he did not stand for Aylesbury.

[4] L.P.L. Sibthorp Papers.

[5] Add. MS 32921, f. 133, per Sir Lewis Namier.

Scrope caused a riot by drawing his sword to head up his men. The Guildhall was stormed, the windows broken, and other damage done.[1] He was unsuccessful, but he polled 373 votes against Monson with 733 and Sibthorp with 486, these two being returned. After the election Scrope published Sibthorp's letter to electors with comments on its grammar and sense, declaring that he would petition against Sibthorp's return.[2] He did so, but withdrew the petition.[3]

Although George Monson was home from India at the time of the next election in 1768 he did not stand for parliament, and there seems to have been no other member of the Monson family available. This fact no doubt explains the appearance of Constantine John Phipps, the future second Lord Mulgrave, a post captain in the navy, who was to win fame for a voyage of discovery towards the North Pole, and notoriety for 'a course of tergiversation which earned him an English peerage, a long succession of richly paid offices, and a couplet by Fitzpatrick worth all the painfully composed and minutely revised speeches that he ever made on either side of any controversy':

> Acute observers, who with skilful ken
> Descry the characters of public men,
> Exchange with pleasure Elliot, Lew'sham, North,
> For Mulgrave's tried integrity and worth.
> For all must own *that* worth completely tried,
> By turns experienced on every side.[4]

When he stood at Lincoln he was a whig, and a year later said he would not act without the concurrence of Lord Monson, mentioning also Lord Scarbrough, both of them supporters of the Rockingham whigs.[5]

It was presumably the country gentlemen who put forward Robert Vyner the younger of Gautby, who had sat for Okehampton in the Parliament of 1754 on the duke of Bedford's interest, and like his father opposed the administration, even after Bedford had taken office in it. Wraxall remarked that Vyner reminded him of the portraits of 'Hudibras'; he was a gentleman of large property, endowed with very good common sense, and of an irreproachable character.[6] Later, after he had won a seat at Lincoln the *English Chronicle* described him as proud and imperious to inferiors, and not at all popular even in the place he represented.[7] He was to become a supporter of Lord North, and to take a high line against the

---

[1] *L.D.B. sub anno.*   [2] L.P.L. Sibthorp Papers.   [3] *C.J.* XXIX, 49, 188.
[4] C. Trevelyan, *Early History of Charles James Fox* (1899 edn), p. 314. For Phipps, see *Memoirs of Sir N. W. Wraxall* (1884), II, 167, 173.
[5] *Correspondence of Edmund Burke*, II (ed. L. S. Sutherland), 59–60.
[6] *Op. cit.* V, 203–4.
[7] Namier and Brooke, *The Commons 1754–1790*, III, 590.

American rebels. Scrope stood again. Vyner was charged with the detestable enormity of telling the freemen that they could vote as they pleased, no matter whose money they had taken. Apparently many of them had taken Scrope's, for his expenses were said to amount to £4,000. He headed the poll with 534 votes, Phipps securing the second seat with 500. Vyner polled 449.

Afterwards actions were brought against Scrope's agents, charging them with bribery. It was declared that during the campaign a rumour that Scrope was giving money had brought all the freemen to the King's Arms. After some had been paid a guinea for voting for him at the previous election, there was an adjournment to a private house. There a person, dressed as a Cherokee chief with a mask, sat at a table with a bag of money before him, the agents[1] sitting at another table. Each freeman was asked his name, whence he came, and whether he voted for Scrope in the previous election. The answer to the last question could be tested from the poll book. The tariff of rewards was, to resident freemen £3. 3s., to those dispersed in the country £4. 4s., to Londoners £7. 7s., and, if they had voted for Scrope last time and not received their arrears, £1. 1s. This process continued until somebody tried to pull off the mask, and candles were blown out, and the great noise and riot broke up the assembly. Next day the proceedings continued at the Spread Eagle. The proceedings for bribery failed, and by way of celebration fifteen hogsheads of ale were given to the populace, and Mr Scrope gave a ball in the downhill assembly rooms.[2]

There was a report of Scrope's death in 1770. Lord Monson was proposing that George Monson should stand again; the latter, being willing, wrote to Sibthorp, who had said that if he, George, were standing he would not oppose him, but if not, then he would offer himself or his nephew to the citizens. Monson informed the mayor of his plans, but the correspondence came to an end with the news that Scrope was not dead after all.[3] The object of the Indian colonel's nomination was, it seems, to hold the seat as a caretaker until his nephew came of age. But before that happened, and before the next election, the second Lord Monson had died (in 1774), the nephew had become the third lord and there was no Monson candidate in the city until 1806. The colonel passed into history as the bitter enemy of Warren Hastings in the Supreme Council of Bengal.

Vyner stood again at the election of 1774, and, there being no Monson

---

[1] Well-known citizens, the Messrs Bullen and Mr Gibbeson.

[2] L.P.L. MSS 5017 and 4807. For details of the corrupt practices see *Lincolnshire Chronicle*, 3 April 1884; *Annual Register* (1768), p. 155.

[3] Monson, xx, 82, 83; xxxi, 84–6.

available, Scarbrough put forward his son Lord Lumley with Monson support. The main purpose then was to be rid of Scrope, as the latter well knew; when in 1779 Monson applied to him for support for his brother in the county election, Scrope replied:

20 July 1779. Having received a letter from your Lordship, which although it be only a circular one, I found myself so circumstanced that I could not forbear giving an answer to it. Your Lordship cannot forget the opposition which I unexpectedly met with last election from your family and friends, the consequence of which was the loss of my election, and the bringing in Mr Vyner, whose political principles and conduct in Parliament I conceive to be totally different from yours, and most certainly from mine. My wish was that Lord Lumley and myself might be chose, and I flattered myself I should at least not be opposed, if not supported, by those who to me seemed engaged in the same publick spirited cause, but I found myself much mistaken.[1]

There was a fourth candidate in Humphrey Sibthorp, the nephew of Coningsby and son of the professor of botany, against whose wishes he was interesting himself in Lincoln politics. He was at the bottom of the poll, Scrope was unseated, and Lumley and Vyner were returned.[2] Sibthorp secured a seat at Boston in 1777, and in the same year had the felicity to be elected recorder of Lincoln and to become the husband of Miss Ellison, whose father was the Fossdyke lessee and one of the proprietors of the Lincoln Bank.

At the election of 1780, Vyner and Lumley were again in the field, and Scrope was threatening to stand. He was, however, no longer taken seriously—he was to receive only four votes—and the freemen, anxious as ever to secure a real contest, approached Sir Thomas Clarges, a Hertfordshire baronet with a house in Minster Yard and property in Lincolnshire,[3] who was a captain in the northern battalion of the county militia. The *English Chronicle* put the matter in the best possible way:

Sir T. Clarges had the good fortune to obtain this representation by means, of all others, the most grateful and honourable by which a gentleman can acquire a seat in the British legislature, the voluntary, unsolicited suffrages of the majority of the electors. The inhabitants of this city have distinguished themselves for a generous independence in the choice of their members, by exempting themselves from the influence of those obligations that had nothing but pre-

[1] Monson, xcviii, 151.
[2] The voting was, Lumley 575, Vyner 522, Scrope 238, Sibthorp 225. In 1776 there were rumours that Lumley was in bad health, and George Monson wrote from Calcutta to Lord Monson, mentioning that this might give him an opportunity of forwarding the interest of Monson's brother George, though the election should not be procured at enormous expense (Monson, xxi, 88). The vacancy did not arise.
[3] He had property in Norton Disney and Bitchfield, and earlier members of the family had land at Deeping St James. Clarges was the third baronet, of St Martin's in the Fields.

scription to recommend them, and making free offers of the honour of their representation to various gentlemen who had not obtruded themselves upon their choice. Besides this instance of their generosity to Sir Thomas Clarges, they made another voluntary offer to Mr Banks, the celebrated botanist and circumnavigator; but the business of science predominated in his estimation above every other consideration, and, like a true philosopher, he preferred the private gratification of his literary propensities to all the suggestions of ambition, and to all the consequence with which such an honour is inseparately accompanied. Sir T. Clarges is a man of good fortune, good morals and good sense. He is of an old family in the county, and is a captain in the northern battalion of the Lincolnshire militia. He succeeded Lord Lumley as member for this city, who was thrown out by some accidental carelessness in the formation of an electioneering compromise between him and Lord Monson.[1]

Clarges headed the poll with 626 votes, and Vyner held the second seat with 616. Lumley polled only 339. Vyner was clearly not well thought of. In 1781 the great wool battle was impending in the House,[2] and Charles Chaplin of Tathwell wrote to Banks:

17 December 1781. I fear our county members will not be willing to undertake it, and more that they would not conduct it ably...the lead must devolve to some other member, perhaps the member for Lincoln, who though a man of business, is not well attended to in the House.

Banks shared this view.[3]

Clarges was a supporter of Lord North. He died in 1782, but not before he had abandoned support of North's government and declared himself a convert to the view that the reconquest of the American colonies was impracticable.[4]

At the ensuing by-election Sir John Hussey Delaval of Seaton Delaval in Northumberland, for many years M.P. for Berwick, the owner of Doddington, 6 miles to the south-west of Lincoln, was able to add to his political influence comparatively cheaply by bringing in for Lincoln un-opposed his son-in-law John Fenton Cawthorne, of Winside, Lancaster. Both were supporters of Fox, from whom Delaval received an Irish peerage; but when Fox's policy became unpopular in court and country

---

[1] Per Sir Lewis Namier.   [2] Below, pp. 115–19.

[3] Banks, Sutro Coll. III, 8. The county members were Charles Anderson Pelham and Sir John Thorold: as to the latter's part see below, pp. 118–19. Robert Vyner wrote to W. B. Massingberd from Gautby (2 Nov. 1782): 'I am going to London about the meeting of Parliament and mean to steal about three weeks for the Xmas recess, which time I should be glad to spend in Lincolnshire; but Gautby is so dirty and so dull at that season that I cannot swallow the Pill immediately upon a return from London, but if it would not be inconvenient to you to lend me your house at Ormsby I could with great pleasure pass the recess there, where I should be in the reach of Mr Chaplin and in a neighbourhood of some society, who like myself, are simple enough to be amused with coursing a hare' (Massingberd Mundy MSS, Society of Genealogists).

[4] Debrett, *Parliamentary Register*, III, 525–6.

he underwent conversion and became a supporter of Pitt, soon receiving from him a British peerage. *The Rolliad* commemorates him:

> The Noble Convert, Berwick's honoured choice,
> That faithful echo of the people's voice,
> One day to gain an Irish title glad,
> For Fox he voted—So the people bade:
> 'Mongst English lords ambitious grown to sit,
> Next day the people bade him vote for Pitt;
> To join the Stream our Patriot nothing loath
> By turns discreetly gave his voice to both.[1]

When the general election came in 1784 Vyner did not offer himself: at a by-election a few months later he was returned for Thirsk. In place of Lumley, who had become fifth earl of Scarbrough in 1782, his brother Richard (who took the name of Savile on succeeding to Savile estates) was urged to stand, and was exhorted by his uncle Sir George Savile not to be fastidious:

[It is] perfect Methodism in politics to talk of the Lumley interest at Lincoln rather as a curse than a blessing (not to be cultivated like an estate but got rid of like a mortgage) and that so far from such a seat *as it has been* being honourable, it is more dirty than a seat in a necessary.... The plan, however, we will suppose to be to start with a most positive and most explicit declaration that you would not give a sixpence.... Do you think that they'll choose you? Their gratitude, you say? Gratitude! I answer you in the words of Shakespeare 'milk of a male tiger'. Gratitude indeed![2]

With this encouragement, Richard Savile stood, and both he and Cawthorne, the other candidate, showed the 'usual civilities' to the freemen. They were returned unopposed. But sterner times approached, and more expensive, and Savile did not stand again. In 1788 Cawthorn entertained some of his supporters at Doddington and, wrote the agent to Lord Delaval:

14 September 1788. They all of them seem both to think and say it is exceedingly fortunate Mr Cawthorn coming to the Races, for there was some underhand schemes going forward, but Mr Cawthorn coming and behaving in the agreeable manner he hath done hath frustrated all their schemes, and Mr Cawthorn hath been exceedingly caressed by all the gentlemen and also the whole city. Mr Cawthorn dined yesterday at the hunting Club, and to-morrow at what they call the Lunitick Club: on Tuesday he dines along with all the aldermen and other gentlemen, it being the day they elect the mayor for the ensuing year.[3]

Every winter Cawthorn, like most city members, gave his annual compliment of coal to poor freemen.

---

[1] Delaval rebuilt Doddington church between 1770 and 1775 in the Gothic of the period, the architects being William Lumby and his father.

[2] Namier and Brooke, *The Commons 1754–1790*, I, 328.

[3] R. E. G. Cole, *History of Doddington* (1897), p. 164.

Another family was about to enter the Lincoln election market. In 1766 Nocton had passed into the hands of the Hobarts of Blickling in Norfolk, and possession had been taken of it by George Hobart, first son of the first earl of Buckinghamshire by his second wife; he had married Albinia, eldest daughter and co-heiress of Lord Vere Bertie and his wife Anne, who lived at Branston. Their son Robert, lately of age, was seeking a seat in parliament, and the duke of Rutland wrote to the prime minister, William Pitt, on his behalf. It was thought that the fifth earl of Scarbrough was dead, and that the succession to the earldom of his brother Richard Lumley Savile would create a vacancy at Lincoln. Pitt replied that Scarbrough was not dead, and that in any case in the event of a vacancy he was committed to a Lincolnshire gentleman named Turnor. This was probably Edmund Turnor of Ponton, who announced in 1802 that he declined to disturb the repose of the county by a canvass, and was confident he would not forfeit the good opinion of his friends on another occasion. In December 1788 Rutland brought Hobart in as member for Bramber, and in 1789 Hobart was appointed Chief Secretary to the Lord Lieutenant of Ireland.[1]

Election rumours were rife at the beginning of 1789, and Hobart was quickly in the field. Delaval's agent reported:

9 January 1789. Your Lordship's agents at Lincoln was distributing the coals amongst the freemen at Lincoln when I received the honour of your lordship's letter. Mr Greaves still keeps rallying up for Fenton as he calls him, and Dick Bullen does the same for Major Hubberd; but Fenton at present is the cry in Lincoln among the poorer sort of freemen. There are upwards of 30 that have told me, if there be an opposition, they will give Mr Cawthorn a single vote. Mr Greaves hath paid, as I hear, for 10 or 12 young men taking up their freedom, on that proviso they vote for Mr Fenton at the next election, which I suppose he takes care to secure before he pays the money. It cost the young freemen 7s. 6d. and Mr Greaves hath given them all 10s. 6d.—to whit, 3s. above what their freedom costs them; he tells them that is to drink Mr Fenton's health. I am told that Dick Bullen went up to London to engage all the freemen of his acquaintance, or whatever he could possibly engage, to vote for Major Hubberd. I only mention these things as I am informed; I cannot answer for them to be matters of fact, only Mr Cawthorn may inform himself, as he is in London.

On 18 April he wrote again:

There is nothing now going forward at Lincoln but electioneering. Mr. Viner by two letters to the aldermen Kent hath declared that he will stand candidate for

---

[1] *Correspondence between the Rt Hon William Pitt and Charles Duke of Rutland 1781–87* (1890), p. 3, where the letter is misdated. It must be dated 30 April 1786, as Sir Lewis Namier has pointed out (see *H.M.C. Rutland*, II, 239). There had been an earlier rumour of Scarbrough's death in 1784, when Scrope Bernard thought of standing (Mrs Higgins, *The Bernards of Abington and Nether Winchendon*, III (1904), 71).

the ensuing election: also young Bullen is also making all the interest he can both in Lincoln and all the places round where there is any freemen for Mr Hubbert: But I am in the greatest hopes if two more candidates offer, Mr Cawthorn is sure to be first Member. Although if your lordship was but one week at Doddington, and show yourself only once at Lincoln before the election, it would assist greatly in strengthening Mr Cawthorn's interest. They have got it entirely into their heads at Lincoln that the Parliament is to be dissolved on Friday the 24th, the day after his Majesty goes in state to St Paul's, and then the election comes on immediately. But however it be, no person can be more assiduous and diligent in strengthening Mr Cawthorn's interest than Mr Graves is. He told me he would spend £500 of his own money before Mr Cawthorn lost his election.

Rumours were still flying on 27 November:

They have got it on foot now that an Indian Nabob hath for this some time past been endeavouring to secure what votes he possibly could at London, and is in a short time to be at Lincoln; and this Nabob at last turns out to be Doctor Petreys brother, that I suppose hath been at the East Indies, and hath accumulated some money which he may very soon spend at Lincoln without reaping any benefit to himself. They also speak of young Mr Viner, and seem to expect a very contested election whenever it happens; but I am convinced Mr Cawthorn will represent the city of Lincoln whilst your lordship thinks good to offer him as a candidate, whatever opposition may happen.[1]

Hobart and Cawthorn were both supporters of Pitt, and opposition had been stimulated by Delaval's and Cawthorn's apostasy; and Major Rawdon was sent down, supported, Delaval thought, by Carlton House money in the interest of Fox and the whigs, and locally by the Vyners. Lord Rawdon, his brother, wrote that they flattered themselves that they had secured the writ for Lincoln, but found that Hobart had not only got it, but gone down to hurry the election, so as to prevent Rawdon's principal force, the out-voters recruited in London, from arriving in time.[2]

In his appeal to the electors Rawdon did not trouble about politics: he stood forth as the third man who made a contest necessary, and so created a market for votes. Without him, he said, the choice of the freemen would be confined, and in fact oppressed. His position as a guarantor of the prosperity and independence of the franchises of the city made a strong appeal to the London freemen, among whom he had more support promised than any other candidate had ever had.

Cawthorn had been told by Delaval (as the latter contended afterwards) that he limited his financial commitment to £300; he added that if

---

[1] *History of Doddington*, pp. 164–6.
[2] *H.M.C. Var. Coll.* VI, 210. A gentleman in office, of great character and integrity, told Oldfield that he was present when 1,000 guineas were given at the dissolution for the writ for the city (*Representative History of Great Britain* (1816), IV, 136).

Cawthorn wanted money for his election he must go before he left Town 'to a certain quarter for it where you have as good a pretension as others to apply, and better than most, upon account of the extraordinary circumstances of your opponents, and the *cause* of the opposition, for it was occasioned by an adherence to the XXXX; there will be the service, not to me, and there will be the expence'. Nevertheless, Cawthorn plunged into the fight with gusto and, two days before polling began, the agent at Doddington wrote to Delaval:

I came to Lincoln this forenoon, but never before did I see Lincoln so crowded with people at such a time, for all three candidates have been walking the streets with their colours flying. By the best information I can receive it will be the hottest contested election that hath been at Lincoln for a great number of years. The City are so afraid of disagreeable confusion that they are altering the town hall for the freemen to go up one way to vote and come down another. . . .

Mr Gibbeson, their chief supporter, wrote that the contest would cost Cawthorn £5,000; carriages full of freemen were coming from all parts.

Rawdon was attacked as a Nabob; his songs contained pointed references which were no doubt well understood at the time:

> The last Election's not forgot,
>   Nor many great Pretences;
> In Street to stand was many a Lot,
>   Waiting for Expences.
> But here, my Boys, its truly said,
>   To Defray he's a Designer,
> According to the promise made
>   To his Honor—*Squire Vyner*.

There is a glimpse of the campaign among freemen resident in the county in a report to Sir Joseph Banks, who supported Hobart, from his agent at Mareham:

I cannot express how anxious Mr Coltman is, and exerts himself, on your account in the behalf of Major Hobart; he had canvassed all Horncastle before I got to market, and I waited on such afterwards as he desired; in the afternoon (on Saturday) he set out for Spilsby, and writes me word he had pretty good success, he has wrote to Mr Somerscales, to intercede with the Walesbys, and I spoke to some who were acquainted with them to do the same; none of them happened to be at Market; Mr Coltman has, lest you should have forgot to do it, wrote to Mr Fydell to let him know your wish; there are 15 freemen in Boston, but am told 12 of them has promised Mr Hobart some time ago; Mr Coltman was to set out early for Alford, this morning, to get what votes he can thereabouts—it is thought it will be a very strong contested election—at Grimsby there are four candidates. I sent Mr Weatherhogg and Mr Hall of Tumby Swan, who is a freeman, from Horncastle on Saturday, to Coningsby, where they got 4 votes, at Tattershall one and at Dogdyke, Wm North; these with 5 more got hereabouts, is to have a treat at Tumby Swan to-morrow; your servant Thomas Nowell is a freeman.[1]

Cawthorn headed the poll with 637 votes, followed by Hobart with 604; Rawdon, though he secured 110 London votes against 20 for Cawthorn and 12 for Hobart, polled only 464. Cawthorn wrote defensively to Delaval to say that £1,000 would pay completely for every treating, though they had had to incur the cost of colours as well. He thought Rawdon's London votes would cost £25 each at least; he had counsel down, sent by Erskine, but he had said nothing. Hobart's friends had tried to get to the top of the poll; the duchess of Rutland had given him all the Grantham votes single. There ensued an angry correspondence with Delaval, who complained that with post-election gifts of £5 each to 600 voters the total cost would be not less than £4,000.

Cawthorn's association with Lincoln came to an abrupt end on 3 May 1796, when, having been found guilty by court martial of misappropriation of the funds of the Westminster militia, of which he was colonel, he was expelled from the House. So died the political influence in Lincoln of Lord Delaval.[2]

[1] Hill, Banks, 3/8.

[2] The correspondence between Delaval and Cawthorn is contained in the Delaval Papers in the Central Library, Newcastle-upon-Tyne. Francis Askham has used them in his *The Gay Delavals* (1955). Cawthorn was returned for Lancaster in 1806 and 1812.

CHAPTER V

GROWING MARKETS

THE city was wholly dependent on the countryside for its living: thence came the vendors at its fairs and markets and the purchasers at its shops. Even its modest industries—milling, brewing, malting, tanning—depended on the produce of the land. It is necessary, therefore, without attempting anything so ambitious as a history of agriculture, to try to form some impression of its problems and prospects, and of the gradual changes which were to make a decisive impact upon the fortunes of the city.

Defoe had given a glowing account of the countryside. He found the Lincoln district a most rich, pleasant and agreeable country. The Lincoln heath, stretching fifty miles to north and south of the city, he called a noble plain. To the west of it he found the pleasant rich Trent valley, and to the east the richest, most fruitful and best cultivated of any county in England so far from London, part of it being fen or marsh ground.

In this short passage he discerns, though a little indistinctly, the four farming regions of the county. There were the uplands, consisting of the limestone ridge to north and south of the city—and known as the 'cliff' to the north and the 'heath' to the south—with which he might have grouped the other uplands, the chalk wolds, to the north-east of the county; the clay lands to the east and west of the heath and cliff; the fens to the south-east of the city; and the coastal marshes.[1]

No doubt he learned, by inspection or inquiry, that the chief corn crops on the heath and the clays—the arable still lying mostly in open fields— were barley, for bread, beer and fodder, and oats, for horses and perhaps for domestic use. There were some peas and beans, and some rye, no doubt to be mixed with wheat for 'maslin' bread. The surplus of all these crops, after domestic needs were satisfied, went to market. There was besides some wheat, which was a luxury, and was grown mostly for sale.[2]

He seems to have been more interested in livestock; he knew about the growing demand for sheep and cattle, and no doubt he saw the sheepwalks and heard something about piecemeal inclosure of land for additional

[1] For this and subsequent references to Defoe see his *Tour through England and Wales* (Everyman edn), I, 84, 98–100; II, 94, 199, 222. On Lincoln heath Lord Harley saw oxen ploughing and drawing carriages, which he had not seen for many years (*H.M.C. Portland*, VI, 84).

[2] On the whole subject of crops and livestock see Joan Thirsk, *English Peasant Farming: the Agrarian History of Lincolnshire from Tudor to Recent Times* (1957).

pasture. He notes, particularly in the eastern half of the county, the innumerable droves and flocks of black cattle and sheep:

indeed I should not have said black cattle. I should have called them red cattle; for it was remarkable, that almost all their cows for 50 miles together are red, or py'd red and white, and consequently all the cattle raised there, are the same.

Great numbers of these cattle were driven to London markets, working havoc with the roads, for they worked through in winter what the road surveyors had mended in the summer.[1] Defoe had much to say about the need for better roads.

Their wool made the sheep at least equally interesting. He found that at Stourbridge fair, at Cambridge, the wool sold was principally fleece wool out of Lincolnshire, where the long staple was found. Its buyers were chiefly the manufacturers of Norfolk, Suffolk and Essex, who bought a prodigious quantity of it.[2] From Lincolnshire came also the great funds of sheep which furnished the city of London with their large mutton in so incredible a quantity.

Clearly Defoe knew, though he did not mention, that while the wool from the fens and the coastal marshes went to East Anglia, that from the Lincoln area and the north of the county went to the West Riding of Yorkshire. There were the growing cloth towns of Halifax, Bradford, Leeds and Wakefield, and the clothing villages of which he gave the classical description. The rapid growth of this market for wool is sufficiently indicated by the increase in the amount of cloth milled at the fulling mills on the Pennine streams in the West Riding. In 1727 there were 29,000 broad cloths; by 1800 there were 285,000 broad cloths and 169,000 narrow cloths.[3] The population so engaged grew hardly enough to feed their poultry, and looked to neighbouring counties for their food, thereby providing a market for Lincolnshire corn. The wool and corn were carried by packhorse, and, when the roads became fit, by waggon; and if only it were kept in repair, there was the Fossdyke canal to carry it from Lincoln to the Trent.[4]

Turning to a subject of lesser moment, Defoe described at length the duck decoys that he found in the fens, and the manner of their operation. Thirty-eight decoys are recorded in the county. As many as 6,000 fowl had been taken in a single season at Ashby near Brigg; at Dowsby decoy about

---

[1] See G. E. Fussell and Constance Goodman, 'Eighteenth Century Traffic in Live Stock', *Economic History*, III, 214.

[2] See H. B. Carter, *His Majesty's Spanish Flock* (1964), ch. 1; M. L. Ryder, 'The History of Sheep Breeds in Britain', *Agricultural History Review*, XII, 11.

[3] H. Heaton, *Yorkshire Woollen and Worsted Industries* (1920), p. 278.

[4] Below, p. 126.

13,000 fowl were taken in 1765–6, the price being 7s. a dozen.[1] In a single season 31,000 wild duck, teal and widgeon were sent to London from Wainfleet.[2] Near Lincoln there were decoys at Nocton and Skellingthorpe to the south-east and south-west, and at Burton and South Carlton to the north-west. Lady Dashwood's steward despatched from Nocton to Leadenhall market from 1 November 1762 to 7 February 1763, 371½ dozen of fowl at 9s. a dozen, and with the cost of carriage first to Lincoln and then to London the account came to £210. 16s. 4d.[3] The first of October was the day appointed for commencing to decoy wild fowl in Lincolnshire.[4] According to Fuller, wildfowl had the reputation of being more dainty and digestible than tame fowl, which he explained by saying that they spent their gross humours with their activity and constant motion in flying.[5]

There was also a trade in tame fowl, or geese, which were reared in the fen in vast numbers. During the breeding season they were lodged in houses and even in bedchambers. There were rows of coarse wicker pens placed one above another; each bird had its separate lodging whilst sitting. A gozzard, or goose-herd, attended the flock, and twice a day drove them to water; he then brought them back to their pens, helping those of the upper storeys without misplacing a single bird.[6] The geese were plucked five times in the year for feathers, and once for quills, and they were sent off in great droves to London markets. Some of the perils from flood in the life of a gozzard are described by William Hall, known as Low Fen Bull Hall, born at Willow Booth, a small island in the parish of South Kyme, who supplied London markets with fowl and warehouses with feathers and quills:

> The poor old geese away were floated,
> Till some high lands got lit'rally coated;
> Nor did most peasants think it duty
> Them to preserve, but make their booty;
> And those that were not worth a goose,
> On other people's lived profuse.[7]

The feathers were used for pillows, eiderdowns and feather beds. According to Arthur Young the feathers of a dead goose were worth 6d., those of three birds making a pound. Plucking alive did not yield more than 3d. a head per annum. From the information given him by Sir Joseph Banks's boatman on East Fen, an average year might show him a profit of £40:

---

[1] Sir R. Payne-Gallwey, *The Book of Duck Decoys* (1886), ch. VIII. There was a decoy at Twigmoor, not there recorded (*Lincolnshire Magazine*, II (1934–6), 136n.).

[2] William Hone, *Year Book*, 1 Oct.

[3] Bodl. MSS, DD. Dashwood (Bucks), B 19/5/2.

[4] Hone, *Year Book*, 1 Oct.   [5] *Worthies of England*, II, 2.

[6] Gough's edition of Camden's *Britannia* (1806), II, 342.

[7] William Hone, *Every-Day Book* (1830), III, 139.

600 geese at 1*s*. 3*d*. for the goose and 1*s*. 3*d*. for the feathers, totalling £75, less £35 for corn. Young suspected exaggeration, because of the current talk about inclosure.[1]

Perhaps rabbits were beneath Defoe's notice, but they were not negligible, either as vermin or as food. Unlike hares, they were not legally game. On a waste they belonged to the lord of the manor, who might claim (if the commoners were provided for) to have the right to let part of the waste as a warren, which came to be protected by law. It can hardly have been possible to prevent the taking of rabbits in snares on the great open heaths and commons. An acknowledgement of the damage done by rabbits, with a degree of toleration for their taking, is contained in a statute in 1765 'for the preservation of fish in fish ponds and other waters and conies in warrens'. A saving clause for Lincolnshire enacted that the provision as to rabbits should not extend to the sea or river banks so far as the flux and reflux of the tide should extend, mischief having been caused by their increase in sea and river banks. Any person might therefore take and carry away in the daytime rabbits within a furlong of the banks, doing as little damage as might be.[2] In later times it was said that there was a custom in Lincolnshire and Yorkshire that anyone might turn out on 5 November and shoot freely, and that landowners and game preservers never thought of hindering; the same applied to Good Friday, but then there was little game to be had, and so people did not turn out in such multitudes.[3] The state of mind in which these concessions were made is not difficult to guess.

Rabbit warrens were the subject of formal tenancies. In 1718 Dame Alice Brownlow let the mansion house at Temple Bruer on Lincoln heath with pastures, warrens and sheep walks; among the tenant's covenants was one that he should keep the burrows in the warren in good repair, and leave 4,000 couple of rabbits there at the end of the term. He must leave sixty good going traps on the premises.[4] The steward at Nocton received £63. 12*s*. for 862 couple of rabbits caught on Nocton heath between 10 August and 31 December 1763; and when Lady Le Despenser (Dashwood) and her husband rented her life interest there to the Hobarts in 1766, the inventory of goods and stock included a sum of £50 for rabbits on the heath, and among the vehicles valued was a rabbit cart.[5] A warren at Skellingthorpe, viewed in 1759, was taken to contain 1,055 couple of rabbits plus 30 in 'the borough upon the dales'. They were valued

---

[1] *General View of the Agriculture of the County of Lincoln* (1799), pp. 394–5.
[2] 5 George III, c. 14.   [3] *Notes and Queries* (7), VI, 404–5.
[4] L.A.O. Misc. Dep. 65/2/2.
[5] Bodl. MSS, DD. Dashwood (Bucks), C48a4, folder 5/57, B19/2/18–19.

according to the 'long hundred' of 120, the price being £7 per hundred, and the value £63. 5s. There were also nine folding nets at 10s. each, six steel traps at 10s., and 7 dozen purse nets at 2s. 6d. a dozen.[1] There must have been some conventional way of computing the numbers of rabbits, perhaps with reference to previous years' catches. Whether rabbits reached the markets by orthodox channels or not they were cheap, and nearer to the means of the poor than other meat. In 1741 Edward Nevile of Thorney paid a shilling for two couple of rabbits bought at Gainsborough.[2]

Although warrens provided rent to the landlord and profit to the tenant they were a nuisance to neighbouring farmers. In 1736 the lord of the manor of Redbourne was paid £60 by the freeholders of Kirton Lindsey to build a wall round his warren.[3] There was growing pressure to remove them from cornfields, but it was to be long before warrens vanished from the scene.

Here, vastly varying in importance, were the principal products of the county. From surviving estate correspondence it is not difficult to imagine the talk Defoe must have heard in the markets and inns, and on the roads. The word 'ruin' was assuredly in constant use, and certainly ruin was always near, both in his time and later. The countryside was desperately poor, and distant markets were difficult and costly to reach. Demand and supply were inelastic, and a small surplus or deficiency in the harvest would be enough to cause a disproportionately large fall or rise in prices; and when so many lived near starvation level even small changes could be disastrous. The complaints of ruin that are so frequently heard were due to a variety of causes, and came from different classes in the community. Sometimes, at least, the cause and the class can be identified.

Distress might be due to disease. In 1719 it was said that there was a bad and mortal distemper in the county, perhaps because of the long dry season, inasmuch that land let at £1 or 25s. an acre was not worth anything.[4] In 1731 the duke of Kingston's agent at Langworth reported that arrears of rent were due to outbreaks of sheep rot; he had laid out money in drainage in the hope of keeping tenants and enabling them in time to pay their debts.[5] There was also rot in the fens in 1730. Distemper raged in the county in 1747;[6] in December of that year the Massingberd tenants were all without money. One of them went into Yorkshire to

---

[1] L.A.O. Lindsey Dep. 71/60.
[2] *Lincs. N. & Q.* x (1908–9), 53; and see Young, *General View*, pp. 382–94.
[3] L.A.O. Redbourne, 1/5/4.   [4] L.A.O. Tyrwhitt Drake, IV, 4.
[5] G. E. Mingay, 'The Agricultural Depression, 1730–1750', *Essays in Economic History* (ed. E. M. Carus-Wilson), II, 314, reprinted from *Economic History Review*, 2nd ser. VIII (1955).
[6] L.A.O. Tyrwhitt Drake, IV, 24.

look for his woolman, who should have taken his wool in the summer but did not; and he could not sell it to anyone else unless the woolman set it at liberty.[1]

Change in farming practice could cause injury; and a complaint from the coastal marshes at Croft in 1723 is a tribute to the enterprise of wold farmers. Substantial men from the wolds, wanting pasture for their flocks, took marshland. When rents were raised they threw up their pasture, which was taken by meaner men who overstocked the land, neglected the drains, and, when there was a bad year, failed. The wold men were improving their own land with turnips and feeding their sheep there, or selling them lean to counties where turnips were used. They had also begun to buy Scots cattle, which, having been brought up in so cold and poor a country as Scotland, found even the wolds so much better that they could pick up a living there. Since their desertion by the woldmen the marshlands were not so well maintained.[2]

The commonest complaints were of course about prices. At Michaelmas 1723 the price of new wheat was down to 28s. a quarter in Lincoln. Such a low price indicated that the harvest was a good one; but from the point of view of the farmer who relied on his corn to pay his rent it was a bad year. That November Mrs Whichcot was told by her agent that times were so bad that as yet he had not received £12 of rent, though he hoped to have some of it in after Martinmas.[3]

In 1727–8 wheat was 44s.–45s. Evidently the crop was poor and, though the larger farmers might be well off, smaller farmers and labourers would be in distress. In November 1727 the incumbent of Holton Beckering and Wragby wrote that his Holton tithe would not be worth collecting, and was worse than the previous year: he added that the poor tenants had not so much barley as would support their families.[4] In 1728 and the following year Mrs Massingberd, whose lands lay in the marsh, was told by agents that she would have to abate two-thirds of her rents.[5]

As might be expected, the complaints of high prices were the loudest, and they are heard especially from the poorest class. The famous riots against the removal of the western spires of Lincoln Minster[6] produced a comment from the bishop who, though an absentee, was well informed, to the Secretary of State, that he thought it was not a Lincoln but a Lincolnshire riot, encouraged by the success of former riots (and particularly of riots in the

[1] L.A.O. Massingberd Mundy, VII/2/91.
[2] L.A.O. Tyrwhitt Drake, 2/2/20, 21. It was said that 30,000 Scots cattle were yearly brought into England.
[3] L.A.O. Aswarby, 10/27/7.   [4] L.A.O. Emeris, 25/13.
[5] W. O. Massingberd, *History of Ormsby* (n.d.), p. 307.
[6] Above, p. 40.

neighbouring fens) and managed by malcontents disaffected to the State.[1] It is reasonable to suppose that the high prices of that year contributed to the causes of the riots. In 1725 the price of wheat rose from 30s. to 34s. a quarter, and in the three following years was 40s., 45s. and 44s. respectively, whereafter a good harvest brought it down to 24s. In the same years rye, formerly 24s., reached 38s.; barley went from 16s. to 26s.; oats from 10s. to 13s.; and beans from 14s. to 20s.[2]

Wheat did not reach 40s. again until 1740, when the export of corn was prohibited for a year. Of that and the following year the *Stamford Mercury* commented in 1795[3] that dear as corn then was, the distress of 1740–1 was worse. Bread, butter, cheese and every common necessity was hardly to be had for money, and not only the people but even the cattle felt the effects of famine: there was no hay or straw, and thatch was taken from the roofs to feed the beasts. It is not surprising that a suspected attempt to export corn provoked a riot at Bourne in 1740.[4]

In 1756–7 wheat reached 40s. again, and the export of corn and flour was prohibited. William Pitt had just revived the militia, and perhaps both facts had something to do with risings all over the county. There was a riot at Boston, whence the mob designed to go to Lincoln races to attack the nobility.[5] On 14 September 1757 the Monson agent at Burton reported:

We have had several mobs rose in this county about the Militia Acts, some much more violent than others. One of the modestest made me a visit, only desired a drink of beer, which I consented to at half a pint, each man drank almost half a hogshead. They demanded of every constable the warrant, obliged them and farmers &c. who they met to go with them to Burton. My Lord was apprised of their coming, met them in the town, and by his prudent management they all dispersed to their own homes. Some of the mobs did great mischief, demanded money and ale, and those that refused their demands, beat them, broke their windows, doors &c. to great damage. Am told Mr Monk[6] was obliged to give them ten guineas and ale, and if it had not been for those farmers they obliged to go with them would have done him much greater damage. They rose almost all over the county. The Lord and Deputy Lieutenants had appointed to meet at Lincoln on Tuesday in the race week to take in lists of proper persons to serve from the several chief constables of the several wapentakes in the county, but his Grace the Duke of Ancaster finding it impossible to do anything of that kind by the rising of these mobs sent discharges signed 'Ancaster' to every chief constable with numbers of printed papers to be dispersed round the county to prevent the meeting which if it had not been done 'tis thought thousands would have appeared on the occasion at Lincoln, and great mischief ensued upon such a meeting.[7]

[1] P.R.O. State Papers Domestic, George I, vol. 63, no. 51.
[2] See Appendix 1. [3] 24 July 1795.
[4] L.A.O. Ancaster, 7/4/14. [5] *L.R. & S.M.* 3 Sept. 1757.
[6] Lawrence Monck of Caenby. [7] Monson, v, 69.

The dean of Lincoln wrote that month that the sympathies of the farmers were with their labourers:

At my return [to Lincoln] I found there had just been very tumultuous doings in this neighbourhood, as there had been in the Peak: but these were made by miners, fellows as untaught as Laplanders, whose faces were hardly ever seen by daylight. Our disturbances were made by farmers and neighbours who insulted the justices, the gentlemen and even their landlords to their faces. Their behaviour showed the greatest licenciousness and cowardice, and an utter contempt of the public authority and welfare. 'We will not fight', they said, 'for what does not concern us, and only belongs to our landlords: let the worst happen, we can but be tenants and labourers, as we are at present.' A divine here preached on the obedience due to civil governors: 'aye', said his hearers, 'he fetches that doctrine out of a book, which our governors do not believe in, and why should we?'[1]

That November over 200 persons assembled in the West Fen with drum beating and colours flying, and were cutting down several dams made by order of the Court of Sewers: the surveyor and his family had fled from their house at Sibsey and gone to Boston. Mr Pitt at once sent down a company of dragoons and two companies of foot to restore order.[2]

Sir Francis Whichcote was told in 1759 by a correspondent in Deeping St James that all the windows and doors of his house had been attempted, and he had been fitting bars and bolts and locks.[3] In that year there was smallpox in Lincoln, and the militia was ordered to muster at Stamford instead.[4] In 1764 wheat was from 44s. to 50s. a quarter, which no doubt explains the entry in the Lincoln quarter sessions records that the mayor and justices fixed wages in husbandry: the scale is not recorded. Prices remained at a high level for several years, and there were riots against inclosures in Holland Fen in 1769.[5]

[1] B.M. Birch 4164, Letters and State Papers, no. 18.

[2] L.A.O. Massingberd Mundy, VII/1/162. The militia went forward: in November 1759 it was ordered to Lancashire to guard against a threat of invasion by French ships. When in July 1761 it was ordered to Hertford, there were many complaints of its despatch when harvest was about to begin. The citizens, except the poor, were able to avoid service for which they were drawn in the militia ballot, by joining to hire substitutes: this was generally arranged through the parish by subscription (*Records of the Cust Family*, III (1927), 51, 53).

[3] L.A.O. Aswarby, 10/79/16. There were four alehouses within little more than a stone's throw, of which two seemed to be without business. Lady Anderson was besieged by rioters in her house at Kilnwick in Yorkshire in March 1758 (L.A.O. Anderson, 5/2/1/28).

[4] L.A.O. 2 Ancaster, 9/40.

[5] For the fen riots see *L.R. & S.M.* 11 July 1769; W. Marrat, *History of Lincolnshire* (1814), I, 138–46; II, 187–9; J. S. Padley, *Fens and Floods of Mid-Lincolnshire* (1882), pp. 39–45. J. T. Bealby wrote a novel about the riots, *A Daughter of the Fen* (1896). At Willoughton wheat, which had been 27s. in 1761, was 50s. in 1766, and 60s. in 1767 (*The Local Historian*, no. 23 (1939)).

Apart from complaints about bad years and high or low prices there were general complaints about methods of marketing. Time was when chapmen had come round buying wool, but times had changed, and graziers were at the great trouble and expense of carrying their wool to market—to Colchester and Norwich, and no doubt also to Leeds and Halifax. If they could not sell it they were put to the cost of warehousing it and employing factors whom they had to trust, and selling to buyers whom they did not know, to whom they had to give long credit, and who might eventually pay by a bill upon someone at a distance.[1] Buyers would combine against the grazier; yet if he broke up his farm for corn, grain would soon become as great a drug as wool. One pamphleteer thought that the farmer's distress was due not only to excess of wool, but to the high proportion of rents spent in London, the money that went into the public funds, and the amount raised in taxes and sent to London without adequate return made to the country.[2]

Poverty put the farmers and graziers at a disadvantage in selling their wool. They could not wait, they did not know how to combine, and they had to run after a purchaser instead of a purchaser running after them. Increasing supplies, including imports of wool and yarn from Ireland, gave the buyers an even stronger hand, and the growers felt an increasing sense of grievance that prices were depressed by a long established deliberate State policy of absolute prohibition of export of wool in the interests of the manufacturer. A long downward trend of wool prices reached a turning point about 1746, at about the very time that the growers found a champion in John Smith, a country parson who lived in Lincoln and held livings in nearby villages. He knew the farmers and their problems.[3]

---

[1] L.A.O. Tyrwhitt Drake, 2/2/21.

[2] 'The Grazier's Complaint and Petition for Redress; or the Necessity of restraining Irish Wool and Yarns; and of Raising and Supporting the Price of Wool of the Growth of Great Britain, considered by a Lincolnshire Grazier, 1726' (quoted by J. Bischoff, *Comprehensive History of Woollen and Worsted Manufactures and the Natural and Commercial History of Sheep* (1842), I, 115).

[3] His father was minister of West Barkwith, and it was by the interest of Lady Cust with Lady Skipworth, the patroness, that he succeeded his father in the living; Lord Tyrconnel (Sir John Brownlow) procured for him the living of Faldingworth (1720); and the Cust family also used their influence with the Crown to get him the living of Sutterton near Boston. Sir John Cust, the Speaker, offered him the chaplaincy of the House of Commons, but, being advanced in years and having lost his wife and his only son, he procured the offer of the post for his stepson Dr Palmer, who accepted it (Sir Joseph Banks's Notes in the Sutro Coll., which correct and amplify the account in *D.N.B.*; and see Venn, *Alumni Cantabrigienses*). There are several references to 'Mr Smith' in *Records of the Cust family*, III. The dean and chapter granted him a lease of a house in the Close for 40 years in 1744 (Chapter Acts, L.A.O. A/3/14, f. 69r). He acted as an inclosure commissioner at Fillingham in 1760. For James Boswell's visit to Palmer, see *The Ominous Years 1774–1776*, pp. 81–3.

He devoted much of his time and money—he had to mortgage his house in Lincoln for the purpose—to the publication of his monumental *Memoirs of Wool*, undertaken, according to Sir Joseph Banks, at the request of Lord Rockingham, who made him promises of reward and support which were not fulfilled. He collected all the references he could find to the growing and manufacture of wool in this country and abroad, and printed with cogent and acid comment the debates and pamphlets of then recent times. The conclusion he drew from his massive survey was that English wool did not obtain its natural price, because it was worth more abroad; that a duty on export should be substituted for the existing prohibition, and that this would be sufficient to protect the manufacturers' supplies of raw material, whilst it would allow the grower a market for surplus wool and make smuggling unprofitable.

The edition of 1747 prints a list of subscribers which includes many of the nobility and gentry of Lincolnshire (but not Rockingham); by 1765, in a second edition, he was speaking pungently about all the parties in the landed interest, presumably as a result of disappointment:

Grasiers and *Farmers*, immediate sellers of that commodity, are to all *political* intents and purposes, a disjointed, mute, unmeaning class of people: while their antagonists, persons they have to grapple with, WOOL BUYERS, a more compact and spirited body, egg'd on by chiefs and leaders, watchful, subtle, enterprising, are ready and strenuous on a signal given, with petitions to Parliament from all quarters of the kingdom—which petitions are seldom counteracted; and, if at any time, very faintly—NOT, *as might naturally be imagined*.

He added that the sellers, who were tenants, were in the nature of factors for landlords; but that the landlords were as wrapped up in their pleasures as the traders were in their gains: 'the LANDED INTEREST hath been frequently a *Rope of Sand*'.[1]

Those who raised livestock for the market also had their problems, which were aggravated for the sellers of cattle at Smithfield in 1749, when, in order to prevent the spread of distemper, it was enacted that no person, by himself, servant or agent, should sell cattle until they had been his property for 40 days.[2] Lincolnshire gentlemen and graziers at once

---

[1] Second edition, 1, p. iv. In 1750 Wood, the Lincoln printer, printed for him *The Case of the English Farmer and his Landlord*, a reply to criticisms of his book. Adam Smith wrote with respect of the author of the *Memoirs of Wool*. Robert Vyner and Thomas Whichcot opposed the bill to permit the export of Irish wool to Britain (*Parl. Hist.* XIV, cols. 1297, 1308). Banks held the same view as Smith about the apathy of the landed interest. Mr H. B. Carter, in his book *His Majesty's Spanish Flock* (p. 36), quotes him on the Wool Bill (see below, pp. 118–19) as saying 'the country gentlemen must outnumber the manufacturers in the House whenever they are sufficiently pinched, but like lions they want a great proportion of hunger to excite them'.

[2] 22 George II, c. 46, s. 27. The first Act in a series against distemper was 19 George II, c. 5.

complained that the clause had been passed without their knowledge. It meant that instead of using their salesmen or factors they had either to go up themselves or send their servants or drovers, who were a very prey to the butchers. The few men in a vast county which supplied the city of London with as much as any other four counties had to attend the selling of their cattle and neglect their other business, and as stock was ready at different times of the year they had to travel often, and so eat up the profits. If they waited from one market to another the value of their goods shrank by 10s. per beast and 1s. 6d. per sheep; and it cost 3, 5, or even 7 times as much to sell by such methods as it did by a letter of advice and payment of salary to a faithful salesman or factor.[1]

Some of these widely varied complaints have specific causes: sometimes political, like jacobitism, or the revival of the militia, or the ban on the export of wool in the interest of the manufacturer, and sometimes physical, like disease in livestock. Behind them, however, is a more general and enduring cause, namely low prices (except of course for exceptional years like 1740–1). For the period 1730–50 corn prices generally were so low as to make farming less profitable than usual. The farmers fell into arrear with their rents, and landlords had to abate them rather than have the farms thrown on their hands. Both landlords and farmers spent less with the tradesmen in Lincoln and other market towns, who largely depended on the landed interest. On the other hand some of the townsfolk prospered because of the cheapness of corn: 'the direct results of those smiling years were being turned into malt, starch, flour, and the indirect into butcher's meat, leather, glue, tallow as a result of feeding corn to stock.'[2] Labourers, whose rate of wages in terms of money might go on for years without change, certainly benefited by low prices, and there can be no doubt that in these years their standard of living was rising.[3]

Writing before this period of low prices, Defoe had been able to take a long view, being detached from the daily and seasonal problems of landlord, farmer and labourer. He saw the growing demand of the market and the scope for improvement in production and transport. The same long view was drawing the attention of moneyed men to the attractions of investment in land: they knew also that land brought social prestige and political influence, and on its ownership a man might found a family. If it were bought at a favourable price it would yield a fair return on the money invested in it, with scope for raising rents, and there was always the chance of improvement in methods of husbandry, or by inclosure and sometimes

---

[1] L.A.O. Monson, 21/12/2.

[2] J. D. Chambers, *Vale of Trent 1670–1800* (*Economic History Review* Supplements, 3), p. 45. [3] Below, p. 156.

by drainage. The Vyners, the Chaplins and the Heathcotes, who had
provided lord mayors of London and directors of the Bank of England,
were settled among the Lincolnshire gentry along with much lesser London
lights, some of whom had come earlier, and about whom little is known:
Monck at Caenby, Burton at Somersby, Dalton at Knaith, Short at
Edlington.[1] They were joined by Joseph Banks, an energetic Sheffield
attorney who bought Revesby and set up his son there as a country gentleman, and then went on enlarging his estate.[2] He saw possibilities in the
fen, and was pursuing a venture there when he died.[3] An attempt was made
to interest Sir Gilbert Heathcote in land in the Sleaford area, which, it was
claimed, would be worth 15s. an acre after inclosure.[4] Sir John Meres, a
local owner, was also a company promoter, and was more fanciful. He
thought his sandy and moorish lands on the Trentside might yield coal or
some other mineral, or grow timber, with quick growing willows and osiers
in suitable places. The tide in the river might work some useful engines and
water the low grounds. French firs would bring game; there might be a
duck decoy; and some places might be fit for woad.[5]

The less fanciful expectations were realised. Men of enterprise were
willing to embark capital in improvement of roads and waterways which
proved justified; when, for example, the Fossdyke was improved by an
undertaker, the revenue from tolls increased fivefold.[6] As the population
of the country grew, and prices rose, farming became more prosperous,
and there was an expansion of building and an increased consumption of
building materials and coal. The scene was beginning to change.

By 1760 corn prices were rising. The steward at Nocton wrote:

3 February 1766. All corn holds up with us at a great price. I bought three
quarters of oats last week, the best I could get, for there are very few good ones
this year, with a view to save some of our old oats. But the price is so high that
I will buy no more this season, and if we spend our stock and be run near,
perhaps they may be better and cheaper next year.[7]

They were in fact a little higher the next year. The general trend of cereal
prices was upwards. In the Lincoln leet jury returns, for the decade

---

[1] These names are taken at random from various dates in the eighteenth century.
Others could be found.

[2] *Banks Letters and Papers* (L.R.S.), ed. J. W. F. Hill, p. xvii.

[3] L.A.O. Ancaster, v/D/1/i and ff., quoted in *Banks Letters and Papers*, pp. xxiv–v, and
see *ibid.* p. 57; in 1718 Banks's steward was in touch with Captain Perry, who had been
engaged on embanking work on the Thames, and who bought land in Deeping Fen in
1729 (H. C. Darby, *Draining of the Fens* (1940), pp. 144–5). There was a project for
draining fenny lands in 1720 (W. R. Scott, *Joint Stock Companies* (1911), iii, 451); and
another in 1725 (copy in Sutro Coll.).

[4] L.A.O. Aswarby, 10/27/7.   [5] *Ibid.* 10/28/11.   [6] See Appendix ii.

[7] Bodl. MSS, DD. Dashwood (Bucks), B19/6/3.

1741–50 wheat averaged 25s. 5d. a quarter; in 1751–60, 32s. 3d.; in 1761–70, 40s. 11d. By 1781–90, after a fall in the late 1770's, it was 47s. In 1741–50 oats averaged 11s. 5d.; by 1761–70, 14s. 7d. In the same period barley rose from 15s. 1d. to 22s. 1d., and rye from 17s. 5d. to 29s. 5d.

Landlords had therefore an opportunity of raising their rents. In 1766 Lord Scarbrough put up his Lincolnshire rents by 30 per cent.[1] When Harmston was inclosed in 1758 Sir Nathaniel Thorold raised his. It was complained that the increases were too great; yet his successor raised them again in 1773. Mr Scrope took like action on two occasions at Coleby. Charles Amcotts wrote: 'If these stand, surely Lincolnshire estates will be found of much more value than many of the proprietors ever thought of'.[2] In 1770 Lord Le Despenser's steward was raising the rents at Dunston and, in referring to the universal discontent of the tenants, he wrote:

I used every method to convince them that there was no room for complaint, and told them how much every article they had to sell was improved, which obliged the landowner to advance his estate, only to put himself in the same state of fortune he was before, and that such advance was returned to the farmer for everything purchased, which method of reasoning made them more easy, and they have all taken their farms again except the fen tenants, and God knows where they are gone, or whether their houses are standing, for the flood is such as was never known before.

After Le Despenser had bought the land of Dr Willis at Dunston, the steward wrote that the doctor had advanced the rents so high that no further alteration could be made until some of the tenants quitted.[3]

Improving conditions brought the subject of inclosure to the fore. The landlord looked at it from the point of view of the return he might expect from his outlay: it was an expensive undertaking. If he had to borrow the money or realise investments, would the increase in rent that would follow be a reasonable return for his money? Le Despenser was considering what to do at Dunston in 1778, and at once received an inquiry from Hobart at Nocton whether he would sell. His steward thought it would cost £3,000 to inclose, with another £2,000 for necessary buildings; and he thought the estate would then sell for £11,000 without the wood. Le Despenser decided not to inclose, and he did not sell. There were many other considerations, one of them being the proportion of land to be allotted in lieu of tithe; the steward thought a clerical demand for a seventh so wrong

[1] Scarbrough MSS at Sandbeck, EMR/9.
[2] L.A.O. Massingberd Mundy, 11/3/6 (17 Dec. 1773).
[3] Bodl. MSS, DD. Dashwood (Bucks), B/19/6/22. Dr Willis had his private asylum at Dunston before he moved to Greatford.

that it might require a Henry VIII to set it right. There was, he reported, a great deal moving. Inclosure was going on at Metheringham in 1777; Sturton, inclosed, was up for sale; Baumber, inclosed about two years before by the duke of Newcastle, was for sale; and Wispington was also.[1]

There were, it appears, twelve inclosure acts for the county in the reign of George II. In the decade 1761–70 there were fifty-four; in 1771–80, sixty-six, of which thirty-four were passed in the years 1771–4, when wheat was 50s.–56s. a quarter. Thereafter, as interest rates rose, and the cost of inclosure increased, the impetus fell away, only to be renewed in the war years.

An Act of Parliament is a declaration of intention and not evidence of achievement. Allowing first a time for the making of the award, then for the physical work of laying out and inclosure, there was a necessary time-lag in effecting improvements in method, and indeed no guarantee that they happened at all. Thomas Stone said in 1794 that inclosure was the first step towards improvement, but, generally speaking, no further improvement had been made.[2]

When Arthur Young reported in 1771 he clearly took a poor view of the Lincolnshire farmer. In the sandy tract on the Trent bank near Dunham ferry the pastures were overcome with holchus grass, a mere weed. At Boultham by Lincoln he found an execrable rotation of crops, scarcely any idea of improving poor moory soils, and only ridicule for a farmer of spirit. The use of lime for manure was abandoned: sheep were never folded at Boultham, though they were at Canwick; fen meadows were undrained and full of flags. On the heath towards Sleaford, where many inclosures were making, and where the soil would yield very fine sainfoin, it was not as much cultivated as it might be. Further south he had hard things to say about fenland cultivation. Only Sir Cecil Wray at Fillingham (inclosed under an Act of 1758) was commended for his experiments with sainfoin and burnet, his mock-gothic summer castle, his planting and other improvements.[3] Two years later he wrote that from Sleaford to Brigg, 'all that the devil o'erlooks from Lincoln Town' was a desolate waste, over which wayfarers were directed by the landlighthouse of Dunston

---

[1] *Ibid.* B 19/6/21, 24, 25.

[2] *General View of the Agriculture of the County of Lincoln*, p. 56.

[3] *Farmer's Tour through the East of England*, I, 433–72. His only acknowledgements of help in Lincolnshire were to Mr John Davis, who gave him information in Lincoln, Wray, and Mr Wallet of Long Sutton. Thomas Ruggles visited the county in 1786, and sought information about the culture of sainfoin, of which there were many fields round Lincoln; but the only farmer he could find disposed to favour him with any communication had rendered himself incapable by conviviality (*Annals of Agriculture*, VIII, 168).

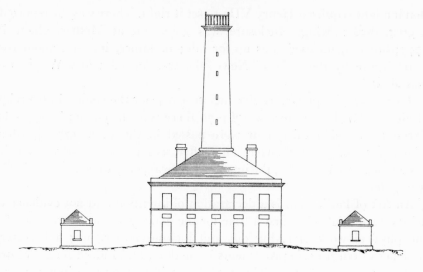

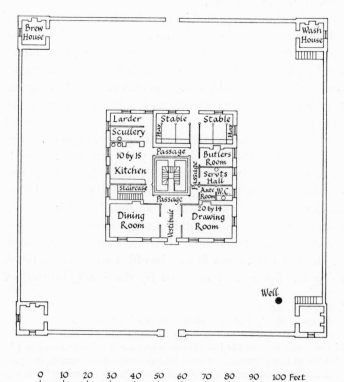

Fig. 2. Dunston Pillar: elevation and plan.

Pillar. No fences were to be seen for miles; only the furze-capped sand-banks which inclosed the warrens. Similarly the high wold ground from Spilsby to Caistor was a bleak unproductive heath.[1] He would tell a different tale a generation later.

But talk had shifted from arable farming to wool, where the grower had a real grievance. John Parkinson, an experienced land agent and inclosure commissioner, calculated for Banks in 1786 that, taking the preceding twelve years as compared with the previous twenty years, there had been a loss of 9s. 4d. on every 20s. per annum of rent of grazing land in the marsh, and nearly the same loss in the inland parts of the county. John Chapman of Marshchapel had a record of prices paid to his father and himself for their wool since 1742. For many years it hovered round £1 per tod; by 1770 it was down to 14s. 6d. and until 1777 it fluctuated between that figure and 18s. By 1780 it was 10s. 10d. and never exceeded 15s. 6d. until 1787, when it was up to 19s.[2] John Bourne, who was agent to Mr Drake in the coastal marsh, wrote in November 1778:

I do not know how things are in the south, but you would be amazed to see what distress impends upon trade and business in Lincolnshire...wool, the support of country business, is fallen from 25 to 30 %, horses and sheep full as much...at present fat beasts are most valuable.

8 March 1779. ...the plough alone can pay the rent...and all future improvement upon it must arise from getting the land into better heart by the turnip system of husbandry, which will carry double the stock...this stock alone... gives improvement to land.

But Mr Drake refused to allow ploughing. He said in 1781 that though corn was at a high price it might be the reverse the next year, and grazing more beneficial.[3] He proved to be wrong. Corn continued to rise, and wool to be depressed. The slump caused by the American war, improved breeding and rearing of sheep, increasing home production and Irish supplies were all contributory causes.

The wool growers became active, issuing pamphlets and calling meetings. 'A Gentleman resident on his estate in Lincolnshire' wrote that long combing wool had fallen in price by one-half from the last fifty years' average, and mounting quantities were left on the hands of the growers. The demand for goods made from long wool had declined owing to changes in fashion; linen and cotton had come in; and wool had increased in

---

[1] *Observations on the Present State of Waste Lands of Great Britain* (1773). At the same time Thomas Quincey saw excellent crops of barley on part of Lincoln heath, but the rest only served as pasture for a few sheep (*Gentleman's Magazine*, XXXIV, 299).

[2] Sutro Coll.

[3] L.A.O. Tyrwhitt Drake, 4/87, 103, 108, 111.

quantity and quality. To the suggestion that graziers should turn over to tillage and supply foreign markets with corn, it was replied that foreign countries had supplied themselves; farmers were ready to sell and merchants to carry, but no markets could be found. The writer pleaded for a temporary suspension of the laws against export of wool under such restrictions as should be least prejudicial to the manufacturers. Wool was a commodity on which so many depended, so universally produced from all land in the island, to a greater or less degree, that a failure in the matter must bring ruin to thousands.[1] Sir Joseph Banks published an historical argument on the same lines and asked:

what genuine Englishman did not feel a more poignant anxiety when he beheld the graziers assembling to inquire into their fallen state, than when he heard of the gallant Cornwallis' fate?[2]

The answer was all too easy.

Attention centred on the statutory prohibition of the export of wool. Adam Smith said that

the cruellest of our revenue laws...are mild and gentle in comparison of some of those which the clamour of our merchants and manufacturers has extorted from the legislature for the support of their own absurd and oppressive monopolies.[3]

It was in pursuance of that view that a county meeting was held at Lincoln castle on 31 October 1781 to consider how to promote the exportation of surplus wool, and a committee was formed. This move at once brought up the manufacturing interests in Yorkshire and East Anglia. Meetings were held to oppose any exportation of wool or ban on the importation of Irish yarn, and the high sheriff and grand jury of York joined in. The Lincolnshire Wool Committee prepared a petition to parliament: it said that the growers were sinking into distress and ruin, others were throwing up their farms, and the landed interest was in peril. It asked for a bill to permit the exportation of long and coarse wool at such a distance of time as would give the manufacturers time to buy up as much as

---

[1] *Considerations upon the Present State of the Wool Trade, the Laws made concerning that Article, and how far the same are consistent with true Policy and the real Interest of the State.* By a Gentleman resident on his Estate in Lincolnshire (1781).

[2] *Propriety of Allowing a Qualified Exportation of Wool discussed historically, to which is added a table which shows the value of the woolen goods of every kind, that were entered for exportation at the custom-house from 1697 to 1780 inclusive, as well as the prices of wool in England during all that period* (1782). It was published anonymously, but there is no doubt that the London Library is correct in attributing it to Banks. *A Letter from a Grower of Long Combing Wool to the Manufacturers of that valuable Staple* (1782) is attributed by the British Museum to T. Chaplin.

[3] *Wealth of Nations* (1822 edn), II, 494.

might be wanted for home consumption, the exported wool to be charged with a duty. This was a very moderate proposal: but moderation was in vain. When the petition came before the Commons it was summarily rejected.[1]

The high price that smuggled wool commanded in France made smuggling inevitable, and it may well have grown in volume. In 1784, 42,000 pounds of wool were seized at English ports, and large quantities escaped detection. Sometimes the material was carried abroad in bags labelled 'hops' or the like, and at other times small boats, laden with wool, put out to sea and met the ships at some distance from port. It was said that few ships left the Yorkshire or Lincolnshire coast towns without having one or two sacks surreptitiously stowed away in their holds.[2] Banks said that over 200,000 pounds of wool was imported into France in each of the years 1782–6.[3] The *Lincoln Gazetteer* commented that sheep were being smuggled to France with greater avidity and success than ever.[4]

With his insatiable appetite for facts Banks inquired of the customs house officers at Hull and Boston whether smuggling was taking place. The officer at Hull, whose district stretched from Grainthorpe haven in Lincolnshire all the way up the Humber, said that small vessels going from Hull upon the river had been supposed to turn about in the night and fall down the Humber, and then put their lading upon board larger vessels ready to receive it and go to the continent; though he had no evidence of the practice. He feared a little was shipped from Grainthorpe and Saltfleet. The Boston district included Saltfleet, Wainfleet, Spalding south to Sutton Wash, to Wisbech, which was a member of the port of Lynn. The district officer explained that the coast was a perfect level, with, in many places, not a bush to interrupt the view for miles; and where it was from one to two or three miles between high- and low-water mark a vessel once laden would have to wait for the tide before she could get off. On the other hand shipping coastwise gave opportunities, and the most elaborate precautions, with sureties for the behaviour of a master of a vessel, might go awry.[5]

---

[1] James Bischoff, *Comprehensive History of Woollen and Worsted Manufactures and the National and Commercial History of Sheep* (London, 1842). Returns collected in the county in the winter of 1781–2 suggested that 250,000 tods of wool were unsold. The manufacturers were able to point out that wool prices were up in 1782–3.

[2] H. Heaton, *Yorkshire Woollen and Worsted Industries* (1920), pp. 326–7; *Report of Parliamentary Committee 1786*, Gen. Coll. Reports, xxxviii, nos. 82–5, 87.

[3] Bischoff, *op. cit.* I, 243.

[4] I, 28 (7 Jan. 1785). Evidence was given before the West Riding justices that 90 tods of wool were put aboard a vessel at Goxhill Haven for export to Dunkirk (*Reports from Committees of House of Commons*, xi, 308, 317).

[5] Three Swedish ships were seized at Hull in 1787.

The belief that smuggling was on the increase prompted a move to make it more difficult. The promotion of a bill to this end seems to have begun in Exeter with a proposal that all wool shorn should be registered and only removed on a certificate. Even when these precautions were limited to areas within 15 miles of the sea there was an outcry. Another county meeting was held in Lincoln on 19 October 1786, which resolved that the parts of a bill tending to impose further restrictions on growers of wool were oppressive and injurious: a petition was drawn up for signature and a subscription entered into. The high sheriffs of other counties were asked to call county meetings: the replies were not encouraging. Only Suffolk and Lincoln seem to have moved.[1]

It is a point of interest that Yorkshire was not in the first place enthusiastic about the bill. Pemberton Milnes wrote from Wakefield that the motion of the bill was to strike at Lancashire and Yorkshire by depriving them from coming at wool as they did then. The trade of the southern counties was on the decline, and of the north on the increase. Wool carried coastwise would be clogged, which would be a disadvantage to Yorkshire, as great quantities were brought up by water up the Aire and Calder. Opinion in the West Riding swung round, however, in favour of legislation. The first bill was abandoned, and a second brought in, and Banks, who had given evidence against it, as Arthur Young had, realised that the best he could do would be to get concessions in drafting. He pointed out to Lord Hawkesbury that the bill contemplated one shearing a year only; whereas in the feeding land in the marshes sheep were shorn and sent to Smithfield every week for a period of 12–14 weeks. He secured a clause—which he called 'my clause'—that if wool were shorn but not removed or disposed of without certificate, it need not be certified until after the general shearing.[2]

Sir John Thorold led for the county in the House of Commons. He said that the allegations of smuggling had been grossly exaggerated. Mr Duncombe quoted Sir George Savile as saying that Halifax and the neighbouring manufacturing towns clothed the hills of Lincolnshire and gave the wool-growers that support without which they could not so long have prospered; to which Mr Harrison, M.P. for Grimsby on the interest of the future Lord Yarborough, replied that the growers substantially paid for

---

[1] Arthur Young acted for Suffolk as Banks did for Lincolnshire. See his *Autobiography* (1898), pp. 163–7, and p. 174, where Banks congratulates him on being burned in effigy for opposition to the Wool Bill. Young pointed out that Birmingham and Sheffield, Manchester and Etruria, prospered without monopoly against the landed interest, and he denounced the landed gentlemen for lying down to be fleeced by the woolmen like their sheep (*Annals of Agriculture*, VII (1786), 165–71).

[2] Sutro Coll.

the benefit, since they sold their wool to the Yorkshire manufacturers at half the price they could get for it abroad.[1]

The bill was passed,[2] and letters to the *Stamford Mercury* told that all the bells in and around Leeds—and at Norwich—were set ringing at the prospect of always having the ready supply of wool which had been denied by smuggling. The factors were saying that the market was full of last year's wool, and trying to force the seller to sell at any price. The writers thought that the remedy lay in local markets; about 30 years ago the grazier had been his own salesman; he now consigned to a factor at a distant market, and was at his mercy. The roads in many parts of the county, especially in the marshes, were almost impassable for three or four months in the year; and if the grower kept his wool at home in expectation of better times he could not remove it for that period. The solution was to build repositories at Louth, Lincoln and Wisbech, and take the wool to them while the roads were passable; and there should be a clerk of the market to receive them. In other counties with less wool production home markets had long subsisted, and their utility was universally admitted.[3]

Banks must have thought the suggestion impracticable, and no such move was made. There were, however, modest attempts at manufacture; but they were undertaken without skill or much capital, and they have the air of poor relief measures. A scheme for making stockings, carpets and blankets was promoted in 1783 by the Rev. Reynold Gideon Bouyer, rector of Theddlethorpe and Willoughby, a philanthropic clergyman who was later to found parish libraries in Northumberland. A general warehouse was to be provided in the county, and a committee set up from among the subscribers; a proper person was to promote the knitting of yarn stockings, and parish officers to set their poor to work in spinning schools as soon as

---

[1] *Parliamentary History of England*, xxvii, 382. Young paid tribute to Thorold's elaborate and able discussion, to which no reply was offered. Sir Peter Burrell and Mr Hobart spoke against the bill, and in the Lords the dukes of Ancaster and Portland, and Lords Exeter, Monson, Boston, Brownlow and Delaval voted against it. Mr Erskine was counsel for the Lincoln and Suffolk petition (*Annals of Agriculture*, x (1790), 1–185). Young advocated county associations to withstand the manufacturing interest (p. 402).

[2] 28 George III, c. 38. Smuggling continued, and it was thought that vessels taking wool out of Lincolnshire brought back geneva and brandy. A cutter was seized at Grainthorpe with such a cargo in 1788. Worsted yarn was found in the custom house in London, described as cotton. The fears of the manufacturers were proved false by the increase in their exports after the ban on the export of wool was repealed in 1825.

[3] Reprinted in *Letters to Lincolnshire Graziers on the subject of the Wool Trade; in which are offered certain hints for the correction of abuses which prevail therein* (Stamford, 1790). Cattle and sheep were, however, sometimes bought by Yorkshire agents visiting graziers at their homes (Stone, *General View*, p. 71).

harvest was over. The weaving of carpets and blankets was to follow.[1] This or a like undertaking flourished in 1787, and in that year the Lincolnshire Stuff Ball was instituted for the encouragement of stuff manufacture, all the ladies appearing in gowns made of stuff grown, spun, woven, dyed and finished in the county. Thomas Stone commented on this enterprise, promoted with spirit by Lady Banks and others during the American war, when long wool had no market.[2]

Statutory discrimination against the grower of wool might have been expected to induce a turnover from pasture to arable, but it was at least partly counteracted by the growing demand for mutton, which doubled its price between 1780 and 1800;[3] though attempts to improve the carcase might reduce the value of the fleece. Much attention was being paid to improvement of the breed of sheep, led by Mr Coke of Holkham and Bakewell of Dishley. Bakewell had taken sheep of the old Lincolnshire stock, and, by inbreeding, had produced the new Leicester breed, which he crossed back on the Lincoln, producing a sheep outstanding for both mutton and wool. The great sheep shearings at Holkham and Woburn became famous, and were attended by Banks and other Lincolnshire breeders. In 1787 Banks tried to heighten interest in the subject by prompting a wager between Charles Chaplin and Sir Peter Burrell as to which could produce the best rams, Chaplin showing his own, and Burrell those of his tenant Philip Wright. A jury were to decide the matter, basing their decision on the value of wool and carcase; when this was demurred to, he substituted the value of the sheep as lamb getters. But the jurymen, gentlemen with practical knowledge and less zeal for improvement, decided that the contest was not in the public interest.

In the following year there is a glimpse of Coke and Bakewell at Revesby.[4] Comparison was made between Leicester and Lincoln sheep, and Chaplin issued a challenge to Bakewell. It was that each party should name on oath two rams of his own breed, to be shown, killed and weighed at the Midsummer following: and to obviate the objection to killing the best sheep he offered to stake £500 on the event. The challenge was declined.[5] The

---

[1] L.P.L. U.P. 595, 596. The *Lincoln Gazetteer* (26 Nov. 1784) announced the sale of blankets, wholesale and retail, strong checked flannels for horse cloths, and stable waistcoats. It was hoped to promote parish spinning schools as well as the manufactory (Mrs Higgins, *The Bernards of Abington and Nether Winchendon*, III (1904), 84–6). There was a small factory in Lincoln in 1772 (*Gentleman's Magazine*, XLIV, 300).

[2] *General View*, p. 96.

[3] W. Marrat, *History of Lincolnshire*, I (1814), Introduction, p. 96; Saunders, *Lincolnshire* (1834), p. 57.

[4] Banks's household accounts for the period 1785–90, in the Sutro Coll., show that he visited Holkham in 1787 and 1790. These sheep shearings were the forerunners of agricultural shows.   [5] Sutro Coll.

incident was recalled after Chaplin's death at the sale of his rams. When criticisms were heard from gentlemen of the Leicestershire tup club, Thomas Chaplin stopped the sale, said that he had told the auctioneer not to make comparisons, and that though he did not wish to recount his victories he renewed his father's challenge. It was not taken.[1] Chaplin's dislike of the Leicester gentlemen came out again in a letter to Banks in 1802:

I have some reason to believe the late duke of Bedford's bailiffs or Mr Walton, a nephew of the late Bakewell's, who sorted and valued the duke's sheep for him, endeavoured to create jealousy of my sheep in the duke's mind and perhaps in some degree succeeded; this said Mr Walton I then understood had the same direction and management of Mr Coke's Leicestershire sheep that not any were exhibited at the show but such as he selected for the purpose, and that he fixed the price each sheep was to be let at; of such is the confidence placed in this man, who is not wanting in any of the accomplishments habitual to the Gentlemen of the Leicestershire Society, viz., *cunning* and *impudence*, it is not impossible he may prevail on Mr Coke not to allow of my sheep coming to Holkham. . . .[2]

Chaplin had shown the previous year at Woburn, when the *Mercury* noted that some judges thought his sheep superior to the New Leicester and South Down breeds, especially as to wool. He did, however, show at Holkham, when the fleece of one of his hoggets turned 15 pounds. It was long stoutly maintained that the Lincoln sheep, to the grazier, was superior to others, and when Arthur Young ventured a contrary opinion, Banks told him roundly that the Lincolnshire grazier did not consider him an infallible judge of the value of livestock: the only judges were the butchers and woolstaplers, and the Leicestershire gentlemen, however much they admired their darlings, must at last carry them to the butcher.[3]

The conclusion of the debate seems to be that the Lincoln breed with the heavier fleece were hardier and better suited to damp situations in the fens and marshes, whilst the New Leicesters were better suited to the uplands: and that the Lincoln breed gave the best wool, the New Leicesters the best meat.[4]

To the improvement of the farming interest above recounted the improvement of transport had made a large contribution, and it is necessary

[1] *L.R. & S.M.* 18 Sept. 1795. One of his rams made £174. 6s., said to be more than double the sum ever given for a ram at any auction, others 150 guineas, second-rate rams £90. For an acrimonious correspondence between Chaplin and Bakewell in 1788, with soothing comments by Young, see *Annals of Agriculture*, x, no. 60, p. 560. Chaplin pursued other controversies by handbill and advertisements in the press, which in appeals to sporting instinct as well as to expert knowledge were no doubt followed by a wide public. Banks collected a number of 'Bakewellisms', the purport of which is that Bakewell was a shifty person and not to be trusted (Sutro Coll.).

[2] Warren Dawson MS 47, 77–8.

[3] Sutro Coll.   [4] Joan Thirsk, *English Peasant Farming*, p. 233.

now to turn to the betterment of roads and waterways, the latter serving the cause of land drainage as well as of navigation.

In Defoe's time the roads were never good, and were sometimes impassable. The journey to London on the Old North Road, for example, involved the crossing of a 50-mile belt of dirty clay land as far as Royston, and road repair was difficult. The road was constantly cut up by the drifts of heavy bullocks going up to London markets. Defoe knew the road well, and wrote feelingly: and he foresaw great benefits from an extension of the turnpike system. Fat cattle would travel lighter and go farther in a day, and not waste their flesh in wallowing through mud. Sheep would be able to travel in winter, and graziers would no longer be obliged to sell their wethers cheap in October to farmers within 20 miles of London, but would bring them to market when they could command the best price.[1]

In spite of all the complaints of ruin recounted above, it is clear that the men who were willing to put capital into roads and waterways had fair confidence that they would get a return on their investment. In Lincolnshire, apart from the north road from Stamford to Grantham, it was the enterprising woldsmen who knew about turnips and how to make money out of Scots cattle[2] who made the first move for a turnpike. The route to their Yorkshire markets lay from the north-east of the county by Wragby to Lincoln, through a clay country where gravel was scarce, and the road had become so 'foundrous' that it was almost lost. Wood and mud repairs soon made it worse, and travellers even had to make a wide detour by the fens rather than bring their horses through. Near Langworth a coach and six horses stuck fast, and the coach was in danger of being broken to pieces. The bill to turnpike the road was passed in 1739,[3] even before the West Riding towns were themselves linked by a turnpike, which was a notable achievement.

After war with France ended in 1748 turnpikes spread more rapidly, and in 1755 the Lincoln common council agreed to subscribe towards the

---

[1] *Tour*, II, 123, 127; and see *H.M.C. Portland*, IV, 332; and for the supply of meat to London and East Anglia, Defoe, *Complete English Tradesman* (1841 edn), II, 73, 189 and 190.

[2] Above, p. 105.

[3] *C.J.* XXIII, 256; 12 George II, c. 10. For the Great North Road from Stamford to Grantham, 12 George II, c. 8; *C.J.* XXVI, 36. The clothing towns of the West Riding were connected by turnpike under 14 George II, c. 19. A traveller in 1743 said that the worst three miles he ever travelled in his life were on the turnpike between Lincoln and Ormsby (W. T. Jackman, *Development of Transportation in Modern England* (1916), I, 89n, 91n). The Wragby road must have been bad indeed if the fen roads, with their added perils of water, were thought better. When Bishop Wake travelled from Horncastle to Boston in the summer of 1709 his coach overturned in the middle of a slough, and he had difficulty in getting it out, and when he found the waters were out and the banks dangerous he took to his horse (Diary, in Lambeth Palace Library, p. 81v).

cost of surveying the road from the north end of Dunsby lane (north of Sleaford) over Lincoln heath, through the city, Bail, Close, Newport and across Lincoln open field; and to lend £500 on credit of future tolls. The roads across Canwick common and from the Stonebow westwards across Carholme and on to Dunham and Littleborough ferries over the Trent were soon added. The southern section of the road, from Dunsby to Peterborough, was also projected, and both bills became law in 1756.[1]

The Act for the northern section of the road included, besides the main roads south and west from Lincoln, the road from Bracebridge bridge to the city, and the road from the gate at the foot of Canwick Hill over the south of Canwick common to Great Bargate at the southern end of Wigford.[2] Liability to statute work on the roads remained with the parishes, and the Act especially provided that no money raised under its powers should be applied to the repair of roads already paved in city, Bail and Close. The line of road ran through the Close, and it was then that the dean and chapter abandoned their ancient right to close their gates at night or otherwise at their discretion: a surrender they were soon to regret.[3] Power was taken to close Little Bargate, and to erect tollgates at the south end of the city and westwards on the Saxilby road, no nearer to Lincoln than four miles. Gentry, clergy and citizens were appointed turnpike trustees.

Other turnpikes were sanctioned in 1765: one between Bawtry bridge and Hainton, which shortened the road from the wolds to the West Riding, and another from Lincoln to Barton waterside on the Humber, where a ferry gave passage to Selby, York and Hull. Roads to the north-east, north, west and south from Lincoln were thus provided for; the initiative for a Lincoln–Newark turnpike was taken at Newark in 1772. The Lincoln council favoured the scheme provided that it ensured that no undue advantage was secured by the Newarkers: if there was a tollbar at Bracebridge there must also be one near enough to Newark to catch the traffic on the road from Newark to Gainsborough. Leave was given by the Commons to bring in a bill,[4] but it did not go forward, and the project waited until the Lincoln turnpike trustees secured in an Act to renew their powers the inclusion of the road from Lincoln to Potter-hill, the point on the Newark road at the Lincoln–Nottingham county boundary, and the road up the Canwick Hill from Lincoln.[5] The road from Potter-hill to Newark was never turnpiked.

[1] 29 George II, cc. 84, 85.   [2] See Plate 13.
[3] Mr Swan said at a Local Government Board inquiry in 1866 that there was no thoroughfare in the Close until about 100 years before (L.P.L. L.C. 612).
[4] C.J. xxxiv, 89, 118.
[5] C.J. xxxvi, 118, 132; 17 George III, c. 109.

The effect of the turnpikes on roads in Lincoln caused much discussion. There had been a proposal to stop up the road through Minster Yard, and to carry it round by 'Mr Glover's garden', to the east of the Close; but the clause was deleted, and the trustees were empowered to buy from the dean and chapter the Potter gate and the East and West Chequer gates,[1] or such part of them as should be thought necessary for the purpose of rendering the passage through them more commodious. This power was not exercised at the time, though the West Chequer gate was taken down about 1800.[2]

The turnpiking of main roads marked a great advance in the conditions of travel, and brought to farmers and graziers the advantages foreseen by Defoe. Travellers of course benefited too: by 1784 there were beginning regular services of stage-coaches to London, Newark and various Lincolnshire towns, which made possible for the first time long distance travel for those who would not walk and could not keep or hire horses.[3] By 1796 Mr Gibbeson had built up and was ready to retire from a service of stage-wagons between London and Lincoln and other parts of the county, with a considerable trade in rum and brandy; wagons leaving London on Saturday morning reached Lincoln on Thursday, and setting out from Lincoln on Monday arrived in London on Saturday. From 1790 Lincoln received a daily post from Newark, where the northern mail dropped the letters which were brought on by the postboy; by 1801 there was a mail-coach from London by Peterborough to Lincoln and Barton, run by the proprietors of the old Lincoln coach.

But the public memory is short: men soon forgot the evils of the pre-turnpike era and began to murmur about the burdens of the tolls, fettering the freedom of travel, and setting up psychological as well as financial barriers between one place and another. The citizens of Lincoln were presently to complain that they were thus cut off even from their own commons.

[1] West Chequer gate stood by the west end of St Mary Magdalene church; there was a square between the two Chequer gates, known as the Chequer.

[2] Of the other main roads near Lincoln, the Grantham–Nottingham was turnpiked in 1758–9, Leadenham–Newark in the same year, Dunham ferry to Markham Common 1765, Bawtry–East Markham via East Retford 1765–6, and Doncaster–Bawtry 1775. In 1766 Mr Drake was asked by John Bourne, his receiver at Croft in the coastal marshes, to forward a proposed bill to widen the road from Boston to Wainfleet, Burgh and the Partney turnpike because 'this is the direct road from London to Croft by which the cattle fed on your estate always go'. Some of the tenants were afraid of tolls, but Bourne thought these were outweighed by the prospect of moving sheep to Smithfield and of shipping wool from Boston to both northern and southern markets at all seasons (L.A.O. Tyrwhitt Drake, 4/1/13–15/48). For road improvements in the city, see below, pp. 145–6.

[3] T. & S.L. pp. 16–17.

Map 1. River and canal communications.

Nor could the turnpiking of roads protect them against floods, which attacked both roads and fields and left villager and townsman alike with a feeling of helplessness. On the south-east of Lincoln the Witham fens came up to the city, and in winter swelled into a sheet of water covering everything east and south of the Sincil dyke, and sometimes washing the east side of High Street. To the south-west the upper Witham drained about 200,000 acres of land, the water from which had all to pass through the gap in the limestone ridge at Lincoln, either under the High Bridge or by the Sincil dyke; and the gap might at any time be appropriated by the Trent flood waters, converting a chain of pools into a vast inland sea. The water from the ridge to the north-west of the city was gathered by the tributary river Till and brought into the Fossdyke, and so either to the Trent or to the Witham.[1]

The waterways were not only channels for drainage of the land; they were also channels of navigation serving both farmer and merchant. Though sheep and cattle had to travel to market on the hoof, the wool to feed the mills and the corn to feed the millworkers could more easily go by water where rivers or canals could be used. The rivers serving the West Riding cloth towns were the Aire and Calder, which were connected by the Ouse and the Humber to the Trent. The Fossdyke canal, therefore, joining the Trent at Torksey to the Witham at Lincoln, resumed its old importance to the city, and the maintenance of the navigation became the constant preoccupation of the council and of traders and farmers alike. Corn, wool, ale and pitprops were sent westwards, and coal came back, which the Lincoln merchants supplied to distant parts of the county.[2]

In the early years of the century the Lincoln common council were struggling to maintain the navigation, of which they were undertakers under an Act of 1671: setting down sluices, cleaning the channel, mending the lock-keeper's house. The revenue was enough to pay for these minor works, leaving a modest surplus which in the 1730's was £50 or thereabouts. For larger works there were no funds, and as the traffic on the water grew the need for major improvements became clamant.[3]

There was a constant clash of interest between nearby landowners who wanted to keep down the water level to prevent flooding, and those who wanted to keep it up to facilitate the passage of boats. The landowners looked to the commissioners set up by the Act of 1671 for the purpose of supervising the undertaking to protect them; but the commissioners had dwindled in number, and the city had not been assiduous in keeping up their ranks. The lord of the manor of Torksey, Sir Jermyn Davers, a Suffolk baronet who had been M.P. for Bury St Edmunds, threatened in 1729 to apply to parliament for redress if he were not given a list of the commissioners, an account of their proceedings, and a promise to appoint

---

[1] *T. & S.L.* pp. 11–12.

[2] See Map 1. It had however to compete with sea-coal from Newcastle, which was plentiful and cheap (*Gentleman's Magazine*, XLIV, 300).

[3] For the earlier history of the Fossdyke, see *M.L.* and *T. & S.L.* (index). In the summer of 1717 the canal was impassable, and Joseph Banks had to carry goods from Scofton near Worksop towards Revesby by land carriage (*Banks Family Papers* (L.R.S. ed. J. W. F. Hill), p. 49). See Plate 15. For the revenue from tolls, see Appendix II.

thirty to be nominated by members of parliament for the county and the boroughs in it.[1]

The Witham below Lincoln presented rather different problems. The Act of 1671 had given the city the opportunity to declare itself undertaker of the river from Lincoln to the sea as well as the Fossdyke, but the power had not been exercised.[2] Nevertheless the city's interest in the river navigation was increasing. Leave was being given by the council to build warehouses on the river bank within the city boundary. In 1724 it was resolved to view the river down to Boston, and get a report on the banks and the responsibility for their repair.[3] Progress was leisurely, but at last a report came from James Scribo in 1733. He found 20 miles of the lower river crooked and winding, in several places not more than 18 or 20 feet wide, and very shallow; and when its tributary streams brought down great quantities of water, the river overflowed its banks and laid several thousands of rich pasture under water to a depth of three feet. The water remained on the land and stagnated for three or four months. The navigation was so bad that only vessels of very small burden could pass from Lincoln to Boston. The attempts of several proprietors to drain and embank their own estates had failed. Scribo gave warning that unless some new method was adopted it would not be many years before the navigation was entirely lost, and draining rendered impracticable. He made proposals to both ends.[4] There followed a series of meetings which issued in agreement between the city of Lincoln, the town of Boston and the owners of low grounds, and a petition to parliament was presented.[5] The move came to nothing.

The Fossdyke was the city's major concern. Its condition was really bad: at Torksey Stukeley saw waggons laden with hay pass over it in 1735.[6] A one-third share of the navigation with which the Lincoln common council had parted in 1672[7] had become vested in Robert Peart, with whom in 1731 they jointly appointed three representatives to co-operate in management for a year. Perhaps it was to finance his share in this

---

[1] L.A.O. Monson, 25/1/24, 25. Several more specific grievances were satisfied. For the manor of Torksey see R. E. G. Cole, 'The Royal Burgh of Torksey', *A.A.S.R.* xxviii (1906), 451.

[2] The navigation undertaken by the city included the 100 yards of the river Witham between Brayford head and the High Bridge, which was geographically part of the river Witham: it later formed part of the Ellison lease.

[3] Earl Fitzwilliam had already undertaken the North Forty Foot drain to improve his lands upon the lower reaches (W. H. Wheeler, *Fens of South Lincolnshire*, 2nd edn, p. 144).

[4] J. S. Padley, *Fens and Floods of Mid-Lincolnshire* (1882), p. 15.

[5] *C.J.* xxii, 661–2.   [6] *Diaries and Letters* (Surtees Society), ii, 275.

[7] *T. & S.L.* p. 209.

commitment that Peart mortgaged his interest to James Humberston for £750,[1] and when the council sought to take further measures it was from the mortgagee that they had to take a lease of the one-third share for £15 at a rent of £21. Having for reasons discussed below[2] decided to seek an undertaker of the navigation they naturally looked among the capitalists who were already interested in the Yorkshire rivers, with which the city's interests were so closely linked. Among them was Richard Ellison of Thorne in the East Riding. He had evidently been in treaty about the Fossdyke in 1739, and after making his inspections and inquiries, at some cost to the city in hospitality, he made alternative proposals: either to provide and maintain a channel of a depth of 3 feet 6 inches and take the tolls, paying a rent of £50 to the city and £25 to Humberston, or to advance half the money required for repair, attend the work, and take half the tolls. The work was estimated to cost £3,000. The common council, which might by a great effort have raised half that sum, nevertheless chose the first alternative, and came to terms with Ellison upon it.

Ellison was a wood merchant, and is described as having been formerly of Almholme in the parish of Arksey, but later of Thorne.[3] Thorne stands on the river Don. In 1725 the Company of Cutlers of Sheffield sought to become undertakers of part of the river, their particular interest being to ease the transport of Swedish ore upstream from Hull, and the export of finished Sheffield goods. In this enterprise they were opposed by Bawtry and Gainsborough, who feared loss to their carrying trade, but they were able to count on support from Wakefield, Leeds, Liverpool, Manchester and Birmingham. The bill was passed in 1726,[4] and the next year Doncaster corporation promoted another bill to improve the river below Doncaster, which was also passed.[5] Richard Ellison took a share in this latter enterprise, and when in 1732 the two undertakings were combined he became a more substantial holder. In 1737 he and two other men

---

[1] L.A.O. Spalding Court of Sewers, bundle 489. The council had already done some work on the canal, so that 5 ton boats could get to Lincoln (Willson, VI, 52).

[2] Below, p. 242.

[3] Ex inf. Mr J. E. Day of Doncaster. The family seem to have retained their timber interests, for in 1744, after Ellison's death, his son entered into an agreement with Doncaster corporation for the sale of a wood in Rossington (*Records of the Borough of Doncaster* (1889), I, no. 713). Later his grandson John Ellison had large interests in timber importing, and was building ships at Thorne.

[4] 12 George I, c. 38; Sheffield Public Libraries Reference Department, L.C. 70/29, 30, 34.

[5] 13 George I, c. 20. The commissioners appointed by the Act included the duke of Ancaster and others of his family, Sir Thomas Saunderson, Sir Nevile Hickman, and Joseph Banks, father and son, an acknowledgement of Lincolnshire's interest in the river.

agreed to take a lease of the tolls for 14 years at a rent of £1,200 a year for the first seven years and £1,500 for the second seven. This was evidently a profitable venture, for in 1751 the tolls were relet at £3,500 a year. In 1740 Ellison gave evidence before a House of Commons committee on a petition for an Act to improve the Don navigation, which Lincoln supported on the ground that it would provide more certain and easy transport to the most populous parts of Yorkshire. The bill was passed.[1] In 1735 Ellison and William Palmer had published 'A Survey of the Rivers Swale and Ouze from Richmond to York; in order to improve the Navigation there'. The survey was made, it seems, with a view to a bill to improve the river above York, but York corporation opposed the scheme, and it was abandoned.[2] Earlier still, in 1728, Ellison had been proposed as 'expenditor' to the Court of Sewers at Doncaster, but not elected; but from 1739 until his death he was called in as their trusted surveyor and engineer.[3] Clearly Ellison was a man well able to cope with the more modest problems of the Fossdyke.

On 18 September 1740 the two-thirds share of the city in the navigation was granted to Ellison by lease for 999 years at a rent of £50, and the other third share was got in and granted to him at a rent of £25. He was bound by covenant to maintain a channel of 3 feet 6 inches, keep up Saxilby Bridge, and indemnify the city against any claims arising on the altering of Torksey bridge. In dry seasons he might take two-thirds of the water coming down from the upper Witham into Brayford or Swanpool into the Fossdyke. The consent of the Fossdyke commissioners was given to the leases.[4] By 1743, as perhaps the council had foreseen or feared, the work had already cost £3,000, and was far from being finished. The canal was navigable in 1744, and the first coal it carried to Lincoln was sold at 13s. the chaldron instead of at 21s. as theretofore. It appears that the lessee had agreed always to furnish coal on those terms, but the promise was not in the leases and could not be enforced.[5]

Richard Ellison died in 1743 and was buried at St Peter at Arches.[6] He

[1] *C.J.* XXIII, 440-1, 445-6; 13 George II, c. 11. The river Don share ledger and minute books are at the British Transport Commission Record Office; they show the Ellisons dealing extensively in shares (see Sheffield Public Libraries, Accessions 35330, 35331; R. E. Leader's notes, L.C. 156).

[2] York Corporation MSS House Book 42, ff. 214...228. The earlier work on the Ouse had been carried out by Palmer.

[3] Records of Sewers, V, 195; VI, 63-4, 66-7, 208-9: Hatfield Chase Papers, now in Nottingham University Library. I am indebted to Mr J. E. Flack for these references.

[4] Lincoln Corporation MSS 598-601.   [5] L.P.L. MS 4973, p. 3.

[6] His wife Susannah was buried at Thorne in 1747. It has sometimes been thought that she was the daughter of Samuel Wesley, whose daughter Susannah married a Richard Ellison: but it is clear that her maiden name was Venoy. She married Ellison at Cantley in 1717.

was succeeded by his son Richard, who controlled the navigation until his death in 1792.[1] The family always regarded the son as the real executor of the work, and he was the architect of the Lincoln family's fortune. The leases were the cause of serious trouble in the future, when the common council were charged, not only with lack of foresight, but with corruption.[2] Indeed, complaints began at once. In 1747 it was said that Ellison (the son) had made a new cut out of the old channel, and erected a new wharf nearby, whereby part of the old river had silted up. Under threat that the council would do the work, he provided a way for keels from Ellison's wharf into Brayford. In 1762 he was pressed to deepen and scour the channel, and John Smeaton was called in by the council to advise, but only a few pottering improvements were made.[3] Ellison temporised on the ground that the Witham promoters would be making a proposal to him to reconcile the two undertakings. Yet when he proposed to proceed with work in 1771, it becoming necessary to close the navigation for a time, the council objected that there was a great shortage of coal, and that to shut the river would put up its price and cause hardship to the poor; and it was agreed to postpone the cleansing for a season.[4]

Meanwhile the council were attempting to make the Witham navigable from the High Bridge to the Stamp at the eastern boundary of the city; and in 1753 the gentry conferred on wider questions, calling in representatives of Lincoln and Boston. They were concerned to make the fens wholesome and habitable as well as to provide a navigation; and they decided that the difficulties could not be obviated without a bill in parliament. They wanted commissioners with powers to levy a tax on proprietors of fens, to erect a grand sluice near the mouth of the river to stem the tide, and to work gradually upstream with improvements. Navigation interests must not unduly prevail over drainage interests, and surface water must not be raised higher than within 2 feet of the natural soil on either side. There were many questions to settle: what should be done with the site of the old river when a new channel was cut; whether the cost of works on tributary drains should be assessed separately on lands affected, or charged to the general fund. The city, wanting to protect the Fossdyke, thought that the river ought not to be made navigable farther up by the commissioners than the east end of Canwick Ings, and they themselves would make it good from thence up to the High Bridge. Sir Francis Dashwood thought that as a shoal of hard gravel had to be taken out, it might be used to make a

[1] See Plate 19.
[2] Below, pp. 243, 254.   [3] S. Smiles, *Lives of the Engineers* (1861), II, 52.
[4] The council seem to have been unreasonable; in opposing the Witham Bill they acknowledged that Ellison had made a convenient navigation to the advantage of the neighbouring people and country.

road from the river to Lincoln heath, and by a bridge over the river communicate with the wolds. He urged that if lands west of Lincoln were to benefit they should contribute, and he asked what Lincoln and Boston would give. As a concession to the city it was agreed that it should be allowed to make a staunch between Stamp End and the High Bridge, but it must be 3 inches lower than the staunch at Brayford head: if it injured lands to the west of Lincoln there was to be an appeal to the commissioners.[1]

Discussion went on for several years, and a new project was advanced in 1761.[2] Many of the gentry and the town of Boston were in favour; owners in Holland fen, not wanting water to come down too quickly, opposed, and so also did Lincoln, Gainsborough, Rotherham and Rochdale, all having an interest in maintaining the water level in the Fossdyke.[3]

Land drainage was the main concern of the landowners, and naturally, for the fens were often deep under water in winter—sometimes, it was said, under 9 feet.[4] In the hope of meeting objections, John Grundy, an engineer, was authorised to negotiate with the city, offering them jurisdiction as far east as Canwick Ings provided they conformed with the plan of the engineers. The staunch at Brayford head was the one stumbling block: the citizens wanted it to keep up the level of the Fossdyke, and owners to the west of the city wanted to lower it to protect their lands from flooding. Grundy saw Mr Amcotts of Kettlethorpe, who was against any deal with the city; he thought a natural staunch was not only illegal but an absurdity. Mr Disney thought the laws of sewers were enough without a bill.[5]

The landowners presented their petition to the Commons, and Lincoln and the Yorkshire towns solidly opposed. Ellison submitted that he and his father had spent great sums of money on the Fossdyke, and that the bill would deprive him of that part of the Witham—a few yards between Brayford head and High Bridge—which was comprised in his navigation; he feared that the latter would be prejudiced if not destroyed. In spite of all opposition the bill received the royal assent on 2 June 1762.[6]

The new Act 'for draining and preserving certain low lands lying on both sides of the river Witham in the county of Lincoln, and for restoring and maintaining the navigation of the said river from the Highbridge in the city of Lincoln through the borough of Boston to the sea' recites that

[1] L.A.O. Monson, 7/8/15; Dashwood MSS; L.P.L. U.P. 582; Padley, *op. cit.* pp. 22–30.

[2] By a committee of which Lord Vere Bertie was chairman; the proposals were based on a report by John Grundy, Langley Edwards and John Smeaton.

[3] Wheeler, *op. cit.* p. 152. Nottingham and Derby supported the scheme.

[4] *Gentleman's Magazine*, xxxiii (1763), 93, 613; Thomas Miller in *Lincolnshire, Notts. & North Midland Times*, 10 Jan. 1860.

[5] Grundy, Plans, Schemes and Reports on the River Witham, Lincolnshire Incorporated Law Society's Library.

[6] *C.J.* xxix, 141...349; 2 George III, c. 32.

the outfall had been obstructed by the sand and silt brought in by the tide, and that great part of the fens (about 100,000 acres) were frequently overflowed and rendered useless and unprofitable. A general commission for drainage was to include two city representatives, and a separate navigation commission four: the latter commission might erect locks and make cuts and clean the river. So much of the Act of 1671 as related to the navigation between the High Bridge and the sea was repealed, and all that the city obtained of its plan for a separate jurisdiction within its boundaries was a proviso that if the commissioners did not within 14 years complete the drainage of the low lands from the east end of Canwick Ings to the western boundaries of the drainage towards Lincoln, and also a navigation along the same stretch of the river, the corporation of Lincoln should have the same powers for 7 years.[1] The common council appointed the recorder (Thomas Vivian), John Disney, John Harrison and John Garmston to be their navigation commissioners. The new bodies seem to have inspired confidence, for Mr Monck of Caenby took up all the unsubscribed shares in 1763, and was willing to take more.[2]

The general commission, wholly dominated by the gentry, at once turned attention to the state of the river between High Bridge and Stamp End. Warehouses had been built there by Lincoln citizens, with river walls to support them, and there were some obstructions of the channel. A lock was begun at Stamp End.[3] This, however, caused trouble with adjoining landowners, as it impeded drainage. The Lincoln frontagers on this short but busy strip of water regularly took their boats into Brayford and the Fossdyke, so bringing up the question whether such trade should take place without payment of toll, which was levied at Stamp End. After argument the commissioners agreed that if the lock did not serve the trade the toll should not be levied.

In 1769 Langley Edwards, the Witham engineer, complained to Ellison that Trent water was occasionally let into the Fossdyke, which raised the water so high in the Witham as to damage the river works: the lock-keeper at Torksey kept haling horses which he hired out to haul the keels to Lincoln, and so was interested in the promotion of the traffic. He either drew the cloughs or connived at others doing so.[4] He also gave notice to the Lincoln frontagers to repair their own walls.

The general commissioners built the Grand Sluice at Boston for the exclusion of tidal waters and opened it in 1766, and they improved the

---

[1] Section 118, 120.   [2] Bodl. MSS, DD. Dashwood (Bucks), B 19/7/8.

[3] It was built about 1770; before that date there was a chain at which tolls were taken, yielding about £300 a year (Willson, v, 55).

[4] Spalding Gentlemen's Society, Banks Stanhope Papers 15, portfolio 2.

lower river. The effect of this operation presumably was to run off flood waters a little more quickly; it could hardly bring other benefit to farmers in the Lincoln area, for it could not prevent floods. The interests of one parish were often in conflict with those of another. There was controversy about the necessity and legality of keeping up the old banks, or erecting new ones, on each side of Dunsdike in Metheringham.[1] When Dunston bank was broken in 1773 Dr Willis wrote that at Tattershall the river was so low that boats could scarcely pass, yet at Dunston the river was over its banks: 'they want the water and we are drowned'. He added that Lady Betty Chaplin, hearing that he went across the fens about a fortnight ago, had twice offered the boatwoman any money to swear that he had cut the bank. The woman replied that if a small cane and a book would do it possibly he might have done.[2]

Work went slowly, and by 1768 the commissioners needed more money, claiming that unless they could complete the work in hand the £42,000 already spent would be lost, though the taxes imposed to pay it off would continue. To lend point to their claim, there were serious floods in 1770 in the low lands to the west of Lincoln, when stacks of hay floating downstream were secured by the mayor's order. There was a great flood below Lincoln in 1773. Though there was no new Witham Act until 1808, from 1785 there was a series of statutes for the draining and embanking of separate parishes from Lincoln down to Billinghay. Windmills were set up for the purpose of throwing out the water: Mr Chaplin of Blankney showed his to Arthur Young. Young printed a table of the drainage improvements in which John Parkinson was a commissioner: there were nine fens below Lincoln, eleven towns in Holland Fen, with Tattershall and Anwick, amounting to 43,000 acres, with an improved value of £42,375, as compared with the old value of £5,982.[3] But the real benefit of this work began to accrue in the war period.[4]

---

[1] L.P.L. U.P. 1081.

[2] Bodl. MSS, DD. Dashwood (Bucks), B19/3/11. Charles Amcotts wrote from Kettlethorpe to W. B. Massingberd in 1774 that 'the water is at this time much higher between this place and Lincoln than I ever remember without a breach of the Trent bank. It is scarce passable with a horse from Mr Ellison's wharff in Lincoln to Burton Fen except the high part of Carholme, and it is also rather dangerous, being quite over the turnpike road in Haddo lane, so much and so that I am prevented seeing several gentlemen from Lincoln who promised to spend the whole of next week at this place' (Massingberd Mundy MSS, Society of Genealogists).

[3] *General View of the Agriculture of the County of Lincoln* (1799), p. 245.

[4] In 1811 the general commissioners were told that soon after the Act of 1762 the drainage commissioners borrowed £53,650 (secured on taxes) and the navigation commissioners £6,800 (secured on tolls), a sum infinitely inadequate, which left both navigation and drainage extremely defective (General Commissioners Entry Books, IV, 215, Lincolnshire Rivers Board office). John Grundy reported on the drainage of the

Thus far the river works had done little or nothing to protect the city from flooding, but in spite of its foreboding they did no harm, and certainly trade was growing. In 1767 a Lincoln vessel was visiting Leeds fortnightly with wool, and it advertised for goods to take back to Lincolnshire or up the Trent.[1] Wharves were being built, and in 1777 the common council directed a committee to view land on the east side of Brayford and consider whether a public wharf could be erected there. Private wharves were authorised, and when Mr Dawber's wharf was found to be so near the natural staunch at Brayford head that it would straiten the outfall and increase the velocity of the current he was given notice to desist.[2] The tolls on the waterways are unmistakable in their meaning. The Fossdyke gross receipts, which a little exceeded £500 in 1750, had reached £2,000 just before the outbreak of war with France in 1793; in 1763-4 the tolls on the Witham at Lincoln and Boston brought in £263; by 1771 £316; by 1782 they had risen to £498; and by 1790 to £898.[3] The Lancashire markets had been brought within easier range by the completion of the Trent and Mersey and the Leeds and Liverpool canals in 1777.

Meanwhile some lesser projects were on the way. In 1774 inhabitants of the Sleaford district wanted a navigation from Sleaford to Grantham, but a bill in parliament does not seem to have gone very far. Ten years later a navigation by the tributary river Slea from Sleaford to the river Witham at Chapel Hill was mooted, and the city of Lincoln sought to ensure that the Witham commissioners should be obliged to impose the same tolls on vessels going down river from Chapel Hill to Boston as up to Lincoln. The project passed into law.[4]

There followed a scheme for the tributary river Bain from Horncastle to the Witham at Tattershall. William Jessop was called in as engineer. Horncastle was in Sir Joseph Banks's country, and there can be no doubt that Banks was the prime mover. Jessop reported in 1791, and with his report was printed another by him which was clearly inspired by Banks. His eyes were on the expanding markets; but his immediate concern on behalf of the district below Lincoln on the river was with the narrow and shallow passage under the High Bridge and the staunch at Brayford head,

Deeping Fen in 1770 and the East Fen in 1774, but the projects had to await the impetus of war (Spalding Gentlemen's Society, Banks Stanhope Papers 1/2 and 15, portfolio 2; Padley, *op. cit.* pp. 14–15). By the end of the century steam-engines were used for pumping; an engine costing £1,000 would drain 1,000 acres 6 feet under the water in 8½ days (*Annals of Agriculture*, xxxiv, 279–80).

[1] Thoresby Society, xxxiii, 203–4.

[2] In 1782 a scheme was afoot for improving the navigation and also draining the lands on each side of it, and Smeaton reported, but this also had to await the war.

[3] Appendix ii; Banks Stanhope Papers, 15, portfolio 2.

[4] *C.J.* xxxiv, 483...647; xlvii, 465...680; 32 George III, c. 106.

which virtually separated the Witham and Fossdyke navigations. Here was the bottleneck. Jessop reported that under the High Bridge there was a passage for small boats or lighters drawing about a foot of water. The width of the passage was about 20 feet, confined between walls for a considerable length. The bridge itself was built upon a wooden floor about 18 inches under the surface in its lowest state. The floor could be taken up without danger to the bridge, the channel deepened all the way through, and the walls confining it underpinned; and it would then admit vessels of the largest size. The bridge below it, Thornbridge, would have to be raised. The great difficulty was the very strong current of water in wet seasons, which for want of a towing path under and above the bridge made it difficult to get vessels upwards. A towing path could be made, but it would still further confine the water. Furthermore, there was not room for vessels to pass each other, or to pass other vessels lying at the wharves. An alternative plan would be to use the Sincil dyke to provide a communication from above to below Lincoln, and to carry off more water. He advised that Sincil dyke should be used to improve drainage, and that High Bridge be improved for navigation.[1]

Armed with this report the Horncastle promoters applied to the Witham drainage commissioners for consent to the inclusion in the Horncastle Bill of a clause empowering them (at the expense of the Horncastle trust and such others as would join) to erect and maintain such works on the Witham below Lincoln as would be needed to protect the low lands there if through navigation were provided at Lincoln. The Sleaford promoters joined in and offered to share the cost.

There were doubts in Lincoln. The project involved the loss of the porterage hitherto needed for the transhipment of goods, and some of the older citizens feared that, if keels or sloops could sail from the Trent down to Boston without stopping or transferring their burthens in open boats or lighters, the trade of the city would decay.[2] Banks pointed out that the reduction of freight charges would increase the amount of river traffic, and that the boat crews would generally leave some of their cash in exchange for good victuals and ale. The city's natural trade would increase.[3] Agreement was finally reached: a meeting of inhabitants resolved in favour of the scheme, and the common council offered to pay the cost of lowering the floor under the High Bridge. On his part the Fossdyke lessee agreed

---

[1] *Report of W. Jessop, Engineer, on the Practicability and Expense of making a Navigable Communication between the River Witham and the Town of Horncastle* (1791); *Report of W. Jessop, Engineer, on the means of making a compleat Navigable Communication between the Witham and the Fosdike at Lincoln*; *C.J.* XLVII, 493...682.

[2] Willson, VI, 60.

[3] Draft in Banks's hand in the Sutro Coll.

to carry out such part of the work as related to his navigation. The cautious Witham drainage commissioners therefore agreed to the scheme provided that the whole cost was met by the Witham navigation commissioners and the proprietors of the Horncastle and Sleaford navigations. The Horncastle Act was passed in 1792,[1] and the Witham drainage commissioners asked for payment of cash before they began. Work was still not completed in 1798, when Sleaford complained against both Ellison and the city. A new Horncastle Bill was needed in 1800 for the raising of more money.[2]

Many other schemes were on the move. There was one for a canal from the Witham at Grantham to the Trent at Nottingham which alarmed the city and Ellison, as water might be thereby diverted from the upper Witham; and they were joined in their opposition by the Witham navigation commissioners and Sir Joseph. Together they defeated the bill in 1792, but on its reintroduction with amendments made to meet objections in 1793 it was carried into law.[3] Another bill for improving the Trent from Wilden ferry (Shardlow) to Gainsborough, providing for a tonnage toll, prompted Lincoln to ask for exemption for persons navigating from Lincoln to Gainsborough; and the toll was lowered for vessels between Torksey and Gainsborough.

Local vested interests were always nervous, and the city was even anxious lest the substitution of a bridge for a ferry over the Trent at Gainsborough should injure its trade. The council were successful in their opposition in 1786, but the bill for the bridge was passed in the following year. This was the first bridge to be built on the Trent below Newark, and in retrospect it is astonishing that such fears should outweigh the obvious convenience of the improvement; by the time that Dunham Bridge was built in 1834 the local attitude had wholly changed.[4] The road beyond Gainsborough, to East Retford, was turnpiked in the same year.[5]

The economic expansion which justified all these undertakings also furnished an opportunity for opening a bank in Lincoln, and it was natural that the Smiths, the Nottingham bankers, who had already opened a bank

---

[1] Witham G. C. Entry Book, III, 91; *C.J.* XLVII, 493...682; 32 George III, c. 107. Mr Tompson, the engineer to the river Don, was engaged to do the work.

[2] The shares were sold at £15–20 in 1796–8; by 1807 they reached £80, and thereafter dropped to a normal £50. The railway brought them down to £15 (L.A.O. T.L.E. Horncastle Navigation).

[3] *C.J.* XLVII, 613...786; 33 George III, c. 94. A boat of coal arrived at Grantham in 1797, and was met by the alderman and corporation and nearly 1,000 spectators; the coal was given to the poor.   [4] Below, p. 196.

[5] By 1811, when the surviving minute books begin, the bridge tolls were being let for £733 a year, a dividend of 6 per cent paid, and £2,500 had been lent by the Bridge Company on mortgage of the Gainsborough–Retford turnpike tolls (Gainsborough Bridge Company MSS, Lindsey County Council).

in London, and were later to go into partnership with William Wilberforce at Hull, should seek a new field there. Abel Smith found a partner in Richard Ellison, son of the original Fossdyke lessee, who already had banking associations. His brother Abraham had married a Heaton, of the family that opened the first Doncaster bank, and Richard's son, John, was a partner in the firm of Cooke, Childers, Swann, Ellison & Co. (evidently the successors of the Heatons) of Doncaster. Smith and Ellison took as a third partner John Brown, a mercer and ex-mayor of the city;[1] he was the resident active partner, and the business began in his house, each of the partners providing £1,000. The bank opened in 1775. When Abel Smith died in 1788 a new partnership was formed, Ellison and Brown each finding £7,000, a like sum being brought in jointly by Robert Smith, later Lord Carrington, and Samuel Smith. By 1786 they had £54,956 of notes in circulation, and the credit they thus created must have contributed largely to the capital investment of the period.[2] Ellison and other private bankers had invested in the Sleaford and Horncastle navigations, and Abel Smith had interests in various turnpike trusts. The Ellisons were constantly expanding their Yorkshire investments. In 1781 Richard Ellison— probably the third of the name—was elected to the committee of the Dun River Navigation, and later was often in the chair. Members of the family also had shares in the Aire and Calder and other undertakings.[3] When Richard Ellison II died in 1792 his personal estate was £35,804.[4] At Lord Carrington's retirement from the Lincoln bank in 1799 the note circulation was about £116,000, and the year's profit £9,867.[5]

---

[1] Below, p. 141.

[2] J. A. S. L. Leighton-Boyce, *Smiths the Bankers 1658–1958*, pp. 139–80; and an unpublished paper on the Doncaster and Retford Bank by Mr A. Robinson, who, through the courtesy of Mr D. Robson of the Westminster Bank, has kindly allowed it to be used.

[3] In 1792 representatives of the Aire and Calder Navigation met those of the Don river, among them Richard and John Ellison; there emerged bills for the Barnsley canal from the Don at Swinton, and the Stainforth to Keadby canal. Richard, Henry and John Ellison became proprietors of both, and all were appointed commissioners of the Aire and Calder, with another Richard. The records of these companies are in the British Transport Commission Record Office. It was not an accident that when Richard Ellison III was high sheriff of Lincolnshire the grand jury presented resolutions in favour of the Yorkshire canal projects.

[4] Spalding Gentlemen's Society, Banks Stanhope papers, 6/1/2.

[5] Nottingham Public Library, Misc. MSS 1700–1800, no. 96.

CHAPTER VI

THE CITY BELOWHILL: ECONOMIC AFFAIRS

LINCOLN, which served the immemorial function of a market centre for a wide and wild but slowly improving countryside, made upon all its visitors the impression of greatness decayed and eaten up by time.[1] Cox's *Magna Britannia*, with its preference for modernity, says of Lincoln:

what it has been for some ages (how splendid soever it was in the most ancient times, when the proverb was verified, Lincoln *was*, London *is*, and York *shall be*, *The finest city of the three*) it still is, and merits no better description than this; It is a large Place, and pretty populous; the Buildings are old, and consequently the beauty is lost, which renders it the more contemptible, not only because London so far outshines it with its new buildings, but many other cities and towns, where the wealthy gentlemen and traders have erected themselves, or built for tenants new Houses of more convenient fashion, as well as better materials.

If Antiquity made a show, Old Sarum might excel all the cities in England. The author conceded that the cathedral was a noble structure, although of the most barbarous Gothic order.[2] This was written in 1719; six years later Lord Harley, perhaps with Cox before him, was prompted by his visit to Lincoln to set down some commonplace reflections on the short continuance of all human affairs.[3]

Defoe, who had a kind word for the upper city, and approved of the countryside,[4] was scathing about the lower city. Lincoln, he wrote:

is an ancient, ragged, decay'd and still decaying city; it is full of the ruins of monasteries and religious houses, that, in short, the very barns, stables, out-houses, and, as they shew'd, some of the very hogstyes, were built churchfashion; that is to say, with stone walls and arch'd windows and doors.

He described the thirteen churches as the meanest to look on that were anywhere to be seen. If he had had more time he might have denounced the survival of such barbarous relics as Roman city walls and medieval gates. He cannot have failed to see some of them. Newland gate to the west, Clasketgate (where the powder magazine was kept) to the east, and at the southern end of Wigford—a long ribbon of houses southwards along the Ermine Street or High Street—the Great and Little Bargates, all remained until they fell victims to the turnpike movement half a century later.[5] It is a sign of the times that he should regard the gothic as peculiarly

---

[1] Camden, *Britannia* (Gough's edn 1806), II, 337; De la Pryme, *Diary* (Surtees Society, 1870), p. 87.

[2] (1720–31), p. 1441.

[3] *H.M.C. Portland*, VI, 84, 86.

[4] Above, pp. 2, 100.

[5] Above, pp. 123–4.

ecclesiastical and backward; he thought stone inferior to brick; he missed the new buildings and the growing population, and it is a pity that he did not see the horse fair or the sheep fair, which would have been more in his line.[1] Nevertheless, he recorded the honest impressions of a lively and able journalist.

John Loveday came soon afterwards. He travelled from Hull across the Humber by ferry to Barton, and along the Ermine Street by Spital to Lincoln, down the steep and difficult descent to the lower town. There he found most of the buildings old and mean, those that were new being built of brick, with some thatched houses.[2] The hints of new building are gradually amplified. William Stukeley had visited the city earlier— probably in 1722—and found it beginning to flourish again very considerably.[3] Thomas Sympson wrote in 1743 that new houses were daily building, and he looked to the Fossdyke undertaking[4] as the greatest improvement of all.[5] The Buck brothers added to their engraving of 1743 a tribute to the magistrates by whose care the city had lately begun to flourish considerably; two new churches had been built, a noble market-house and very handsome dwellinghouses. When all allowance is made for the flattery of prospective patrons, a firm basis of fact remains.

Lincoln was, in fact, very slowly emerging from the decayed medieval shell in which it had languished since the sixteenth century. The change was so slow as to be almost imperceptible. After half a century of growth a visitor could still find more antique than modern buildings, and carry away an impression of ancient greatness.[6] The city had no industries of its own; it was wholly dependent on the countryside which it served through its markets and fairs and its shops; besides being the capital of the county it stood at the junction of roads and waterways, and had no rival in Lincolnshire. As the countryside was stimulated by the growing demand for wool, meat and corn in the London markets and in the West Riding, and, as far as the south of the county was concerned, also in East Anglia, so the city was correspondingly benefited.

[1] *Tour through England and Wales* (Everyman edn), II, 91–4.
[2] *Diary of a Tour in 1732* (Roxburghe Club), pp. 204, 210.
[3] See Plate 12. *Itinerarium Curiosum* (1724), p. 85. For the date see Stuart Piggott, *William Stukeley* (1950), pp. 63–6. He noted that large pieces of the Roman wall remained standing, and where the stone had been robbed ample evidence remained of its foundations and ditches. [4] Above, p. 128.
[5] *Lincs. N. & Q.* IX (1906–7), 83. He noted in his Adversaria, p. 287, a brick kiln on the site of old St Faith's churchyard near Carholme: stone coffins had been dug up and used as horse troughs. In 1742 the common council proposed to allow the digging of clay on the south commons for making brick and tile.
[6] 'A Tour of the Midland Counties in 1772' by T(homas) Q(uincey), *Gentleman's Magazine*, XLIV, 299.

A new, modest affluence is reflected in a water-colour painting by the elder Pugin of the houses of the earlier Georgian period in the High Street south of the Stonebow, and just outside the walled city.[1] They are brick houses of quiet dignity, some of which might on evidence of style be dated rather earlier than 1730; but it may be that they are later, and that building fashions were slow to penetrate to country areas. Four sketches made of different stretches of the High Street in 1818 not only show Pugin's meticulous accuracy: they show also that the rebuilding of the eighteenth century stretched as far south as St Peter at Gowts Church, with a few houses of earlier date surviving; to the north of the Stonebow, inside the walled city, there was some rebuilding, in marked contrast to the Steep Hill, where many of the medieval houses survived.[2]

On the High Street, on both sides of the Stonebow, near to Brayford pool and the river Witham, were the shops and houses of the leading citizens: the drapers and mercers, the grocers and tallow-chandlers, saddlers, ironmongers, cabinet-makers and liquor merchants. Among them was the growing class of merchants concerned with agricultural products: millers, brewers, maltsters, tanners. As the century proceeded they were to gather on the river banks, building wharves and turning Brayford pool into an inland port, flanked by warehouses and coalyards instead of gardens. The number of inns slowly increased, providing for travellers, coaches, and carriers' wagons; their satellite ostlers, porters, coachmen and stable boys lived in the poorer parishes. The inn names reflected not only the trades, but the means of travel: the Coach and Horses, the Horse and Groom, the Packhorse, the Ship, the Sloop. Interspersed in the central area were the houses of the doctors and lawyers, and small private schools. Each trading establishment had its own apprentices, and perhaps journeymen, living in, with numbers of women servants; among them the sons and daughters of farmers, come to learn a trade or to train for domestic service.

There was a constant interchange of people between country and town and the ranks of the citizens were always being recruited from neighbouring villages. The story of one notable family is of especial interest, and may be taken as an example. Hezekiah Brown, probably from Yawthorpe, in the

---

[1] See Plate 2. Augustus Charles Pugin (1762?–1832) was a Frenchman who had been employed by Nash, the architect of Regent Street. He married one of the Welbys of Denton near Grantham, and is said to have made many paintings of Lincoln (B. Ferrey, *Recollections of Welby and Augustus Pugin* (1861), pp. 5–7); F. Gordon Roe, 'Elder Pugin' in *Old Water Colour Society's Club*, XXXI (1956). In these architectural matters I have been helped by the comments of Mr John Harris.

[2] See Plates 10 (*a*) and (*b*), 11 (*a*) and (*b*). They have been identified by the late Iolo A. Williams as being by William Henry Brooke (1772?–1860). They are in the Usher Gallery, Lincoln.

parish of Corringham, in the Gainsborough direction, became a mercer in Lincoln. He married Justina, the daughter of Alderman Thomas Nicholson, an apothecary of St Peter at Arches, who had been mayor in 1688 and again in 1716. Brown was chamberlain in 1706, sheriff in 1708, and mayor in 1712 and 1716. He had four sons. The eldest, Thomas, inherited property at Yawthorpe. The second, John Brown, was, like his father, a mercer and no doubt joined him in business. He married Anne, the only daughter of Alderman John Hooton. He too served the civic offices: chamberlain in 1747, sheriff in 1750, mayor in 1756 and 1772. In 1773 he became a partner with Abel Smith and Richard Ellison in the Lincoln bank.[1]

The third son, Broxholme Brown, was an apothecary. He married, at Burton, Jane, the daughter of Gervase Raines, who had been mayor in 1739. He was chamberlain in 1750, sheriff in 1752, mayor in 1757 and 1773. He had two sons, Hezekiah and Broxholme, who seem both to have lived in the Close, the elder becoming the heir of his uncle John the banker. They were ascending in the social scale; the second Richard Ellison could also live in the Close. This Broxholme Brown took Holy Orders and became rector of Scotton.

The fourth son of the original Hezekiah, also named Hezekiah, was a grazier who apparently farmed at Cammeringham. A daughter Susanna married the Rev. Gilbert Benet, rector of St Peter at Arches; another, Elizabeth, married John Haw of South Carlton, who was probably the steward of the Monson family; Amy married John Davies, a linen draper of St Peter at Arches.[2]

But the trading, middle class of leading citizens grew only slowly. The area that they were improving was small, and the improvements were modest in scale. The area to the south, which remained untouched, is described by a writer at the end of the century. He gave an account of a journey from the south along the dirty road from Bargate at the southern extremity of Wigford, with the rustic church of St Botolph on the right, and the small but rude cottages which seemed to enclose the village green, all conspiring to give it the appearance of village scenery. He saw church after church, the illusion still continuing, having crossed the little streams of the Sincil dyke, which were hardly passable either by the ford or the two inconvenient bridges called the Gowts. Brayford he thought an incommodious basin, almost joining itself to the Swan and other pools, and the Waterside was a dirty place. It was not until he had travelled more than half a mile along the street that he began to think himself in Lincoln. He then reached the High Bridge—which spanned the river

[1] Above, p. 137. [2] Lincs. N. & Q. IX, 197.

Witham—and saw shops and commodious inns, and found himself in the centre of bustle and trade.[1]

Bustle and trade it was, at least when the country folk came to town, as they did on Friday, which was market day. Some came on foot; some in market boats, hauled by one or two men, or in shouts, little narrow cock-boats holding two people, which they moored on the river bank; some in carriers' carts, both horse and carrier sometimes going to sleep on the journey. Perhaps the most uncomfortable vehicle was the cart, drawn maybe by an ox, with chairs in it. Thomas Miller's grandmother used to say that her last two teeth were jolted out of her head while coming down Lincoln Hill in such a contrivance. Miller would see a jolly farmer lifting down from his horse his buxom wife, and hear him say 'Thee an' they sins weighs a featish lump, my old lass'. An old song ran:

> The farmer doth to the market go
>   To sell his barley and wheat;
> His wife on a pilloring seat rides behind,
>   Dressed up so clean and neat.
>
> With a basket of butter and eggs she rides
>   So merrily on I'll vow;
> There's none so rare that can compare
>   With the lads that follow the plough.
>
> And when from the market they do return
>   That is the best comfort of all;
> We have a lusty black pudding in the pot
>   And a good piece of beef and all.
>
> And then after supper a jug of brown beer
>   Is brought to the table, I'll vow;
> And there's none so rare than can compare
>   With the lads that follow the plough.[2]

Or the farmer's daughter might come in to market on a pony.

Though Lincoln lived largely by its market it was one of the badges of its antiquity that it had no market-place. It was too old, and had been confined by its walls, and, south of the Stonebow, by its waterways and the risks of flood. If it had grown up a little later it might have provided a fine open space, like Boston, or King's Lynn, or Cambridge. But it did not, and the markets were held in the streets, which, already narrow, provided a scheme of indescribable confusion. The oat market for oats and

---

[1] *Lincoln and Lincolnshire Cabinet* (1827), pp. 8, 18.

[2] The song was repeated to the vicar of Stixwould in 1892 by one of the oldest women in the parish (*Notes and Queries*, 8th ser. II, 43–4). Black pudding was a form of 'pig cheer': it consisted of fresh pig's blood, milk, barley and suet, and sometimes other ingredients, baked in a sausage skin.

ground meal was held 'on the old hill' by the churchyard wall of St Mary le Wigford; the corn market, for all other grain, had appropriated the churchyard of the vanished church of St John the Evangelist, which became the Cornhill; between High Bridge and the Stonebow was the fish market, which was well furnished twice a week, with sea fish on Wednesdays and fresh-water fish on Fridays, the former brought chiefly from the Yorkshire coast, the latter taken in the Witham; the river provided plenty of pike, carp, tench, eels, barbots and others, and those, said Thomas Sympson, the best of their kind. Inside the wall, north of the Stonebow, was the butter market, to which the farmers' wives and daughters resorted with their baskets of butter and eggs, and above that was the butcher or flesh market. The swine market was held near the foot of the present Lindum Road.[1]

The sheep market was held on the south side of the Greyfriars, in the south-east corner of the walled area, and the annual fair extended across the old eastern ditch—which had become Broadgate, a wide road divided by an open drain running down the middle—into the field outside. Here and far beyond there would assemble, at April fair, perhaps 20,000 sheep. The hurdles, or trays, in which the sheep were folded, were fixed some weeks before the fair, for sheep were sold on several preceding market days. The adjoining Greyfriars was the home of the grammar school,[2] whose boys were allowed to leave school half an hour earlier, in order to gain health and exercise by leaping over the trays. Both hillsides, and the pastures beyond, were studded with sheep. An old boy recalled the scene when the fair opened:

Then to rise at five in the morning, to witness the bargains and the more than diplomatic acuteness of the honest farmers, eager to gain or to save sixpence a head on the bleating imprisoned fold near them, on which each looks with an eye expressive of other feelings than those of pastoral poetry! At length, money in the hand of the one is struck against money in the hand of the other; the bargain is *struck*. The pen is opened: the sheep long compassed so closely as to be but one united mass, recover the privilege of individual existence: they start forward; the shouts, and hats, and sticks of the farmers' men; the barking of dogs; the mimic efforts of school-boys, urge them on: hinderances, entanglements of every kind oppose: a waggon, a fruit stall, an open gate, a closed passage— worst of all, an encounter with another flock: at last all is surmounted: our fleecy care again breathes the air of the country: we school-boys feel that we have done our duty to them, and bid them a kind farewell.[3]

The fair lasted four days: horses on Tuesday and Wednesday, sheep on Thursday, and cattle on Friday. The horse fair, on a smaller scale, was

[1] Adversaria, *passim*.   [2] *T. & S.L.* pp. 103–4.
[3] Henry Best, *Personal and Literary Memorials* (1829), pp. 256–8.

held in Newland, the space between the old south wall and Brayford pool.[1] Early in the century there were two fairs described as well frequented, one on Midsummer day (still held in 1803), the other on St Hugh's day (17 November). In 1827 the September fair was said to last three days, but later references are all to the April fair, which traditionally has been and until lately was held in the last whole week in April, though only a pleasure fair now survives in that week. The *Stamford Mercury* said in 1786 that it was one of the biggest fairs in the whole year, and was proclaimed by the mayor, sheriffs and officers on horseback.

The market traffic was growing, and with more people and more carriages and laden packhorses among the stalls in the narrow streets a demand arose for something better; and the cries of the women about the butter market were the loudest. Their butter, cheese, poultry and eggs were sold on both sides of the High Street by St Peter at Arches Church. At last in 1736 the common council declared that experience had shown the road to be too narrow

not only by reason of carriages and loaded horses frequently passing that way to the indangering of people's lives or maiming of them, but also by hindering a free communication of the other markets and persons going backward and forward, and frequent complaints have been made of the same.

The parishioners of St Peter at Arches therefore agreed to grant to the city a piece of land on the north side of their churchyard for the market. The city on its part was to level and pave the market-place, and the parish on its part to provide forms and chairs and take a half-penny of each person using them.

The countrywomen were not appeased. They had the common council on the run. They were no longer content to remain in the open, even sitting, with their baskets in all weathers. They demanded a market-house, and the council agreed. Bishop Reynolds cordially sanctioned the taking in of a narrow strip of the churchyard in exchange for an annual payment of £6, handsomely remarking that the citizens' forebears had probably given the whole precinct. The little market-house, the charming façade of which is preserved in the modern market-house on the Waterside South, was built in 1738.

Money was always short, and men's minds moved very slowly, but they were beginning to move, and other improvements followed. The High Bridge, whose medieval vault still carries modern traffic, had houses on it on both sides. The number of carriages using the narrow roadway greatly increased, and it was agreed in 1758 that the passage over it was so strait that the houses on the east side, which all belonged to the common chamber,

[1] Adversaria, p. 288.

should not be relet. By 1769 they had fallen vacant and were being pulled down, and John Dixon of Hull was employed to build a conduit in the form of an obelisk on the site. The fish market was moved from the street to a new fish and butchers' shambles in the old St Lawrence churchyard, built according to Dixon's plan: the western part of the present Clasketgate was long known as Butchery Street. Some of the bridges, too, needed attention. The middle arch of Bracebridge Bridge, over the upper Witham, was the city's liability;[1] it was repaired in 1751. St Mary's Bridge, a rustic wooden affair, was difficult to keep up, and a new bridge of brick and stone was ordered in 1755, to the plan of John Hayward, at a cost of £35.

The markets and the bridges were the property and the responsibility of the city, but the roads were the responsibility of the parishes. Tudor legislation had treated urban and rural parishes in this and some other respects alike. The parish vestries, consisting of the heads of a few dozen families, might keep up the lesser streets and lanes with an occasional load of stones or brushwood, and ask the justices' approval of a parish highway rate to meet the cost; but the main roads were a more serious matter, especially in Wigford or on Carholme, when at the most only a ribbon of houses existed to bear the burden of the rate. Already at the beginning of the eighteenth century the common council were sharing the cost of the High Street south of Gowts Bridges, and some of the roads on Lincoln hillside, and Cross Cliff hill, which were difficult to keep in repair. Legal liability however was unaffected, and in 1726 St Botolph's was indicted for a bad highway from Bargate to Bracebridge Lane. The burden was too great to be borne by the parish, and the cost of its proper discharge was rising all the time as traffic, wheeled and otherwise, increased. Old-style repairs, the throwing down of stone or gravel, were no longer enough. In 1738 the common council addressed themselves to the highway from the Old Packhorse inn pavement in St Mark's parish to Great Bargate in St Botolph's parish—a distance of 1200 yards—and declared that the mud was so deep and so cut up that in the winter season wagons and carriages and loaded horses could not get through. Other parts were dangerous to travellers and frequenters of the market. The ordinary law was not enough; and the parishes could not pay, because materials for repair lay at a great distance.

And forasmuch as the repairing the said highway tends to the welfare trade and advantage of this city, and to the intent that the same may be with all convenient speed amended,

it was ordered that the middle part of the causeway, 18 feet wide, be paved with 'coggles'—a Lincolnshire version of 'cobbles' or round stones—and

[1] *M.L.* p. 358.

an outlay of £200 a year was authorised until the work should be finished. The work went slowly on; the road was 'excessive bad' in 1752; and another £400 was voted in 1759. Coggles being found inconvenient (perhaps they meant expensive) it was ordered that gravel be used instead, in the same way as on the turnpike roads to London. Over 7,000 tons of gravel were brought from Skellingthorpe at the price of a penny a load. The causeway was known as the Rampart, or ramper, a phrase still used by Lincolnshire folk for a high road. Evidently the new standard was appreciated, for in 1769 it was ordered that the Rampart be extended from St Mark's parish northward to St Mary's and paved with coggles in the same way.

During these years some of the main approaches to Lincoln, notably from London, were turnpiked,[1] including Pottergate, which was the name given to the whole length of the present Pottergate and Lindum Road. This was the principal road connecting the upper and lower cities. Like the Rampart, it carried a growing volume of traffic, and the slope made it more costly to maintain. Moreover, the gradient, which in places was over six inches in one yard, made it both inconvenient and dangerous. The turnpike trustees were unwilling to undertake its improvement without help, and accordingly a subscription was opened to which the gentry, headed by Sir Joseph Banks, gave handsomely.[2] The turnpike commissioners were allowed by the common council to remove what remained of the Clasket gate—they first removed the armour stored there, relics of an earlier age, consisting of helmets, back-plates and breast-plates, and sold them to a blacksmith as old iron—together with a pinfold opposite, throw the ground into the new road, and also take part of the site of the old Blackfriars to the east of the old town wall and ditch. The new road was finished in 1786. It was a triumph. It was the greatest improvement yet carried out, and the first attempt since the Romans to ease the problem of getting horse-drawn vehicles up and down the Lincoln Hill. It was long called the New Road.

All these evidences of growth imply a greater demand for labour, and although at the end of the century the city was still a small market town, the proportionate increase of population was considerable. The first official census was taken in 1801, but there are available for comparison the returns made by the clergy to their bishop about their parishes, including a statement about the number of families: estimates, no doubt, but there is no reason to distrust their accuracy. According to a return of 1705 there were in Lincoln as a whole, including Bail and Close, 735 families. About 1721, according to another return, there were 981 families. In 1801 the first census return gave 1,603 families, or 6,949 persons.[3] As in each instance

---

[1] Above, p. 123.   [2] *Lincoln Gazetteer*, 17 Sept. 1784.   [3] See Appendix III.

the figures are given by parishes it is possible to say in what parts of the city the increase of population occurred. In the period 1705–21 much of it occurred in the upper city, in St Michael, St Paul and St Peter in Eastgate: this was the area of the gentry and cathedral clergy and their servants, and their growing establishments as their fortunes recovered from the Civil War may account for it. Belowhill St Martin doubled; no doubt increasing traffic on the Fossdyke, with old enclosures available for building, accounts for it. St Swithin grew only a little; improvements on the Witham came later. St Botolph, at the southern extremity of Wigford, doubled; perhaps increasing traffic on the roads and the need of getting farm produce to market explains it. By 1801 there was a general increase of population throughout the city.

To move from population figures to figures of baptisms, marriages and burials as recorded in the parish registers is to move from the reasonably secure to the precarious. Not all births and deaths reached the registers, and, furthermore, there is no certain way of calculating the number of inhabitants from parish register entries. These do, however, indicate trends, and some inferences can be drawn from them. Taking decennial averages for all the Lincoln parishes so far as registers and bishops' transcripts survive, there is a continuing rise in the number of baptisms from 1711–20 to 1731–40, followed by a fall, recovering in 1761–70, notably in St Martin and St Swithin, the waterside parishes. In 1711–30 the number of burials exceeded the number of baptisms, so that the earlier increase of population must have been due to immigration. From 1731 to 1740 baptisms took the lead over burials, so that there was a natural increase, which could have been added to by immigration or reduced by migration.

The city's marriage figures are far from complete, and figures for separate parishes are misleading because some of the parish churches were unfit for service or not regularly served by clergy. Nevertheless it appears that there was a fall in the number of marriages in 1741–60, followed by a climb which may have been continuous.

It is significant that in the earlier years when the city was clearly growing, the population of the county as a whole was falling slightly. The ecclesiastical returns point to a small fall in the number of families from about 31,900 to about 30,450.[1] Rickman, who had charge of the earliest census, attempted to calculate the population of the county at the beginning and the middle of the eighteenth century; his method involved the double assumption that the baptism rates in each county remained constant throughout the century, and that the effects of immigration might be ignored. His calculation, as revised by recent research, gives a population

---

[1] *Speculum Diocesios Lincolniensis* (L.R.S.), p. viii.

of 179,000 in 1700, 153,000 in 1751, about 200,000 in 1781, comparing with 215,000 in 1801.[1]

Like the county, the city passed through a period of decline, and it is reasonable to suppose that both were linked with the agricultural depression of 1730–50, though it was only in 1741–50 that baptisms declined in Lincoln. Perhaps there was an influx into Lincoln during the earlier days of the depression; baptisms increased by 270 as between 1721–30 and 1731–40.

After 1760 not only was the number of baptisms on the increase in Lincoln, but the excess of baptisms over burials was also growing: by the war decade 1791–1800 it had grown to 429. This was probably partly accounted for by a fall in the death rate. It has been suggested that the fall may have been partly due to a gradual disappearance of local famines and greater resistance to infection connected with the more regular supply of food. These results might be expected to flow from improvements in transport and a rise in agricultural income.[2]

The city or parish authorities had no wish to prevent the entry of immigrants—and the law of settlements did not stop them—but the parish overseers were very much concerned to ensure that they should not become chargeable to their new parish. An Act of 1697 had provided for the issue of certificates from the parish of origin which were, in effect, a promise entered into by the parish to take back without demur the person whom the certificate named, should he or she become chargeable at any time. The overseers of the city parishes insisted that the intruders should produce such certificates, as is shown by surviving parish books: no doubt they are representative of the whole. In 1735 St Botolph's vestry determined that those newcomers without a settlement in the parish must bring a certificate, adding two years later that money was not to be taken from those without a settlement without the consent of the vestry. The overseers of the parish might well be tempted to avoid trouble by accepting money instead of insisting on a certificate. St Benedict, who opened their register of settlement certificates in 1701, took a like line in 1739. In 1744 St Swithin laid a rate of 2s. in the £ to cover the expense of removing paupers to their own parishes; and in 1749, to stimulate his zeal, its officer was promised a shilling for every certificate he caused to be brought in by intruders; if he favoured any person by neglect he was to pay a fine of 5s. In 1764 their officer had a shilling if he brought in a certificate, or caused any resident not being a parishioner to swear to his settlement. Clearly some of the immigrants were slipping through the poor law net.

[1] Deane and Cole, *British Economic Growth 1688–1959* (1962), p. 103.
[2] *Ibid.* p. 134.

Vagrants were a serious problem. In 1730 the common council agreed to petition parliament against the growing number of hawkers, pedlars and petty chapmen, who were beggars thinly disguised. Another glimpse of a like problem is provided by the council's decision to apply for an Act of Parliament for the more speedy recovery of small debts. The petition recited that great numbers of artificers and handicraft people, who were employed in the city, could not support themselves without credit; dealers came and took stalls at fairs and markets, and had to give credit in order to get business, though they were discouraged from doing so because they could only collect their debts by the slow and costly methods of the common law. It was claimed that a more speedy method would promote industry. The council rather unwillingly agreed, at the request of Mr Sibthorp, to include the Bail and Close in their bill. Evidence was given before the Commons by John Garmston and Francis Bernard, and the bill became law: the new court it set up had cognisance of debts not exceeding 40s.[1]

A new chance of employment for labourers was provided by William Pitt's revival of the militia in 1756. It was the business of the parishes to conduct the ballot by which individuals were selected for militia service; those who were chosen could make their own arrangement to provide substitutes, or the parishes might provide and pay for them, and levy a rate for the purpose. Lincoln clearly had a supply of able-bodied poor who were willing so to serve, and did so, not only for city parishes, but for rural parishes also. Their wives and children then became the responsibility of their own parishes which were reimbursed from the county stock, which, in Lincoln, a county of itself, meant the city stock. This was a grievance on which the mayor and inhabitants petitioned the Commons in 1760. The grievance was admitted, and a clause was added to a bill then under discussion covering the case of men serving in the militia for a parish other than that in which they lived.[2]

Any attempt to measure the standard of living of the poorest inhabitants, or to assess changes in it, is beset with difficulty. The evidence of actual wage rates is scanty, and even so it tells little unless it is related to the cost of living. It is dangerous to convert yearly wages into weekly or day rates, because rates varied according to the time of the year, and perquisites— such as food or board—varied too, and seasonal unemployment is an

---

[1] *C.J.* xxvi, 66, 88, 111, 263. The *Gentleman's Magazine*, xxi (1751), 135 said that the petitions were for a bill on the same lines as those of Westminster and Southwark. Charles Monson gave £200 towards the cost of the bill. The new Court of Requests was not always held regularly, and it was ordered in 1757 that it be held once a month and oftener if necessary. Among the dealers who came to Lincoln for the market, out of eleven with stalls on St Benedict's church pavement, five were from Newark.

[2] *C.J.* xxviii, 916–17.

unknown quantity. Furthermore, there is little known of the extent to which town labourers augmented their income by exercising their rights of common, or keeping pigs or poultry, or getting fish or game either by buying it cheaply or acquiring it by less orthodox methods.

First of these possible factors must be mentioned right of common. The common fields of the city, which lay fanwise in a northern semi-circle, resting on the Fossdyke towards the west and on the Witham to the east, were unenclosed. The arable lay in common fields, subject to common pasture rights in seasons when it lay fallow. The pasture lay mostly to the west, where several small commons were together described as the west commons. After inclosure this pasture had an area of 266 acres. On it every freeman living north of the waterways might pasture three head of cattle, and every unfree inhabitant one head. In addition two small commons, the Holmes, lying south of Brayford, and rescued from its waters, at least in summer, and the Monks Leys, to the east, were exclusively reserved to the freemen.

Residents in the transpontine suburb of Wigford had never acquired rights of pasture in these fields. This ancient division, older than the social division between the upper city and the lower, or the enclave of the Bail and Close, was marked by two wooden posts at the foot of the High Bridge, one on each side of the street, once connected by a chain. The chain had yielded to increasing traffic, but the phrases 'above the chain' and 'below the chain' still had meaning. In 1725 the common council ordered the wooden posts to be removed, and erected two neat stone columns of the Doric order.[1]

Below the chain the inhabitants never had any arable, though the closes that lay behind the houses straggling along the High Street, reaching westwards to the Witham and eastwards to the Sincil dyke (a drain probably of Roman origin), provided garden space on a large scale. The men of Wigford acquired rights of pasture over a large tract of land between Sincil dyke, the river Witham and the villages of Bracebridge and Canwick. The common council had long since enclosed part of this waste and let it to freemen, the rents being in aid of the common chamber. On the remainder, known as the south common, the inhabitants intercommoned with the men of Canwick, freemen and inhabitants having the same rights of pasture as those above the chain.[2] It was inclosed by an act of 1786, and the part appropriated to the city had an area of 244 acres.

These rights of common were well used, and those entitled to them might purport to let them to others, though this was a practice that the common council were trying to stop in 1753. The commons were under the super-

---

[1] Adversaria, p. 262.   [2] For the open fields and pastures, see *M.L.* ch. xvi.

vision of the chamberlains of the west and south wards. They provided a town bull, paid the pinder who impounded straying cattle, and they attended to fencing and kept down moles. Part of the south common, the swine green, was set apart for pigs to root in. The fishing and fowling on Brayford was let, the rent being paid partly in cash and partly in kind: part of the rent of a half share was 'one fat sweet pike, two fat sweet pickerels, two fat sweet bream, and twenty good sweet perch'. The fishing in the river between High Bridge and Thornbridge was let at 4s. in cash, and two roasting eels, sweet and fat, in Lent, or, in lieu, 2s.:[1] but it cannot have been easy to defend the rights of lessees against illicit fishing.

There seem to be no means of knowing how far the poorer inhabitants used their rights of common. The evidence as to the keeping of pigs in their own yards is a little better. Arthur Young wrote enthusiastically that land, gardens, cows and pigs were generally in the hands of the poor in the Lincolnshire villages, and a part of the cottage system.[2] Banks and Charles Chaplin reported in 1795 that the rural poor mostly fed a pig themselves.[3] The urban and rural poor were so closely akin, that it seems reasonable to assume that they shared this habit: they were equally addicted to 'pig cheer'. It is certain that when a century later complaints about sanitary conditions in Lincoln became so loud that action upon them was being considered, it was found that piggeries existed amongst the poorest cottages.[4] It would be still easier to keep poultry.

One of the many things that town and country had in common was an interest in game. Long afterwards a visitor to the county was told by a country parson that 'To get on in Lincolnshire before all things it is necessary to believe in game, and not to trouble too much about the Catholic faith'.[5] About the importance of game he was certainly right. With it as the subject of sport it was chiefly the gentry who were concerned;

[1] See W. de Grey Birch, *Catalogue of the Royal Charters &c. of the City of Lincoln* (1906), e.g. p. 29.
[2] *Survey*, p. 419. For the details of the number of cottagers with land in 40 villages in Lincolnshire and Rutland in 1801, see *Annals of Agriculture*, XXXVII, 514. The villages had an average population of 226, and the average number of cottagers with cows was 15·45, the average size of family being 4·5. The cottagers had on an average 1·55 cows, 0·84 pigs, 1·83 sheep, and 0·16 horses (p. 596). Enlightened landlords like Lords Brownlow, Winchelsea and Carrington provided the land, and in one of his parishes Carrington had started and supported a cow club, a system of mutual insurance against the loss of cows. Lord Scarbrough's agent wrote that it was an advantage to the farmers to have industrious labourers in their parishes (*Annals*, XXXIII, 535).
[3] *Annals*, XXIV, 119.
[4] *Report made to the Sanitary Committee of the Corporation of Lincoln on a General Underground Sewerage of the City*, by George Giles (1849).
[5] J. J. Hissey, *Over Fen and Wold* (1898), p. 222.

but the citizens were concerned with fowl and fish, hares and rabbits in the market at a cheap price. An account published in 1700 writes of Lincoln that

for Provision it affords great plenty, for 'tis replenished every Friday, which is their chief market day, with such variety of fish and fowl, to be bought up at easy and cheap rates, that there is hardly the like in any other city of England.[1]

And of the later years of the century, when prices were rising, Charles Dibdin wrote of the county:

The soil of this county is in many places very fruitful. It produces corn very abundantly, and the pastures are rich and fattening, witness the Lincolnshire oxen that have been shown in London for money. The fen geese are only to be matched by the Norfolk turkies, and for rabbits I should suppose there is no such county in the world. I have seen them by hundreds in the market at Lincoln, in numbers of large lots strung upon poles and each of them borne by two men. I speak of what I saw fifteen years ago, at which time I dined where they were brought to table roasted, boiled, fricassed, and made into pies; and I understand that even the poor regaled upon them, they were so cheap.[2]

Other visitors found it a 'cheap country'.[3]

There was many a nocturnal expedition to the heaths for hares and rabbits, the river for pike, to the fens for wildfowl, to the woods for pheasants, and perhaps even to the parks for deer. It is not an accident that one of the most famous of county songs is *The Lincolnshire Poacher*. The song has been traced back to 1776, and may well belong to an earlier date.[4]

When I was bound apprentice, in famous Lincolnshire,
Full well I served my master for more than seven year,
Till I took up with poaching, as you shall quickly hear:
Oh! 'tis my delight of a shiny night, in the season of the year.

[1] James Brome, *Travels in England, Scotland and Wales*, p. 142.

[2] *Observations on a Tour* (1801), I, 371.

[3] *A Journey through England, In Familiar Letters from a Gentleman here to his Friend abroad* (2nd edn, 1724), II, 212, 262–3.

[4] *Ancient Poems, Ballads and Songs of the Peasantry of England*, ed. Robert Bell (1862), p. 216. The editor writes: 'This very old ditty has been transformed into the dialects of Somersetshire, Northamptonshire and Leicestershire; but it properly belongs to Lincoln- shire. Nor is this the only liberty that has been taken with it. The original tune is that of a Lancashire air, well known as *The Manchester Angel*; but a florid modern tune has been substituted. *The Lincolnshire Poacher* was a favourite ditty with George IV, and it is said that he often had it sung for his amusement by a band of Berkshire ploughmen. He also commanded it to be sung at his harvest homes, but we believe it was always on such occasions sung to the "playhouse tune", and not to the genuine music. It is often very difficult to trace the locality of countrymen's songs, in consequence of the licence adopted by printers of changing the names of places to suit their own neighbourhoods; but there is no such difficulty about *The Lincolnshire Poacher*. The oldest copy we have seen, printed at York about 1776, reads "Lincolnshire", and it is only in very modern copies that the name is removed to other counties. In the Somersetshire version the local vernacular is skilfully substituted for that of the original; but the deception may, nevertheless, be very easily detected.'

As me and my comrades were setting of a snare,
'Twas then we seed the gamekeeper—for him we did not care,
For we can wrestle and fight, my boys, and jump o'er everywhere:
Oh! 'tis my delight of a shiny night, in the season of the year.

As me and my comrades were setting four or five,
And taking on him up again, we caught the hare alive;
We caught the hare alive, my boys, and through the woods did steer:
Oh! 'tis my delight of a shiny night, in the season of the year.

Bad luck to every magistrate that lives in Lincolnshire;
Success to every poacher that wants to sell a hare;
Bad luck to every gamekeeper that will not sell his deer:
Oh! 'tis my delight of a shiny night, in the season of the year.[1]

There is another version:

Come all ye lads of high renown,
That love to drink good ale that's brown,
And pull the lofty pheasant down
With powder, shot and gun.[2]

It used to be said that in the days before drainage of the fen starvation was unknown. Geese flourished, pike, perch and tench were in the dykes, shell fish, dabs and herring were free to the marsh fishermen, and seabirds were shot and netted wholesale.[3] Some of them must have come to market. Cranberries, blackberries and elderberries grew abundantly in the countryside; and cranberries were so common that they were sold by the bushel in Lincoln market.[4]

The poacher in the song was interested in hares, which were guarded as game, and were coursed by the gentry, providing them with much sport. Cox wrote that the greyhounds of Lincolnshire were said to excel those of other counties as the first hunting hounds, especially those that lay about Ancaster heath, which, though smaller in size, were twice as swift as those in the valleys and plains of the county.[5] Dr Willis, who was a tenant of Dashwood at Dunston, said that a hole in his wall was a great preservative to the hares against coursers.[6] The value of these various ways of augmenting wages cannot be measured, and even the evidence of wage rates is scanty. At Ormsby in 1700 a labourer's wage was 8d. a day; and in 1754 this was still the lowest rate for a labourer in husbandry in winter. In 1775 the

---

[1] A less robust and less convincing version substitutes for the first line of the last stanza: 'Success to every gentleman that lives in Lincolnshire.' Bell suggests that the printer was afraid of the justices.
[2] *Notes and Queries*, 9th ser. IX, 492.
[3] *Lincolnshire Magazine*, II, 115.
[4] Sir Charles Anderson, *Lincolnshire Pocket Guide* (3rd edn, 1892), p. 33.
[5] *Magna Britannia*, pp. 1456–7.   [6] Above, p. 18.

labourer's rate was a shilling, and by 1811 it was 3s. 6d.[1] At Nocton in 1765 the rate was 8d.[2]

Skilled rates were of course higher. At Ormsby in 1700 a carpenter was paid 1s. 3d. and a mason 2s. At Revesby in 1717 the chief carpenter was paid 2s. 8d., a journeyman 2s. 2d. and an apprentice 1s. 8d.; and though Joseph Banks thought the rates unreasonably high—and they were higher than those in the south—he did not get any cheaper labour. The lowest rate on mill repairs in 1718 was 12d.; and among builders in 1725 a 'trowel' was paid 2s. 3d. and a labourer 1s. 4d.[3]

Sometimes there were seasonal variations. In 1721 Burrell Massingberd of South Ormsby signed an agreement with his labourers to pay them 7d. a day plus 6d. during 1 July to 7 September, and 1d. a day from 1 May to 29 September, in lieu of small beer, with penalties for neglect.[4] Payment was frequently higher in summer, especially during harvest time. There was often piecework, with higher earnings, as at Boston in 1754:

labourers in husbandry, the best in summer, 1s.; with meat 6d. In winter 8d., 9d., or 10d.; with meat 5d. Mowers 1s. 6d. to 2s., according as they work by the acre; grass upland or marshland, 1s. 8d. Oats and barley 1s. 6d.; wheat by the acre, reaping, binding and stooking, 5s. Oats and barley the same as wheat. Reaper, best man per day 2s.; with meat 1s. 6d. Best woman per day 1s. 6d.; with meat 1s. Harvest man, best sort, per day, 2s.; second sort 1s. 6d. Thrashing and dressing, wheat and rye, per quarter 2s. Oats by the quarter 6d.; barley by the quarter 1s. 2d.[5]

Labourers were not afraid to grumble, and they were sometimes in a position to bargain. Scarcity of labour strengthened their hands, as the steward at Nocton testified when he wanted to take some decayed alders out of the pipes in the duck decoy:

but the charge of getting these would hardly have answered, for labourers are scarce, and they would not work there at the same wages we give the rest of our labourers, so I told John Hudson to get them as cheap as he could, and I would pay them their 8d. a day as I give the others, and what more he was to give them was to be as out of his own pocket to get his work forward, for if I paid one more than another of a Saturday night I should have had a clamour, so thought it best to let him pay them weekly the overwages, and I have paid him the whole again.[6]

---

[1] W. O. Massingberd, *History of Ormsby*, pp. 311, 317.
[2] Bodl. MSS DD. Dashwood (Bucks), B 19/5/15.
[3] *Banks Family Papers*, ed. J. W. F. Hill (L.R.S.), pp. 42, 60, 84. Cf. Phelps Brown and Hopkins, 'Seven Centuries of Building Wages' in *Essays in Economic History* (ed. Carus Wilson), II, 178.
[4] *Lincs. N. & Q.* VI (1900–1), 92.
[5] Pishey Thompson, *History of Boston* (1856), p. 766.
[6] Bodl. MSS DD. Dashwood (Bucks), B 19/5/15.

Evidently 8*d*. was for a long time the standard daily wage for a labourer, and it is easy to understand the steward's reluctance to make exceptions. The rate in Lincoln may have been a little higher; by 1771 it was 7*s*. a week on an average all the year round, which was 1*s*. 2*d*. a day. Arthur Young was given a budget by a gentleman at Lincoln for a poor family consisting of a man, wife and two children as follows:

	£	s.	d.
1 quarter of wheat	2	8	o
2 quarters of rye	3	12	o
Fuel		13	o
Candles and soap		8	o
Furniture		10	o
Working tools		5	o
Rent	1	6	o
Man, coat, waistcoat and breeches	1	2	o
3 pairs of stockings and a hat		3	o
3 shirts		10	o
2 pairs of shoes		8	o
Wife and two children, clothing	4	6	o
Butcher's meat and other provisions	6	17	o
	22	8	o
He receives for 52 weeks at 7*s*.	18	4	o
His wife earns	5	4	o
Total	23	8	o
Total expenses	22	8	o
[In hand]	1	o	o

Young's own comment on this budget was that such a family could not eat so large a quantity of wheat and rye. On the other hand he thought the stockings and hat would cost more. Something, he added, should be included for the earnings of the two children, for on an average of such families both could not be too young to earn something.[1]

The presence of butcher's meat is significant; and the proportions of rye and wheat suggest that they normally ate maslin bread, a mixture of the two, which was generally baked in these proportions. It seems that they fared better than country labourers. In the wolds, certainly, a common diet of the poor was barley bread; one woman from the Louth area recalled that in her grandfather's time they never had but barley bread. On the day of his funeral, however, they had a wheat cake; and the children wished the old man had died long before, as they would then have had

[1] *Farmer's Tour through the East of England* (1771), I, 445-7.

wheat cake.[1] Willson said that in the wold villages peas were once much used in the diet of farmhouses and cottages, and that it was customary for a large quantity of rye bread to be made at Martinmas, enough to last until Candlemas: this great baking was kneaded by the men. An occasional loaf or two of maslin bread was a delicacy.[2] But by the time that war broke out with France wheaten bread was usual, partly because it was best with tea.[3] Apparently the poor drank tea in town and country alike; it was still frowned upon as a luxury and a drug, but it was ousting ale for domestic use. Joseph Burtt owned the first tea kettle in Welbourn, keeping the displaced punchbowl as a memento of the milk and ale posset formerly served at breakfast. A Quaker who died in 1741 decided not to leave his property to the Burtts, as they would drink it all in tea.[4]

Young said in 1771 that labour had risen by a third in 20 years; as his figure then was £18. 4s. for the year the corresponding figure for 1750 would be £13. 13s. By 1794 the annual income, taking an average of all his village returns, was £31. 19s. 1d., or 12s. a week. He concluded that labour was probably higher than in any other county in the kingdom.[5]

The price of cereals fell in the quinquennium 1741–5, and only began to rise in the period 1761–5. The wage rate of 8d. a day having become a conventional figure, it would seem that the standard of living of the workers rose. If the poor continued to eat maslin bread the comparable figure for wages and the cost of bread meal would be:

| | Wages per annum | | | Price per qr. |
	£	s.	d.	wheat/rye
1751–60	13	13	0	25s. 1d.
1771–80	18	14	0	34s. 8d.
1791–1800	31	19	1	48s. 6d.

This scanty and in itself not very satisfactory evidence is consistent with the accepted view that the rise in wages rather more than kept pace with the cost of living up to and including the earlier years of the war with France.[6] The grain prices here used, however, are the Michaelmas prices found by the Lincoln leet jury, after harvest, when they were relatively low; and even a relatively satisfactory average wage rate left vast room for

---

[1] *Lincs. N. & Q.* (1890–1), II, 233. 'Burying with wheat' evidently preceded the later custom of 'burying with ham'. An old inhabitant of Somersby told H. D. Rawnsley that they ate mostly barley bread when he was a boy. Wheat was little known or thought of (*Memories of the Tennysons* (1900), p. 48).

[2] Willson, XIII, 62–3.

[3] *Annals of Agriculture*, XXIV, 120–3, Elmhirst's evidence.

[4] M. B. Burtt, *The Burtts* (1937), pp. 73, 76–7.   [5] *Survey*, pp. 397, 403.

[6] It is the conclusion of Professors Ashton, Chambers and others, summarised by A. J. Taylor in *Essays in Economic History*, III, 391.

hardship in a bad year for all labourers, and in all years for those in irregular work. Poor rates and charitable doles, moreover, are not so elastic as prices, and rising prices must always have brought hardship. On the other hand it is right to recall that the poor may not have been so sorry for themselves as a later generation would be, as hardship was more often part of their lot.

The administration of the poor law was supervised by the justices, who fixed the poor rate and enforced its payment: the parish overseers of the poor collected the rate and laid it out in doles by way of outrelief. St Benedict, and probably other parishes, insisted that recipients, who might get a shilling or 1s. 6d. a week,[1] must wear the parish badge; it was a precaution against fraud. There was a new departure in the law in 1723. A statute of that year[2] authorised the setting up of parish workhouses for single parishes or groups of parishes; and it established a workhouse test for relief. This meant that those who refused to enter the workhouse must be refused outdoor relief. So could they provide a powerful deterrent to applications for relief, and spur the able-bodied to find work. A charge of harshness met with the reply that many who had to pay the poor rate were little better off than the paupers themselves; and even a kindly woman like Mary Yorke could balance individual hardship against the burden on the parish.[3]

It would seem that the common council, who were dominated by the aldermen, most of whom—those who had passed the chair—were the justices for the city, decided that the provision of a workhouse could be better undertaken by the city than by the parishes separately; and they no doubt had it in mind to reduce the cost of poor relief by enforcing the workhouse test. In 1729 they agreed to buy a house in St Martin's parish, called the Corporation House, with all the materials, at not more than £200, to be used as a city workhouse: and it was bought at the beginning of 1731. The project did not however proceed, and the house was put to other uses.

In fact the parishes were moving independently. St Swithin was building its own workhouse in 1736; St Mary Magdalene had already moved in 1731, and soon had a house; in 1737 St Benedict was in treaty with St Peter at Arches for a joint workhouse, which was in being two years later; and in 1754 St Peter in Eastgate was negotiating with St Swithin.[4]

---

[1] Clearly these doles were not meant to be lived on. More likely they were meant to augment low wages, perhaps of disabled or old casual workers (see Dorothy Marshall in *Essays in Economic History*, 1, 304).

[2] 9 George I, c. 7.   [3] Bedfordshire Record Office, L30/9.

[4] The accident of survival of some parish books has preserved these and following details; other parishes probably made like provision.

There had long existed a Jersey School, held in the lower storey of the Greyfriars, for the purpose of teaching the poor to knit, and providing them with work. In 1661 the master had been provided with stock on condition that he paid spinners 5*d*. and knitters 4*d*. apiece weekly during their first six months in work, and afterwards according to agreed rates. Henry Stone of Skellingthorpe, whose will was proved in 1693, had left £700 to be invested to yield an income for the support of the school. The gift led to some expansion: by 1705 the master's salary had risen from £20 to £35—presumably 5 per cent on the bequest—and in 1708 the mayor and senior aldermen were bidden to treat with the dean and chapter and the gentlemen abovehill about making an addition to the school.[1] In 1732 the council agreed to make an extension from the conduit pipes—the city's water supply—to the Jersey School at the city's expense. The school's usefulness is attested by Thomas Sympson, who wrote: 'Here all are employed that either can spin, or are willing to learn: and are paid the customary prices in proportion to the goodness of the work.'[2] It is easy to imagine therefore the horror that would be caused among the poor by any suggestion that the school should be turned into a workhouse with a workhouse test.

On 9 December 1741 the common council resolved that such alterations should be made in the Jersey School as would render it a convenient place for a general workhouse for the use of the poor of the city, according to the plan proposed by William Johnson, the expense to be defrayed by the city. On 25 March 1742 the mayor was authorised to buy such materials of pewter, brass, iron, earthenware and woodenware necessary in housekeeping as were wanted to 'replenish' the general workhouse; which seems to suggest that operations had already started. On the 30th Henry Gildon was elected master out of a panel of four candidates.

The cry of despair of the poor woolcombers reached the Secretary of State, the duke of Newcastle. A petition sent to him recalled that Henry Stone had given them the Jersey School, and that the mayor and aldermen had wronged them by taking it away. Stone, they said, had left £35 per annum for a master tradesman to employ them, and £50 in cash for him to trade with, and had left the governors of Christ's Hospital in the City of London trustees for the school:

But for want of due care, or through neglect of the Governors, The Mayor and Aldermen hath quite taken away our rights and privileges of our Jersey School, and hath converted the same into a Parishes Poor House, and will not let a Master Tradesman have and employ it, as Esquire Stone's Will directs; And for want of our Jersey School, we poor Wool Combers And us poor people in general are almost ready to starve, And our Children which usually was taught to spin Jersey now wanders up and down the streets like vagabonds.

[1] *T. & S.L.* pp. 92, 214.   [2] Adversaria, p. 307.

They begged that the school might be restored to its former and usual employment; and that the governors of Christ's Hospital might send down an order by the next Judge of Assize.[1]

What steps were taken upon the petition does not appear, but the Jersey School was reinstated, and the wool combers had their way. Perhaps one of the compassionate clergy or gentry had helped them with their petition.

Apparently William Johnson was the author of the scheme, and he was a marked man. He became mayor in 1746. During his year of office his house was robbed, and some of the city's money taken. It is even more significant of the sympathies of his colleagues that when a motion was moved in the council to allow him £50 towards his loss it was defeated by 16 votes to 14.[2] Of course other considerations may have played a part in this decision. Certainly the common council still favoured a general workhouse, and it was proposed in 1762 to promote a bill in parliament for this and other purposes. Here again the project did not proceed, and the Jersey School continued until 1831.[3]

These were years of rising prices, and clearly the council felt that the efforts of the parishes must be supplemented by other measures. In 1752 proposals were read to them for establishing a manufactory of camlets and shalloons. In the distressed winter of 1756 they agreed for the benefit of the public in general and the poor in particular that the common crier should not take tolls of corn or grain brought to market, and during the suspension of the tolls he was allowed £20 a year instead. He was to keep the corn market hill and the oat market clean, and to see to it that corn was brought to market and sold publicly: the bad practice of selling it in public houses was denounced. This suspension of tolls continued until June 1759, when prices were falling again. In February 1757 the council had given £21 to a public subscription for relief of the poor, owing to the dearness of provisions and especially of corn, and of fuel because of the severity of the season. They gave £21 again in 1762. In 1765 the mayor was authorised to lend the master of the Jersey School £100 for the purpose of encouraging him to carry on a woollen manufacture.

A small factory for camlets was in being in Lincoln in 1774.[4] A philanthropic project was taking shape in 1783, apparently in conjunction with the plans of the Rev. R. G. Bouyer for spinning schools in parishes,[5] a broadsheet being issued under the heading: 'New Woollen Factory, Lincoln.'

---

[1] P.R.O. S.P. Dom. 36/157, f. 252.

[2] The mayor's ring also was stolen, and after it had become the subject of another robbery in Surrey it was recovered by the city.

[3] Below, p. 249.   [4] *Gentleman's Magazine*, XLIV, 300.   [5] Above, p. 119.

After declaring that there had been 20 young persons, from 8 to 18 years old, taught to card and spin coarse wool, with constant work at their own home, as a trial whether the most distressed part of the poor were willing and able to earn their bread without loss to their employers, it continued:

This is to inform the Overseers of the respective Parishes in, or near Lincoln, that there is room for a fresh set of Learners, and also a settled intention of carrying on the Manufacture, but that those only will be taught or employed for the future, whose parishes subscribe (as recommended by the Rev. Mr Bouyer) the small sum of One per cent. yearly out of their Poor Rates; which is requested solely for the purpose of providing a Teacher, constantly to attend the Spinning School; whereby a large number of children may be admitted, and kept in good order.

When the subscriptions are sufficient they may also be taught to read in the manner usual in Yorkshire, and in Mr Bouyer's Spinning Schools: going by turns both morning and evening: they will be found materials, and implements to learn upon, and after they are taught, constant work.

It is much to be wished that they should learn during the spring and summer months to earn their subsistence before the approach of winter, as, with the assistance of the excellent School, already established to teach Jersey Spinning, it would certainly keep from idleness and beggary, most of the children above 8 years old who now loiter in the streets; and thereby afford a convincing proof to each parish, and the town in general, of the utility of so plain and easy a plan.

A postscript added that any gentleman or lady who subscribed 5s. might send two poor children to be taught.[1]

Mrs White was an enthusiastic supporter of the scheme, and she wrote to her brother Scrope Bernard, who was also a subscriber, on 8 November 1785:

It goes on exceedingly well and with a quiet steadiness that does it honour, and will during this winter have the effect of introducing the Parish Spinning Schools in the manner recommended by Mr Bowyer, so earnestly desired by us all, and they will be independent of the Factory and almost in opposition to it, which is for particular reasons still more desirable, as nothing can hurt it but too great a load of poor, which lay heavy on the fund last winter, but is now removed without detriment to them, and the City Jersey School taken up to assist in the great work of making the poor *industrious and comfortable*.[2]

The same philanthropic impetus was prompting Dean Kaye and others to open Sunday schools;[3] the manufactory was flourishing, though standing still for want of wool in 1787; but little more is heard of the spinning school, and it is to be feared that it did not last long or amount to much. Arthur Young found (1799) that most of Mr Bouyer's spinning schools had been discontinued.[4]

[1] L.P.L. Broadsheet 1240.
[2] Mrs Napier Higgins, *The Bernards of Abington and Nether Winchendon*, III (1904), 86.
[3] Above, p. 71.   [4] *Survey*, p. 441.

The Jersey School itself went on, but otherwise the poor had to depend upon their parishes. Sometimes the parishes farmed them out. In 1744 Henry Gildon, who had been appointed to the general workhouse which had temporarily displaced the Jersey School, contracted with St Swithin to take all the parish poor for a 2s. rate, and deal with removals to other parishes and charges for trials about settlements unless they exceeded £1. St Benedict farmed out its poor in 1777. For £50 the farmer was to collect the rate required to raise that sum, and to have the benefit of the work done by the poor. It was made a condition of admission to the workhouse of the parish that the poor should take their goods with them, and might remove them when they left; no doubt this suited both pauper and farmer. When Widow York went into the house she took with her one half-head bedstead, red and white check hangings, sacking bottom, feather bed, narrow stript tick, two pillows, bolster, four blankets and a flesh-coloured quilt, a cradle and pillow, a wainscot screen, table, one round deal table and a painted corner chair, an old oak chest of drawers, a glass with painted frame, peck basket, deal box, a red leather trunk, one quartern basket, a copper pint can, four pewter spoons, a tea kettle, a brass bell, metal pan, tinder box, candlesticks and snuffers, a black hafted knife and fork, one common chair, one child's common chair, a child's wanded chair, and two large sharp pointed flat irons. Clearly she had come down in the world. Sarah Barley had only a bedstead and cord, new mat, feather bed, a bolster and pillows, two blankets, a new rug, a pair of sheets and two pillow covers. Three children were taken with bedding only. When the parish had to provide furnishing it consisted only of bedding and the apparatus of work and punishment: in 1782 St Margaret had in its workhouse three bedsteads with beds and bedding, a worsted wheel with reel, a strait waistcoat, lock and chains.

The poor who had not acquired a legal settlement were at the mercy of the parish overseers, who wished to relieve their own parishes' finances at the expense of some other parish to which the poor could be traced. Canon Cook has described the activities of the overseers of St Peter in Eastgate, and especially of the redoubtable Mrs Mompesson. She went to Gainsborough, the parish hiring a horse for her, and later she went to Boston for the purpose of ridding the parish of undesirables. One family was traced to York, and ultimately deported to Horncastle.[1] The treatment of the poor who sought relief was deliberately made hard in order to discourage idleness, and if their lot was to be harder than that of the poorest who earned their living it must be hard indeed. But it was not wantonly cruel.

[1] *A Glimpse of the Parish of S. Peter-in-Eastgate in the Eighteenth Century*, by Rev. A. Malcolm Cook.

Boys were put out as apprentices, and premiums paid with them to their masters: one of St Mary Magdalene's boys went to a worsted weaver at Spaldford and another to a tailor at North Clifton. The girls were equipped with clothing when they went out to service.

But there must have been many cases where the law failed to protect the poor, especially children. One such case is recorded by the city quarter sessions minutes. In 1767 Esther Johnson, a poor child of St Martin's parish, aged about 14, was apprenticed by the churchwardens and overseers of the parish, with the consent of two justices, to Mark Johnson of St Mary le Wigford's parish, as a labourer, to learn the art and mystery of a housewife, to stay until she was 21 or married. In October 1769 Mark Johnson agreed with John Morley of St Peter in Eastgate—though the parish officers of St Martin were neither party nor privy to the agreement —to assign Esther to him. She there continued for six months and upwards, after which Morley agreed with Thomas Mastin, master of a cold bath, who had married his daughter and lived in St Margaret, to lend Esther to him. After 18 months Mastin turned her out of doors, whereupon she offered herself to Morley, who refused to receive her and gave her her indenture. Being destitute she went to her father, who was a very poor man living alone in St Mary's parish. He received her into his house, but not being able to maintain her he applied several times to the parish officers of St Mary to get her removed to her place of settlement. After six months, and before her indentures expired—she was then about 19— the officers took her before two justices, who made an order removing her to St Margaret. Johnson and Morley having both refused to receive her, St Margaret appealed to quarter sessions, where the order of removal was confirmed.

There was a constant trial of wits between the poor who sought to acquire a settlement in the parish of their choice—the only social security known to them—and the parish officers who sought to prevent them from doing so, and deport them, or at least charge them, to some other parish. In this contest even parochial charities might work against the parish by making it more attractive to the poor. John Smith, a London merchant— whose local connections are attested by the fact that Charles Dalison, recorder of Lincoln at the outbreak of the Civil War, was his nephew—by his will made in 1653 left lands in the county for the benefit of the poor of St Swithin and St Peter at Eastgate in the proportion of two-thirds to the former and a third to the latter. In 1786 there was £112 to divide. By the time that the charity commissioners were making inquiries in 1836 the income—over £700—was distributed in sums varying from £1 to £12 a year; in St Peter 32 received pensions and in St Swithin 89. The parish officers then stated that the effect was injurious to the parish, and not particularly beneficial even to the recipients.

The parish of St Swithin is heavily burdened with paupers resident and non-resident, and the poor-rates greater there than in any other parish in the city. This arises from the anxiety of the poorer classes to obtain a settlement in that parish, and thus to qualify themselves as recipients of Smith's Charity; and it has been stated to us, that some few years ago a speculator erected there a row, consisting of 12 tenements, not worth at all more than £4 each per annum: these, however, he was able without difficulty to let at £10 each per annum, the tenants hiring them just long enough to acquire a settlement in the parish, and then being replaced by a new set, who hired them for the same purpose; having thus acquired a settlement, the parties take care not to lose it, although they probably remove very many of them into other parishes. By this and similar means an abundant supply of paupers is kept up, and whenever they require parochial assistance they come upon St Swithin's and cause a very heavy burden in consequence.

The abuse ceased under the New Poor Law of 1834, but not before the parish had suffered severely.[1]

Many other charities had been founded in the seventeenth and eighteenth centuries for the benefit of the poor in specified parishes or in the city generally. Dr Peter Richier, a doctor living in the Bail, by will dated 1728, provided £4 a year each for three poor widows living abovehill, to be chosen by the dean and chapter, and three belowhill, to be chosen by the mayor, recorder and town clerk. John Harvey, town clerk, provided £12 per year to be divided between four poor freemen. George Westby, of St Peter at Arches, by will dated 1786, provided for three poor men and three poor women. Mrs Elizabeth Garmston, by will dated 1798, bequeathed a number of separate funds for the poor of St Martin's parish. Another town clerk, Samuel Lyon, by will dated 1804, provided for a number of annual pensioners of £3 each. Mary Durance, of St Martin, also left money for the poor of her parish.

The charity of Sir Thomas White calls for special mention. White, an alderman of the city of London, gave (by deed of 1566) a fund the income from which was to be paid to 24 corporations, of which Lincoln was one. The city ought to have received £104 in its turn for the purpose of making interest-free loans of £25 each to four young freemen (clothiers preferred) for 10 years, finding sufficient sureties for repayment. Income accumulated in the hands of the corporation, although, as Samuel Lyon wrote, they never refused proper applications with offer of security. He thought the fall in the value of money, coupled with the difficulty of finding

---

[1] Samuel Lyon's MS Account of the Charters and Charities of the City of Lincoln; *Report of Charity Commissioners* (1839), Lincs. p. 368.

sureties, explained the lack of applications: clearly he thought there was a need to be met.[1]

Charitable revenue grew steadily, not only by reason of new benefactions, but because the income from land in which the funds were invested was increasing; by 1786 the income from public charities in Lincoln amounted to £1,069.[2] The distribution of this sum must have had some effect in keeping down the poor rates, but, as was pointed out to the commissioners inquiring into the poor law prior to the Act of 1834, the greater part of it was bestowed upon a class of persons not likely to become chargeable to the parishes.

It seems generally to be true that over the century as a whole the prosperity of the city was increasing, though its growth was so slow as to be hardly perceptible save in retrospect. The population too was growing, but the poor were increasing out of proportion to the trading classes and craftsmen, and although their standards were gradually improving the community was more vulnerable, and would suffer more acutely when bad times came. They were soon to come.

[1] Lyon's MS. Moneys accumulated in the hands of the Corporation, and the Charity Commissioners thought they should be compelled to account (*op. cit.* p. 361).

[2] The *Report from H.M. Commissioners for inquiring into the Administration and Practical Operation of the Poor Laws*, App. A, Reports of Asst. Commrs. Part II, gives the total as £1,035. There might have been expected a substantial increase on the earlier figure; perhaps the local witnesses erred on the side of caution.

CHAPTER VII

YEARS OF WAR

THE events of the French Revolution were retailed on the foreign page of the *Lincoln Rutland and Stamford Mercury* every Friday—and of course in other newspapers—and reviewed in the inn parlours during the following week: the tale of massacre and guillotine was received with horror of mounting intensity. Seen from a distance all the issues were simplified, and the red cap of liberty, rendered into English, spelt murder. In revulsion, a jacobinical flavour was detected in the mildest liberal utterance. Even silence was suspect. When a meeting was called to consider petitioning Parliament against the slave trade—although the corporation had petitioned against it in 1788[1]—the mayor of Lincoln published a counter notice cautioning people against the meeting. In December 1792 a general meeting of inhabitants of Lincoln and the district was called to consider the most effectual steps to be adopted to check the spirit of disaffection to King and Constitution. It was resolved to try to discover the publishers and distributors of seditious writings, or persons who should scribble any treasonable or unconstitutional inscriptions on walls or other places. Clergy were invited to call vestry meetings to nominate members of a committee for the purpose; and innholders were urged to be vigilant in reporting suspicious persons to the justices.[2] Leading dissenters were summoned to the Guildhall to take the oath of allegiance.[3]

Detestation focused upon Thomas Paine's *Rights of Man*—a textbook of jacobinism—and still more upon its author. It was recalled that he had been an exciseman set to watch smugglers at Alford 28 years before, and that he had been dismissed for misconduct. According to the *Mercury* he had been reproved for inattention by his supervisor, on whom he had retaliated by obliterating figures in the official journal, and so procuring the supervisor's dismissal.[4] Here was clear evidence that he was a bad lot, and nothing

---

[1] *C.J.* XLIII, 243.

[2] Thomas Smith was desired by Colonel Sibthorp to attend, because, as he wrote, 'I am one of those who are charged with disaffection to Government, and I am branded with the infamous names of Republican and Painite' (J. F. Todhunter, 'Thomas Smith of Waddington, 1765–1823', *Lincolnshire Historian*, II, no. 5).

[3] This was recalled by William Bedford, who was one of them, forty years later.

[4] According to his biographer he fell into the common practice of 'stamping', setting down surveys of work in his books at home, without always travelling to the traders' premises and examining specimens (M. D. Conway, *Life of Thomas Paine* (New York, 1892), I, 16–17).

good or true could be expected from such a source. William Gardiner, writing with the benefit of hindsight after the defeat of the French, wrote:

Lincolnshire was so imbued with high tory principles that it was dangerous to drop a sentiment leaning towards liberty, and my silence excited a suspicion against me. Although Mr Pitt had been a great advocate of reform, and Burke's opinions had accorded with those of Paine, it was a common and disgusting sight to witness the figure of a man whipped, and dragged through the streets, and afterwards hung up and burnt, with a label in his hat, printed in large letters, 'Tom Paine'. This was to frighten the *few* persons in every town who chose not to join the mad Tory party. Printers and booksellers were hunted out for prosecution, and the habeas corpus bill was suspended, merely on the supposition that treasonable conspiracies did exist.[1]

On one occasion Paine's effigy was hanged on a gallows in the Corn market, and afterwards burnt to ashes in the presence of members of the corporation and hundreds of others.

When war with France began early in 1793 the corporation paid the expenses of a meeting of Friends of the Constitution, and the celebration included a dinner for themselves and ale for the populace. After the execution of the French queen Marie Antoinette members of a book club at the Spread Eagle inn ordered a pamphlet upon her life and trial to be burnt as a libel on her and the whole human species. The Reverend William Hett, whose tongue and pen were ever ready to defend the established order, published the pamphlet *The Genuine Tree of Liberty, or, The Royal Oak of Great Britain*, whose title tells enough about it. When the news reached Lincoln in October 1794 that Thomas Hardy and Horne Tooke had been acquitted of a charge of high treason, great disappointment was felt, and execration against the jury was loud and long.[2] About the same time the city newsroom was founded to keep citizens informed of current affairs.

But though the arch-jacobin could only be burnt in effigy, the leaders of the county had to reckon with the father of parliamentary reform, Major Cartwright, in person. He had married Anne Katharine, daughter of Samuel Dashwood of Well Vale, and settled on a farm at Brothertoft near Boston, which he had bought in 1788, and on which he cultivated woad. He spoke and wrote on matters of agriculture and the defence of the flat Lincolnshire coast against invasion; but his chief interest was the reform of parliament. He could always be relied upon to break the unanimity of a county meeting. He held a reform meeting at Boston in 1797, in the middle of the war, at which it was said that there were seventeen

---

[1] *Music and Friends* (1838), I, 221.   [2] *Ibid.*

listeners at the end of his speech: if a placard were posted by authority he could be relied upon to post a counter-notice.[1] He was regarded as a public nuisance.

On the outbreak of war the raising of the militia began, and both the corporation and the public gave bounties in addition to those given by the government. In the spring of 1794 the announcement of the name of the new high sheriff was postponed for a week, clearly to secure the appointment of Sir Joseph Banks, who had procured exemption on a previous occasion from what he had called 'a troublesome and useless office'.[2] He came to the task with his accustomed zeal, and letters and memoranda poured from his pen. At the Lent Assize he laid before the grand jury papers from the Secretary of State relating to defence. The jury resolved that the landed proprietors ought to make provision at their own expense for the defence of the county and kingdom, and the country people ought to learn the use of arms, and place themselves under the command of half-pay officers. Instead of a county meeting there followed a meeting of nobility and gentry at the Thatched House tavern in London under the presidency of the lord lieutenant, the fifth duke of Ancaster, at which £4,000 was subscribed. But the home-dwelling gentry took this amiss, and Banks felt obliged to comply with their requisition of a county meeting. It was there resolved to raise bodies of cavalry, with companies of infantry to man the batteries on the seacoast. A city meeting decided to contribute a company of cavalry, for which purpose the corporation voted £300 and the dean and chapter £50.[3] The government had set the press gangs to work for the needs of the navy, and a quota of men had to be found by the parishes.[4]

The lively fears of enemy landings and of discontent among the labourers in the coastal marshes are described by Edward Walls of Spilsby to Banks:

30 May 1795. The farmers immediately on the coast have exposed to me their fears that smuggling piratical vessels will land merely for pillage and plunder. They proposed a petition to the Admiralty. Petitions, in my idea, indicate at

[1] *C.J.* LII, 621, for a petition from the meeting, and p. 598 for the reply, which arrived first (Lindsey C.L., Banks, 3/2/26, 3/1/27). See *Life and Correspondence of Major Cartwright*, edited by his niece F. D. Cartwright, 1826, and, for his family, *The Ancestor*, x, 1. His brother Edmund, who became a prebendary of Lincoln, invented the power loom, and his niece Elizabeth, who married John Penrose, was the Mrs Markham of the famous history of England for children.

[2] B.M. Add. MSS 38223, 273–4; Banks to Lord Hawkesbury (18 Nov. 1788).

[3] L.P.L. U.P. 603, 1145.

[4] See F. W. Brooks in *E.H.R.* XLIII (1928), 230. Banks refused to promote an appeal for funds for naval volunteers, on the ground that it would interfere with the raising of yeomanry.

present too much timidity. The labourers at Burgh, 27 in number, have entered into and signed a league under pretence of wages—wages are increased! They threatened the inhabitants, the mills, and shops. My advice was not to show the least fear, but calmly propose coming before a magistrate and state their grievances. This they waved, and am in hopes it will end here: but a very few armed men poured out of a vessel of the above description would cause serious alarm and do infinite mischief, joined by those men.

A cutter carrying 8 or 10 guns, properly manned, continually cruising between Wainfleet and Saltfleet Haven would effectually prevent all this. Is it unreasonable for an extent of coast of 20 miles to ask from Government such slender protection?

Some smugglers pretending to have a French commission set the Customhouse officers at defiance and retook a high booty. We are certainly in danger of free-booters of that kind....The open boat in the pay of Government at Boston is the height of burlesque, and we wish to avoid all Corporation connection of this sort...a cutter would...be a security to the small collier craft, and our neighbours the Dutch are not to be much relied on. They well know our coast.[1]

There were riots in October 1796 when meetings were held for the raising of a supplementary militia. At Caistor the mob (chiefly farmers' servants) took the lists of men to be balloted for from the constables and destroyed them, shouting 'God save the King, but no militia', and there was like trouble at Horncastle, Spilsby and Alford. The men wore smock frocks, and under them carried small hatchets or furze bills; some had sticks, scythes or clubs. The discovery of a pike on the road between Spilsby and Louth was enough to raise an alarm: it might have been a specimen sent from Sheffield to instruct the local jacobins how to forge pikes.[2] The riots were put down by the despatch of cavalry from Lincoln, and the calling out of the yeomanry, but they were symptomatic of a widespread discontent, and they inevitably affected the public nerves. Banks had early pointed out that the danger of offering pikes to the multitude as arms, was that it would 'teach them that they may for twopence a piece arm themselves with weapons of which the blacksmith will manufacture several hundreds in a day'.

It appears that the rioters thought that they would be drafted for service overseas, whereas the purpose of the supplementary militia was to provide for local defence only, requiring twenty days of training a year. They were paid a shilling a day, and their families were provided for. Banks blamed Ancaster for not calling proper meetings, in a moment of exasperation calling him a dupe and a fool, and his son-in-law, Lord Gwydir, for

[1] Hill, Banks, 3/16. French privateers were off the coast in 1803, and several colliers and trading vessels were captured and taken into Ostend.

[2] Tennyson's reference in his *Walking to the Mail* to 'A Chartist Pike...a venomous thing' may preserve some memory of the incident.

'execrable carelessness and mismanagement':'if I am peevish, excuse me.
I do not think I am.[1]'

The gentry felt strongly that the supplementary militia should not be
attached to the regular militia battalions and commanded by their officers,
but should be officered by the gentry themselves, whose own men would
follow them. Banks thought that those gentlemen who were not given commissions should enrol, and provide farmers' sons as substitutes: vagabonds
should not be used in these units, as their proper place was the army and
navy.[2] In deference to local pressure it was laid down by the government
that if a number of volunteers amounting to three-fourths of the numbers
required was forthcoming, then appointments and ballots for men and
horses under the Act should cease. A volunteer troop of cavalry, consisting
of tradesmen and neighbouring gentlemen, was formed under the command of Richard Ellison. 'Armed Associations' were called for in 1798 to
put down riots or insurrections, and apparently the volunteer troop
satisfied official requirements.

The Peace of Amiens in 1802 interrupted the career of the citizen soldiers.
The militia was disembodied and the yeoman cavalry discharged, and the
peace was suitably celebrated at the Reindeer and in the other public
houses. On the resumption of war the fear of invasion became graver as
Bonaparte's army encamped at Boulogne. The militia was called up,

---

[1] Lindsey C.L., Banks, 3/1/1–43, 3/2/1–46. At a county meeting for defence in
1792 Mr Coltman of Hagnaby proposed to petition government to fortify the coast.
Mr Alington proposed that the surveyors of the roads should be continued in their office
for the term of their natural lives, as he was sure the roads were so bad that if the French
landed they would never get into the interior. It was said that Coltman would never
speak to Alington again (Anderson, Notes in *Lincoln Date Book*, L.P.L.).

It is apparently to the year 1797 that a story told by Henry Best relates. An invasion was
so seriously apprehended that a military man was sent down to Lincoln by government
to organise the defence. It was feared that the enemy might land on the flat coast, and
so penetrate across to the manufacturing midlands, in which it was feared that many
would join them. A public meeting was called, at which the lord lieutenant presided.
The commissioner of government was a German; he conducted himself with great good
sense and imperturbable phlegm, answering all questions without any sign of impatience,
unless, indeed, taking snuff were one; this expedient certainly gave him time to recollect
himself. It was amusing to hear with how much coolness he talked of driving cattle,
burning corn stacks, destroying mills and ovens. To reconcile us to these measures
repayment of damages was promised on the part of government, and the son-in-law of
the lord lieutenant, he himself being infirm and deaf, made a speech. This was Lord
Gwydir: he called the French 'our atrocious and implacable enemy'. Best remarked to
Subdean Paley that *implacable* was too humble; and of *atrocious* Paley remarked 'they
have a right to come, and we have a right to knock 'em on the head: there's nothing
atrocious in all that; it is fair in war. We have done them as much harm as we could,
wherever we could: they have a right to serve us the same sauce' (*Personal and Literary
Memorials* (1829), pp. 189–90).

[2] Lindsey C.L., Banks, 3/1/21.

Ellison taking command of the northern Lincolnshire battalion, and the supplementary militia was placed under Lord Buckinghamshire. A volunteer corps of cavalry was raised, Philip Bullen taking command of a Lincoln company, and Hezekiah Brown of four companies of infantry. Subscriptions were raised, and patriotic ladies provided the infantry with flannel waistcoats. Pending delivery of other weapons they were armed with pikes: 'it is an excellent weapon' said the *Mercury*, 'and with it freeborn Britons will feel no difficulty in defending those privileges which are the objects of admiration and envy to the rest of the world'.[1] In 1806 a military arsenal capable of holding 10,000 stand of arms was built near the north-west corner of Brayford. The Southern Lincoln Militia spent some years making a military canal in Kent, and the Northern Battalion served in Ireland. As the war danger receded both the numbers and the subscriptions of volunteers declined: the volunteers were disbanded in 1813, and the militia welcomed some of them.

It was only the economic effects of the war that touched everyone. A trade boom had ended even before the war broke out, and there was much distress in 1792. Current troubles are illustrated by a pamphlet entitled *The Fiddle of Corruption playing the Tune of Misery to the Poor* which may be the work of Cartwright.[2] In it the author attributed the high price of corn after a good harvest to the smuggling of corn and flour 'to feed our natural enemies' in France. It was certainly Cartwright who published *Plain Truths for Plain Men: by a Holland Fen Farmer* in 1791. Farm labourers having combined against the farmers in consequence of their jealousy of the poor Irish who came over every year to work in the harvest, he recommended that the farmers should arm themselves to support the magistrates. It appears that an association to this end was formed, and peace restored.[3]

Clearly there was distress and discontent even before war broke out. When it did, there was an instant contraction of credit. Good trade had prompted speculation in wool at high prices, aided by the large number of country banks, which readily issued their notes. The bankers now tried to call in their loans; wool was forced on to the market and sold at any price that the manufacturers would offer. Depositors wanted their money, and demanded payment from the banks. The manager of Garfit and Claypon's Spalding branch wrote in his journal that he feared the bank would be included in the general wreck of the times

. . .that confidence which is the only support of commerce failed—the Bankers in London dare go no further. This contagion having affected the country who

---

[1] *L.R. & S.M.* 16 Nov. 1803.

[2] 'In a letter addressed to the Free Burgesses of Boston', 1790 (L.P.L. U.P. 1427).

[3] F. D. Cartwright, *Life and Correspondence of Major Cartwright* (1826), i, 186–7.

had lodged money in the Bank, they not only brought in the notes for immediate payment, but also demanded what was lodged at interest. All these circumstances united together, and brought on the stoppage of the Bank. . . .

The consequences of the war with France, and the embargo upon the shipping caused so much alarm with the merchants and farmers that in the course of a few months the whole course of the trade seemed changed, and the universal want of confidence had drove things into quite another channel.

In this panic atmosphere banks at Newark, Louth, Barton, Stamford and Gainsborough stopped payment. Garfit and Claypon at Boston sustained a run of £81,000 at a time when graziers could not repay the sums advanced to them until the spring fairs and markets. A committee of gentry investigated their affairs for the reassurance of the public, and found them solvent, and they soon resumed payment.[1]

There was also a run on Smith Ellison's bank at Lincoln which lasted for seven weeks, and gold was repeatedly brought from London to meet it. Happily the bank held: on the initiative of the bank partners the local nobility and gentry advertised their confidence in the bank, and their willingness to take its notes in payment of rent.[2] Nevertheless, many of the tradesmen were bankrupt.

The agricultural interest reacted vigorously. Wool growers were urged to postpone their sales, and do without dishonest factors who acted in the interests of manufacturers. To the like end a fat stock market was set up at Lincoln, with the same charges as at Rotherham. The graziers supported it, and it was soon noted that the Yorkshire dealers were finding it worth while to attend. Within a few years the market was declared to be one of the best in the country. Recovery of trade was expedited by large government orders for cloth and blankets for the armed forces and allied armies.

Trade dislocation brought unemployment and fearful hardship to the poor. In the especially severe winter of 1794–5, the crops being deficient by a quarter, 932 families in Lincoln were relieved by a charitable subscription: a few months later over 3,000 people were helped by a fund to provide bread and flour at 3s. a stone. The city bought coal for the poor. There was a campaign for cheap food and its economical use. A prescription for making bread from oats was published, and millers ground oats and wheat together. The governors of the County Hospital directed that bread used there be made as to one-third of barley meal.[3] The Lindsey justices, for the sake of example, publicly pledged themselves to reduce the

[1] Spalding Gentlemen's Society, Addl. List, Claypon and Garfit, Hawkes MSS, no. 8.
[2] National Provincial Bank, Smith Ellison Papers; J. A. S. L. Leighton Boyce, *Smiths the Bankers* (1958), pp. 154–6.
[3] This is the only reference in their minutes to the war.

consumption of wheat in their own households by a quarter. Before the harvest the price of wheat had reached 120s. a quarter.

Throughout the war there were wild fluctuations of supply. There was an abundant harvest in 1795, but alarm again, and nervousness about the banks, in 1797; and there were disorders in the fens. The country gentlemen, who disliked the moneyed interest, were blaming all their troubles on the banks. Mr Coltman of Hagnaby wrote to Banks:

29 March 1797. Corn is very low in price both from the quantity and the want of money. It is a London idea that there have been two years' scarcity. There never was any scarcity but what the merchants made. I know there was always great plenty, and if the Bill Trade (which is more to be dreaded than the war) could be put under a due regulation we might have a market price for the necessaries of life again. The country bankers will ruin this kingdom. Their speculations and their bills raise the prices of everything.[1]

But this was prejudice; there was recurrent shortage. Wheat, having fallen in price, rose, and reached 80s. a quarter in 1795, after which it fell again as far as 46s. because the government permitted the import of corn. This measure brought the gentry and farmers of the county to petition the Commons. They claimed that in reliance on the import control under the Corn Law of 1791 they had laid a large area of land down to corn, and now found that the price did not pay the cost of production. Poor rates had risen, and wages so far that during the 1796 harvest upwards of 8s. a day had been paid. Corn was left in the hands of the growers, and it was being hoarded by dealers, and with the promise of a good harvest it was feared that the price would fall further. The petition lay on the table.[2]

Although in the 1790's one or two harvests were good, more of them were bad. Four of the six seasons before 1801 were so wet that most of the newly inclosed fens on the Witham were flooded and the crops lost or injured. In 1795, when the waters were very high from snow and frost followed by a thaw, the right bank of the Trent broke at Spaldford, and nearly 20,000 acres of land to the west of the city were flooded. The water found its way to Lincoln, where the High Street—the Roman causeway across the valley—being 10 feet higher than the adjoining lands, acted as a dam. The area was under water for three weeks.[3] Disaster came again

---

[1] Lindsey C.L., Banks, 3/2/20.   [2] C.J. LII, 598.

[3] Padley, Fens and Floods of Mid-Lincolnshire (1882), pp. 2–5. Ellison described the flood to Banks. The Trent had been higher than it had ever been known: the Spaldford break caused a rush of water to Lincoln from the prodigious quantity of back water which came in torrents to Torksey lock. The lock gates were open, the Trent having been higher than the Fossdyke, and fastened back to the walls. The current of the back water was so violent that the gates could not be shut. The back water poured over the walls upon the back of the gates, and there was fear lest the walls should give way. Fortunately the gates rose from their sockets, broke their collars, and floated away. The navigation

in 1799. Hundreds of acres were reaped by men in boats,[1] or standing up to their middles in water, and clipping off the ears wherever they appeared.[2] Not a grain of corn was ripe in August, when the snow lay unmelted, and that very month the snow began to fall again.[3] The air was filled with foreboding.

But the tale of woe was soon forgotten, as weather troubles are, and by the summer of 1800 the prospect looked better. Banks wrote to Lord Liverpool (15 August) that the harvest was expected to be favourable. Old wheat was abundant, and had been sold at £20 a load. In his opinion the scarcity of the previous year was due to the small quantity sown because of the low price paid in 1798 in consequence of the ports being open (that is, to the importation of foreign corn), which deterred the farmers from sowing. He thought the new crop would suffice for the nation's needs. His advice was that the import of wheat should be prohibited during harvest and seedtime so that English prices should find a natural level, and that returns might be made of the quantity of land sown with wheat.[4]

Whether Banks's advice on public policy was sound or not, his hopes of the harvest were dashed. On 6–8 September, on a journey from Chesterfield to Boston, he wrote:

Corn everywhere on the ground and almost universally grown in the mush. If this weather continued the consequences cannot be estimated. I saw oats about an inch long in the sheaf. Large quantities must be rendered absolutely unfit for human food. Dry weather will however save the fens which are very late.[5]

And Sir John Beckett wrote: 'in that part of Lincolnshire where I resided the crops of 1799 and 1800 added together fell far short of the single year 1798....'[6] The price of wheat in Lincoln at the New Year 1800 was 83s. 8d. By July it was 113s. (The corresponding prices for Middlesex were 100s. 6d. and 143s. Lincoln prices were normally lower than the London ones, but in 1800 rye, beans and oatmeal were substantially higher in Lincoln than in London.) In March 1801 wheat was 178s.

Urgent measures to relieve distress were needed. In Lincoln in 1800 a

was left completely without lockage (Spalding Gentlemen's Society, Banks Stanhope, 16 Portfolio, 3/18). 'There was a boat sent down from Clifton to Wilford to help the people; we got it to go to the stable to fodder the horses. They had many of the people to take out at the thatch of their houses, and several of the poor houses tumbled down' (Letter to Samuel Smith the banker, who lived at Wilford, Smith Ellison papers).

[1] William Chapman, *Observations on the Improvement of Boston Haven*, II (1801), 8n.
[2] Wheeler, *Fens of South Lincolnshire*, p. 160.
[3] Thomas Miller wrote a series of articles entitled 'Sketches of English Country Life' in the *Lincoln Notts and North Midland Times* in 1859–60; this and a few other details are taken from them.
[4] *Banks Letters*, ed. Warren R. Dawson (1958), p. 463. Liverpool's own view is given on p. 464. This was the first Lord Liverpool, the father of the prime minister.
[5] *Ibid.* p. 464; B.M. Add. MS 38234, 140–1.   [6] *H.M.C. Lonsdale*, p. 149.

subscription paid for a pound of meat every fortnight and a quartern of potatoes—a vegetable which had not made much headway in Lincolnshire —every week to each member of a family. By 18 April soup kitchens had distributed 25,000 quarts of soup. A public meeting exhorted the citizens to reduce the consumption of bread, not to use flour in pastry, restrict the use of oats for horses, and seek substitute foods. The merits of peas and potatoes in bread were preached, and the use of more vegetables, carrots, turnips and broccoli. The workhouse was crowded. In the country Sir Joseph Banks sent rice and herrings from London to be sold cheaply to his tenants. It was said in 1800 that the poorer classes in Lincoln, who within living memory had exchanged the use of barley bread for wheaten, had in the previous year returned to barley bread.[1]

The national need for food, and the years of famine prices, sharply accelerated the movement towards inclosure, especially of waste lands, which in the fen meant drainage as well. Gardiner remarked that when he visited Lincolnshire, thousands of acres in the fens produced nothing but reeds, peat, geese and wildfowl; and he never entered the White Hart at Spilsby without dining off a wild duck, which was the finest thing, in his estimation, that the country produced.[2] Happily Banks, as lessee under the Duchy of Lancaster of the manorial rights in East and West and Wildmore Fens, and also as a considerable landowner, was directly concerned with the vast possibilities of improvement there, and he wrote in 1799 that he must hasten into Lincolnshire to reconcile the fencing interests of the landholders of twenty-three parishes, and to engage them in doing— what they had neglected to do for 700 years—to divide a common of 10,000 acres of valuable land.[3] This was Wildmore Fen, and at the same time the drainage and inclosure of East and West Fens, with an area of over 29,000 acres, was being discussed. By 1801 Banks could tell Lord Liverpool that arrangements for the inclosure of 40,000 acres of common land, involving fifty parishes, were complete, together also with the cultivation of 20,000 acres of private land. In 1805 he added:

We do not think much of the defeat of the Austrians [at Austerlitz] because the calamity is distant and the consequences to us remote; we think most on the progress of our drainage, which is very prosperous. Our land sold at first for

[1] See C. R. Fay, *Great Britain from Adam Smith to the Present Day* (1928), p. 223. Banks wrote to C. B. Massingberd from Soho Square on 19 Feb. 1800: 'We hope here that the economy arising from the high price of grain and the great saving of wheat owing to the multitude who have under the present pressure resumed the use of barley bread, will remedy the deficiency which the last bad harvest has occasioned' (Massingberd Mundy MSS, Society of Genealogists).   [2] *Music and Friends*, I, 114.

[3] Birmingham Assay Office, 71. He wrote in 1801 that he thought he did not receive 1/20 of the rent he would make if the drainage were complete (Royal Society, Misc. MSS, I, 25). For John Cragg's account of the inaugural meeting see L.A.O. Ancaster, 9/6/27.

somewhat more than £30 an acre. The second sale it brought £40. The sale of £75,000 worth lately brought £50, and a small sale since has brought £60 an acre, although there has been no particular convenience of situation, and in all cases the buyer pays auction tax, and all costs of enclosure, as we deliver only the surface of the commons marked out by surveyors' stakes.

The quantity of land which is to be won to the public from thistles in summer and wild ducks in winter as you have seen, and which did not, I am confident, on an average of years bring to the occupier 5s. an acre or indeed 1s. to the landlord, is 40,000 acres at £50 an acre, that is, £2,000,000 of money....[1]

Thus a chain of lakes from 3 to 6 feet deep, bordered by crops of reeds, with adjoining land which flooded in winter, was drained; and the soil was so generous that it yielded two and even three crops in succession of not less than 10 quarters to the acre. In 1812 seven new townships had come into being.[2]

A lesser scheme which more closely affected the city was launched in 1804, Sir John Rennie being the engineer, to drain the low lands to the west of Lincoln on both sides of the Fossdyke.[3] It concerned an area of nearly 4,000 acres, growing only gorse and ling, and supporting myriads of wild duck, for which there were decoys at Burton, South Carlton and Skellingthorpe.[4] It became the Lincoln West Drainage. Lord Monson was the principal owner.[5] The corporation consented to the bill, drainage through the city being involved; and the cost of new bridges over the Great and Little Gowts drains in High Street was to be shared equally between the city and the commissioners. It had some immediate success; in 1806 a correspondent in Lincoln noted that fat beef was growing on Swanpool, where fishes lately swam.[6]

In 1858, when the drainage trustees complained that they might be prejudiced by the improvement of the Upper Witham, the clerk thus described the project:

the lands within the level and now constituting what is called the Lincoln West Drainage and which in ancient time lay open to the Rivers Witham and Foss,

[1] National Library of Wales, MS 12415.E34; *Banks Letters*, p. 466. Later he told Sir Charles Blagden that this improved value cost £600,000, and he had gained about 2,000 acres, which let for £2,000 a year (Royal Society, Banks MSS, 51). It was reported in 1810 that East Fen sales averaged £32. 3s. per acre, West Fen £67. 3s. For the complicated common rights see *Annals of Agriculture*, XXVI, 484.

[2] W. H. Wheeler, *Fens of South Lincolnshire*, pp. 216–22; *V.C.H. Lincs.* II, 350, 399.

[3] It had been mooted earlier, but was perhaps not practicable until the channel through the High Bridge was improved (see above, p. 136).

[4] *T. & S.L.* p. 13.

[5] 44 George III, c. 87. Its southern district was bounded by the upper Witham on the east, the high lands in Boultham and Skellingthorpe on the south, other lands in Skellingthorpe, Saxilby and Broadholme on the west, and the Fossdyke and Brayford on the north; the northern district by high lands in Lincoln, Burton, South and North Carlton, Broxholme and Hathow east and north, high lands in Saxilby west, and Fossdyke south.

[6] Mr Savage's Letter Book in L.P.L.

being much on a level with the beds of those rivers, were about the year 1808 reclaimed from flood at considerable cost...partly by means of embankments against the said rivers and partly by catchwater drains to intercept the upland waters. Thus protected against floods from without, these low lands...had still to be relieved of their own internal springs, rainwater &c., and this was effected under the same Act by means of main drains in the centre or low parts of the fen through a sunken tunnel under the Witham in the parish of St Peter at Gowts into the [Sincil Dyke]....

The scheme was eventually of great benefit to drainage, but it did not go smoothly, wanting perhaps the energy of Banks. Lord Monson and other owners in Skellingthorpe appealed against the drainage rate, and Colonel Ellison complained that the burden in Boultham was excessive, and his high land wrongly included. By 1809 he was saying that the estate was in worse condition than before the works began, and the Fossdyke banks could not be raised because there was no money. When the war ended the work was unfinished, and it was not until 1816 that the award was complete.[1]

These drainage works would, however, have been of little avail unless the newly channelled waters were suffered to escape downstream. Their success depended upon the improvement of the river; and at the same time there was pressure from the navigation interests to the same end. The making of a through navigation from the Fossdyke to the Witham under the Horncastle Act[2] had quickened trade. Brayford had been a pool of mud and sand without wharves or warehouses on its banks, surrounded by gardens and orchards. As traffic grew, the gardens turned into coalyards or were covered by warehouses, and the pool became an inland port. Access to it from Newland was bad, and until a new bridge at its north-east corner was built by Ellison in 1801 there was a bank of earth at the junction with the river across which people could walk in summer with the aid of a few loose stepping stones.[3] In the first printed history of Lincoln, Adam Stark could in 1810 describe the continuous improvement of the Fossdyke under the Ellison lease, and commend it for bringing wealth to the lessee, benefit to the city's commerce, and employment to the poor; of Brayford, he said:

a spacious lake, forming on its shores a commodious quay, covered with vessels, and skirted halfway round with warehouses, exhibits, by its contrast with the distant country, a scene more beautiful and sublime than might be expected in the neighbourhood of Lincoln.

The special interest of the city in the Witham between High Bridge and Stamp End is also explained by the fact that this half mile

can only be considered as an extensive wharf, on each side. To this place the inhabitants of the villages below Lincoln bring up their productions to market,

---

[1] Lincoln West Drainage papers, L.A.O. T.L.E. 37; Lincoln Court of Sewers.
[2] Above, p. 136.   [3] Willson, v, 12; vi, 60.

in schuyts, or small boats, and take back their various purchases in the same way. The continual bustling of porters and watermen, the creaking of carts, the rolling of drays, the lowering and raising of masts, and the bawling and not very decent language of the sailors, render the waterside, if not one of the most delightful, at least one of the most noisy parts of the city.[1]

By 1820 Brayford head was deep enough to admit vessels of 50 tons alongside the quay, and the pool was no longer dry in summer.[2]

Despite all the loud complaints about prices and trade depression the volume of traffic upon the Fossdyke was, with annual variations, trending upwards all the time. Between 1746 and 1750 the revenue ranged between £400 and £600; in 1751 it first passed £700; in 1755 it passed £900; in 1757 £1,000. In 1764 it reached £1,370 and in 1774 £1,499. In 1789, in the boom that preceded the outbreak of war with France, it was £2,367; in 1794, on the outbreak of war, it dropped to £1,523, but thereafter it never fell below £2,000 again, and at the end of the war (in 1814) it was £5,908.[3] The increase in revenue from tolls on the Witham was even more dramatic. About 1790 the tolls between Lincoln and Boston were let for £300; by 1810 for £3,000.

In 1801 the Drainage Commissioners declared in favour of the complete embankment of the river, which was impossible without power to levy additional taxation on the lands within the trust. The only alternative was for gentlemen to embank their own estates and look to the commission for reimbursement: several of them, indeed, did embark upon their frontage work. The channel was obstructed by weeds and shoals. On the other hand, more money was coming in from the freshly enclosed fens. John Rennie was consulted, and he advised a level bottom between Stamp End lock and the Grand Sluice at Boston: only so could the clash between drainage and navigation interests be avoided. Wind engines in the fens would no longer be needed, and in lieu of the cost thereof proprietors might be asked to pay an additional shilling an acre. The scheme was estimated to cost £106,000. A new Act, obtained in 1808, failed because it did not provide enough funds. Flooding and distress in 1809 provided new stimulus to action and there followed the Act of 1812.[4] It fixed tolls, provided for deepening the river and the carriage of flood waters of the river above Lincoln by the Sincil dyke to the river below Lincoln. A new Company of

---

[1] Pp. 263, 290–1.

[2] Willson's notes in B.M. copy of Drury's *Lincoln*, p. 85. Banks wrote that large supplies of oats went by the Witham to Chesterfield and so to Manchester (Banks Corr. xviii, 184). And see Sir George Head, *Home Tour of the Manufacturing Districts of England* (1836 edn), p. 142.

[3] L.A.O. BS. 12/3/1/3/149. See Appendix ii. Lincoln registered 110 river boats under an Act of 1795 (35 George III, c. 58; L.A.O. Lincoln City, L/1/5/9).

[4] 52 George III, c. 108.

proprietors was authorised to raise £120,000 in shares and borrow £60,000 on mortgage of the tolls and dues.[1] The story of their operations belongs to the following chapter.

After the disastrous years 1799–1801, which set in motion so many large measures of agricultural expansion, prices fell again. In 1802–4 wheat did not exceed 65s. a quarter. In 1805 the trend was reversed, and it rose to 84s., and barley rose from 36s. to 60s. A great flood caused severe distress in February 1809, and that autumn wheat reached 110s., rye 56s., and barley 68s. In the following year conditions were so unsettled that the Lincoln leet jury made no return of prices at all. In March 1812, following floods again, wheat was 142s., and by August the best quality was 155s. That summer a good harvest brought the price down by 60s. in 14 days. Even so, wheat at Michaelmas was 103s. In the summer of 1813 there were prospects of good corn crops, and the planting of potatoes had gone beyond all former example, holding out promise of low prices. In fact wheat fell only to 92s. By December the *Stamford Mercury* thought prices too low: yet there was distress.

Urgent measures of charity were called for in these last war years of high prices. For example, in April 1813 the mayor of Lincoln was authorised by the common council to buy potatoes, which were 10d. or a shilling a peck, up to a limit of £50, and sell them at 6d. a peck: so prices were brought down. It was complained also that Lincoln bakers did not bring down the price of bread as bakers in other parts of the country did; clearly some of the distress was attributed to overcharging. In February 1814 1,100 families in Lincoln were relieved by charitable subscription.

Much of the distress was seasonal. There was work for all at harvest time, and indeed there was a shortage of labour in the fens, where in 1808 it was feared that because of the scarcity of labour part of the crop would be lost: the *Mercury* remarked that men from manufacturing counties would earn more in a day than their usual earnings in a week. There were hundreds of Irish labourers in the fens.

The labour shortage was caused partly by migration and partly by the fen drainage schemes. Already before the war new tracts of land—such as Holland Fen, of 22,000 acres—had been brought into cultivation. The wartime schemes have been described. The new areas of cultivation being still unpopulated, labourers flocked in from elsewhere. Banks described how, standing on the bridge at Boston or Wisbech, they were hired by the day: he had even heard of 13s. a day being paid, and a magistrate had had to enforce a contract to reap 6½ acres of wheat at £9. 10s.[2]

---

[1] Wheeler, *op. cit.* pp. 164–6.

[2] 18 Oct. 1792, *Annals of Agriculture*, XIX, 187 ff. The contract price might normally have been 11s. an acre. See also A. Young, *Farmer's Calendar* (1804 edn), p. 426.

It was said in 1801 that in Lincolnshire harvest wages had risen absurdly, but not the regular employment: the former because although immense tracts of marsh and fen had been brought into cultivation, the building of cottages had been neglected.[1] It has already been noticed that wages paid during the harvest of 1796 were upwards of 7s. a day, and when the Witham General Commissioners advertised for canal cutters in 1802, they said that wages were 6s. to 7s. a day. This would be heavy navvying work, no doubt on a piecework basis.

Ordinary wage rates seem not to have fallen behind the cost of living up to the last years of the eighteenth century.[2] The Rev. Samuel Partridge of Boston wrote (16 January 1796) that the increase of wages seemed to make up for the increased price of bread, and that poor rates had not generally risen. He added, 'alehouses (full, as usual, every evening) seem to be the grand cause of distress—crimes and poor rates'.[3] Young's Lincolnshire correspondents had reported in 1795 that in spite of high prices no substitute for wheaten bread had been introduced, and Mr Elmhirst said that since tea had been much used the poor liked the finest white bread, though some might use rye and barley bread and potatoes.[4] By 1799 substitutes were being urged.[5] In Lincoln workhouse in 1797 meat was given to inmates every day:[6] perhaps they fared better than the desperately poor outside, but they are not likely to have fared better than those in regular work.

There is less evidence about regular wage levels after 1800. Young had given 10s. 5d. as the average all-the-year-round wage. Mr Amos of Brothertoft near Boston said in 1799 that labourers had been able to support themselves and their families decently on from 10s. to 12s. a week, but that they began to murmur as wages fell to the winter standard of 9s. to 10s.[7] The only available later evidence is that in 1813 wages were said to be 12s., and later it was said that during the war they had been 15s.[8] Perhaps something had been learnt from the dread years 1799–1801. No doubt the increase in wage rates was regarded as having some relation to the cost of living, and it may be that after adjustment of wages to prices a man in regular work was no worse off in the last years of the war than he had been earlier.[9] For the seasonal and casual workers, the unemployed,

[1] *Annals*, xxxvii, 610. [2] Above, p. 156. [3] *Annals*, xxvi, 1.
[4] *Ibid.* xxiv, 119. [5] *Ibid.* xxxiv, 284. [6] Below, p. 186.
[7] *Annals*, xxxiv, 284.
[8] A. L. Bowley, *Wages in the United Kingdom in the Nineteenth Century* (1900), pp. 32–3, and table at end; *State of Agriculture, Second Report 1836*, p. 78.
[9] Gayer, Rostow and Schwartz, *Growth and Fluctuation of the British Economy 1790–1850* (1953), i, 108, say that in 1807–11 general indexes of labour's position show that the rise in money wages was a more adequate counter-weight to the rise in living costs than in 1797–1802; and G. D. H. Cole, *Short History of the British Working Class Movement*

and perhaps for all at times of famine prices, it seems to have been accepted that distress should be dealt with by charity on an organised scale rather than by subventions from the poor rate. It could be argued that the resort to charity did not fall on the poor as the poor rate did, and that relief in kind was safer in the hands of the improvident than money, which could be squandered in the alehouse. And if wages rose only when abnormally high prices showed signs of becoming normal there must have been a considerable time-lag involving a temporary fall in the standard of living. A time of rising prices inevitably meant some hardship all round.

Increasing demand for agricultural produce and the high price it made in the market did not immediately promote improvement of method. The new ideas spread gradually and casually; the process is illustrated by a letter from Henry Dalton, the intelligent squire of Knaith, to George Tennyson, in 1808:

I rather intend to take Norfolk on my way from town, chiefly for the purpose of calling on my relation Mr Wyndham... I think of giving my farming man the amusement of Smithfield and the Norfolk husbandry. Very possibly he may gain something. At least we shall get some turnip seed, and if you should wish to have any, I can get you some at the same time.[1]

When Arthur Young made his second Lincolnshire tour he was full of enthusiasm and propagandist zeal. He found the farmers industrious, active and enlightened. Cultivation of turnips had spread, and drainage gave a new chance to tenant farmers. In some parts rents had risen fourfold. He spoke highly of the condition of the heath, studded with new farm houses and buildings, the progress being so great in twenty years that very little remained to do. The wolds were still to be tackled.[2]

His critics soon followed in his footsteps. Thomas Stone said Young could have seen part of the heath which had been enclosed and quicked twenty years, and afterwards 'ploughed out' and returned to rabbit warren.[3] And when Marshall travelled between Lincoln and Sleaford in 1810 he saw hundreds of acres in the veriest state of waste he ever saw land in, whether appropriated or unappropriated:

Half a dozen wild rabbits were all the stock I observed upon them, with scarcely a blade or leaf of herbage to keep even these alive; doubtless thro the folly or madness of the first occupiers (after appropriation) in converting them to 'arable farms' instead of *sheep walks* or *rabbit warrens.*[4]

(1948 edn), p. 135, says that the real wages or agricultural purchasing power of agricultural labourers rose. He gives as real wages: about 1800, 67; about 1805, 78; in 1815, 100.   [1] L.A.O. Tennyson d'Eyncourt MSS.

  [2] *General View of the Agriculture of the County of Lincoln* (1799), pp. 10–11, 40, 43, 67, 77, 224.

  [3] *Review of the Corrected Agricultural Survey of Lincolnshire by Arthur Young Esq.* (1800), p. 76. He described Young as the Baron Munchausen of the age.

  [4] *Review of the Reports of the Board of Agriculture from the Eastern Department of England* (1811), pp. 81–2 n.

On a longer view, however, there was great progress—a Lindsey Agricultural Society was in being in 1803—and high prices drove the margin of cultivation to the top of the wolds, as well as across the heaths and fens. A Worlaby farmer recalled in 1848 that his family had settled in 1812 on land just broken up from heath: the first wheat yield was not more than two quarters to the acre. A farmer on Lincoln heath said that the yield had risen there from almost nothing to 32–36 bushels of wheat to the acre. By 1813 rents in the south of the county were being raised owing to the high price of corn.[1] Most of the parishes were enclosed by 1800, and all by the end of the war. The young Tennyson must often have listened to the tales of farmers and labourers of the great enterprise. The best-known witness is his *Northern Farmer (Old Style)*:

> Dubbut loook at the waäste: theer warn't not feeäd for a cow:
> Nowt at all but bracken and fuzz, an' look at it now—
> Warn't worth nowt a haäcre, an' now theer's lots of feeäd,
> Fourscoor yows upon it an' some on it down i' seeäd.

H. D. Rawnsley records the words of an old inhabitant of Somersby, told in the same speech: 'the wold in them daäys was just a complete wilderness, a mask of rabbits, nowt nobbut rabbits.'[2]

Edward James Willson, looking at the war period in retrospect, described the great improvement of the wold and heath districts of the county, consequent on the high price of corn. In a few years a poor and neglected country surpassed those counties which had always been more forward in cultivation and produce. The introduction of new manures, particularly bones, assisted the improvement; and a small population allowing the land to be thrown into a few large farms occupied by wealthy tenants with large establishments made farming appear quite the occupation of a gentleman. Several respectable families, he added, might be mentioned who speedily arose from poverty to wealth by the great increase in the price of corn after the outbreak of the French Revolution and the consequent improvement in the price of land. The purchasers were greatly benefited, and those who were able to procure money to purchase an entire manor or township, especially if its fields were uninclosed, and then subdivided the estate and sold it in parcels, in most instances acquired very great profit.[3]

It has been suggested by Sir Charles Anderson that there were circumstances peculiar to Lincolnshire which gave unusual opportunities to attorneys and surveyors and other professional men serving the landed interest to set themselves up as landowners, and so to mature into gentry. Thomas Stone wrote in 1794 that estates in the county had been sold within

---

[1] *Report from Select Committee on Agricultural Customs* (1848), pp. 16–36, 386–91, 401, 410.
[2] *Memories of the Tennysons* (1900), p. 47.   [3] Willson, XIII, 63.

a short distance of time by non-resident landlords without full inquiry about the value of their property; and that it was only since the American war that the idea that the county was a duckpool had been dispelled.[1] William Dixon of Holton le Moor and John Cragg of Threekingham were two such professional men; George Tennyson, the poet's grandfather, was another. The Huttons of Gate Burton, into which family George's younger son Charles was to marry, were attorneys at Gainsborough: Thomas Hutton had been agent for an absentee landlord, Lord Abingdon, from whom he bought the Gate Burton estate. Anderson, who had all the prejudices of the gentry, noted that the Elmhirsts raised themselves by land and agency business and laying inclosures:

I was once told that they never planted a tree in the hedgerows, and that was one reason why the Lincolnshire enclosed lands are so bare of timber. I believe that the real reason was that the agents and farmers played into each other's hands, which was generally so easy in a county where so much land belongs to non-resident owners. I have long been of opinion that the county of Lincoln is ruled chiefly by agents and attorneys, and that in no county have they such power: and several have raised themselves into the position of landowners by buying the estates of their employers.[2]

It must surely have been in the public interest, however, that land should be in the hands of more active owners who were willing to put it on the market when prices were favourable.

There is no doubt that the city's trade was prospering in spite of severe fluctuations in prices and distress among the poor and the seasonal workers throughout the war. The population was not only growing: it was growing at an increasing rate. The number of baptisms had begun clearly to exceed the number of burials per year in 1781 (206 to 153), though in bad years like 1783-4, when there was much fever, and 1789, burials exceeded baptisms. Even in the years 1799–1800, when distress was especially acute, baptisms exceeded burials (225 to 185, 250 to 160), so that there was an increase by natural growth apart from any net immigration.[3] Solid ground is reached in 1801, when the first census return for the parishes in city Bail and Close was 6,949.[4] It was stated in 1811 that the first return for St Swithin was inaccurately taken and much understated, probably not less than 300 below the actual number.[5] A comparison of the figures for separate

---

[1] *General View of the Agriculture of the County of Lincoln*, pp. 10–11. In 1817 a writer in the *Mercury* attributed the slow progress of the county to absence of proprietors, who spent their money elsewhere, leaving local affairs in inferior hands.

[2] Note in his interleaved copy of the *Lincoln Date Book*, sub 1810, in L.P.L.

[3] These figures relate to the old municipal borough and the four towns (*Abstract of Answers and Returns to the Population Act 1 George III*, p. 174).

[4] See Appendix III.   [5] *L.R. & S.M.* 21 June 1811.

parishes with the ecclesiastical returns of 1721[1] shows that all the downhill parishes had increased by from 50 to 100 per cent, save St Peter at Arches, which was probably already fully occupied by the shops and houses of the most substantial citizens, who were not to be cramped by further building. The greatest increase was in St Martin, which lay along the Fossdyke. The total return for city Bail and Close in 1811 was 8,486; in the decade 1801–11 the central parishes had increased little, but St Swithin grew from 940 in 1801 (or perhaps 1,240 if it was understated as claimed) to 1,553 in 1811 and 1,869 in 1821. It lay upon the northern bank of the Witham, and its increase was due to river and fen drainage works and to the growth in river traffic; watermen, navvies, porters and labourers made up great part of the population. The southern Wigford parishes also were growing: there was room for building behind the long ribbon of houses in High Street, and the side-streets of small houses and courtyards were beginning to appear.

Increase of trade meant that the city could sustain a modest increase of tradesmen and professional men, but most of the increase of population was due to the growth of the poorer classes. With it came increase of crime and disorder, which presented problems both to the common council and to the parish vestries. The increase in the number receiving poor relief cannot be calculated from the increase of the total relief paid out, for the scales of relief must have been raised when the cost of living rose so rapidly. Even so, the figures are striking enough. In 1776 the money raised by assessment in city Bail and Close and the four towns was £1,087; the average of the three years 1783–5 was £1,311; in 1803 it was £3,096. The proportionate increase in the latter period in the county as a whole was even higher: £47,000 to £146,000.[2]

The city increase was however large enough to pose serious problems for the parishes, who were in the first instance responsible for problems of order, poverty, and highways. An initiative in dealing with the poor was taken by residents in the Close. Gilbert's Act, passed in 1782, had given parishes power to join in unions, and the rates collected by parish overseers to be distributed by guardians appointed by the justices: only the old and infirm and orphans or babies with their mothers should be sent to poorhouses: and work must be found for the able-bodied.[3] The local promoters thereupon took a lease of a building which had been put up as a glue

---

[1] Above, p. 146.

[2] *Abstract of Answers and Returns relative to Expense and Maintenance of the Poor in England* (1804), p. 290. The average annual amount raised in the county in the years 1748–50 was £14,851 (*First and Second Reports from Select Committee on the Poor Laws*, 1818, App. 1B).

[3] 22 George III, c. 83. The machinery of the Act was devised to transfer real control to the justices and visitors from the less competent parish officers.

manufactory, and set up there a house of industry, where the poor of subscribing parishes might be housed and employed. By 1789 it was full, chiefly from rural parishes, only one city parish (St Benedict) and two in the Bail (St Mary Magdalene and St Paul) contributing to it. It seems that other parishes used it sometimes, but the proprietors insisted that all the poor receiving relief from a subscribing parish must be sent in: they might otherwise get only the worst cases.

Sir Frederic Eden reported upon this enterprise. At first the paupers were paid for at so much a head, but then the association of parishes was formed.

It was agreed to pay the proprietors of the house a rent for receiving all such poor as should be sent thither: and that the house and out-poor expense should be paid out of the general stock, towards which each parish pays the average of its annual expenditure for the five years before the union, to be paid in four quarterly payments. Seldom more than three of the quarterly payments have been called for in a year. There is, moreover, a surplus in hand of £400, which it is proposed to spend on an Act of Parliament to incorporate the parishes and make some improvements in the house. At present the union consists of 19 small parishes. There are 40 male and 41 female inmates, of whom 30 are children under 12, and 25 above 60. They are chiefly employed indoors in spinning flax and wool, in making stockings and other clothes. The worsted spinners earn about £25 a year. The house is kept clean: its situation is very healthy.[1]

The common council had been considering this and other problems. As they were to say in a petition to the House of Commons, the poor were numerous and burdensome, and a house or houses for them were needed. The streets were ill-lit, watched and cleansed: there were disorders at night, and nuisances made the streets dangerous. As to street lighting, a committee estimated that 224 lamps at least would be needed, and that the annual expense of lighting them would be at least £164, and of watching the streets £53. A rate of 6d. in the £ on all houses, and 3d. in the £ on lands near the streets, with 6d. a yard for all public buildings, would bring in £168, and would cost the corporation £12 for public buildings. So far from quailing at this cost, the corporation proposed to contribute £30. After two attempts, a bill was carried to the royal assent for the lighting, watching and cleansing of the streets, the part dealing with the poor not being proceeded with.[2]

Road maintenance had theretofore been the responsibility of the parishes, though the corporation had contributed to the larger maintenance costs, and the streets had been paved in two parts, without footpaths, with a

[1] *State of the Poor* (abridged edn 1923), pp. 238–9.
[2] 31 George III, c. 80; *C.J.* XLV, 186, 353; XLVI, 183...686.

channel running down the middle. Now, in specified main streets, the frontagers were to pave footways on their own frontages, and in default the commissioners might do the work and recover the cost. Other streets might be admitted to the benefit of the Act on the application of two-thirds in number and value of the owners. Lamps were to be provided, and might be lit by contract; watchmen were to be appointed with watch-houses, and there was to be control of nuisances, signs, encroachments and sweeping of pavements. The rate was limited to 6*d*. in the £, and the poor might be exempted. The corporation were to give their £30.

There was some excitement in the city when the streets were lit for the first time, and some paving of streets was done, but the total results were small. No regular public watch was kept, though private places were sometimes watched in winter at private expense. Lamps in globe glasses were set up, sufficient to light the streets fairly well. In 1800 tenders were invited for lighting 200 lamps for about 120 nights in the year, when the moon failed the commissioners. Soon they ran into debt, and the number of lamps was reduced.[1] Public hatred of a rate outweighed considerations of comfort and safety.

Long afterwards, in 1855, Richard Mason said, on his retirement from the clerkship to the Lighting and Paving Board, that he remembered the first flagstone being laid for a pavement in Lincoln. The gutters then ran down the middle of the street, and the butchers' stalls on market days stood in the narrow part of High Street. Until oil lamps were brought in under the Act, public lighting was voluntary, and the council repeatedly begged inhabitants to hang out lights. The inconvenience of badly paved streets and lanes on dark nights might be imagined.[2]

A new Act for dealing with the poor was obtained by the corporation at the request of the parishes in 1796.[3] It contained most drastic penal powers for the directors. According to Sir Robert Heron the bill had been promoted by Richard Ellison, one of the city M.P.s, whom he blamed for these clauses; certainly a year later, when another poor law was impending, the city asked Ellison to oppose it. Men could be detained for failing to maintain or even threatening to desert their families, with penalties of detention with correction, solitary confinement, abatement of diet and distinction of dress. Poor persons wandering abroad could be brought in by a warrant of three directors or a justice. Children were to be bound apprentice, and pauper labour might be contracted out. If persons following a trade or occupying land in the city refused to employ the poor of their own parish and took instead people with settlements else-

---

[1] Willson, vi, 60*a*.   [2] *L.R. & S.M.* 13 July 1855.
[3] 36 George III, c. 102.

where, a justice might order that they be found work in their own parishes, and that in default the parish must bear the cost of relieving him in addition to its payment to the workhouse. Some of these rules were to cause trouble later.[1]

By-laws were made in 1797 defining the duties of parish officers and the governor and the matron of the house. The house diet prescribed: for breakfast a pint of milk porridge and 6½ ounces of bread to each adult; for dinner 8 ounces of meat and 6 of bread, a trencher of roots or greens and a pint of beer; for supper a pint of broth and 6½ ounces of bread, or a trencher of potatoes and a pint of beer or 3 ounces of cheese and 6½ ounces of bread. The most striking fact about this diet table is that it contains meat for every day. Three meat days were customary, and had been the number in the house of industry at the gluehouse; there were three at Louth, four at Spilsby, six at Alford.[2] (Evidently the bread supplied was white bread, for brown bread was given in 1825 as a punishment.) By contrast under the New Poor Law of 1834 there were only three meat days in the Lincoln workhouse, new emphasis being laid on deterrence from entering the house. Perhaps the earlier provision was generous, and the inmates might be better off inside than they had been outside, but it cannot have been markedly better than the standard of living of labourers in work.

A modest incentive for inmates was provided by allowing them a gratuity of a sixth part of the value of their work, except in cases of misconduct. Visitors were only allowed by leave of the governor or matron, and the poor could not go out without leave; when they did so they must wear a medal inscribed *Lincoln House of Industry*. Children not at work in the house were taught for six hours a day. Profanity or drunkenness incurred the stocks for not more than four hours.[3]

The directors bought the gluehouse, and arranged to receive the poor of contracting parishes. In 1809 Skellingthorpe was allowed to have its parish poor remain in the house on a fresh contract for ten years at an average rate of £72, or for 21 years at £90, at the option of the parish. Two years later an offer was made to Saxilby at £120 a year; and as Scampton was trying to avoid performance of its contract, after an abortive attempt to enforce payment the sole parish pauper was sent home. Reepham was given a three-year contract at £105. St Paul's had not become an incorporated parish, and in 1828 the directors offered to contract with it on payment of £100 and an annual rate to be ascertained on reference to their annual expenditure for the last seven years.

---

[1] Below, p. 207. [2] *State of the Poor*, pp. xlvii, 229–39.
[3] L.P.L. Local Pamphlets, xv, 18.

The women in the house were usually set to spinning hemp, and flax was given to the outpoor to spin. The dress of every female was to consist of a black bonnet, cotton white cap, dark cotton gown and slip, red flannel petticoat, black stockings and blue neckerchief; and when Sarah Toyn was hired for a year at wages of 2s. 6d. a week she was provided with a frock, a pair of stockings, a white flannel petticoat and a check apron.

The men were often let out on hire for gardening or breaking stones; in 1809 Joseph Lee was sent out to work for a ropemaker at 4d. a day. The poor were forbidden to hire themselves out to work. Casual paupers were encouraged to take themselves off at the earliest moment by putting all of them pronounced by the surgeon to be in a good state of health on bread and cheese and water.

A growing population in a time of social upheaval and distress meant a great increase in crime. The surviving quarter sessions records for the city break off at 1785; when they resume in 1802 the volume of crime had markedly increased. In the 1770's a county rate[1] of £60. 1s. 2d. might suffice for a year for purposes of justice and police. In 1802 that amount was being levied quarterly. Conditions in the gaol were therefore worsened at the very time when a new humanitarianism was calling for prison reform. The old gaol at the Stonebow consisted of two storeys, the lower one forming two dismal dungeons, the prisoners in which could be seen and spoken with by passers by. The upper floor was all one room. The gaoler could increase his income by selling ale to the prisoners. The gaol had been denounced in the *Gentleman's Magazine* in 1805 as the sepulture of the living, to whom were denied the benefits of religion and the services of a chaplain. At an inquest on the body of a woman who died there, Mr Bedford, a juror, moved for a verdict that the woman's death was caused by the damp and bad state of the prison. Mr Hunnings, the coroner, overruled this for fear of the expense of building a new prison.[2]

After years of complaint a new sessions house was begun in 1805, and the first sessions were held in it in 1809. There were probably complaints not only about the cost of building at all but also about extravagance. Adam Stark remarked that the building had more the appearance of a gentleman's house than of a prison, and the interior was as comfortable and convenient as was compatible with the safe custody of those confined there: which seems to imply that he thought it too comfortable.[3]

The provision conformed to the principles laid down by Howard the prison reformer; and so also did the new county prison at the castle, where extensive alterations and improvements were carried out about

---

[1] Below, p. 241. [2] Willson, v, 62.
[3] *History of Lincoln* (1810), p. 304.

1790, for the same reasons of rising standards and growing crime as in the city.[1]

The last years of the war were troublous. In 1807 the common council asked the Postmaster General to have the postboys armed as they were in some other parts of the country. The *Mercury* reported in November 1808 that there had been more robberies throughout the city that winter than perhaps was ever known in a year before; and besides the crimes reported there was petty thieving of poultry and linen. In 1809 the county rate for the city was £420. 8s. 2d. plus £300 for the new gaol and £99. 18s. for the relief of militiamen of the Royal South Lincolnshire Militia. The rate remained at this level until the end of the war. For the protection of tradesmen and householders an association for the prosecution of felons was formed for the city Bail and Close and the neighbouring villages. There were frequent prosecutions for keeping disorderly houses. A man so convicted was placed in the pillory on the Cornhill for an hour before being sent with his wife to his own parish of settlement. In another such case a woman was imprisoned for a month and set in the pillory for an hour. The number of bastardy cases had greatly increased, and the number of soldiers involved prompted the directors of the House of Industry to ask the clergy that all the soldiers they married should be sworn to their place of settlement. The provision of a ducking stool was proposed by the magistrates, though it appears that the proposal was not carried out. A treadwheel was provided at the new gaol: the gaoler thought the work was not severe, but beneficial to the health of the prisoners.

The troubles of these last war years at Lincoln culminated in February 1814 when the bank of Sheath, Son, Steel and Wray of Lincoln—one of the several partnerships of the Sheaths of Boston[2]—stopped payment, and like its associated firms was thrown into bankruptcy. The city was in utter confusion, and panic grew with the news that other banks at Stamford, Boston, Leicester and Derby also stopped payment. The peace celebrations therefore came at an inauspicious moment.

[1] Spalding Gentlemen's Society, Banks Stanhope papers, 20; L.A.O. County Committee, 3/1/1, p. 199.

[2] The Lincoln bank of Sheaths was open by 1806. Besides being a banker, Abraham Sheath was shipowner and timber merchant, and he overreached himself (*Lincolnshire Magazine*, III, 165–8).

CHAPTER VIII

DEPRESSION AND RECOVERY

SINCE the Restoration it had been accepted national policy to encourage the exportation of corn, and to permit its importation only when it reached a certain price in the home market. The price at which the ports were opened to foreign corn depended upon the price above which the home corn grower was thought not to need protection against the foreigner. The system, including the method by which an average price was ascertained, had been varied from time to time; as also had the price at which the ports were opened. Restriction on import had not generally made bread dearer. The end of the war, however, made the 'corn laws' an important question. During the wartime period of increased production and high prices both landlords and farmers had enjoyed an improved standard of living, which they were concerned to maintain. Laws which had originally been devised in the interest of the consumer were now looked to partly for the defence of the landed interest, and partly to prevent the country from becoming dependent on foreign supplies which might be interrupted in the event of war.

When at the end of the war Banks was making a case to the prime minister for a high corn law he depicted the results of inflation with his usual clarity. Bonaparte's continental system had strengthened the country, whose resources had increased in proportion to the increased prices of agricultural products. The farmer received 100s. a quarter instead of 50s. for his wheat; he employed more servants and paid more in wages; he spent more in the shops and he paid a higher rent. Tradesmen and manufacturers benefited, and the government had a swollen revenue. The growth of population, he said, was a proof of the well-established prosperity of the nation.

In fact the prosperity was highly vulnerable, as Banks knew, for he went on:

Peace, dreaded by all men who possessed talents capable of calculation, found the country in the state of prosperity described above, and in a few months reduced it to the precarious situation in which it now stands: corn fallen below the cost incurred in raising it; the farmers abridging themselves of all their usual comforts and of many indulgences grown by use almost into necessaries; the young men who used to be their servants returning from their statutes unhired and unable to procure service, crowding from mere necessity into the poor-houses; the gentlemen beginning to reduce their customary expenses, under a well-founded apprehension that the Lady-day rents will be very ill paid; and the tax gatherers returning from their collections with a small portion of the sums which at this time last year they collected without difficulty.

He dismissed the argument for cheap food by saying that manufacture was no longer dependent on it, and that if the necessaries of life were cheaper, the greater would be the indulgences in liquor insisted upon by workmen: 'if a 15*d*. loaf allows Saturday and Monday to be kept as holidays, a 10*d*. loaf will add Tuesday to the number.' Even 80*s*. as the import price of corn (of which he had little hope) would mean that many farmers would lose a third of their income.[1]

Some of the Lincolnshire members of parliament, though they all belonged to the landed interest, did not go so far as Banks. When the Corn Bill was debated in the Commons—whilst foreign wheat was pouring into the country, and the manufacturing interest was doing its best to prevent rapid action—Sir Gilbert Heathcote thought rents should be reduced; Colonel Ellison that 76*s*. would ensure that in the future the country would not depend on foreign powers. Henry Dalton of Knaith wrote privately that he thought 74*s*. or 75*s*. would have passed without great opposition, and would have been enough.[2] Nevertheless the rule that foreign corn could not be imported until the price had reached 80*s*. was carried into law.

The general fall in prices brought serious distress to farmers, said to be aggravated by the delay in enacting the new Corn Law. Rents fell into arrear. Agricultural wages were reduced. Millers were attacked for keeping up the price of bread though flour had fallen; landowners were criticised for not spending their money at home, and for leaving local affairs in inferior hands; and an attempt was made at Lincoln to reduce the burden of outdoor relief by publishing a list of recipients.[3] The corn law did not relieve the want of money, taxation did not come down, and the malt and leather duties in particular were felt to be injurious. It was said that poverty turned many consumers from meat and wheat to gruel and potatoes. Corn factors were charged with rigging the price averages in order to open the ports, and labourers complained that more Irishmen than ever were coming in for harvest, and taking their work from them. There was a general contraction of trade: even the mail coach so proudly started was discontinued, and Lincoln letters were brought from Market Deeping on horseback, until the old way of bringing them from Newark was brought back, and they arrived $1\frac{1}{2}$ hours earlier. The mail coach was restored in 1822. The three-day-a-week coach also ceased for a time.

[1] Banks Corr. XIX, 139–44. The government already had a protective price of 80*s*. in mind (Yonge, *Life and Administration of Lord Liverpool* (1868), II, 136).

[2] *Parliamentary Debates*, XXX, 15, 19; L.A.O. Tennyson d'Eyncourt (6 March 1815). Sir Robert Heron was so roughly used by the mob demonstrating against the bill that he was driven to declare his support of it. And see *Report from Select Committee on Petitions relating to the Corn Laws* (1814), p. 49.   [3] L.P.L. U.P. 484.

Some of the preoccupations of the farmers are illustrated by letters of Henry Dalton to his friend George Tennyson, both of them owner-occupiers of land:

22 June 1819. We are laying on lime profusely, are meddling a little with new bones (Sir J. Banks told me he used no other manure for his garden crops, and that they answered to perfection). In short we are striving hard for a turnip crop.

23 April 1820. I hope you are distraining your own stock for the rent of your own farm—ruined, both as fancied landlord and tenant. My farming accounts, I am sure, if I had spirits to cast them up, would be far worse than ever.

9 May 1820.....the vaunt of the Willingham breed is no recommendation to me. I am by no means a Collings fancier. I address this to you as a decided grazier. I expect that at our agricultural meeting you will propose as a toast 'D—— the plough'....I am convinced that it was your clodhopping that brought on your gout, and that on your altered establishment you will have no return.

That October he added that he had large quantities of wool on hand and unsold.[1]

Agriculture gradually recovered. Payments by the bankrupt banks on account of debts to customers put money into circulation. The iron trade at Sheffield improved, and hosiery at Leicester and Northampton. In the Yorkshire cloth towns, though half the population were in relief in the summer of 1820, by the autumn trade was stable and there was a shortage of workmen. The markets for farm produce were thus recovering. The Lincolnshire Agricultural Society was established in 1819 for the encouragement of improvement in methods. It was the low price of wheat that brought distress to the farmer: if he could keep sheep he was not so badly off. It was said in 1821 that more wool had passed through Stamford than old wagoners could remember. The Lincoln fairs grew to vast size: in 1823 there were said to be over 40,000 sheep, with the largest show of horses for many years. A wool market was started at Gainsborough, and another mooted at Grimsby, and a depot was set up at Lincoln, to the alarm of the Wakefield wool factors. The grinding of bones for manure became common, and created a new industry. Turnips, which had been grown on the wolds for a century, had only lately been introduced for winter feeding, though there was always anxiety lest the crop fail, there being no substitute.

Disaster returned in 1825. Trade was bad, the country swarmed with beggars, and alarmist rumours about the banks were justified when Ingelows of Boston stopped payment. A run on the Lincoln bank lasted for eight days, but the bank stood: Charles Anderson wrote that he could not pay his bills on the road, as no one would take the notes of country banks.[2]

---

[1] L.A.O. Tennyson d'Eyncourt. [2] Wilberforce MSS.

In 1826 there was an appeal for the distressed workmen of the West Riding, who were said to be sleeping on rotten straw and raking dunghills for food; Lincoln, it was said, had suffered less than most places in the universal depression. Distress was accompanied by alarm about a proposed amendment of the corn law, and petitions poured into the Commons, the corporation and 700 tradesmen of Lincoln declaring that when corn was at a low price the trade of the city suffered in consequence. The price of wool, too, was very low: farmers were sending their sheep to market earlier and not keeping them to a mature age. For lack of demand, it was said, the quality of Lincolnshire wool was declining, and more Scotch and Irish wool was coming in; and although the ban on the export of wool had at last been lifted, little or none was being sent abroad.[1]

Lincoln was wholly identified with the agricultural interest, and Tennyson was speaking for it as well as for the countryman when he said:

Saw I turn'd in ageän, an'I thowt o' the good owd times 'at was goän,
An' the munney they maäde by the war, an' the times 'at was coomin' on;

Fur I thowt if the Staäte was a gawin' to let in furriners' wheät,
Howiver was British farmers to stan' ageän o' their feeät.

Howiver was I fur to find my rent an' to paäy my men?
An' all along o' the feller as turn'd 'is back of hissen.[2]

There were cries of distress again in 1830. Taxation and tithe were denounced, and relief was demanded. Lincoln swarmed with beggars in the winter season, and in the workhouse casual paupers found to be in good health were placed on a diet of bread and cheese and water without meat to encourage them to depart. There was an outbreak of incendiarism in the countryside. In December, Edward Bromhead[3] was told, a man was going round selling matches, and asking whether the farmers used thrashing machines and employed Irish labourers; and Bromhead himself was busy swearing in special constables and issuing proclamations. He feared no danger among themselves. Lord Brownlow told Bromhead that he had had a fire, but it was limited to one stack of oats, and he was forming an association of mounted volunteers, for whom he wanted 100 swords and bills. Charles Anderson also wrote of fires in his district, where yeomanry were being enrolled and arms distributed; he thought it was dangerous to give arms to people who lived in isolated places. He too was surprised at

[1] *Report from Select Committee of House of Lords appointed to take into consideration the state of the Wool Trade* (1828), pp. 17–29.

[2] *Owd Roä.* The reference is of course to Sir Robert Peel's repeal of the Corn Laws in 1846, but the other sentiments were applicable earlier. The poem was not published until 1889. See Sir Charles Tennyson, 'Tennyson and His Times' in *The Lincolnshire Historian*, ii, no. 11.

[3] As to whom, see below, p. 277.

outbreaks in Lincolnshire, where 'we have always been a Noah's Ark in time of disturbance'. In the Ormsby neighbourhood there were stories about fireballs being fired at stacks from passing coaches, but it was thought that the stories were set up by countrymen to divert the scent of justice. Irish labourers, come over for the harvest, were attacked by country labourers, who also threatened farmers who wished to engage them. As they passed through Lincoln on their way home the mayor relieved them with bread.

In June 1831 Bromhead reported several incidents to Lord Melbourne, the Home Secretary, remarking that one of the farmers whose wheat was burnt

never used a machine and is very popular, so that the excuses usually invented by the London press are unfounded. I hope that vagrants may be the guilty parties. I have sent to search a vagrants' lodging house at Coleby.[1]

Agricultural wages, which had been 12s. a week in 1813 and 15s. in 1815,[2] fell during the peace years to 9s. to 10s. It was said in 1825 that they ranged from 8s. to 12s. Prices also fell, slightly in 1816, decisively in 1822. But the wage reduction came first, and there was for a time a fall in the labourer's standard of living. By 1830 the position had recovered. Bowley gave 13s. 4d. as the rate for 1833. By 1836 labourers' wages averaged 12s. in the county.[3] A man thrashing corn by piecework might take 18s. home.[4] In 1838 an official of the Poor Law Board said that the weekly wage of an able-bodied man in Lincolnshire was 13s. 6d., and in some places more; and earnings at task work had been stated to amount to 15s., 16s. and 17s.

The official also made comparisons. He said that the district was more favourably circumstanced than Berkshire or Oxford, and more than Nottinghamshire.[5] A writer in the *Stamford Mercury* noted at the Lincoln hiring statutes in 1826 crowds of servants in healthy and well dressed groups, and he contrasted them with the emaciated thousands in other districts. Thomas Cooper, whose sympathies with the poor cannot be in doubt, testified, after seeing the plight of the stockingers in Leicester, that

[1] Bromhead MSS; Wilberforce MSS; L.A.O. Massingberd 1/80, 91. And see the Countess Brownlow, *The Eve of Victorianism* (1940), pp. 152–6. There was stack firing round Orby in 1834, which the parish clerk seemed to attribute to the king's dismissal of his whig ministers (*The Local Historian*, no. 26, Jan. 1940).

[2] Above, p. 179.

[3] A. L. Bowley, *Wages in the United Kingdom in the Nineteenth Century* (1900), table at end. G. D. H. Cole, *Short History of the British Working Class Movement* (1948 edn), pp. 134–5, gave as an index of real wages: 1815, 100; 1820, 87; 1825, 77; 1830, 106.

[4] J. E. Coulson, *Memorials of Mr Charles Richardson* (1865), p. 57.

[5] *Fifth Annual Report of Poor Law Commissioners for England and Wales* (1839), pp. 18–19.

the Lincolnshire labourers had wages which amounted to double the earnings the stockingers said were theirs: in Lincolnshire

I mingled with the poor and saw a deal of their suffering—yet witnessed, not merely the respect usually subsisting between master and servant, but in many instances the strong attachment of the peasantry to the farmers, and of the farmers to their landlords.[1]

Lincolnshire folk wore leather to their feet, and when Samuel Bamford left Lincoln castle after his imprisonment there he left his Lancashire clogs with the turnkey as curiosities.[2] Edward Bromhead, whose judgement is entitled to the highest respect, wrote:

4 December 1830. The labouring classes in the whole of this country are better off than they have been within memory; wages are high compared with the calls upon them; in general there is even a *want of labourers* occasionally.[3]

Furthermore, good landlords, like Mr Chaplin, gave their labourers a rood of land to provide vegetables and potatoes to feed a pig; and all but the improvident among them had a pig in the stye and bacon in the chimney corner.[4] In the Brocklesby neighbourhood nearly all the cottagers kept a cow, some of them two cows; and they generally kept a pig.[5] There is poetic evidence from Witham on the Hill in 1834 to the like effect:

> If we survey with an attentive eye,
> The cots of those who're termed the lab'ring poor,
> We find a pig in almost ev'ry stye
> And in each hovel one milch cow or more.[6]

It is a remarkable fact that the Lincoln Savings Bank was founded in 1816, at what might have been thought a most inauspicious moment, under the patronage of gentry and clergy. Its deposits grew throughout the period. In 1828, in spite of reduced wages, £200 more was deposited than on any previous statute day, and there was less drunkenness. By 1829 the bank could take temporary premises, and it so far prospered that in 1836 it was able to buy the Wesleyan chapel for its use.

---

[1] *Life of Thomas Cooper, written by himself* (1872), pp. 139, 143. Cobbett wrote of the stockingers of Derby, Notts., and Leicester who had scarcely means of a bare existence. Weavers might get 4s. 6d. a week (*Rural Rides* (ed. Cole), II, 572).

[2] *Passages in the Life of a Radical* (ed. Dunckley), p. 329.   [3] Bromhead MSS.

[4] W. H. Hosford in *Lincolnshire Historian*, II, no. 7, p. 35. There is much evidence to the like effect in *The Agricultural State of the Kingdom in February–April 1816, being replies to inquiries by the Board of Agriculture* (London, 1816).

[5] *State of Agriculture, Second Report* (1836), p. 73.

[6] C. W. Friend, *The Village Muse*. Thomas Miller, who placed his hero in *Gideon Giles the Roper* (1841) in a Trentside village between Newark and Gainsborough, gave him a kitchen garden with neatly built stye and cowhouse; even the comic and improvident character Ben Brust had a pig (pp. 24, 29).

By 1833 the worst was over for agriculture. It was reported that it was doing better in Lincolnshire than elsewhere.[1] Cobbett was in the county in 1830, and declared, having travelled its length, that he had never seen a single acre of waste land, and not one acre that would be called bad land in the south of England. When he reached Lincoln:

It was the third or fourth day of the Spring fair, which is one of the greatest in the kingdom, and which lasts for a whole week. Horses begin the fair; then come sheep; and to-day, the horned cattle. It is supposed that there were about 50,000 sheep, and I think the whole of the space in the various roads and streets, covered by the cattle, must have amounted to ten acres of ground or more. Some say that they were as numerous as the sheep. The number of horses I did not hear; but they say that there were 1,500 fewer than last year. The sheep sold 5s. a head, on an average, lower than last year; and the cattle in the same proportion. High-priced horses sold well; but the horses which are called tradesmen's horses, were very low.

Then Cobbett mounted his hobbyhorse, and charged his political enemies.[2]

In 1836 glowing accounts were given of the improvement of wold land, which had begun when high war prices prompted the conversion of sheep walks and rabbit warrens into good cultivable land; and in the fen improved drainage due to the installation of steam pumping engines had expanded the arable area. On the new land in both parts of the county oats had first been grown: Lincoln was described in 1821 as a great oat country, but oats gave way to wheat over a great area. The amount of wheat sold in Lincoln market more than trebled between 1825 and 1834.[3] It was in the post-war years that the custom spread of compensating an outgoing tenant for improvements. In 1826 William Hesseltine's father's rent was doubled; and the tenant objected unless he could have covenants to protect him. The practice grew out of this type of bargain, and became general; but the improvements came before the custom, because the tenants trusted their landlords.[4]

[1] V.C.H. Lincs. II, 351.

[2] Rural Rides (ed. Cole), II, 644, 658. And see J. H. Clapham, Economic History of Modern Britain, I, 16, quoting Meidinger's Travels. Anderson said that in 1828 it was still partly rabbit warren on the heath between Ashby toll bar and the Green Man (L.A.O. Anderson, 5/2/2, p. 124).

[3] Report on Agriculture of United Kingdom (1821), p. 210; State of Agriculture, First Report (1836), pp. 59, 64–5, App. 4. The Lords Committee (1837) were told that Irish imports drove the farmers out of the oat market, p. 61. For the growing of oats on land ploughed for the first time, see D. B. Grigg, 'The 1801 Crop Returns for South Lincolnshire, in East Midland Geographer, x, 44. In 1812 one-third of all the oats imported into London for stables came from Boston.

[4] Reports from Select Committee on Agricultural Customs (1848), evidence of Lincolnshire witnesses (pp. 16–36, 386–91, 401, 410). But by 1814 and earlier Banks was allowing for improvements in his Revesby estate. Buildings put up by the tenant were estimated at 18 years' purchase, 1/18th being deducted for every year that the tenant had enjoyed

In spite of the grave depression through which farming had passed, there is no sign that much ground had been lost to cultivation. Small pieces of land were bought at a high price for building small tenements. Eight or ten acres so parcelled out would soon contain as many families as the whole village besides; and Willson, writing in 1827, said that this increase had mostly taken place since 1820.[1] There was similar development in Lincoln. In 1824 a small paddock of $2\frac{1}{2}$ acres on the waterside was sold for little more than £1,100. This was considered a great price, but it was sold in small building lots at 10s. a yard or £2,420 per acre.[2]

A broad indication of trade fluctuations is given by the yield of turnpike tolls. In 1815 the tolls at Great Bargate, at the southern end of Lincoln, were let for £1,600. The rent fell at once to £1,350; with a few ups and downs it climbed to £1,550 in 1837, and the next year the tolls were let for three years at £1,605. Cattle tolls in Lincoln fairs and markets were let for £395 in 1826, or £290 more than they fetched for many years. Gainsborough bridge tolls were let in 1814 for £815; in 1817 for £785; in 1821 and 1822 for £855; and by 1827 had crept up to £1,055. Thereafter the rent fluctuated between £700 and £900.[3] Even if prices were bad, the volume of traffic in farm produce was growing fast.

In these years the case for a bridge over the Trent at Dunham was being debated; it would provide transit from the north-east of the county to the manufacturing districts of Derby, Manchester, Sheffield and Rotherham, in place of a dangerous, expensive and tedious ferry; and it would bring the trade of the East Fen through Lincoln. The initiative came from the city, where ideas had changed since the citizens opposed the Gainsborough bridge;[4] powers were obtained by statute, and the existing ferry, which had yielded its owner Mr Angerstein a net £60 a year, was bought for £1,000. By 1834 the bridge was open, and the tolls were let for £362. The

---

them. Underdrains he put at 20 years; and an outgoing tenant ought to leave all the manure needed for next year's crops in the usual course of cultivation. Banks had often found arbitration grossly partial to the outgoing tenant: in 1801 an incoming tenant was charged for a pump on the lead of which was the date 1765 (Hill, Banks MSS 1/5). In 1795 John Parkinson, a Lincolnshire valuer who worked for Banks, was examining evidence respecting right between landlord and tenant in the produce and interest in their following crops (*Annals of Agriculture*, XXIV, 123). See also D. B. Grigg, 'Development of Tenant Right in South Lincolnshire', *Lincolnshire Historian*, II, no. 9, p. 41.

[1] Willson, XIII, 63. But in fifteen parishes in the Alford area, where between 1801 and 1821 the population had increased by 1,283, 176 cottages had been demolished and only nine built (E. Dawson, *An Attempt to Develop the Causes of Pauperism and Distress* (1831); L.P.L. U.P. 1413). The writer commended Mr Dashwood of Well Vale and Miss Manners of Bloxholme for letting land for labourer's allotments.

[2] *L.R. & S.M.* 2 July 1824. Though there were many houses in Lincoln to let in September 1831 (L.A.O. Massingberd, 1/129).

[3] The rents were reported in *L.R. & S.M.*   [4] Above, p. 136.

rent varied between £300 and £390 until the shadow of the railway fell across the bridge.[1]

But even the turnpike roads were far from good, and in particular the fen roads in winter were bad for wheels, though practicable on horseback.[2] Transport by water was therefore the more important. There were horse-drawn packets on the Fossdyke in 1805, and on the Witham in 1809,[3] and a steam packet appeared about 1814; in the following year the *Stamford Mercury* heard that Mr Merryweather's patent for improved means of propelling vessels was to be fitted to a steam packet on the Witham. This portentous threat produced notices of better service by proprietors of the old packets. The steam packet *Witham* was plying regularly between Lincoln and Boston in 1816, and others followed. The *Duke of Sussex* was launched in Lincoln in 1822, and it was proclaimed that 'this large and handsome vessel' presented 'a spectacle of commercial grandeur'.

Clearly the service met a need, for it developed rapidly. By 1832 the Steam Packet Company could advertise that their steam packet would leave Boston at 7 a.m. in time for coaches to Hull, Leicester, Nottingham and Gainsborough the same day. Another company did the journey from Gainsborough to Hull in five hours.[4] Coaches plied to connect with the packets. In 1824 it was claimed that Lincolnshire was no longer behind most other counties:

Not long since, a mail coach to London and Hull, and another thrice a week to Nottingham, constituted all the means it could afford to a traveller; now it offers him two coaches daily to London and Hull, two to Nottingham (one of which is a mail coach to Derby), a daily coach to Manchester in one day, by

---

[1] 11 George IV, c. 66. Among the shareholders were Lincoln corporation, Sir Edward Bromhead, Sir William Ingilby, Dr Charlesworth, Joseph Collingham, Robert Cracroft, William Dawber, E. B. Drury, John Fardell, Dean Gordon, the two Pretymans, Rev. William Hett, Lord Monson, Colonel Sibthorp, and Aldermen Winn and Wriglesworth, most of whom appear elsewhere in these pages. It was a remarkable mixture of gentry, clergy and townsmen. No dividend was paid until 1887, the profits having gone in repayment of the company's borrowings. The records are in the possession of Messrs Danby Eptons and Griffith of Lincoln, who kindly allowed access to them. Charlesworth said that Angerstein had demanded £80 per annum to be secured for ever upon the tolls (Bromhead MSS).

[2] L.A.O. Massingberd, 1/105.

[3] One of the owners of the horsedrawn packets was Nathaniel Clayton. After his death in 1827 his widow Mary carried on the business, taking her son Nathaniel into partnership to work a steam packet of which he was to be captain at a wage of 30s. a week apart from his share of the profits. (A copy of the partnership agreement was given to me by the late Richard Mason. Mary signed by making a mark.) Later the son was also agent for the Steam Packet Company. At the same time there are references to the schooner of Mr Shuttleworth and his boat yards near the locks at Lincoln and at Dogdyke, farther down the river (see three articles by Arthur Smith in *Lincolnshire Chronicle*, 1 Jan. 1927 and following weeks). [4] L.P.L. U.P. 922.

way of Gainsborough; and last, though to the district not least in interest, a daily coach to Horncastle and Louth; this, though long wanted, would not sooner have been undertaken with any prospect of success. The several established coaches above mentioned, the improved state of the roads, and the growing opulence of the county have all co-operated to justify the undertaking.[1]

In 1829 a traveller could go from Hull to Gainsborough by water (if the tide were favourable), reach Lincoln by coach, and take the packet to Boston, completing the journey of 102 miles in a day for 3s. 6d. By 1835 the journey to London could be made between 7 a.m. and 10 p.m. the same day; and by 1838 the London coach had only to reach Denbigh hall on the Holyhead road in order there to join the railway to London.

The Lincolnshire Steam Navigation and Insurance Company projected the ambitious scheme of carrying fatstock by water to London. Its prospectus stated that 18,000 head of beast and 230,000 head of sheep were sent yearly from the Lincolnshire marshes and parts adjacent to London markets. The beast and sheep lost in weight and value in travelling by road.[2] Business began in 1837 in spite of the protests of the drovers. A few ships even made the journey between Lincoln and London, and there was a dry dock near Stamp End lock where Mr Shuttleworth was building a schooner for the London journey.

The possible effects on the river banks of steam packets hurtling up and down stream at as much as eight miles an hour caused anxiety to the Witham commissioners. This was not their only trouble. In spite of all their work, under the Act of 1812, since whose passing they had spent some £200,000 on the river, the banks between High Bridge and Stamp End were in disrepair, and the water reached almost to the houses. In 1825 they were indicted for non-repair. In 1826 the river was still being widened and deepened, and Stamp End lock enlarged. They needed more money and new powers, which would require an amending Act. There were conflicting opinions among the proprietors which broke into open quarrels, described with his usual zest by Dr Charlesworth[3] to Bromhead:

30 August 1827. Major Brown tells me that £150,000 have been thrown away in the management of the Witham, and that an engineer, paid £2,000 for directing, would have been a cheap purchase. Yet the concern will turn out well.

19 September 1827. The Witham in its course through Lincoln is the greatest botch I ever beheld: I call it the 'serpentine river'. This great concern required for its good conduct a man with a hard head and a soft heart; it has been managed by one who has a soft head and a very hard heart; who tramples upon all rights, public and private; and never winces at the hottest iron applied to his neighbour. Tell me what ever prospers that he touches (except his own purse)—all that is good shrinks from his grasp.

---

[1] *L.R. & S.M.* 1 Oct. 1824.   [2] L.P.L. U.P. 1941.   [3] As to whom, see p. 277.

This was his favourite enemy and fellow medical man, Dr Cookson.

23 July 1828. I have seen Burcham to-day, fresh from the Witham meeting, C. Chaplin in the chair. I could find that Cookson had been noisy and over-bearish even for Burcham, who told the party that their bill for money would be opposed in parliament by gentlemen who thought that enough money had been made ducks and drakes of already. Humphrey Sibthorp asked the meeting to guarantee any sums of money the committee might lay out. This was too monstrous for Chaplin, who negatived the request. Humphrey must have some view ulterior to the Navigation; he cannot be so bitten by Merryweather as to wish to waste the Company's (and his own) gold. Burcham tells me the interest, and the price, of shares will fall. . . .

A possible explanation of Humphrey Sibthorp's action, which eluded the sharp eyes of Charlesworth, may be found in the account of Fossdyke affairs which is soon to follow.

On his part Bromhead was anxious that no impediment should be put in the way of the full development of steam navigation on the river, and he wrote to Richard Mason:

4 May 1829. I am deeply impressed with the vital importance of the steam navigation to the interest of the city and county, and indeed to the ultimate interest of the Company itself. It appears to me essential that you should be personally present in Town on this business. If a restriction should be demanded on the ground that it will save some immense outlay to the Company, of course they will tender to the public in exchange for the sacrifice some reduction of toll in limitation of profits, but it strikes me that nothing whatsoever could be adequate compensation.[1]

The Witham Bill went through parliament in that year. In the debate in the Commons Charles Tennyson said that the company had narrowed the banks when they deepened the river, and had caused accidents by removing posts and rails. A corporation petition said that sixteen lives had thereby been lost in a short time. There was a compromise on the cost of fencing, the company to bear a third, and the rest to be borne by public subscription or otherwise. Clauses for the regulation of steam navigation in the interests of the river banks, and against steam-engine pumps in the fens, were abandoned. The jurisdiction of the city justices over the river within the city was preserved in spite of a proposal that the county justices should have concurrent jurisdiction.[2]

The city's commercial interest in the Fossdyke was greater than it was in the Witham, and as the demands upon the navigation grew the complaints about its condition grew also, and indeed more loudly. The making

---

[1] Bromhead MSS.

[2] 10 George IV, c. 123; W. H. Wheeler, *Fens of South Lincolnshire*, pp. 164–6. The Little Bargate bridge was taken down to facilitate work in the Sincil dyke.

of a through navigation from Witham to Fossdyke under the Horncastle Act[1]—complete by 1795—was followed by the extensive work on the Witham mentioned already; where by 1824, it was said, there was a 6-foot navigation from the High Bridge at Lincoln to the Grand Sluice at Boston. Even if, therefore, the Fossdyke was maintained at the regulation depth of 3 feet 6 inches, there was— all things being relative—ground for discontent.

The artificial waterway had always been difficult to maintain. The banks stood 10–14 feet above the water, and being of sand—part of them quicksand—were constantly falling in, especially if a vessel ran against them. Some work was done in 1805, when, on the making of the West Drainage embankment,[2] Colonel Ellison emptied the Foss for a mile and a quarter from Lincoln and deepened it. Apart from considerations of cost he did not like drying the river, for he feared that when the water was run off the high and heavy banks would press up the bottom of the river. From that date until 1818 little was done save by the use of sand pans for the removal of shoals; and conditions worsened until 1819–20 when 'Hamer's machines' were brought into use. In 1826 an exceptional drought brought complaints to a head.

On the side of the lessees the position was not simple. When Richard Ellison II died in 1792 he settled a two-thirds interest in the navigation on his son Richard (Colonel Ellison) and his heirs male, and the remaining one-third on his son Henry (of Beverley) and his heirs male. Henry left the management entirely to his brother, who, having only a life interest, did not spend a shilling unless he was compelled to do so. The colonel died in 1827 without lawful issue; and his brother Henry, who then became solely entitled for life, left the management of his interest to Humphrey Sibthorp, the rector of Washingborough, who had married his daughter Esther. Henry died in 1836, leaving his son Richard, the fourth of the name, solely entitled to the income. Richard acknowledged privately that the navigation had been grossly neglected until 1827; in that and the preceding year the lessee spent £6,000 in providing a 4-foot navigation, and not less than 3 feet 6 inches at all seasons. Although this measure satisfied the terms of the leases it did not satisfy the rising demands on the river. Not only were ketches 72 feet long and drawing 3 feet of water coming from Nottingham down the Trent and into the Foss; with the deepening of the Witham vessels drawing 4 or even 5 feet of water were trying to get through the Fossdyke. Delays meant financial loss to the merchants, and as the trade grew the financial losses, and hopes of gains, grew also. It was contended for the lessee that if the Witham had continued in its old state, and the fens

---

[1] Above, pp. 135–6.   [2] Above, p. 175.

had not been drained, the Fossdyke tolls at their old level would not have been sufficient to maintain the navigation and pay interest on the money expended on repair.

Complaints had become vigorous in 1819. The traders said that the channel was so silted up that they could not pass up and down even with empty vessels drawing only 2 feet of water, which was far below the standard depth. They had to land their goods at Torksey or lighter them up in small quantities, to their great loss. Colonel Ellison claimed that the trouble was due to the extraction of water from the upper Witham and the Till by the improvement of the lower Witham. The contract for the deepening of the navigation had been partly acted upon already; which suggested hope for the future.

There was much resort to legal opinion about the provisions of the leases of 1741. Counsel advised the corporation that the leases were good in law and equity, but that the Act of Charles II under which the citizens were undertakers authorised only such tolls as were necessary for completing and supporting the navigation. This meant that the commissioners under the Act must have authority to call for the accounts of the corporation and their lessees, and that the tolls should be fixed in the light of the evidence.

The point was seized upon, as it was well known that the navigation was highly profitable to the Ellisons. Public meetings were held, new commissioners were appointed, and accounts demanded at common law. On his side Colonel Ellison gave the corporation notice that he would hold them responsible under the covenants in the leases. Throughout the proceedings the Ellison influence was strong,[1] and party spirit and personal hostility on the other side were correspondingly vigorous. A 'careless and ineffectual cleansing' of 1827 did not appease the public; and a middle party, which included Dean Gordon and Bromhead, came to a compromise with Ellison on a bill to make the navigation capable of drawing five or six feet of water, half at the cost of the lessees (estimated to amount to £40,000 or

---

[1] 'Colonel Ellison possessed great influence in the Council. He had been for many years their Representative in Parliament, their recorder, chairman of their quarter sessions, and a colonel of the city cavalry. The corporation account was kept at the bank of Messrs. Ellison and Co., who occasionally advanced them money. The influence derived from these circumstances was further increased by making the town clerk his election agent, and thus attaching to his own interest the legal adviser of the corporation' (*Report of the Municipal Commissioners* (1835), p. 2363). The newspaper account of the proceedings at the inquiry adds that he was a large Witham shareholder and lived near Lincoln. 'It was not pretended that the Corporation as a body could be influenced by being on the debit side with their banker, but many of the individual members of the Corporation undoubtedly did business with Colonel Ellison's bank, and might require advances. (More demonstrations of assent)' (*L.R. & S.M.* 27 Sept. 1833).

£50,000), whose lease should be confirmed and established, and half at the cost of the public, to be raised by an additional toll of 6*d*. per ton. The extreme party, however, raised a fund to file a bill in Chancery praying that the leases be declared void and the tolls adjudged public property; and the compromise bill, which had no hope of success unless it was generally accepted, was abandoned.

The legal proceedings dragged on wearily year after year, with parties and persons taking sides, and a sense of frustration found expression in verses sent anonymously to Tallents of Newark, the Ellison solicitor:

> Who but the Fossdike, let me ask ye,
> Makes pot to boil, or bakes the pasty?
> Furnish'd the city feasts (that *were*)—
> Alas! we *now* have no such cheer,
> *Nor* shall again (so are my fears)
> These many long and tedious years;
> For *Lawyer's bill* and *Lawyer's fee*,
> Will starve both *Lessor* and *Lessee*.
> The Dean and Chapter too, no more
> Give dinners (as they did before);
> The audit ale, the sparkling wine
> (Choice product of some happy fine)
> No longer on their table shine.
>
> It stirs up all one's very liver
> To think that *they* so ill should use thee,
> Thy Guardians too, who thus abuse thee;
> Try all manoeuvres and devices,
> To carve thy income into slices,
> And take each one a golden pill,
> M[ayo]r, A[lderme]n, and C[ommo]n C[ounci]l.
> (A job too rank to be conceal'd
> By doors hermetically seal'd,
> By some misgiving wight reveal'd).

By 1837 the heat had gone out of the battle. The Ellison brothers were dead; it was increasingly realised that some of the troubles lay not in the Fossdyke itself but in shoals in the Trent, and that the Fossdyke could never be made fit for the modern volume of traffic; and there was a disposition on the part of the promoters of the proceedings to propose a new channel for the Fossdyke, bringing it to the Trent nearer Gainsborough and below the offending shoals. Richard Ellison IV—the whistle of a railway engine already in his ears—did not want to be committed to new expenditure, and would welcome a chance to sell out. He could not however negotiate while proceedings were pending; and at last the proceedings at law were abandoned, and judgement was given in Chancery against the city in 1839.

It was thought that the Witham Company might buy the leases; perhaps Humphrey Sibthorp, with a foot in each waterway, was trying to bring this about.[1] The corporation also were disposed to treat, and a price of £120,000 was mentioned, which, said Charlesworth, would be out of the frying pan into the fire. When the railway promoters came on the scene no conclusion had been reached; and meanwhile the canal was kept in better condition with the aid of a steam dredging machine.[2]

The growing importance of the Fossdyke, even in its defective condition, is most eloquently shown by the account of receipts. They first passed £5,000 in 1813; in 1818 they passed £6,000 for the first time; in 1825, a year of great distress, they passed £8,000, and thereafter, up to 1832, they only once fell below that figure. However bad the prices of their products might be, the farmers were producing and the merchants handling a steadily increasing volume of goods for despatch to Yorkshire and Lancashire; and it is no wonder therefore that there should be such concentration upon the problems of the navigation.[3]

This trade was largely in the hands of a group of merchants whose yards and warehouses flanked the river and Brayford pool, where the ownership of the wharves, partly built by them, was to give rise to legal questions. These men were often simply described as 'merchants', which meant that they would turn to any activity in which they saw prospect of profit. In White's *Gazetteer* of 1826 John Maltby and William Rudgard appear as bone merchants and crushers; John Rudgard and several of the Winn family as brewers; Keyworths, Dawbers, Winns and Rudgard again as coal merchants; Dawber was also a corn merchant; Rudgard was a miller; Dawbers, Rudgards and Winns were maltsters; John Keyworth was a timber merchant; Dawber and Keyworth were wine and spirit merchants. By 1842, the date of a second White's *Gazetteer*, the lists were lengthening, but many of the same names appear; among them were the men who (after reform) took the lead in politics and municipal affairs, and their money made them leaders of the social world belowhill. The census of 1841 shows that they and the principal shopkeepers could keep two or three female servants and perhaps a man servant or a boy as well.[4] Some of their establishments were considerable, with journeymen and servants living in.

---

[1] Above, p. 199.

[2] The Ellison papers in L.A.O. B.S. 12/3/1/3. The Witham Company minutes, the newspapers, and many printed pamphlets and broadsheets have been drawn upon for this highly abridged account of the battle. In 1836 the High bridge was undergoing 'a rather *severe* and dangerous operation' (W. A. Nicholson to Charles Tennyson d'Eyncourt).

[3] See Appendix II.

[4] Charles Seely had already moved uphill, and kept four female servants.

This group dominated the business life of the city until the rise of the engineers later in the century. The family of Keyworth provides a link between the periods. The father had been managing clerk in the Smith Ellison bank; on his retirement he embarked with two of his sons in the river trade; one of them, Thomas Michael, was to take Charles Seely as a partner in his mill, and together they were to become sleeping partners with Nathaniel Clayton in the manufacture of thrashing machines.

The growing prosperity of farmer and merchant, and the professional men who prospered with them, meant that there was enough business for more than one bank; and there was a strong disposition to form one because the old bank of Smith Ellison was based on the support of the gentry, to which its partners had come to belong, especially since Samuel Smith had sent his son-in-law Alexander Leslie Melville, a son of the Earl of Leven and Melville, and an advocate of the Scottish bar, to Lincoln as the resident partner. Furthermore, there was the Fossdyke feud. The division that would be created between the old and a new bank would therefore be social, partly political and even partly religious, for the dissenters would go with the whigs and liberals, and the higher clergy with the tories.

All legal restrictions upon the formation of joint-stock banking were removed in 1826, and Bromhead at once began to think of forming a Land Bank; and a neighbouring squire, Samuel Solly, wrote to him with a view to helping small freeholders in particular.[1] He did not go on, but various other projects were being discussed in 1831. In the following year the Stamford and Spalding Joint Stock Banking Company was formed, and in 1833 the Hull Banking Company, which at once opened branches in north Lincolnshire. In March 1833, largely through the initiative of Richard Mason, solicitor and town clerk, there was issued a prospectus of the Lincoln and Lindsey Banking Company. The promoters were at once accused of political motives, which they hastened to disown publicly; though E. B. Drury (a radical citizen) told Charles Tennyson that he and Mason had started the undertaking as a means of emancipating the liberals from the control of tory money influence.[2] The promoters declared that they held no opinions in common (though in fact most of them were whigs), and that they did not purpose to establish the bank in rivalry, far less in hostility, to the highly respectable private bank in the city. They held that in the capital town of a large county and agricultural district there was room for two banks, one a public company. The nominal capital was

---

[1] Bromhead MSS. Samuel Solly presently became a director of the Lincoln and Lindsey Bank.

[2] L.A.O. Tennyson d'Eyncourt (22 Jan. 1836).

£200,000 in shares of £200, of which only £20 was called up. The shares were fully subscribed, and the bank opened in premises opposite St Mary's church in August 1833. As London agents the bank appointed the firm in which George Grote, the radical banker and historian of Greece, was a partner; he had connections with the county through his wife and through an estate at Long Bennington.

The bank soon had branches in other towns, and its agents attended a number of markets. Its annual report in 1834 said that not only had the bank to contend with old-established firms of the highest character and respectability, which for years had engrossed the almost entire banking business of the city as well as of the northern part of the county, but it had further had to contend with a rival bank of a nature similar to its own, which in every town where the company had set up branch banks and agencies had met it in opposition. It had also had to contend with those doubts, fears, jealousies and prejudices which would always affect the public mind in relation to establishments of a novel description such as joint-stock banks even then were.

Its joint stock rival was the Hull Banking Company; but a run on its Lincolnshire branches brought their closure, and the Lincoln and Lindsey Bank succeeded to much of their business. By 1835 the debtors in its ledger reached nearly £100,000, and it called up another £10 per share. It agreed its interest rates with Smith Ellisons, and it was soon paying a dividend of 10 per cent. In 1837, in spite of general distress, it doubled its profits, and it was well established before the depression of the 1840's came upon it.[1]

All this commercial expansion was accompanied by a growing population. In 1811 the number of people in city Bail and Close was 8,486; in 1821, 9,875; in 1831, 11,116. Thereafter the rate of increase was more rapid. In the 30 years (1811–41) the number of houses grew from 1,775 to 3,254. Some of the increase of population was due to natural increase, that is, to the excess of births over deaths, and some to immigration. In the decade 1801–10 there was an excess of baptisms over burials of 621. The population, however, had grown by 1,650, so that there was a balance of immigration; and as some must have gone out, the actual immigration must have been larger. In the same period the county as a whole showed a small balance outwards. (Natural increase, 30,628; increase of population, 26,599.) In the following decade, 1811–20, the natural increase of Lincoln was 1,003, and the population increase 1,396. There was thus a net immigration of 393. In this period the county also showed a net

---

[1] Crick and Wadsworth, *A Hundred Years of Joint Stock Banking* (1936), pp. 209–10, 253–5, and notes kindly lent to me by Mr Wadsworth.

immigration of 6,587. (41,247 compared with 47,834.)[1] Of the city population in 1841, 2,607 were born out of Lincolnshire, and no doubt a considerable further number were born in the county but outside the city.

Between 1801 and 1841, of the two parishes north of the Bail, St John in Newport doubled, and St Nicholas grew from 147 to 1,053, mostly in 1831–41. Following the inclosure of the common fields, land in this area was broken up for building, mostly of small houses. An increase in St Michael was due to rows of terrace houses packed tightly on the steep hillside; the other uphill parishes changed little. Belowhill there were three chief areas of growth. St Martin grew from 1,187 to 2,285, small houses being built on old inclosures and on the hillside; St Botolph nearly doubled and St Peter at Gowts increased by half, no doubt by the building of courts off High Street. St Swithin grew from 940 to 2,634, the river traffic being the reason. The scene in that area is depicted in 1827 as follows:

What is called the Waterside, on the lower side of the High-bridge, particularly about the Turn-bridge, affords many happy combinations. The houses are old and ruinous; the ground rough, broken and almost impassable; these when united with the dirty coal-lighters, in a canal of the most impure water, with the watermen and other idlers constantly grouped on the Turn-bridge, the haling-horses, boatmen's wives, and other accompaniments of a canal, give a study worthy of Hogarth, or of any artist skilled in delineating the lower *grades* of human life. The scene much resembles some of those views transmitted to us from the Netherlands: but it wants the trees, and above all the cleanliness of a Dutch picture.[2]

This increase of population meant a great increase in the number of poor; and this increase and the increase of prices meant more poor relief; and the burden of poor relief was correspondingly greater when at the end of the war and in the first years of the peace there was serious unemployment. In 1812 the amount paid out in outrelief was under £200; in 1817 it was £1,300. The House of Industry itself cost £4,800 a year, and had 175 inmates. The contributing population at the most was 12,000, namely the city Bail Close and the four towns and a few rural parishes. The workhouse was in danger of breaking down. In 1820 the cost of poor relief in city Bail Close and the four towns was £2,660 and in 1821 £3,476.[3] More money was called for, and lists were printed of persons receiving out-relief as a precaution against fraud. Lodging houses were searched, and forty vagrants were put in gaol pending despatch to their places of settlement. The great volume of crime was a grave evil. Sheep stealing, robbery and drunkenness were rife, with vagabonds at the races, gambling and riot and disorderly

---

[1] See Appendix III.   [2] *Lincoln and Lincolnshire Cabinet* (1827), p. 7.
[3] *Supplemental Appendix to Report from Select Committee on Poor Rate Returns* (1822), p. 99.

houses. Beggars tried to evade the law by posing as hawkers, and some resorted to violence and abuse. Parish constables were given their orders, and some of the offenders soon found themselves on the treadwheel.

In St Swithin's parish the amount spent on the poor rose from £138 in 1820 to £601 in 1824.[1] It seemed that the poor law was breaking down, and presently the whig government produced its new poor law measure. In protest against the rate burden in 1832, the mayor and others refused to grant a poor rate, and quashed three rates granted before the magistrates. Many families within the city and from the villages to the north and south of it, described as respectable small capitalists, were emigrating to the settled parts of the United States.

There had been much discussion about the penal clauses in poor law bills such as those in the Lincoln Act of 1796.[2] When in 1811 the Spilsby Poor Law Bill was read in the House of Commons the reformer Sir Samuel Romilly opposed it, and Mr Chaplin, one of the members for the county, proposed to postpone it, in order that some objectionable clauses might be omitted: Mr Ellison agreed, and disclaimed knowledge of them on the part of the magistrates. The bill was rejected.[3] In 1813 an attempt was made to repeal such clauses in local Acts, and limits were placed on the powers of authorities to confine the poor or administer corporal punishment.[4] Another attempt at amelioration was made by Sir Robert Heron, then M.P. for Grimsby.[5] He was a strong partisan, and his account was written, or at least published, long afterwards, so that it must be received with due reserve:

I had long witnessed the evils occasioned to the lower orders, within twenty miles of Lincoln, by a local poor bill, passed in 1796, and which had been smuggled, in some extraordinary manner, through both Houses; as it contained clauses oppressive and tyrannical to a great degree, and contrary to the principles of common law, as well as of justice. The workhouse was managed well as to food, cleanliness and order, but it was ruled with an iron rod, and chains and dungeons were in constant use for trivial faults, and at the will of the governor; it was, also, totally without the means of complaint for the unfortunate inhabitants. The last of these inconveniences must, I fear, remain; the rest I had determined to remedy. With the assistance of Sir Samuel Romilly, I framed a bill for that purpose, which has also the advantage of repealing all similar clauses in other local acts.

---

[1] *Report from Select Committee on Poor Rate Returns* (1821), p. 99; (1825), p. 131.

[2] Above, p. 185. In 1809 an inmate was ordered to be confined in a cell for four weeks for leaving the house without permission. Other offenders were whipped or put in the stocks for an hour a day.

[3] *Parliamentary Debates*, XIX, 514–15.

[4] 54 George III, c. 170; *Memoirs of Sir Samuel Romilly* (1840), II, 381–3.

[5] *Parliamentary Debates*, XXXIII, 850.

He censured Ellison—said to have been the author of the Lincoln Act of 1796—for furtive opposition to his bill. Ellison, he said, had told him he had always disapproved of the Lincoln bill, but was satisfied with Heron's bill as amended, adding, 'but as soon as I had left Town, he threatened to oppose my bill, and told Sir Samuel Romilly that there was neither sense nor legislation in it'. He did not, however, oppose the third reading.[1]

Generous allowance must be made here for political hostility. Heron's bill was discussed at a meeting in Lincoln in April 1816. The protection of paupers from improper treatment was not opposed by the meeting. An impression that Heron had reflected on the Lincoln house was however challenged by the deputy town clerk, who reported that Heron had said a good deal in commendation of the house and little against it.

The bill was passed.[2] In repealing provisions in local Acts it ensured that no person who had not applied for relief could be compelled to go into a workhouse, or any person be kept there after he was capable of maintaining himself; and that no child might be apprenticed to the governor of the house. No parish could contribute to a workhouse more than ten miles away, and no adult could be hired out. Chains and manacles for the sane poor were forbidden.

Individual parishes were more concerned to see that they did not bear more than they need or ought of the total cost of the house. The relative distribution of the population had so changed since 1796 that in 1820 there was proposed a bill whereby each parish should maintain its own poor. This proposal was not adopted, but instead an amending Act provided for contributions according to seven-year averages.[3] This sharing did nothing for economy in the house, and the guardians complained in 1821 that although prices had fallen expenditure was nearly the same; and it was thought that was due to grants of out-relief to persons to help them to maintain themselves. One parish had made applicants for out-relief work for their pay, and so had cleared their books of more than half.

When later the time came for reviewing expenses on account of parish averages, it was noted that they were working equitably. As each parish paid according to expenditure on its own poor, it had an incentive to care, and St Peter at Arches, reaping the benefit of careful management, had dropped from £328 to £135 in four years. But the state of the house gave cause for anxiety, for there was no means of separating the young from the old. A new building was considered, but the difficulty was that part of the

---

[1] *Notes* (2nd edn 1851), pp. 71–3. Ellison opposed a bill to enable overseers to relieve deserving poor without rendering them liable to removal (*Parliamentary History of England*, xxxv, col. 199).

[2] 56 George III, c. 129.   [3] 1 & 2 George IV, c. 49; *C.J.* LXXVI, 49…309.

site was the freehold of the dean and chapter, and terms could not be reached for purchase. There were as always complaints about the burden of the rate, and there was talk of farming the poor, but Charlesworth commented that he did not understand how the poor could be maintained at so low a rate.

The treatment of pauper children by the guardians is of particular interest. A schoolroom had been fitted up in 1798, and a schoolmistress advertised for. By 1826 the children were attending the National School in Lincoln, and some of them could be used as monitors for teaching the younger children. Presently relations with the schoolmaster became strained. He was removing manure from opposite the school, and so interfering with the monopoly of the House of Industry under its scavenging contract with the Lighting and Paving Commissioners. Then he so severely flogged one of the boys that two guardians were sent to see him, the subscription to the school was stopped, and the children withdrawn. Thereafter they were taught on the workhouse premises, and one of the inmates was allowed extra meat on meat days, cheese for his supper every night, and 2s. 6d. a quarter for teaching them, and another inmate had a like allowance of meat and cheese for helping him.

Some of the boys were apprenticed to framework knitters at Bingham beyond Newark; the master of one of them was summoned to appear at the house to answer a complaint of ill-treatment by his apprentice. Others went to watermen, ropemakers, masons and bricklayers, and one at least to a chimney sweep. Boys might be hired to brickmakers with the stipulation that they could be withdrawn at any time to be apprenticed. Girls generally went into domestic service. In 1797 twenty-two boys and girls were apprenticed to cotton manufacturers at Bolton in Lancashire, £5 being granted towards the cost of removing them; but as employers found that they could employ free child labour at little extra cost the employment of pauper children became less popular.[1]

When in 1832 the whig government appointed a Royal Commission to investigate the poor law administration, the commissioner who visited Lincoln approved of what he saw. He found that without any apparent advantages beyond the ordinary sources of employment, the directors and guardians of the poor had steadily resisted the spread of pauperism; and he thought that when this was done the existing law was sufficient. Evil practices found elsewhere did not prevail. Rents were not paid out of the

[1] The minutes of the House of Industry have only survived in part; the volumes for the 1809–13 and 1824–32 periods are in L.A.O.; these, and another volume for the period 1796–1800, since lost, were described by the Rev. E. R. Milton, rector of St Paul's, in the *Lincolnshire Chronicle* on 28 Aug., 4 and 11 Sept. 1948.

poor rates; wages were not augmented; roundsmen were not known; and the poor rate was at the moderate level of a shilling in the pound. The house, not having been built for its purpose, was not well adapted for separation of the different classes of inmates, but what could be done to this end was done. Inmates were not allowed to leave the house without permission. As the idle and dissolute, if able-bodied, were restricted in their diet, and employed in laborious work, such paupers seldom remained long in the house. The offer of the house was highly useful in checking pauperism.

He added that the anti-pauper system was completed by the honest and honourable distribution of parochial charities, which were very consider-able in amount, and by schools, a sick hospital, a lunatic asylum, a savings bank and a friendly society, as well as several sick clubs. Several of these institutions had, however, only come into being after the war.[1]

Another body, the Lighting and Paving Commissioners, were eventually to do good work, but only after a very slow start. Their scope under their Act of 1791 was small, for they were limited to a 6d. rate: in 1794 they invited tenders for lighting 250 lamps in the streets for 130 nights in the year, and by 1796 they were ready to contract for sweeping the streets. Street improvements however were hardly attempted. The turnpike com-missioners who were responsible for the road approaches to the city and also to the main roads through it—though the charges for the latter were borne by the city parishes—had been active and successful. The contrast between the two results became pointed. The *Mercury* noted in 1823 that the roads at the entrances into Lincoln had greatly improved, but the angles and turns of the old town were highly dangerous, and a new Lighting and Paving Act was necessary. Greatly daring, it went on to suggest that gas for lighting the streets should not be discarded as impracticable. In the following year it reported that the Gainsborough road was to be widened, and hoped that this would lead to an improvement of Newland, to which it led, and the approach from the west to the Stonebow. It seems that the idea was acted upon, for about 1826–7 a house north of the Reindeer was taken down, and the present Guildhall Street doubled in width.[2] Most of the complaints related to the inadequate lighting of the streets; the moon,

[1] *Report of H.M. Commissioners for inquiring into the Administration and Practical Operation of the Poor Laws*, App. A. Reports of Assistant Commissioners, Part II (Major W. Wilde R.A.). Of Lincolnshire as a whole, the Poor Law Commissioners thought it one of the most pauperised counties when they entered upon their work in 1834. In that year one in four of the paupers relieved was able-bodied; by 1839 the proportion had fallen to one in five. The number of able-bodied relieved had fallen by 61 per cent, and the total number relieved by 47 per cent (*Fifth Annual Report of the Poor Law Commissioners for England and Wales* (1839), p. 14). The relatively humane treatment of the poor under the old system must have increased resentment against the New Poor Law.

[2] Willson, v, 67.

even on its good nights, was not enough; the pavements were broken and dirty, and things were at their worst on Sundays when the crowds left church, because there were no shops open. It was even suggested that if the commissioners could not afford more lights, a voluntary subscription should be raised.

Bromhead and Charlesworth were of course members of the turnpike trust, and Charlesworth was pressing for more efficiency. He complained that the farmers on the trust were determined to dismiss any pinder who did his duty and impounded stray cattle, and he wanted to advertise the powers of the trustees; he noted that the farmers entering Lincoln from the north got in without paying toll, though the farmers from the south had to pay; and he wanted a weighing machine at the foot of the New, or Lindum, Road.

The trustees were having trouble with the dean and chapter, who disliked having the turnpike road through the Close, and would have liked to be rid of it. Russell Collet, one of the trustees, wrote to Bromhead:

24 October 1825. I am one appointed with a doctor and a nobody to meet the Dean and the devil to consult on the rights of the Church and the claims of the trust. Why were you not named? You have more words and wit at will than your humble servant, besides more leisure at this important season of the year, and far more knowledge on the subject. If you have any true Christian charity you will impart some of the latter to me, and let me shine in borrowed feathers, by informing me what *we* (the trust) want from the Church and what we can give them in exchange: for without a *double* equivalent nothing is to be got from them, and also tell me what power we have to give up old or make new roads... on Friday next... at 12 I am to meet the Dean and *his friend.*

Presently the turnpike surveyor, Brocklesby, got his trustees into trouble by pulling down the western wall of St Nicholas churchyard in Newport, taking up the dead bodies, and throwing part of the churchyard into the public highway; and all this without the authority of the dean and chapter, the patrons of the living. The chapter stood on their rights, and though Charlesworth thought Dean Gordon would give way if he could, he added that the dean

15 October 1826....loves his money dearly, and his abettors will *not one of them* help him with a guinea...he takes his stand upon two grounds...as a trustee who disapproves the conduct of the surveyor and the application of the funds, and as a Churchman protecting the rights of the Church which have been infringed.

He wrote later that the dean had forced the surveyor to sign a document of submission acknowledging his fault; though Subdean Bayley thought Gordon's action harsh, and that a great public improvement had been effected, though in the wrong way.[1]

[1] Bromhead MSS.

Meanwhile the Lighting and Paving Commissioners, watched by the corporation, were struggling with their own inadequate powers. They were limited to a 6d. rate; the parish watchmen were not on a permanent footing, and the streets were dirty and ill-lit, though the corporation were paying £35 a year towards the sweeping of the streets. This payment had gone since 1818 to the House of Industry, which got the job done with pauper labour. Disgraceful disorders in 1827 led to a determined move for a new Act; the mayor suggested that the Bail and Close should come into a new commission, and others suggested that the streets should be lit by gas, the cost of which was estimated to be £6,300 for the city and £700 for the Bail.

Action was taken. A petition was presented to parliament, and an amending Act for lighting, watching and paving city Bail and Close, and for regulating the police, received the royal assent on 9 May 1828.[1] The new Act recited the Act of 1791, and continued that since that date the population of the city and the numbers of houses and buildings in it had been greatly increased, and several of the streets had become considerable thoroughfares. It provided (*inter alia*) that such parts of the turnpike roads as were within the city Bail and Close and had houses on both sides should cease to be parts of the turnpike and come under the commissioners.

The clerk to the turnpike trust made his comments on the new Act to Bromhead. He pointed out that many places had houses only on one side and would remain under the trust, and that the whole of each road ought to be under one body or the other. He noted also that Pottergate and Chequergate and indeed all future contact with the dean and chapter would under this ruling be cut off from the Lincoln turnpike, and the roads within the Close be brought under the commission. He added that there was another bill, then in the House of Lords, authorising the removal of the Great Bargate tollgate to the foot of Cross Cliff Hill, and the erection of another at the foot of Canwick Hill, which there had been no previous power to do.[2]

Churchwardens and overseers of the poor duly called meetings in their own parishes to elect two commissioners for each parish. The *Mercury* commented that in this unfamiliar experience of popular election at the vestries, the ambitious thrust forward, and the more deliberate receded. Enthusiasm was not universal. One parish, St Nicholas, made no election return, several commissioners were soon disqualified by non-attendance, and one declined to act. The new body set assessors to work to value

[1] 9 George IV, c. 27; *C.J.* LXXXIII, 32, 116, 167, 333. An Act for lighting city Bail and Close with gas went through all its stages at the same time.

[2] Bromhead MSS (10 June 1828).

property for rating purposes, paid off the small debt of the old commissioners, and took over their books and papers. There was jealousy lest the new Gas Company, just formed under its new Act, should make high profits out of street lighting; though, as was pointed out, even this was better than sending cash to Hull for oil and St Petersburg for tallow.

Serious limitations were soon discovered in the new Lighting and Paving Act. The actual work on the highways was carried out by the parishes under their own surveyors, and one parish would do the work well and another neglect it. The footpaths were still the liability of the frontagers, and so were unequally maintained. A recital in the Act that the city Bail and Close comprised fifteen parishes was construed to mean that the Act did not apply to extra-parochial places, of which there were several in the city. Finally, no work could be done in the Close without the consent of the dean and chapter; this limitation became a cause of increasing friction after the Bail and Close were brought into the municipal borough by the Municipal Corporations Act of 1835.

Nevertheless, within their limited powers, the commissioners set to work with a zeal that must have startled the corporation and indeed the inhabitants generally. They proposed to divide the town into eighteen beats for the purposes of the watch, and to appoint twenty-one watchmen with three inspectors. In fact they did not go quite so far, and they set up a force of ten watchmen with two superintendents and a surveyor, with additional constables from time to time, and a reserve of fifty for the races. The watchmen were to go on duty at 9 p.m. and quit at a time according to sunrise, and to be paid 12s. a week, though within a few weeks it was found necessary to raise the wage to 14s. The public were called upon to sweep their pavements twice a week, and the Witham Proprietors to rebuild the walls and parapets of Bargate Bridge. Coal porters were licensed.

It was proposed to increase the number of street lamps by 142 to a total of 500, with five lamp-lighters at the same wage as the watchmen; but this programme also had to be cut down after negotiations with the Gas Light and Coke Company. Eventually, after considering an offer to supply gas at £3. 3s. per lamp with batswing burner, abating five full nights in each full moon, terms were reached for the lighting by gas of 181 lamps and by oil of forty; averaging ten hours per night, September to April, deducting four nights in each moon, at a price of £525.

The commissioners also tried to get tenders for sweeping the streets, but failed, and were thrown back upon the House of Industry, whose directors seized the chance to put up the price of pauper labour; and rather than pay the new rates the commissioners first made a contract with the superintendent of police to do the job, and then found a private contractor.

One of the greatest needs of the city was a market-place. Stark had complained in 1810 that

the street from the cornhill to the butter market is, on a market day, literally choaked up with stalls and standings, to the great annoyance of passengers and inconvenience of the neighbouring housekeepers: it is indeed a nuisance which calls loudly for removal, and a grievance which it behoves the magistrates seriously and speedily to redress.

Farmers and others turned the main street into a corn market, and

notwithstanding repeated admonitions to the contrary, after sometimes being played upon by the fire-engine, will continue to stand in the main street. In consequence of which, they subject themselves to be gored by cattle and run over by carriages, passing and repassing, which cannot work their way through without much trouble and interruption.[1]

There was another point of view, which surprisingly appealed to Charlesworth:

15 September 1829. Snow has reasoned me into a belief that it is not good for Lincoln to have a market place at all. He says we are highly privileged in being without one, by which we can prevent all houseless travelling dealers from coming to rob of their custom the inhabitants of Lincoln, who purchase the perishable fruits of the earth from the neighbouring inhabitants, and have a right to receive their money in return. That the impoverishment arising to the tradesmen of Lincoln by an unnatural exchange recoils upon the country people; and that the absence of travelling traders would presently create a competition among the Lincoln traders which would bring prices nearly as low as they were before.[2]

The commissioners had no such doubts. On 1 September 1828 they addressed a memorial to the corporation representing to them the absolute necessity of some proper place being appointed as a general market-place, and warned them that the commissioners were resolved to enforce the Act by removing stalls from the streets on market days as well as other days.

The corporation did not dissent from the view that a market-place was necessary, but presently added that the cost would be so high that nothing could be done; they also thought that a total ban on street stalls during markets and fairs would be prejudicial to public and private interests. The two bodies compromised on 'judicious regulation' of the stalls by the commissioners' surveyor and by making by-laws. All sales in the street by 'auction, outcry or blast of horn' were forbidden; High Street as far south as High Bridge must be kept clear;[3] earthenware and vegetables were

---

[1] History of Lincoln, pp. 286 n., 287.　　　[2] Bromhead MSS.
[3] The fish stalls were removed from the bridge in 1830.

allotted to the east side of the corn market, agricultural implements to the south, fruit to the north, and vegetables again in front. The rules must refer to the open space known as the Cornhill. Auctions were allowed on Castle Hill. The by-laws remained valid until the building of a corn exchange in 1846 by a public company.

Many of the streets had no official names, and the commissioners set up a committee to choose them. The Bail from Castle Hill to Newport Arch was named Ermine Street; St Paul's Lane became Westgate, the lane from the present Steep Hill to the New Road, Danesgate; the New Road itself, Lindum Road; the middle lane from Bullring terrace to Silver Street, Flaxengate; Corporation Lane became Saltergate; two branches of East-gate became Greetwellgate and Langworthgate, and the lane between them St Leonard's Lane. The names were all suitable, and some were in keeping with ancient usage; and they no doubt derived from the anti-quarian knowledge of Edward James Willson, who was one of the assessors. Nevertheless they are a snare to the local historian.[1]

The assessors were hustled into completing their valuation, and the revised assessments were entered on the quarter sessions minutes on 13 September 1828; the total valuations of many parishes had increased threefold, some fourfold, over the former assessments. By April 1829 a rate of 2s. in the £, payable half-yearly, was levied. There followed a crop of pleas for relief from the rate on the ground of poverty (as was contem-plated by the Act) and some were granted.

As might be expected, the new impost produced an instant and continu-ing demand for economy. In 1834 a motion that public streets should not be swept and cleansed by the trust was only lost by 11 votes to 10; and when a labourer came forward offering to cart away dirt on Saturdays, when it was swept together, and to provide scavengers for the manure without payment, for one year, the offer was accepted. The next year a rate of 1s. was ordered. Tenders for sweeping the streets twice weekly were sought; clearly the previous experiment had failed. A new contract was made with William Scorer, farmer and publican, for £42 a year, 2s. weekly to be withheld and forfeited if the work was not properly done.

Complaints about the rate were balanced by complaints that everything was not done at once. The mud in the streets was still very bad; Waterside was a quagmire; the bridges at the lock were left in darkness. But by 1833 the *Mercury* acknowledged that there were improvements in many back streets and courts, and that the respectable were displacing the disorderly.

The burden of the main roads, and especially Lindum Road on the hillside, was felt to be considerable, and moves were made to throw them

---

[1] See *M.L.* p. 33.

upon the turnpike trust, which in its turn wished to wash its hands of the
city completely. When the trust reduced its urban commitments in 1828,
the country parishes wanted to reduce their parish compositions, but
Charlesworth pressed that these should be maintained in order to provide
a fund for the improvement of Cross Cliff Hill and the lowering of the
gradient, which was proposed in 1831. He had several comments to make
upon the doings of the new commission. He thought the moneyed interest,
concerned to keep down the rates, was trying to bully the commissioners
into tameness; and he noted that the 'under £6 houses' belonged almost
wholly to wealthy proprietors, who had forced the burden of their rates
upon the inhabitants, their tenants being likely to obtain exemption from
payment. Of course he tilted at his *bêtes noires*, the dean and chapter:

31 May 1831. The Dean arbitrarily stops every public improvement in the Close,
with the same daring defiance of opinion as in the best days of the Church. The
chapter is outrageous at Beaty for having accommodated the public by lowering
his footway, and protects Hill in withholding a similar accommodation, there is
an opportunity to widen the road without inconvenience or expense: but the
chapter is determined to act upon the contrary principle of keeping the road as
inconvenient as possible; that the public may more readily consent to their desire
of 'gating' the Close and turning the road.[1]

In 1835 the police function passed to the new corporation, but the
Lighting and Paving Commission's other functions continued into the new
era.

These new measures of administration did not include any provision for
the protection of public health, though occasional efforts were made under
fear of epidemics. Typhus fever was prevalent in 1825. In November 1831,
faced with fear of cholera, the mayor requisitioned a public meeting with a
view to forming a Board of Health and raising a subscription for it.
Charlesworth, full of enthusiasm, prophesied that the whole would end in
a general purgation, underground sewers, a Mendicity Society, and a
Dispensary Standing Board of Health. Dr Cookson called attention to the
foul state of the lodging houses of the vagrant poor, where they slept four
or five in a bed, with others on the stairs.

The Board was formed, and it issued warnings of the danger of cholera
carried by vagrants. It proposed a Mendicity Society to isolate them, and
repaired the Jersey School to receive them; and it gave flannel belts to such
of the poor as had houses certified to be properly limewashed and cleansed.
It was claimed that working-class houses had been improved. Several
cases of cholera were reported in the city in the summer of 1832. The fatal
lodging house was ordered to be cleaned, the windows barred and left

---

[1] Bromhead MSS.

open, the tenants bought out and the clothes and furniture burnt at the cost of the Board. But it had no powers, and subscriptions were not likely to be kept up after the panic had passed; and Charlesworth, bitterly disappointed, declared that the Board would continue to be only a name, for there was not an active man amongst them, though they might rise into jobbery.

The appointment of directors and guardians of the poor and lighting and paving commissioners reduced the amount of work to be done in the parishes by the parish officers, and instead it became a principal function of the vestries to elect their representatives to the new bodies. On the other hand they still had to levy their rates both for their own purposes as well as to pay their due share of the expenses of the new bodies. The burden of collection of the rate and the keeping of accounts grew as the population grew, and as it became too much for the annually elected and unpaid churchwardens and overseers, permanent paid overseers or deputies were appointed. The traditional assessments of house and shop property had long been inadequate and inequitable, and the work of revaluation became, not only greater in volume, but more difficult as properties like mills, coalyards, dissenting chapels and a billiard room came into valuation lists. This work too fell to paid experts. But the framework of parish administration remained intact for a long time, though its importance continued to decline until it vanished from the sphere of secular administration when the city was declared to be one civil parish in 1907.

CHAPTER IX

THE APPROACH OF REFORM

IN 1794, just after the outbreak of war with France, Charles Anderson Pelham, one of the members for the county, a whig who then supported the government, was created Lord Yarborough,[1] and at the resultant by-election there were the usual efforts to avoid a contest.[2] Sir Gilbert Heathcote came forward, and then withdrew in order not to disturb the peace of the county, with a hint that he would be in the field next time.[3] Robert Vyner the younger was elected unopposed.

Meanwhile, in the city, Major Hobart, one of the sitting members, and Major Rawdon, who had been defeated at the election of 1790, were distributing coal to the poor freemen each Christmas, and Rawdon was cultivating the London freemen. When therefore Cawthorn, the other sitting member, was expelled from the House,[4] Rawdon, having a long start of any newcomer, was returned unopposed. He seems to have had the support of Pitt but not the approval of Banks, for when Banks was organising the militia and ran into trouble, he wrote:

3 December 1796.... possibly the new member, whose interest among us was so warmly espoused by Mr Pit ought to do something, but he did not attend the county meeting, as I have been told, till the second day, when he came to Lincoln to attend a ball, and he is now busy in running Poney Races in Leicestershire.[5]

It was becoming evident that Richard Ellison had parliamentary ambitions. He was the third generation of Ellisons in Lincoln—his father died in 1792—and no longer a merchant, but a banker and a country gentleman, though some of the established families looked askance at his arrival in their circle. He was able, ambitious and energetic, though his speeches were commonplace and pompous; his habit of parading his own independence and honesty aroused derision, as when, opposing Fox's motion for repeal of the Treason and Sedition Bills, he invited the respectable and

---

[1] About this time Pelham, who stammered, was staying with the Vyners at Gautby, and was overheard by his aunt talking to himself: 'LLLord YYarborough bby GGGod! I think it sounds very well' (L.A.O. Anderson, 5/2/2, p. 45*b*). He was said in 1784 to want a peerage. (Namier and Brooke, *The House of Commons, 1754–90*, II, 22).

[2] Banks wrote in August that he was much occupied in labouring to keep the peace of the county (B.M. Egerton, 2641, pp. 153–154).

[3] Pitt was favourable to him. A draft letter announcing his withdrawal contained the admission that he was not of age, but this was deleted (L.A.O. 3 Ancaster, 9/4/1–8). He was born 6 October 1773, so was not of age when the vacancy occurred.

[4] Above, p. 99.　　　　　　　　　　　[5] Lindsey C. L., Banks, 3/2/1.

independent members to form a broad and firm phalanx around himself, uninfluenced by faction, and doing their duty to king, country and God.[1] In 1794 Banks wrote to him in irritation about the militia, charging him with seeking to display his abilities; to which Ellison replied that though he had parliament in view he did not look for promotion in Lincolnshire, but had a better project. Banks did later, however, assure an official of the Secretary of State's office that he would answer for Ellison's courage and discretion.[2] He was in fact seeking to represent the city and welcomed a chance of figuring in county affairs. The *Stamford Mercury* referred in glowing terms to his part at a county meeting:

His speeches were replete with good sense, sound argument, a firm and inviolable attachment to the King and Constitution; and were received with the most unbounded applause. We cannot omit this opportunity of felicitating our fellow citizens on the prospect of this gentleman's becoming a candidate to represent this city at the next general election. We wish not any longer to behold the loyal, ancient and respectable city of Lincoln, a cypher in the scale of representation, the mart of venality or the bear garden of aliens; and we are bold to say that a candidate will not be found in whom the necessary requisites of great abilities, unwearied activity, strict integrity and a firm attachment to the sound principles of our most excellent Constitution are more eminently united than in this gentleman.[3]

It is a passage that so resembles Ellison's speeches and letters that it seems likely that he was the composer; but whoever wrote it, it was well understood that his methods of procuring support would only be different from those of others in being more lavish.

A general election followed quickly upon the by-election, and in spite of efforts to find a third candidate, no other came forward, and Rawdon and Ellison were returned unopposed. The celebrations that followed included a party at Canwick on the invitation of Colonel Sibthorp, Ellison's brother-in-law. His hospitality was rewarded sooner than might have been expected, for Rawdon died in 1800, and Sibthorp, absent on service with the militia, addressed the electors:

A Stranger I am not, but one born and nursed within the walls of your ancient City—a needy and bold adventurer I am not, but of fair fortunes, fairly acquired and preserved.

Freemen in Lincoln and London tried to find another candidate; they especially disliked the idea of both their members representing the same interest, which they regarded as the corporation interest. They tried to

[1] *Parliamentary History of England*, xxxiii, cols. 631–3. He was a staunch supporter of Pitt, whom he described after his death as being without spot or blemish.
[2] Lindsey C.L., Banks, 3/1/5, 11/2/5, 7.
[3] 4 Dec. 1795.

persuade Sir Gilbert Heathcote to put forward a member of his family, but without success.[1]

Sibthorp was elected unopposed, and he invited the inhabitants to dine with him at Canwick. Provision was made for at least 2,000 people. It was not enough. A rabble seized the food, broke open the kitchen, larder and other offices, and pillaged the eatables and furniture. No doubt they were hungry: this was one of the worst years of the war.

The freemen's committee declared their firm intention to present a third man to the electors, but the sitting members had evidently discouraged such an adventure by the scale of their expenditure. Their canvass at the election of 1802 was attended by a band, flags, flambeaux and tar-tubs; the public houses were opened for three days, and the inhabitants had wine and punch without stint or fee. The *Mercury* declared after the election without a contest that 'here the freemen were all of one opinion—the gentlemen elected are neighbours, independent, connected with no party, and generous to an extreme'.[2]

When an election was called in 1806 Sibthorp retired from the contest, making reference to his decline in health and faculties, and to his limited means and numerous family; he was sore about the wilful extravagance of the last election without the shadow of an adversary. Ellison spent lavishly; the freemen resident in the villages round Lincoln did not regard him as their favourite representative without reason. Ellison stood again, and with him John Sullivan, a stranger put forward on the Hobart interest. Colonel William Monson, an Indian veteran, son of the second Lord Monson, appeared on the scene, claiming to be the third man. It appears that the fourth Lord Monson did not favour the entry of the family into the election field, and that the colonel's friend and emissary, Captain Fraser, concluded that the fight must therefore be abandoned; but he changed his view when as the candidate's representative he was received in Lincoln

with such acclamations and *Monson for ever* that I resolved on calling a meeting of his friends (not the Burton ones) previously to taking any other measures, and found them so numerous and respectable that a committee was formed and a deputation sent to meet him (he having set out for Newark at that hour) and to solicit his becoming a candidate. He entered the Town at ½ past six yesterday evening, and was met at the Bargate by upwards of a thousand of the inhabitants with torches, colors, musick &c., and the air resounding with every thing that was most flatring, the horses unharnessed and the carriage drawn in triumph through part of the Town.

The freemen were happy again, and Fraser was confident of success. Later he reported that the house of Burton began to relent, but 'neither their interest nor their support is at all necessary'.

[1] L.A.O. 3 Ancaster, 9/6/29–31.
[2] Even so, Ellison's expenses amounted to £4,042. 2s. (*L.R. & S.M.* 29 Jan. 1858).

In his election address Monson repudiated aspersions on his character, and declared himself a true Protestant, and an adherent to church, king and constitution.[1] His committee produced the song 'Monson for ever', which, after alluding unkindly to Sibthorp's retirement:

> The wearied Member's gone to bed,
> Empty purse and empty head,
> Deficient strength and failing voice,
> Then Monson honour with your choice,

invoked the new candidate's military glory:

> See him on Indostan's Plains,
> Parch'd with heat, delug'd with Rains,
> Holkar's Rebel Force subdue,
> His honor, Freemen, rests with you.

Monson and Ellison were returned, and Monson was reconciled to Burton. In writing to his wife, Monson noted that

the county election came on on Tuesday, and I have not yet learnt whether there is to be any opposition, great talk of it. They wish at Burton there may be, for they were not pleased with Mr Chaplin's conduct at my election, going plump against me.[2]

Nevertheless, Chaplin and Heathcote were elected for the county un-opposed, as they had been in 1802. There had been a threat of a contest, for Sir Robert Heron of Stubton near Newark had requisitioned the sheriff to hold a nomination meeting before the election. Banks, who was trying again to avoid a contest, wrote to Heron dismissing his claim to represent the county, adding that the promoters of his candidature

can have acted on no other principle than that of the freemen of Lincoln, who cry out at every election for a third man, and it is more than possible, Sir, that you had a view of being called upon as a third man, if not by the large bodies of freeholders who solicited you to become a candidate, at least by a complaisant troop of yeomanry whose voices, if well posted, would evidently issue from every part of the space occupied by the surrounding multitude, and might have the effect of terrifying one or other of the old members from entering into a new contest with a man whose popularity could command so extensive a vocifera-tion....

Banks warned him that if he persevered £50,000 would not cover his expense, and that his rash and inconsiderate enterprise would end in failure.[3] Heron withdrew: in 1812, after he had been returned for Grimsby, he wrote

[1] Monson, LIX, 73–4.
[2] Monson, LIX, 91. Lord Buckinghamshire and Sullivan spent a very large sum of money at the election (*H.M.C. Fortescue*, IX, 56).
[3] Hill, Banks, 1/48. Banks added that if Heron put himself forward again he would publish his letter.

that he was convinced that he could have sat for the county, but a contest was certain, and he was too ignorant of the strength of the enemy to calculate its duration or expense, and that he ought not to repent having declined it.[1]

On the death of William Pitt in January 1806 there had come into being the coalition government of 'All the Talents', which presently became involved in a clash with the king. Thinking that they had the royal consent they brought in a bill to allow Roman Catholics to hold commissions in both armed services. The king refused to consent, and they withdrew the measure. The king then demanded a written pledge that they would never press for further concessions to Catholics, which they refused to give, and resigned. A tory government was formed under the titular headship of the duke of Portland.

Thus when an election came in 1807 there was an issue of principle to discuss. Heathcote declined to stand for the county again, and it was expected that Ellison would stand along with Chaplin, in his place. On nomination day upwards of 500 horsemen assembled near Blankney in the joint interest of Chaplin and Ellison, and made a grand entry into the city. Charles Anderson Pelham, Lord Yarborough's son, had declared himself a candidate, and had arrived with a large party the night before. On the question of the hour, Chaplin was declared to have supported the king against the Catholics; Ellison's cry was 'No Popery and no wooden gods'; for Pelham it was said that the late ministry had withdrawn the Catholic Bill, and that to have supported them was no imputation.

In his speeches Ellison protested that he was not a tory or a bigot, but an independent man. He had been attached to Mr Pitt, but had opposed him time and again. Sir Robert Heron was on the scene once more. He said that he disapproved of Chaplin's tame support of every administration, and wished he would follow the dictates of his own understanding: but he much preferred him to Ellison on both political and other grounds. Ellison did not represent the landed property of the county. It was honourable to have raised himself to the high mercantile consequence of a banker; but the landed interest was the best representation. He supported Pelham.

This objection to Ellison was put into ballad form and printed by Weir, the Horncastle printer, and this would hardly have happened without Banks's approval. It was called *Tumble Down Dick*:

> With paper wings
> And such like things,
> Like Temple, fat and greasy,
> A Banker sly
> Began to fly,
> And found it mighty easy.

[1] *Notes* (2nd edn 1851), p. 4.

The final stanza ran:

> Ye Bankers all,
> Mark well his fall,
> And learn by the disaster,
> A Borough's Seat
> Is Bankers' Meat,
> A County's for his Master.

Another song, also printed by Weir, referred to old Ellison as a dealer in timber and bark. His son sent a bailiff to canvass Sir Joseph's tenants—a breach of the recognised courtesy between gentlemen—and the bailiff was criticised because, although a Methodist, he arrived on a Sunday, and did his master no good.[1]

Major Cartwright, the veteran champion of parliamentary reform, who was standing for Boston, also had his say. He advised Ellison to remain member for the city, though he was surprised to hear his city constituents described as 'loyal and independent':

I care not who is offended. A pander of corruption who some years ago had dealings with them publicly said he could sell them like swine. Many will remember that some years ago a person who answered the description and did the work of the Devil came and held a levée in the city, and that his arrival was hailed with joy. They were added to His Majesty's presence one by one; and he went away grinning with delight that he had bought all the souls he came for. This was what they were some years ago; and what are they now?

Ellison's voters of the last election had only lately, he said, had their reward; and he alleged that Ellison was a friend of the slave trade. Both charges were denied by Ellison.

The sheriff declared on the hustings that a show of hands was in favour of Chaplin and Ellison; and Pelham said that he reluctantly demanded a poll. For the first time for eighty years a poll was held, and it ended in Ellison's withdrawal. About 2,000 freeholders voted, which was not more than a fifth of the electors in the county.[2]

Ellison was however successful in the city, where he and Monson were returned unopposed. The religious question came up again in the following year, when Monson died. In his place was nominated the earl of Mexborough, Lady Monson's brother; and against him Colonel Harcourt, the king's godson, who declared his support of the tory ministry. He said he had been with the late member in battle; as to Mexborough, he supported the late government in an administration subversive of the quiet of the country, and offensive to the king. The London voters and the Sheffielders among the freemen supported Harcourt, but the countrymen were for

---

[1] Spalding Gentlemen's Society, Banks Stanhope MSS, 6/1, 6/11.
[2] The figures were: Chaplin 1,602, Pelham 1,168, Ellison 955.

Mexborough, who was successful. The expense of the election was estimated at not less than £20,000. Aftewards the usual 'compliment' money
was paid to the Mexborough voters, but it was carefully explained that the
money came, not from the new member, but from Lady Monson's private
purse. Harcourt went off leaving some of his debts unpaid.[1]

When the next election came in 1812 Ellison was in the field again, and
John Nicholas Fazackerley was nominated by the Monsons in place of
Mexborough. He is described by Greville as a sensible man and a moderate
whig, and he was often at Holland House; Sydney Smith said that nobody
was more agreeable to him than Fazackerley.[2] The Hobart interest was
also active. The Major Hobart of Nocton who had represented the city in
1790 had since been Governor of Madras and Secretary of State for War
and the Colonies; he had been an adherent of Addington, and, with him,
Fox and the whigs, in the coalition ministry of 1806. He succeeded his
father as fourth earl of Buckinghamshire in 1804. Ellison unexpectedly
withdrew after his committee had begun work; his reasons were declared
by them to be sufficient, but they were not disclosed. There is a hint that
the reasons were financial in a letter from Francis Bernard Morland, who
had been sent down to Lincoln with two brothers by his father, Scrope
Bernard (who had taken the additional name of Morland), son of Sir
Francis, to take up their freedom, and vote:

Lady Monson's party with Mr Fazackerley the candidate and three or four of
Tom's schoolfellows were ushered into the White Hart by one of the Common
Council, entered our room, and asked for our votes; we told them we had
proffered them to Lord Bucks (tho he did not intend to try his interest against
Colonel Ellison whose friends were canvassing about the same time). Shortly
after, Osbaldeston and two or three others were mentioned as candidates, but
he was solicited by Lord Fitzwilliam to stand for Retford on the Monday. We
heard that in consequence of Colonel Ellison neither wishing to stand nor to
pay the expenses Mr Hobart had introduced Mr Ellis as proxy for Sir Henry
Sullivan, who is in Spain, in Colonel Ellison's room.[3]

There were thus two candidates only, nominated by the Monsons and the
Hobarts. The circumstances of the election were described afterwards by
Oldfield:

These noblemen nominated at the last general election in 1812. The expense of
a contest is estimated at twelve thousand pounds to each party. This arises from
the number of non-resident freemen, who are to be collected from all parts of the
kingdom by the candidates and their agents: from the sums given to the voters,

[1] He died in 1815 a major-general. Under a Chancery decree creditors were called
on to prove debts, which the *Mercury* said would be pleasant to many citizens.
[2] *Letters of Sydney Smith*, ed. Nowell C. Smith (1953), p. 565.
[3] Mrs Napier Higgins, *The Bernards of Abington and Nether Winchendon*, IV (1904), 173.

which vary according to circumstances; and the enormous demands for ribbons and treating. The dread of incurring these expenses left the electors with only one candidate at the last general election in 1812. The friends of the Earl of Buckinghamshire were fearful of naming their man till the morning of the election, when they proposed a gentleman who was abroad on military service in Spain, who was totally unknown to the people, and unconnected with the place. It is generally understood that if any independent candidate could have been found, he would have been chosen without opposition, but expresses were sent off to several gentlemen, and no one could be prevailed on to encounter the danger, in consequence of which the nominees of the two noble families were returned.[1]

The unknown gentleman, Sir Henry Sullivan, who had also been returned for Rye but chose Lincoln, visited the city soon after his election. In 1814, in one of the last actions of the long war with France, he was killed at Bayonne in a sortie of the French garrison. His brother Charles, then serving in the navy on the American station, was expected to stand in his place. But the freemen revolted against another stranger, and sent a requisition to Richard Ellison to stand again. He replied that he would do so if he could vacate his seat—he had been returned for Wootton Bassett—in time; as he could not, he commended his nephew Colonel Coningsby Waldo Sibthorp. The friends of Sullivan declined to proceed, and Sibthorp was returned unopposed.

By the end of 1817 the freemen were seeking a candidate again, and a London alderman was approached, though he declined the honour. Fazackerley withdrew; he was standing for Grimsby. In his stead the Monson interest produced Robert Smith, brother of the famous whig clerical wit, Sydney Smith, and the 'Bobus' of his letters. Robert's marriage had made him a connection of Lord Lansdowne, through whom he became Advocate General of Bengal. He returned to England in 1811, and became member for Grantham. Sir William Manners, on whose interest he sat, had been told he was to be a second Pitt.[2] He was a friend of Canning, though not an avowed Ministerialist. When Canning died he might have joined the government, but preferred to act on his own views of each particular matter.[3]

Sibthorp stood again, and at the request of the London freemen, organised by a jobber in seats named Stanbury, there appeared as third man Ralph Bernal, a barrister of the Court of Chancery and a complete stranger. The contest was one of the closest ever known, with one of the highest polls. Sibthorp headed it, followed by Bernal, who defeated Smith

[1] Oldfield, *Representative History of Great Britain and Ireland* (1816), IV, 133.
[2] L.A.O. 3 Ancaster, 9/7/1.
[3] *Transactions of Royal Historical Society*, 4th series, XVII, 179. His brother Sydney once said to him: 'Brother, you and I are exceptions to the laws of nature. You have risen by your gravity, and I have sunk by my levity.'

by the aid of the London freemen.[1] The horror and shame felt at this result had a dramatic effect at the next election.

In the county Chaplin and Pelham continued to sit without opposition until the death of Charles Chaplin in 1816.[2] His son declined to stand; Heron would have liked to do so, but he was member for Grimsby and could not vacate his seat in time, and Lord Brownlow's brother William Cust was elected without a contest, and, said Heron, 'with every possible mark of disapprobation'.[3]

When the general election came in 1818 Charles Chaplin, son of the late member, angrily charged Lord Brownlow with procuring his nomination as high sheriff, in the interest of his brother William Cust, to prevent his becoming a candidate; but the quarrel was settled, Cust withdrew, and Chaplin came forward. Pelham was standing again, and Heron, who had long wanted to stand, did so at last. Sir Charles Anderson noted that Pelham's speech differed very little from Chaplin's, so mild were whig politics in that day. He added 'Heron was called a radical. He was a conceited fellow without much in him. After the election we (Pelhamites) all went to the Minster on Sunday with purple favours.'[4] After a contest of nine days Heron was left at the bottom of the poll, attributing his defeat to not having paid agents.[5] Pelham and Chaplin were returned.

A vivid memory of a county election of the time, with the freeholders converging on Lincoln—the only voting place—from all parts of the county, has been preserved:

A county election was a very different affair to what it is now. It was a grand sight, such as I shall never witness again, to see the fine tenantry of those men of broad acres, such as Chaplin, of Blankney; Pelham, of Brocklesby; and many others of that class, ascend the steep hill at Lincoln like cavalry regiments, and enter the old Castle Yard to tender their votes at the polling booth. It was an imposing and a magnificent sight to behold these robust, healthy, ruddy-faced men mounted on fine horses, three abreast, men and horses decked with a profusion of ribbons of different colours denoting the candidate these men supported. Every evening there would be bands of music, lighted flambeaux and

---

[1] The voting was: Sibthorp 742, Bernal 733, Smith 596.

[2] C. A. Pelham wrote (10 April 1812): 'We have been lucky this time, my Father having carried two members at Grimsby, kept one at Beverley and no opposition for this county' (L.A.O. Bradford, 2/5/9).

[3] *Notes* (2nd edn 1851), p. 75.   [4] L.A.O. Anderson, 5/2/2, p. 44 *b*.

[5] In 1819 Lord Fitzwilliam returned Heron for Peterborough, which he represented until 1847, though he continued to play a part in county affairs. He was chairman of the Newark Guardians until shortly before his death in 1854. The *Quarterly Review*, in a review of the second edition of Heron's *Notes* in 1851, said that 'he has been a somewhat obscure, though, it appears, abundantly zealous and superabundantly rancorous member of that Whig opposition which had so long, so factiously and—luckily for the country—so fruitlessly arrayed themselves against the principles of Mr Pitt...' (xc, 206).

burning tar barrels; the occasion being still more enlivened by the ringing cries in every direction of 'Chaplin for ever!' 'Pelham for ever!' 'Heron for ever!'. . .

I was permitted, now and then, to attend a county meeting in the old City Castle Yard. These meetings were not much less exciting than a contested election. They were convened to discuss some public question of the day, and the leading men who took a part in them were supported by a large retinue of adherents. It was on such occasions the peasantry indulged in rustic wit and humour, and would tell a bit of their minds to the great men of the county, which they dared not venture to do except on these occasions. More than fifty years have passed away since I attended one of these county meetings, yet I have a very vivid recollection of some of the leading men that took part in them, notably that veteran—Major Cartwright, who at that time was styled 'The father of Reform'. There was also 'Charley Chaplin', who, although not a great orator, was a fine handsome man and every inch a country squire; Sir Charles Anderson Pelham, as plain in person and dress as the plainest of his tenants; Sir Robert Heron, with his thin Saturnine face and Roman cast of countenance. These men were celebrities in their day. They have long passed away, but their names live in the history of the county.[1]

Before the city election of 1820 Mr Bernal's friends among the Lincoln freemen met again, but there was a demurrer about renewal of support for him, as some complained that they had not been *complimented* in the same way as Sibthorp's voters some time before. The London freemen, again marshalled by the jobber Stanbury, who had changed his client, announced that Mr E. D. Davenport, a gentleman of independent means, had declared himself third man. Bernal withdrew; he was standing for Rochester. A meeting was held at the Royal Oak, at which Stanbury took the chair. It was solemnly resolved that Davenport having presented himself before Bernal had retired, Davenport was in fact, as the Londoners had said, the third man; and thanks were voted to over a hundred freemen who had promised their support to him. This piece of jugglery provoked a storm of indignation. The *Mercury* boldly described Stanbury as a sort of broker for seats, or agent between those voters for cities and open boroughs who resided in London, and such parliamentary adventurers as might choose to risk a few thousands upon a trial of the strength of that species of miscalled 'Independent Interest'. It was thought that the Burton hunt might produce a candidate, but as the day of election approached, and no other candidate offered, the respectable part of the freemen began to feel that disgrace awaited them in the open sale of a seat to the jobber's nominee. Conversations led to a meeting at the Reindeer, at which it was determined to try to arouse the spirit of the city. A public appeal was issued:

Surely, the City of Lincoln, which for many years stood distinguished for the respectability of its Members, will not stoop to the degrading situation of

[1] Joseph Pacy, *Reminiscences of a Gauger* (Newark, 1873), pp. 21–4.

becoming an object of traffic with mere mercenary Borough Factors—Surely, this ancient and loyal City, which was represented for ages by its Monsons, its Saviles, its Hobarts, its Vyners, and its Sibthorps, will not allow itself to be sold by a contemptible Dealer in Seats to the highest bidder among his Parliamentary Adventurers.

There followed a proposal to nominate Robert Smith again, in his absence and free of expense to himself. Sibthorp and Smith were elected, leaving Davenport far behind.[1]

Davenport, the victim of the jobber, lost no time in denouncing him: he had 'deceived and abandoned both his friends and me'. Smith was later entertained by his supporters at the Reindeer. He declared that their aim had been to assert the right of the great majority of the electors against mercenary jobbing. The freemen residing in and around Lincoln were four-fifths of the electors, and they ought to have the greatest weight. Power ought not to be abandoned to a small club of men meeting at a porter-house in London, enlisting themselves under the banner of a common jobber, and ready to receive from him anybody whom he might recommend as the best bidder for the representation of the city.

Smith meant precisely what he said. He was certainly not preaching democracy, and he was not even urging parliamentary reform; and after the election his supporters received the usual reward for *past* services. But the disgust aroused among the citizens at the jobbery and corruption of the system must have given impetus to a feeling in favour of reform.

In the county Pelham and Chaplin were returned unopposed. They entertained over 1,000 people at the White Hart, and no fewer than 2,000 bottles of wine were consumed.

The chief themes of public discussion in the years after the death of George III in 1820 were, according to Croker, corn, currency and Catholics: to these must be added, for a few years, the relations of the new king George IV with his queen Caroline. Broadly speaking the whigs and the 'lower orders' sided with the queen, and the tories and churchmen supported the king. A public meeting was requisitioned, and called under protest by the mayor, at which a petition in favour of the queen was carried by the 'Low-City Party'. As Colonel Sibthorp declined to present it, it was sent off to Robert Smith, the other member; it seems he also declined, and it was presented by Mr Bernal. The petition also called for parliamentary reform, a subject which Smith said he approached with apprehension rather than hope. Another meeting to carry a counter address to the king,

---

[1] The votes were: Sibthorp 748, Smith 523, Davenport 263. The list of subscribers to Smith's fund is impressive: it includes Charlesworth, Richard Mason, three aldermen and William Bedford, the leader of the dissenters, who were coming to the fore.

led by Sibthorp and Dean Gordon, miscarried, for a hostile amendment was passed by a large majority. During the queen's 'trial' there were parades of the 'lower orders' in the streets with torches and tar-barrels and 'transparencies'; and when news of the defeat of the bill against the queen arrived it put the mob in high good humour, and 300 special constables sworn in for the occasion were not needed. The precautions were, however, justified, for a day or two before several of the clergy and 'Foxhunter Smith' of the Burton hunt had their windows broken. In the following year the coronation celebrations in Lincoln were marred by the mob, and the streets were cleared by the troops. These must have been among the first political demonstrations in Lincoln other than at election times, and they proved to be rehearsals for the great reform struggle soon to begin.

Coningsby Sibthorp, one of the city members, died in 1822 from the results of an accident caused by the removal of a lynch-pin from the wheel of his carriage. It so happened that the day after his death Mr Denman, a learned counsel on the Midland Circuit who was solicitor-general to the queen and associated with Brougham in her defence, arrived at Lincoln for the assizes. He at once sent off to John Williams, who had been one of his juniors at the trial, to come to Lincoln, and procured his nomination. Williams declared himself in favour of reform and retrenchment. The tories approached the late member's brother Captain Charles Sibthorp, who declined, and then their uncle Richard Ellison, but the latter was too much depressed by his nephew's death. Williams was therefore returned unopposed.[1]

Reform was coming to the fore.[2] A great county meeting in 1822 carried a petition, couched in strong language, with hardly any opposition. When

[1] Williams afterwards became a judge of the Queen's Bench, looking, according to Sir J. Arnould, like Punch in ermine (*Memoir of Lord Denman* (1873), II, 18). Denman wrote (I, 197) that he had secured Williams's return at a very moderate expense. Denman had much local influence: he was a Nottinghamshire man, and had sat for Newark and Nottingham; he married a niece of the Rev. Sir Charles Anderson, the squire-parson of Lea, who was the father of the Anderson so much quoted in these pages.

[2] The reform movement received considerable stimulus from events at Stamford. In 1809, at a by-election there, Lord Exeter's nominee, Charles Chaplin, was opposed by Joshua Jepson Oddy, a Russia merchant and writer on political economy, who told the electors that in matters of opinion they were in a state of slavery worse than the inhabitants of a West India plantation. In that year John Drakard started his weekly *Stamford News*; and in 1810 he published an article denouncing flogging in the army. Leigh Hunt and his brother reprinted part of it in the *Examiner*. Both the Hunts and Drakard were prosecuted for seditious libel, and defended by Henry Brougham. The Hunts were acquitted by a Middlesex jury in spite of a hostile summing up by Lord Ellenborough, but Drakard was convicted by the Lincolnshire jury, which had been packed with special jurors, and he was sentenced to 18 months' imprisonment in Lincoln castle, and fined £200. He paid himself a handsome tribute in his *History of Stamford*, printed in 1822. In his later years he was provided with a home by Sir William Ingilby at Ripley.

it was presented to the House by Pelham he made clear his reason for support. It was not a democratic one. He thought that the landed interest was not duly represented in the House, and it would gain by the abolition of rotten boroughs. In supporting him Heron referred to the most severe and menacing distress in agricultural districts, and said that reform gave the only hope of relief in taxation. Another meeting in 1823 seems not to have been so successful, though the resolution was carried against a radical amendment of the veteran Cartwright.[1]

Pelham and Chaplin had continued to hold the two county seats, until the death of Lord Yarborough in 1823 removed Pelham to the Upper House as second baron. He was the leader of the whigs in the county.[2] After an unsuccessful approach to Sir Gilbert Heathcote's son there came forward as a candidate for the county Sir William Amcotts Ingilby, a Yorkshire baronet who had inherited Kettlethorpe from his mother. Ingilby wrote at the time that it had been decided by his friends at Brocklesby that he was to fight the county against Heron as Heathcote had declined.[3] The tory candidate proved to be Sir John Thorold, whom Ingilby defeated after a poll lasting ten days. Charlesworth said that the election was kept going unnecessarily long at Ingilby's expense, all for the honour of the House of Brocklesby.[4] Ingilby was to prove too radical for many of his supporters, especially the clergy, whom he was to attack with vigour, and the loss of support from Brocklesby and elsewhere was eventually to cost him his seat, but all this lay in the future: at this contest his sister complained of his treatment by the radical jacobins.[5]

About this time an agitation against the corn laws was alarming the

---

[1] The *Mercury* printed a rhyme which began:
> 'Three thousand souls flock'd to see three rascals hang,
> While scarcely three hundred heard Heron's harangue.'

Cartwright thought he had not been well treated by Heron, and wrote him a letter which is printed in F. D. Cartwright, *Life and Correspondence of Major Cartwright* (1826), II, 395.

[2] Yarborough had a survey made by a local lawyer of the electoral position in the county. The survey paid special attention to the parts of Holland, which, owing to the extensive fen drainage of the war years, contained a large number of freeholders not subject to any territorial influence, whose support would be especially important if the tories tried to return two members. It was thought that the estimate of 12,000 freeholders in the county was near the truth, and that there were at least 1,000 freeholders who had not been entered in the land tax returns—the test of eligibility to vote—and who were not very anxious that they should be (L.P.L. 'A List of the Freeholders of the County of Lincoln with explanatory remarks etc. 1825. By J. G. Stapylton Smith').

[3] L.A.O. 3 Ancaster, 9/4, 9/7/22.

[4] Bromhead MSS. The majority was certainly decisive: Ingilby 3,316, Thorold 1,575.

[5] L.A.O. Massingberd, 1/12. Anderson declared that Ingilby had been a professed tory, and was brought in as an intended warming pan for young Pelham. He presented Colonel Sibthorp's brother Humphrey to the rectory of Washingborough. Ingilby and two of the Sibthorps and Charles Tennyson were all at Louth School.

agricultural districts. A Lincoln meeting declared that landowners and occupiers had only just emerged from the ruinous embarrassments lately overwhelming the agricultural interest; rents had that spring been fixed on the faith of the corn laws, and the very agitation for change had already paralysed the sale of produce. A county meeting followed suit.

On the surface the issues at the general election of 1826 were different. No candidate would have had the temerity in an agricultural county to denounce the corn laws. In the city, Williams and Smith, the retiring members, both withdrew, and Fazackerley reappeared in the Monson interest. Colonel Charles de Laet Waldo Sibthorp, who was a brother of the former member, had served in the peninsular war, and on retirement from the army became a colonel of militia, and was destined to become famous in his own odd way, came forward in effect as a tory, being opposed to Catholic emancipation and parliamentary reform, though he never owned to a party label. A third man was promised who proved to be Thomas George Corbett of Elsham Hall near Brigg: he stood for religious toleration and political freedom. He had the support of the Heneages and the young Charles Tennyson. Fazackerley headed the poll, and Sibthorp secured the second seat.[1] According to Sir Charles Anderson, Sibthorp was very angry at not being at the top of the poll, which he said was his birthright; he did his utmost to get there, being aided by huge shoals of Reverends and Right Reverends, who enlisted under his banners on account of the Catholic question.[2]

Corbett was a portent. The Monsons, the reds, and the Sibthorps, the pinks, were both parts of the old landed interest, one being whig and the other vaguely tory; but now there was emerging against them a generation of whigs who were moderate reformers. Dr Charlesworth, who supported this new interest, wrote:

13 June 1826. The next contest will be a very severe one: Mr Corbett lost this time *only* by coming too late: he has gained the personal respect of all persons of all parties: he is determined to try again: one of the neighbouring interests will then be thrown out: all the powers of darkness will be moved to ward off this blow from Canwick: if Burton be not tenanted in the meanwhile, the blow *must* fall there. We have come off with great credit this time for fair and manly conduct in our canvass and polling: for half the atrocities and littlenesses which the pinks committed *we* should have been characterised diabolical and infamous.[3]

---

[1] The voting was: Fazackerley 806, Sibthorp 797, Corbett 612.

[2] Wilberforce MSS. Charlesworth wrote that if Sibthorp had not come forward Goderich (as to whom see p. 276) would have sent a man. In the course of the contest Sibthorp was struck by a stone. At a hearing before the magistrates the accused was defended by Charles Tennyson: it emerged that he was committed on a blank warrant without any previous examination, for which irregularity the town clerk admitted responsibility (L.P.L. Sibthorp MSS).   [3] Bromhead MSS.

He was right about the Monson decline, due not only to a long minority following the death of the fourth Lord Monson in 1809 at the age of 24. They had deprived the citizens of the long-enjoyed pleasure of rook-shooting at Burton, and they had built a wall to separate the park from the highway; and there were added complaints of rough treatment of a farm tenant. It was said that their nominee Fazackerley had dead rooks in various stages of decomposition hurled at him during the election contest, and, although he was successful, the Burton interest did not recover.[1]

Talk about the Corn Laws was still making the agriculturalists' flesh creep, and petitions against their amendment were presented in both Houses. Lord Yarborough presented one from the mayor and corporation and about 700 resident tradesmen of Lincoln: he moved that it be read to show that it was not the agriculturist alone who was interested, for when corn was low the city trade suffered in proportion. He said that at that moment (1827) foreign wheat could be bought at Hull under 22*s*. a quarter, and it was natural to suppose that the merchants would wait until the price reached 65*s*.; upon payment of a trifling duty they had it in their power to flood the market with foreign grain, and this would lower the price to 55*s*. in the following week, and perhaps in a fortnight to 50*s*. Such fluctuating prices were the ruin of the landowners.

During Canning's ministry, Huskisson sought to amend the Corn Law, but failed, and a sliding scale was enacted under Wellington's government in 1828. The local outcry continued, and the wool-growers joined in by offering to relinquish their power to export wool if they might be protected against foreign wool. There were loud outcries of distress in 1830, and there was much unemployment. City and county petitions against the malt tax, which affected the price of barley, were presented, declaring that excessive taxation, including tithe, was weighing the country down.

As the election of 1830 approached Fazackerley announced his withdrawal, and there was a general impression that the young Lord Monson would not offer another nominee: it was even rumoured that his views were not the whig views hitherto held at Burton. Nevertheless Monson's uncle Lord Mexborough emerged. Sibthorp was in the field—none could kiss the girls better than he[2]—and both made an approach to the London freemen. The latter had also been in touch with Charles Tennyson. They liked him, but the Lincoln voters did not, for they disapproved of his reformist views; as M.P. for Grimsby he had come latterly into prominence by moving to transfer the seats for East Retford, disfranchised for corruption,

---

[1] In the election squibs Fazackerley was described as a crow, and Sibthorp as an ape or chimpanzee, a personal allusion.

[2] L.A.O. Massingberd, 1/50.

to Birmingham. Reformist views were a serious handicap in an election on the old franchise. Tennyson, having visited Lincoln, therefore abandoned the idea of standing, and pressed young Gilbert Heathcote to meet the London freemen's committee at the Bell at Smithfield. Heathcote missed his chance.[1]

Mexborough withdrew, paying for single votes promised him £2, and for plumpers £4. Charlesworth had written in 1828 that the red interest was terribly down, 'much below Sibthorp's, with all his faults. He has continued to get the popular cry in his favor, by coming down from London once or twice to be reconciled to Mrs Sibthorp, who refuses'.[2] An incident at Monson's coming of age celebrations had been used against Mexborough. When a roasted ox was distributed, some of it had been spoiled for eating, and, as the *Mercury* acidly commented, those who took a money dole in February cried stinking beef in July.

The Lincoln reform committee, headed by Mr Bedford the dissenter, without a candidate, persuaded a pleasant nonentity, John Fardell, to stand; he was believed to be a reformer. Charlesworth wrote that 'Jacky suffered himself to be dragged down in his carriage to do "third man" for the Blue committee, driven to their wits end for somebody to pay the expenses they had incurred'.[3]

There was in fact no third man, and Sibthorp and Fardell were returned unopposed. Anderson summed up the result:

9 August 1830. The Monson interest is gone for ever at Lincoln. His uncle Lord Mexboro' canvassed, but so unsuccessfully that he gave up without coming to a poll, so the Lincolners have been disappointed in not having a contest as they wished. Jacky Fardell the new Member is son to the late Registrar of the Dean and Chapter, a good natured man who will be sufficiently happy in franking letters at the old Dame's *routs* in the Minster Yard.[4]

Sibthorp was asked to contest the county, but declined. He had no higher ambition than to represent the city; from that height, he said, he could just as well look down on ministers, and watch with regret their apathy and rapacity.[5] There was a fine impartiality about his denunciations of all in authority.

[1] L.A.O. Ancaster, XIII, B/5 *bb*, 5 *cc*, 5 *dd*, 5 *ff*.

[2] Bromhead MSS. Mrs Sibthorp obtained a separation from her husband in an undefended suit in 1828.

[3] Bromhead MSS. Earlier, Charlesworth had written: 'I know Fardell well, and have kept him out of mischief hitherto (at the Asylum). I humour him in little points: his mind cannot grasp a large one, which saves me much trouble.'

[4] Wilberforce MSS.

[5] Benjamin Bromhead said that as Sibthorp had been avoided by the country gentlemen he had made common cause with the city and the agricultural interest, and thence drew his companions.

That November Lord Grey formed his whig government, and rising excitement found expression in meetings about slavery, the ballot, economy and reform, and they were not prevented by the prevailing dread of cholera. There was a spate of local newspapers on behalf of each of the contending parties. On 1 March 1831 the Reform Bill was introduced in the Commons. It would have disfranchised the freemen and given the vote to £10 householders, and Sibthorp claimed that it would reduce the number of eligible voters in Lincoln to 434 (1,233 had voted before). His figures were disputed, but certainly the electorate would have been reduced. On 23 March the bill passed its second reading by one vote. Charlesworth reported to Bromhead:

24 March 1831. I suppose when you heard the bells of St Peter at Arches ringing so merrily this morning, you would be surprised to learn that it was for the majority of *one* upon the question of reform in the House of Commons. Beaty set the clappers going. Both Sibthorp and Fardell were in the minority.... Already the blues anticipate a coalition with the reds to turn out the sitting members. Fazackerley is the man the reformers have fixed upon. (I personally dislike him, but will work for him politically.) The reds are in a buzz, laying heads together. They have condemned (and executed in anticipation) Sibthorp and Fardell, who are no doubt the beau ideals of the London voters, to whom, and their own *real* party, they have sold themselves.[1]

The blues were the reformers, the reds the whig or Monson party; the pink or Sibthorp party and Fardell had accepted the tory label by voting against the bill. Mrs Massingberd wrote that the Lincoln people were all radicals, and had hung Sibthorp in chains and beheaded Fardell for voting against the bill.[2] Fardell had said he had been converted to opposition to it on the spot by the speech of 'Sir Edward somebody'.[3]

The king dissolved parliament, and Charles Tennyson again pressed Heathcote to stand for Lincoln:

I think Fardell and Sibthorp will meet with a rough reception—indeed I should think Fardell will scarcely make another attempt. There is a large body of outvoters who may not like a reformer, but they will vote for *any third man*.[4]

Heathcote did not come forward, in spite of an application from the local reformers, and Fardell withdrew, saying that the bill went too far. The electoral committee—the reformers—secured George Heneage from the Whig Club, and sent for Fazackerley, but he was secure at Peterborough. General Hall was sent down by the Treasury, carried out a canvass, and withdrew. Sibthorp, who was refused a hearing by the mob, declared that he believed in reform of a safe and salutary kind, but he would not

---

[1] Bromhead MSS.　　　　　　　　[2] L.A.O. Massingberd, 1/10.
[3] Bromhead MSS.　　　　　　　　[4] L.A.O. Ancaster, xiii, B/6c, 6d.

rob the poor man—meaning the poor freeman who was not a £10 house-holder—of his right. He secured so many promises that no third candidate could be found, and Sibthorp and Heneage were returned unopposed.

In the county Ingilby did most of the campaigning. Anderson described him as an *ultra*: he had had Cobbett at Ripley Castle, his Yorkshire seat. He was both violent and whimsical in his speeches, inveighing against place-holders, the squirearchy and especially the clergy, whom he de-scribed as 'the sable gentry'. As a second reform candidate Lord Yar-borough brought forward his son Charles Pelham, who had sat for Newport, one of the four boroughs in the Isle of Wight which his father had sold to the government for £4,000. Pelham was a moderate whig, and opposed to the ballot, which Ingilby supported. He observed the convention which forbade a candidate to canvass tenants without first obtaining the consent of their landlords, and when he made such an application to Lord Brownlow and was refused, he preferred to rely on public opinion to prevent landlords from abusing their power rather than break the convention. The young Lord Monson took no part in the election, and left his tenants to vote as they thought fit.[1] The tory candidate Charles Chaplin, fearing a costly contest, withdrew, and Ingilby and Pelham were elected without opposition.

The government introduced a second Reform Bill, and Lord Chandos got the credit for an amendment which had originally been moved by Sibthorp, extending the vote to £50 tenants-at-will in counties: the radicals accepted it on principle, the tories because of the influence the landlords would have on such voters. The struggle continued until a third bill was carried into law in June 1832.

When the victorious reformers celebrated at the City Arms hotel (formerly the Reindeer), and welcomed Ingilby, who was their especial hero, there were loud denunciations of notorious boroughmongers, base apostates, truckling whigs, and, above all, a wicked hierarchy. Anderson commented that his private hope was that they would kick Ingilby out for ever next time. He had abused the Church in a speech to the mob, and that could have been for no good reason but to gain a little popular applause.[2]

---

[1] He was one of the twenty-two diehard peers who voted against the third reading of the Reform Bill. He was small and childish in appearance, and is depicted as a boy minstrel attending on Queen Adelaide, who was the patroness of the opposition, in a caricature of 1832 (*B.M. Catalogue of Political and Personal Satires*, XI, no. 16957). The sixth lord wrote of him that he was D.C.L. at Oxford at the installation of the Duke of Wellington. 'He was a great patron of the fine arts, and brought many valuable pictures marbles &c. from the continent. He purchased Gatton, but alas! sold and spent the proceeds of more than half the Lincolnshire property' (Ross Corr. v, 11 Sept. 1862).

[2] Wilberforce MSS.

The non-resident freemen had vanished from the political scene, leaving the city franchise in the resident freemen (who had been reprieved) and the £10 householders. Sibthorp lost his seat at the ensuing election, but he recovered it in 1835; his greatest days lay in the future.[1]

[1] Charlesworth said that Sibthorp talked incessantly. The mayor of Lincoln called on him after dinner, and Sibthorp was called away to receive him. 'I daresay it is my friend the Mayor of Lincoln—I'll *ride* him in. Gentlemen, I have the pleasure of introducing the Mayor of Lincoln. Mr Mayor, your good health &c. Gentlemen, you have done yourselves the honour to drink my health individually, for which I have the honour to thank you collectively, and to drink your good healths. Rum drum a drum drum!' On another occasion Charlesworth said he talked oceans of nonsense, and got very drunk.

CHAPTER X

LATTER DAYS OF THE OLD CORPORATION

THE civic constitution was founded in custom evolved through the Middle Ages,[1] with small help from statute or charter; during the sixteenth century, a period of decay, it changed little, and it was amended and for the first time formally defined in its details by the charter of Charles I in 1628.[2] Thereafter, except during the brief years when the charter of Charles II was in operation, it remained unchanged until the Municipal Reform Bill. The town clerk, writing in 1784[3] and the Municipal Commissioners, reporting in 1835, testified that the governing charter of Charles I had been scrupulously observed. Through the legislative, economic, political and social changes of the eighteenth century it remained the same, and there was neither the local means nor the inclination to alter it. Judged by the modern concept of democratic local government it became, as the years went on, increasingly absurd and out of touch with reality: but it was not so judged. It is remarkable that there was no demand for its amendment, and even after the repeal of the Test and Corporation Acts, which had imposed religious tests, in 1829, and the passing of the Reform Bill in 1832, there was no great enthusiasm for impending municipal reform.

In essence the civic constitution still enshrined the medieval conception of a protected and self-regulated community. Royal charters had secured to it rights which had been dearly paid for and must therefore be carefully defended. Admission to citizenship was gained only by defined channels: a man born the son of a freeman was entitled by patrimony; or a man who had served a seven-years' apprenticeship duly enrolled, to a freeman; a man who had bought admission at a price fixed by the corporate body, or who was given it freely for reasons of public policy. No woman could become 'free' or transmit the freedom of her father to her husband. Once admitted, the new member of the commonalty was eligible to participate in several privileges and property rights. He might vote at elections for the two burgesses in parliament for the city, he might be admitted to civic office and dignity, he might obtain leases of corporate property at ancient rents which, with the fall in the value of money, had become nominal, he might enjoy larger rights of common than other householders and inhabitants, and he might on proof of need benefit from various city charities. There were imposts such as tolls from which he became exempt. Residents

---

[1] *M.L.* chapter XIV.   [2] *T. & S.L.* p. 120.
[3] Samuel Lyon's MS account of the charters.

who were not members of this privileged class might grow, as they did, in numbers and wealth, they might become leaders in church or chapel or in social assemblies, they might serve parish offices and break into the freemen's monopoly of the crafts, but they were not citizens in the full sense, 'free' of the city. In the eyes of the corporate body they were foreigners. The distinction could not go on for ever; and when once it was established that money would buy admission to the freedom as a matter of course, it could only be a matter of time before the entrance fee was abolished.

In an older static society the rigidity of the constitution had had some advantages. It left little scope for disputes and, in a depressed and declining community such as Lincoln was in the seventeenth century, civic life could continue to run in a well-worn groove with a minimum of energy. The mayor and aldermen in particular were a civic aristocracy, which was valued for its influence and social distinction, and it provided an incentive to ambition.[1]

A young freeman could always hope to move by successive steps to the mayoralty. Every year the mayor chose four young men 'of the better sort'—they must be acceptable to his worship—to be chamberlains. Each of them was assigned to a ward. Acting chiefly by deputy—the town crier or other officer—they paid expenses arising within their wards, erected fences, killed moles on the commons, provided a town bull, mended conduits and bridges, and paid such wages and other outgoings as by custom were charged to their ward accounts. They received rents from the corporate lands within their own wards, and accounted, when the mayor accounted, to the incoming mayor at Michaelmas. Having served the office of chamberlain, they were eligible for the shrievalty. There were two sheriffs each year, as there had been since the charter of Henry IV made the city a county of itself: one was chosen by the mayor; as to the other, the mayor and those aldermen who had passed the chair presented to the common council a calendar of five ex-chamberlains, and from them the mayor, aldermen and common councilmen chose one to be sheriff. A freeman who had served either office of sheriff or chamberlain was eligible for election to the common council. When there was a vacancy the mayor and those aldermen who passed the chair presented a calendar of three from whom the common councilmen chose one. He held office for life. Seniority was the general rule.

The common councilmen, who varied from 40 to 45 in number, were the outer body, greatly inferior in dignity to the mayor and aldermen, who were the inner council. When there was a vacancy among the aldermen

---

[1] As was remarked by an observer a generation after 1835 (Edward Peacock, *Ralph Skirlaugh, The Lincolnshire Squire* (1870), III, 103).

(twelve in number), the mayor and aldermen prepared a calendar of three common councilmen, from whom the common councilmen chose one. He was elected by ballot,[1] and he too held office for life.

In accordance with Charles I's charter the senior alderman who had not held the office was always chosen mayor. On Holy Cross Day (14 September) the aldermen with the town clerk, assembled in the inner hall, made the election and entered it in the minute book; then after the bell had rung three times they entered the outer hall. There the minute of the election was read to the common council, who nodded their assent. The new mayor took office on Michaelmas Day (29 September). The events of the civic year were prescribed by custom, and the mayor went through the courts leet and quarter sessions and other occasions as his predecessors had from ancient time.[2]

The mayor and those aldermen who had passed the chair were the justices of the peace for the city; and the steady increase in the duties laid by parliament on magistrates tended to exalt the aldermanic bench at the expense of the outer council. They supervised the administration of the poor law and the highways by the parishes; they had jurisdiction in apprenticeship, fixed a scale of wages in husbandry, dealt with weights and measures and nuisances, alehouse licences, market offences and a host of other matters. In quarter sessions with the recorder (appointed by the council) they dealt with all but the gravest crimes. They controlled the city gaol and the house of correction. A ducking stool had once been at their disposal, but although a new one was proposed in 1809 the proposal was not acted upon; but the whipping post was in frequent use, and public or private whipping as a punishment had the advantage of being cheaper than imprisonment.

As a result of parliamentary legislation some of the duties which the medieval common council would have discharged had passed to the parishes. The poor law grew by stages from voluntary contribution to compulsory rate; and whereas in the earlier statutes parliament seemed indifferent who did the work so long as it was done,[3] the system was

---

[1] In 1749 the ballot was criticised as repugnant to the charter, which implied that voices must be given, but on a vote the ballot was upheld.

[2] It was customary for an ingoing mayor or sheriff to be provided with a summary of the annual civic timetable, of which numerous copies have survived. The 'Instructions to the Town Clerk' printed in Appendix IV, which are similar but briefer, are printed from a copy in my possession.

[3] Duties relating to the impotent and vagabond poor were allotted to the governors and ministers of cities, shires, towns, hundreds, wapentakes...and parishes (27 Henry VIII, c. 25). The mayor and other officers of towns were referred to in two poor law statutes of Edward VI (1 Edward VI, c. 3, 5 & 6 Edward VI, c. 2). Two of the earlier Acts of Elizabeth referred to county justices or town magistrates (5 Eliz. c. 3, 14 Eliz. c. 5). In 1576 justices in towns were required to appoint collectors and governors of the poor (18 Eliz. c. 3).

adopted in 1597 of giving the administration of the poor law to the churchwardens and overseers of the parishes in boroughs as well as in the rest of the country, and the supervision to the justices everywhere.[1] There was no other course available in the countryside: there were unintentional effects in the boroughs.

The parish having been thus established as the unit of assessment and collection of rates for poor law purposes, it was natural that it should be used for other secular purposes, such as highways: all rates created later were moulded on the poor rate, and earlier levies were brought into conformity. These rate-levying powers of the parish having been created by statute and constantly exercised, the levying of contributions on the whole city by the common council, the old town scot, which had been practised down to the sixteenth century, fell into disuse. There is no sign that the charter granted to Lincoln by Edward IV, requiring the inhabitants to pay scot and lot and other burdens as theretofore,[2] was ever cited upon the point. In 1610, only a few years after the poor law had been codified, a special assessment was made by the common council for the benefit of sufferers from the plague—the sanction as usual being disfranchisement (expulsion from the freedom)—one of the chamberlains disputed the mayor's power to make out a warrant.[3] It is not clear whether he opposed the levy because it was a poor rate and therefore the business of the parishes, or because the council were levying a rate at all; but there is no evidence that the council ever made the attempt again, though it stood behind parish officers who were resisted, and used its authority and resources in other ways to reduce the burden of the poor.[4] The charter of Charles I made no reference to a power to levy a rate.[5]

[1] 39 Eliz. c. 3, virtually re-enacted in 1601, 43 Eliz. c. 2. See E. Cannan, *History of Local Rates in England* (1912), pp. 56–77.

[2] Birch, *Royal Charters of the City of Lincoln* (1911), pp. 134–5.

[3] *T. & S.L.* p. 134.   [4] *Ibid.* p. 137.

[5] A study of the reports made in 1835 on individual boroughs makes it plain that with a very few exceptions the old 'town scot' had disappeared, and it was accepted that the borough council had no power to levy a rate for general purposes. In their *First Report* the Municipal Commissioners did not suggest that they had the power; if they had thought otherwise they would have been quick to allege a breach of duty against councils which had incurred debts instead of levying rates, or neglected their work for lack of means. They noted that many of the corporations had become indebted to the patrons of their borough for money advanced to them, adding, 'we are at a loss to understand from what sources even the inconsiderable expenditure of money of the smaller Corporations can be provided for, since the passing of the Reform Bill' (*First Report of the Commissioners of Municipal Corporations in England and Wales*, 1835, p. 46).

It is true that borough justices had been authorised by a statute of 1784 (24 Geo. III, c. 54) to levy a rate 'in the nature of a county rate' for purposes of justice and police. But although this was sometimes called a 'borough rate' it differed from the borough rate in the modern sense, not only in that it was levied for special and not for the general

A general rate of this kind is not to be confused with a rate for purposes of justice and police: this was levied by the magistrates and not by the common council, and it was not available for the general purposes of the city. It was the county rate, and Lincoln being a county corporate there could be no doubt of the power of the city justices to levy it. An attempt was made in 1731 to secure contribution not only from the parishes, but from extra-parochial places, towards the cost of transporting felons, and in 1759 rates were made upon parishes for reimbursing the charges of maintaining and conveying vagrants to and from the city and transporting felons from the gaol to the colonies and plantations in America. The levy was based upon an ancient assessment of the parishes: a rate consisted of £30. 0s. 7d. or a multiple of that sum. It was said in 1828 that no fresh assessment had been made for 100 years.

There being no borough rate, the common council had to make do for general purposes with its own revenues. Besides the revenues collected by the chamberlains within their wards—he of the south ward also collected

purposes of the borough, but also in that it was levied by the justices and not by the council. These distinctions were sometimes blurred in practice. At Stamford a 'borough rate' was imposed by the magistrates, and it was a matter of complaint that charges for the repair of bridges, pumps, drains and for street lighting were thrown upon the rate without authority of the statute (*M.C.R.* IV, 2531); and at Hereford the Wye bridge was maintained out of it (I, 262–3). At Liskeard and Saltash the corporation had at one time kept the poor (I, 528, 607), and at St Ives the aldermen constituted the ancient select vestry and directed parochial affairs (I, 620). At Banbury and Buckingham gaol or sessions expenses were paid out of the poor rate (I, 12, 29). At Pevensey a town scot was imposed by the magistrates nearly every year, and paid to the treasurer of the corporation as part of the corporate income (II, 1019). Such anomalies are found mostly in the smallest boroughs, and would arise most easily when the parish and the borough were co-extensive, and the same few burgesses held sway in both.

There were few survivals of the old town scot. Folkestone was levying by virtue of a Cinque Port Charter of Charles II, for the sake of keeping up evidence of the prescriptive right to levy (II, 983). At Brading in the Isle of Wight the corporation levied on lands for the repair of corporation buildings, and after taking advice whether the rate could be levied the owners submitted (II, 681). It was mentioned at Faversham that before a county rate was levied in 1830 an occasional rate was levied from house to house according to ancient custom (II, 972–3). At Tenterden it was said that the town scot once levied by the mayor jurats and freemen had for many years been levied by the justices (II, 1068).

The *Analytical Index to the Reports of the Commissioners*, 1839 (compiled by Joseph Fletcher; see *Journal of Statistical Society of London*, V, 97), gives a list of the boroughs in which rates were levied by the magistrates, but the list is not complete. These were rates in the nature of a county rate. Under 'Rates levied by authority of the Common Council' it names, besides Brading and Folkestone, five boroughs. On examination these break down. Of the five, Derby's rate was a county rate; Romney Marsh was making a special rate for drainage and seawalls; Harwich, Bristol and Lynn were declared once to have levied borough rates under charter powers but no longer did so. The index was mechanically and not very intelligently compiled. It would seem that in 1835 there were only two real exceptions. Mr and Mrs Webb, *Manor and Borough* (1924), II, 703–4, are confused on the subject of the borough rate.

the Canwick rents—the mayor as treasurer received rents from other city properties outside the city, at Hanslope and Castlethorpe in Buckingham-shire, and Belton-in-Axholme and Hemswell in Lincolnshire;[1] and receipts from fines, fees, tolls and payments for the freedom. There was no distinc-tion between income and capital; when expenditure of a capital nature was incurred it was charged to the same account as routine items, and although there is an occasional reference to the common chest, the chest seems to have become exhausted and not replenished. Money was raised on mortgage or on bond—a promise to pay under the common seal—and the capital debt was to mount until interest upon it was to absorb a considerable part of the annual income. Yet the income rose. Early in the century it totalled about £700; by the end it had reached £3,000.

Special expenses were incurred for the mending of High Street or a subscription to the turnpike trust,[2] but it was the grants towards the building of St Peter at Arches Church which led the way in large non-recurring outlays.[3] The bells cost £381. 16s.; £300 was taken out of the city chest and brought into account, and at the end of the year there was a balance on the right side. When the new market house was built, some arrears of rent helped to balance the mayor's account for the year. But when the 'great causeway'[4] was made, and £663 spent in one year for digging gravel, carrying it by boat, laying it down, and paving and draining, £400 was raised on bonds.

The next major project to be considered was the restoration of the Fossdyke navigation.[5] The problem had been before the council for some years, and small repairs had been carried out; but major works were another matter. Enterprise, money and technical skill were all lacking, and they had not the vision to enable them to assess the future prospects of the navigation. They may have learned that other towns, Bath, Salisbury and Chester, had undertaken river works and abandoned them to a private undertaker.[6] Furthermore, financing canal works presented two difficulties which turnpikes, soon to follow, did not. Turnpiking could be done by stages, and partly paid for by tolls as the work went on, but the canal was useless until the whole channel was clear. Secondly, on the roads the interest of the gentry was the same as that of the citizens, and they could and did provide both leadership and money;[7] on the canal it was to some extent adverse, for landowners wanted to keep down the water level to

---

[1] For the city's purchase of the manor of Canwick in 1456, see *M.L.* p. 273; the others were granted to the city by Henry VIII (*T. & S.L.* p. 52).
[2] Above, p. 123.   [3] Above, pp. 63–4.
[4] Above, pp. 145–6.   [5] Above, p. 128.
[6] T. S. Willan, *River Navigation in England 1600–1750* (1936), p. 74.
[7] Above, pp. 122–3.

prevent flooding, whilst the navigation interest wished to keep it high to provide a channel. How many of these considerations were present in the minds of the council it is impossible to say: but no doubt some of them prompted the council to seek and find a private undertaker. Having done so they relinquished their interest to him at a fixed rent equal to the revenue they had been accustomed to receive. Now, of course, they received it without deduction for repair, but they left to the undertaker the whole benefit to be derived from improved navigation and increasing traffic.

Seen in retrospect the decision was deplorable, and a few generations later there were loud denunciations by reformers, with suggestions of corruption for which no evidence was ever produced. It is more profitable to understand than to condemn.

It did not escape the notice of later critics that in 1742, soon after the grant of the Fossdyke to Ellison, the common council had enterprise and capital enough to buy the Reindeer inn for £600, raising £400 on bond for the purpose. They thereby invited the charge that they were more concerned with their own pleasure and comfort than they were with the commercial well-being of the city, though the two projects were totally different in scale. The inn almost adjoined the Guildhall, and the informal discussions held there were partly formalised in 1752, when the mayor and aldermen agreed to meet there on the first Tuesday in every month, at 7 p.m. in the summer and 6 p.m. in the winter, 'to deliberate upon such matters as may most tend to the well-ordering the interests and concerns of the said city in particular, and to the good government thereof in general'. The mayor or his appointee was steward, and there was a fine of 6d. for non-attendance, to be applied as the company should think fit. By the end of the century the attendance had become irregular, and the semi-official body seems to have been succeeded by a gathering of clubable men discussing and practically deciding matters of public interest. It was under a thin disguise that Thomas Cooper described it in his novel *Alderman Ralph*:

...the Wheat Sheaf parlour company, that *imperium in imperio* in the affairs of ancient Willowacre; that choice collection of intelligences which had for so many years ruled the borough; that select band into which none could find admittance, however high his rank or official status, unless by goodwill of the members....[1]

But while the select body in the Guildhall, and the still more select one in the inner hall and the parlour at the Reindeer stood upon the old ways, the privileged position of the resident freemen was being undermined by

[1] (1853), I, 241.

economic change and political corruption. One of their most cherished privileges had been their monopoly of the crafts and trades, which had been protected by the craft gilds or companies, whose right and duty it was to prevent infringement of the monopoly by non-freemen. The authority of the crafts had been shaken during the Civil War, and although some of them had afterwards resumed their functions, by 1739 only two of them, the tailors and cordwainers—the only ones to have had royal charters— remained.[1] Though the companies had mostly lapsed, the common council continued to defend the craft monopoly, and from time to time ordered prosecutions for its infringement.[2] Proceedings to this end were ordered in 1719, but without much conviction, and an attempt was made to persuade the offending non-freemen to buy the freedom: this course would have the double advantage of bringing them into conformity, and getting the purchase money into the city coffers. In 1723 a linen-draper and a woollen-draper were admitted freemen on payment of £50 each, £20 of the price being returned: no doubt the net figure was the result of hard bargaining. Candidates for admission by purchase were sometimes re-jected, but it was coming to be recognised that the great barrier between freemen and non-freemen could be removed as a matter of course by a cash payment. But the price was high, and few of the non-freemen paid it.

The latter days of the cordwainers' company were mirrored in their surviving minute book. They continued to prevent non-members of the company from following the craft until 1772. Then resolution failed: their hall was partitioned and let, and the brethren continued until 1785 as a dining club meeting on licensed premises. Their feast was held on St Ambrose Day (4 April). One of the brethren was elected king of the craft for the ensuing year; one year the feast was held abovehill, when those in the upper town chose him, and the next year in the lower town when those living there chose him. Many people dined with the brethren. The tailors also had an annual feast; in 1784 112 dined and spent the day together with the greatest mirth and friendship.[3]

As the unfreemen grew in number and consequence, the common council, recruited by co-option from a relatively narrowing circle, found their claim to representative capacity declining. The dissenters too were growing as the Methodists not only grew themselves but revitalised the older dissenting bodies, and while they could be freemen they could not hold corporate office because of the religious tests.

---

[1] Adversaria, p. 290.   [2] *T. & S.L.* pp. 204–5.
[3] L.P.L., Cordwainers MS; Willson, VI, 60; *Lincoln Gazette*, 3 Dec. 1784. The Friendly Institution of Cordwainers was formed in 1807.

The institution of the freedom was moreover being rendered farcical by another development: the establishment of the claim to the freedom by non-residents on the ground of patrimony, in order to share in the market for parliamentary votes. The common council took a stand in 1737. They declared that persons born and living out of the city were claiming the freedom on pretence that they were the sons of freemen born after their fathers were admitted; that their claim was prejudicial to the freemen living in the city who undertook all charges and expenses, and bore all the burthensome offices. Furthermore, the claim was contrary to the freemen's oath to be levant and couchant—that is, to keep house or chamber in the city—and bear charges and offices laid to them.[1] The council accordingly ordered that no person born out of the city and liberties from and after a given date should be admitted to the freedom unless he was entitled by service (that is, apprenticeship) or purchase, and should reside therein according to his oath. It was added in 1739 that no person thereafter taking an apprentice and living out of the city and liberties should be allowed to enrol his apprentice, nor the latter be entitled to the freedom. A later attempt to make an exception for residents in the Bail and Close was defeated; and it was laid down that the whole apprenticeship must be served in the city, not even service in His Majesty's forces being admitted as an exception.

The common council stood their ground for some years. But as political corruption grew, and the quest for votes by parliamentary candidates and their agents, or political jobbers trafficking in seats, became keener, the pressure increased. In 1775 three writs of *mandamus* were issued against the corporation in the name of claimants to the freedom, commanding them to show cause why they had not admitted the claimants. The council set up a committee to examine the whole matter; it was resolved to defend the actions, and to consult counsel.

---

[1] The freeman's oath ran: 'You shall be true, and faith and allegiance bear to our Sovereign Lord King George III, and to his heirs Kings or Queens of Great Britain, and be meek and justifiable by the Mayor of this City that now is, and his Successors that hereafter shall be; And that that may be for the Common Profit of the City you shall do; And all Liberties and Franchises thereof you shall maintain to your Power; All Ordinances and Customs made, and to be made, you shall keep; You shall be Levant and Couchant to keep House or Chamber within this City; and all Manner of Charges and Offices laid to you, for the Common-weal Worship or Profit of this City, You shall bear and be contributary to your Power; You shall have no part of Merchandise with any Merchant-stranger, to sell or colour it by any Means, but you shall pay toll for it; You shall colour none of Unfranchised Men's Goods, whereby the Sheriffalty or Commonalty should lose their right; You shall nothing do nor labour that shall be to the Prejudice, Derogation or Hindrance of the Common-weal or Profit of this City; But all these Points and Articles, and what else belongs to be done by a Free Man of this City, You shall keep and maintain to your Power. So help you God.'

Three learned counsel agreed that their clients had a poor case. The duty of residence of a freeman, they found, arose from the freeman's oath, and so only became a duty after admission. A freeman might be disfranchised for breach of it, but every man must be dealt with separately. Freemen were not to be disfranchised in the lump, and the number of non-resident freemen who had been allowed to enjoy the franchise without objection required the corporation to proceed with care. One lawyer thought that apprentices of freemen living in the Bail or Close ought to be admitted.

Nevertheless the common council resolved to fight. The claim of the 'freemen outeners' against the corporation was heard before Baron Eyre at the Guildhall, and after a hearing of $3\frac{1}{2}$ hours judgement was given for the plaintiffs.[1] The council accepted defeat: their by-laws were repealed, and it was agreed that if the son of a freeman had been wrongly excluded the grandson might still be admitted.

The number of unfree residents and the number of free non-residents were therefore increasing at the same time. Clearly a common council recruited from a body constituted according to medieval custom could not speak for the inhabitants as a whole. When new public duties had to be undertaken they had neither the means nor the inclination to undertake them. The machinery for assessment and collection of rates was in the hands of the parishes, whose vestry meetings were free from these anachronistic rules. When bills were promoted in parliament for care of the poor or for lighting, watching and paving the streets, the duties were laid upon bodies elected by, and precepting upon, the parishes. So far from being hostile, the common council promoted the bills.

These moves were made necessary by growing population and especially the increase in the number of the poor. Some of the problems had been discussed in 1762; and by 1782 the common council were setting up a standing committee to examine street nuisances. The subject was resumed, as conditions deteriorated, in 1789, when a committee of the council reported in favour of an Act for lighting, watching and cleansing the streets and preventing nuisances, adding that if it extended to the general regulation of the poor it might soon relieve the poor rates. The council were willing to contribute to the cost, the major part being of course borne by parish rates. The plan was approved, but it was decided by 25 votes to 2 not to extend the bill to include the Bail and Close.[2] The

[1] 7 March 1779; L.P.L. 4938. The nominal plaintiff was Mr Harrison, a tenant of the Manor farm at Fiskerton (Marrat, *History of Lincolnshire*, VI (only parts published), 17).
[2] Whose inhabitants had experimented in a voluntary subscription towards the cost of watchmen, but the scheme did not last long.

committee were instructed to confer with the inhabitants, by which was meant the parish vestries.

A petition was duly presented to the Commons for both purposes, but it did not proceed; a like petition in the following year led to a bill for lighting, watching and paving, which went to the royal assent.[1] Perhaps the bill for the poor was dropped because of the gluehouse project.[2] The functions of the new body were under the control of members of the corporation and the commissioners elected by the vestries.

Perhaps it was because the proprietors of the House of Industry were proposing to apply for a bill that the citizens moved again. A number of parishes requisitioned a meeting of inhabitants, which resolved to promote a bill, the corporation agreeing to make the application and meet the expenses. The Act was passed in 1796, and related to the city and county of the city and the parish of St Margaret in the Close. The 'guardians of the poor' were to be incorporated, and directors elected at vestry meetings, the corporation adding three aldermen. Other parishes might 'contract in'.[3]

The common council, having stood behind the vestries, were called upon also to stand behind the magistrates, though herein they were much slower to move. Conditions at the city gaol at the Stonebow had been exposed by John Howard, who described it as having

one large room for men-debtors, one smaller for women, both upstairs: in each a fireplace. The rooms for criminals are two dungeons down three steps: with bedsteads, that they may not sleep on the damp earth floor. In one of them is a cage for closer confinement when necessary. These prisoners are sometimes taken into the keeper's house. No court yard: no water accessible to prisoners: no straw.

At one time there were three debtors and two criminals imprisoned there; at another one debtor and no felons.[4]

The city magistrates were not as open to the movement of humane opinion as the county magistrates, and a quarter of a century later the gaol survived to be denounced as one of the worst prisons in the kingdom. There was no chaplain, and no work was provided for the prisoners; a blanket and a rug were found for each prisoner, and there was straw on the floor. Passers-by in the street could talk to the prisoners, and, as a pot of beer would go through the bars, they often were able to drink to excess.

[1] 31 Geo. III, c. 80; *C.J.* xxxxv, 186, 353; xxxxvi, 183...686.
[2] Above, p. 183.
[3] 36 Geo. III, c. 102; *C.J.* li, 376. The four towns asked to be excluded (p. 650). The Act provided that they were not to be incorporated without the consent of four-fifths in value of the owners of land.
[4] John Howard, *State of the Prisons* (2nd edn 1777), pp. 303–4.

Water and a privy had at last been provided, and a visitor was assured that land had been bought for a new gaol.

A house of correction had been provided in the sheep market: its inhabitants were employed in spinning and carding wool and were allowed 2d. of every shilling they earned. There was no religious attention. The inmates were allowed a plank bedstead with straw, with two blankets and a rug.[1]

At last a new sessions house and gaol were undertaken. To pay for it the corporation raised the sum of £4,380 on bonds, the interest on the loan being met from the county rate.[2]

Similarly, when the inhabitants north of 'the chain'[3] sought in 1799 to inclose the open fields of the city they conferred with the common council. Terms were reached, and an inclosure bill promoted, into which the council inserted a clause for the erection of a stand for the races.[4]

It is evident that the common council did thus acknowledge some general responsibility for promotion of the well-being of the city, as indeed their freemen's oath required; though the modern concept of 'local government' was certainly unknown to them. When it came to rights of property, however, they saw these as handed down through the ages, succession to which was defined by law and custom; and it would have been difficult to persuade them that changing social and economic conditions had any bearing on their right to beneficial leases of corporate land, or that the rents ought to have been raised as money values fell. It was not their fault that the world was changing round them. It was upon such questions that controversy was soon to arise.

In a body where seniority reigned and the members held office for life, and in which, moreover, powers were small and revenues limited, it might be expected that there would be many members whose interest in its proceedings were slight. At a meeting of the common council in 1813, for example, there were present only the mayor, three aldermen, one sheriff and thirteen common councilmen. Attendance had theretofore been by verbal summons of the crier, and in the hope of securing an improved attendance it was decided to substitute a card of summons.

Nevertheless a good deal of useful work was done by the old corporation in its last years. It investigated the condition of the grammar school;[5] it passed over the mayoral claim of an alderman who had misapplied public funds; it promoted the Lighting and Paving Act of 1828, and revised the

---

[1] James Neild in *Gentleman's Magazine*, LXXV (1) (March 1805), 195–9.
[2] Above, p. 241.   [3] Above, p. 150.
[4] Above, p. 17
[5] Below, pp. 281–2.

freeman's oath, removing references to freemen being levant and couchant in the city and the promise not to trade with strangers;[1] it took shares in the Gas Company, the Dunham Bridge Company, and the Witham Navigation, the activity of whose proprietors it watched to see that the interests of the citizens were protected; and in 1826 it appointed a committee to investigate the affairs of the Jersey School.[2] They found that the master had let the school decline to such a degree as would still give him a colourable claim to his post. They found only one miserable old woman employed in spinning half-dressed locks by which she could earn $2\frac{1}{2}d$. a day, and even she, they suspected, had been sent there in haste when the master learnt of a probable visit of the committee. Jersey spinning had been virtually abandoned for two or three years, the fact being that the master was engaged in weaving linen, and had four looms on the ground floor of the school for that purpose; in spite of his assurances to the contrary, the committee thought that there was still a market for hand-spun worsted, and

they entertain no doubt that under the care of a proper master the poor would gladly avail themselves of the benefits of the establishment, and that it would be of essential service to many necessitous and industrious people and would tend to give habits of industry to poor children and preserve them from idleness and profligacy.

The council accordingly agreed to dismiss the master and engage a new one. The master made trouble; in 1828 the corporation began proceedings to eject him from the school house and premises, and refused to comply with his attorney's demand for documents; after another long delay he gave up his keys and was paid for his fixtures. By that time the school had been closed for several years, and the council abandoned the intention of resuming it, and agreed to repay to the trustees of their benefactor's will the capital sum with which it had been endowed.

In view of high prices, the council had also sensibly abandoned the tolls on agricultural produce and all goods passing into and out of the city (except on cattle), proclaiming the city free and open, and it gave up the tolls in the butter market, and freed the fisheries to all citizens by letting the leases run out.

The various capital projects upon which the council had entered raised serious financial problems. It had a large debt. By 1829 it had borrowed

---

[1] The new oath ran: 'You shall be faithful and bear true allegiance to H.M. King George, and shall be true and faithful to the Mayor Sheriffs Citizens and Commonalty of the city of Lincoln and to your power maintain and defend the franchises privileges jurisdictions and charters of this Corporation, and perform execute and do all such duties offices and things as you are liable and ought to do as a franchised man of this city. So help you God.'   [2] Above, p. 158.

charity moneys in its hands amounting to £3,802. 10s.; it had borrowed on bond £24,740; and it owed to the bank without security £700: the total being £29,242. 10s., and the interest payable being £1,330. 8s. 6d. Ordinary income amounted to £4,010. 11s. 2d., and ordinary expenditure to £3,590. 12s. 4d., leaving a balance of £419. 18s. 10d., which was not enough to pay loan charges. There had been £5,900 invested in the Witham Navigation shares, and £500 in the Gas Company, and £500 in the Dunham Bridge. Improvement of the race-course and the building of a stand had cost £6,652. Other money had been spent in the purchase of land, improvements to corporate estates and redemption of land tax; and, in 1781, £1,000 for the purchase of the remaining city fee farm rent.[1] There was no suggestion that the debt had been improperly incurred. With a view to economy all corporate dinners, save one at Michaelmas, were stopped, allowances and salaries were reduced, and sessions dinners given up. The great question which had not been faced was that of rents from leases of corporate property.

Fortunately Sir Edward Bromhead and Dr Charlesworth came on the scene, and the latter's letters fill out the story. In August 1821 Bromhead was elected Steward of the City Courts, and paid £50 for the freedom, which was returned to him. Evidently it was assumed that he was a whig, such as would be approved by the 'red' interest of Burton, and he gave offence to the reds in 1822 when he was thought to have intervened on the tory side. Meanwhile the restless Charlesworth was meditating entry into the corporation:

2 December 1823. I have serious thoughts of entering our Corporation. Snow mayor, Fardell my chamberlain. The Corporation cannot long remain what it is: two changes which may fairly be expected, namely in the City and Navigation leases, must add greatly to its funds and importance.

In the following year he reported that the radical Wrigglesworth had been elected an alderman, Snow coming second, and he thought that if the red interest would be satisfied with one triumph, Snow would come in next time. He was right, and when Snow became mayor in 1825, he appointed Charlesworth one of his chamberlains, and one of the latter's friends George Marr another. He had got his foot in, and one of the tories, Bruce, was alarmed:

23 June 1825. I have heard to-night that Bruce has expressed himself very strongly on the subject of my entering the Corporation, including Mr Marr's name: he says 'one must not expect to rule that body'. Mr Mason will probably soon be town clerk, and then many things will be brought forward. The truth is, I suppose, the knowledge of my intention, coupled with that of Mr Marr's, has

---

[1] For the fee farm rent, see M.L. (see index) and T. & S.L. pp. 25–9, 53–5, 72–3.

excited a sensation *above*, and it is thought necessary to begin to excite a party feeling *below*. A party feeling against me will make a party for me....I hear my enemies are very angry at the step I am taking, and my friends are very sorry.

The expected subjects came up for discussion.[1] The corporate lands had probably once all been let at rack-rents, but in the course of time the fall in the value of money had made the rents nominal, and if they had been revised as leases fell in the financial difficulties of the corporation would have been solved. The lessees had in fact come to regard them as customary freeholds; in a memorial presented against alteration of terms, presented in 1826, they said:

That the uniform and unvaried practice of the Corporation in renewing their leases from time to time...has therefore induced a high confidence on the part of the public in the value and security of such leasehold property, which has long been freely purchased, not only for immediate convenience, but for permanent investment at prices equal to freeholds, and that large sums of money have been expended by the lessees in buildings and other improvements. That this description of property has been made the provision for widows and children under wills and marriage settlements, and has been pledged as security for money for nearly the value at which it has been heretofore estimated, and that in many instances honest and industrious individuals have invested the savings of their whole lives in such leaseholds, which constitute their sole property and resources.

Any variation of terms would be an invasion of the lessees' property and a violation of the tacit understanding derived from the practice of ages.[2]

In 1821 the question of renewal on the old 'very moderate terms' had been considered, and the council voted as to 11 votes for increase of the fines, and 18 against. When the subject came up again in 1825, legal opinion was taken; counsel advised that the corporation were not bound to renew on the old terms, though he thought they should search for further evidence: but he added that they had the fee simple and could alienate without restraint. On a motion for renewal, the voting was equal, and the mayor refused to give his casting vote; and the old practice continued. Another effort was made in 1828, when the radical Wrigglesworth moved for a committee to investigate the leasehold question, but was defeated by 22 votes to 14. The reforming interest was receding.

Meanwhile the death of Richard Ellison had created a vacancy in the office of recorder. The young Lord Monson, who would otherwise have been regarded by the whigs as the obvious choice, was not yet of age. The pink, or Canwick, interest brought forward Lord Goderich, who lived at Nocton, and Bromhead also was nominated. The great question was what the red interest would do. They supported Goderich, who was elected.

---

[1] For the Fossdyke, see above, p. 243.   [2] L.P.L. U.P. 581.

Charlesworth thought that Richard Mason, who was agent for the Burton interest, had been outwitted, and that Lady Warwick (formerly Lady Monson) would have been sharper. He consoled Bromhead for his defeat by saying that 'it took two Lords to beat you, with Canwick and the Minster to boot'.

As Charlesworth laid down his office of chamberlain and took up that of sheriff he reflected:

27 September 1827. I have opened a door into the Corporation thro' which men of a higher class than formerly will walk in. An attempt will be made that these shall be principally Goderich men, to counterbalance me, who have evidently excited a panic. I mean to lay the axe to the root of every tree in that Corporation that shades the light: and that immediately while I have the chance. The chamberlains will all vote against me.

He used his chance by proposing periodical meetings of the council. But the charter vested the power to order meetings in the mayor alone, and the council could only request him to summon one: and Charlesworth could get no further. He found a party was forming to defend the old leases, and to increase the party's numbers by introducing none but 'old lease' sheriffs. He was all 'for daylight', printing documents, and publishing accounts. His year of office ran out, and he was no longer a member of the council, but he hoped to be elected a common councilman, and to attain the mayoralty, and sooner or later to clean the Augean stable. He would have fared better if he had not been so dictatorial and quarrelsome.

He looked on sourly while Mason sought to pull down the Reindeer, doubtless to save money:

4 December 1831.. . .it was built to enable the Aldermen Brickmakers &c. . . .to bone the funds intrusted to their tender care. The repairs now form an annual revenue to Foster (the builder); the Corporation, as a trust, deriving no revenue at all. It has been a millstone upon the legitimate purposes of the trust.

A majority of the council decided to keep the inn standing, and let it if possible; and, if not, to keep the large room in hand and let the remainder. Nothing was right for Charlesworth if other people did it: his comment was: 'the affair is a job on both sides'.

In July 1832 he was proposed as a common councilman and rejected, and he was rejected again in December 1833.[1] The stable was not to be

---

[1] According to the press report of the inquiry of the Municipal Commissioners, 'Dr Charlesworth was in rotation for being elected on the Common Council, a ballot was demanded, and he was passed over. His was the only instance of the kind that had occurred for perhaps a century: his sentiments were known to be in favor of an alteration of the leases. It did not appear that others had been objected to on the same account' (*L.R. & S.M.* 27 Sept. 1833).

cleaned by him, and he could only pay tribute to Bromhead and himself for their disinterested but unsuccessful efforts at reform:

15 September 1834. . . . there cannot be a doubt that all the honest voting which we at one time used to admire in the lower town was a mere passive following of our lead, given because it cost nothing. If ever there had been any right feeling in these men it could not so utterly have disappeared and left no trace behind.[1]

It may well have been true that these men were too weak to act without a strong lead.

Reform was at hand. In September 1833, when the Municipal Commissioners appointed by the whig government were expected, a local committee was formed to furnish them with grounds for inquiry. The radical printer E. B. Drury was preparing questions for them, and Charlesworth was giving him some hints. There were the city leases: property worth perhaps half a million of money[2] was let at nominal rents, even including the west end of the Guildhall, which was let as a butcher's shop. There was the licensing money charged to non-freemen.[3] There was the expenditure of the corporation: was it all for the public benefit? Accounts and records should be made public. There was the manner (and motive) of distributing city charities. Persons in public office should be regarded as trustees, and ought not to derive benefit from their offices. There was plenty of scope for inquiry.

When the inquiry was opened in Lincoln Guildhall the public attendance was small. The mayor at once agreed when it was put to him that the grand jury at sessions, which might have to consider indictments against the corporation, should not be composed of members of the corporation, as by custom it was. The facts about the leases of city land were not in dispute. It was found that charity moneys were distributed according to the will of the donors. The mayor, the town clerk, and some of the aldermen and councilmen were in favour of election of the council by the £10 householders, the magistrates being elected for life. It was complained that the town clerk had acted as agent for parliamentary candidates, though he destroyed the party value of the complaint by disclosing that the complainants had also tried to secure his services in that capacity. In their licensing jurisdiction the magistrates had shown excessive tenderness to one of their own number who had a bad record as a licensee.

---

[1] Bromhead MSS.

[2] This figure was ridiculous. Willson suggested a figure of £60,000.

[3] See *T. & S.L.* p. 94. These payments were challenged by the publicans in 1835, and on counsel's advice the common council ceased to exact them. For some forty years no children of poor freemen had been apprenticed with the aid of the fund, which had accumulated to £600. It is an example of customs continuing merely because they existed: but it was not the corrupt practice it was alleged to be.

The commissioners declared themselves satisfied with the corporation's treatment of them, and they thanked the gentlemen who had given evidence. Even the tory *Lincolnshire Chronicle* declared that the commissioners had gained the respect and esteem of the inhabitants. In their report, though they made no allegations of corruption against individuals, they exposed the system in all its absurdity. The great majority of citizens and inhabitants were excluded from the corporation. Little less than half of the freemen and three-quarters of the whole corporate body (by which they meant the citizens and inhabitants) were not ratepayers. It appeared that owners and occupiers of more than four-fifths of the property rated were excluded from chartered rights. No local responsibility attached to the exercise of official power; and while the community was governed and taxed by functionaries over whom they had no control, the revenues 'entrusted to those functionaries for public purposes' had been converted into private property. Presumably they were here referring to the Fossdyke and city leases. They were adhering strictly to whig principles, without concession to history or custom.

There was more excitement when the Municipal Reform Bill was published. The leaders of the local reform movement were described by a hostile pen. There was Alderman Wrigglesworth; there was Henry Blyth, 'who, like his brandy, is warranted genuine and perfectly harmless', Dr Boot, 'whose patriotism, like ginger beer, spurts out the best in warm weather...muttered something about the Star Chamber', 'the Jack of Clubs, the Bacchus of Sir William Ingilby, a Scotchman'—evidently Mr Northhouse, who was Lincoln correspondent for Drakard's *Stamford News*, and whom Ingilby called the Gin Orator—and others. After a second public meeting held on requisition to the mayor, the anti-reformer wrote:

Oh, ye holders of City Lease Property, many of whom have assisted to bring on this measure by your wild advocacy of the Reform Bill, had you been present, and seen this goodly company, these Electors of the Town Council, and possibly many of them forming a portion of the Town Council—how would your hearts have died within you at the idea of being compelled to trust in their hands as the Town Council the property which had descended to you from your forefathers, and had been purchased with the earnings of an industrious life; men whom in private life you would not have trusted one shilling. The Bill declares that no qualification shall be required....Had you seen their mouths open, their eyes widen and glisten with delight...'Tis said, the new Corporation intend to dine weekly at the house of one of the future Town Council, Mr Allen Bouch, as he has placed in the window of the Duck Tavern a Notice that a good Dinner and a Pint of Ale may be had for 9*d*. I know not whether this is a fact.[1]

[1] L.P.L. U.P. 1484.

A crowded public meeting, refused the Guildhall, was held in the Butter Market, and petitioned for the bill.[1] The corporation sent the town clerk to London to observe its progress in parliament and make such representations to members as he thought fit, to remove wrong impressions of the conduct and character of the corporation. The resolution was carried by 16 votes against an amendment approving the bill, which had only four votes.

The lessees of city lands had made a final bid to save something from the wreck of their hopes, and the council agreed that the property should be enfranchised on fair and equitable terms. A compromise on exceedingly generous terms was proposed, namely that the lessees should pay 25 per cent of the gross value of property consisting mainly of land, and 20 per cent of property for the greater part houses and buildings.

Edward James Willson wrote a despairing letter of protest to the *Stamford Mercury*,[2] and invoked the aid of Charles Tennyson, then Liberal member for Lambeth. If the property were sold before the bill was passed, the power of revision reserved to the future council would be evaded.

July 1835. If the property must be made available immediately, the value of every lease ought to be separately taken, and the term of the lease be duly considered. Instead of this the Corporation are going to sell to all the lessees at the same price: which is making *a mere scramble* for the property: just like the scene of a country fair, when a basket full of apples is thrown amongst a crowd of boys.

Upon the advice of Tennyson he wrote to Lord Brougham; he had already written to Lord John Russell and Mr Hume.

31 July 1835. I am much afraid that this iniquitous measure will be effected: for the lessees amount to above 150 in number, and amongst them are almost all the principal persons in the city, members of the Corporation &c. Colonel Sibthorp is a lessee, and so is Mr Mainwaring. It is not liable to be made a political question, for it so happens that three or four of the staunchest reformers are lessees, and join in opposing any reform of this abuse of public property.

2 August 1835. The valuations are going on with all possible haste, trusting to the alienations being confirmed either by *a packed town* council, or by the higher powers to whom these bargains are referred.... For Justice sake, my dear Sir, do try to stay this sack of poor old Lincoln! The Corporation have kept this property in an unprofitable state, but there was always a hope, up to this period, that it would at some time be made useful. To have this hope cut off, under a ministry who are endeavouring to remedy these abuses of our municipal governors at the very moment that remedy is held out to us—is bitter indeed.[3]

It was in vain. The sale went through, and on 24 August the council directed that moneys received for enfranchisement of corporation property

---

[1] There were two petitions for, and two against, the bill from Lincoln (*C.J.* xc, 369, 547, 465, 469). [2] 10 July 1835.
[3] L.A.O. 2 Tennyson d'Eyncourt, H/31/1–3.

should be applied in discharge of corporation debts. The bill became law on 9 September. The only business at the last meeting of the old common council on 21 December was to seal conveyances of the old leasehold properties. If the bargains were referred to any 'higher power' as Willson mentioned, there was no result. Private vested interests had triumphed.

At the Lincoln meeting in favour of the bill Dr Beaty and Mr North-house were appointed a deputation to concert with other deputies soon to meet in London as to the best manner of forwarding the bill. On his return Northhouse issued *Hints to Municipal Electors, A Test for Candidates, with directions....* He proclaimed that a man should not be chosen because he was a politician on one side or other, but he ought to be a friend of the Act of Parliament by virtue of which he was elected: which well-sounding doctrine led plainly to the right conclusion.[1] In the result the reformers won every seat on the new council.

Disillusion followed, as it always follows exaggerated expectations of reform. Thomas Cooper had been a vocal and aggressive member of the reform party in Lincoln; but a few years later, when he lay in gaol for being involved in Chartist disorders, he looked back and remembered the general tendency to exaggeration in judging the old corporations:

How witty were the newspaper people in their conceits of conserving, or pickling, or embalming an alderman, and having him placed in the British Museum, as a curiosity for antiquaries to form profound speculations upon, some ten or twenty centuries into futurity! Ay, and how eloquently abusive was the prevailing Whig strain about 'nests of corruption', and 'rotten lumber', and 'fine pickings' and impositions, and frauds, and 'dark rogueries of the self-elect'. And how the scale has turned, since in the greater share of boroughs, where the poor and labouring classes threw up their hats at 'municipal reform'—and now mutter discontent at the pride of upstarts become insolent oppressors—or openly curse, as in the poverty-stricken and hunger-bitten manufacturing districts, at the relentless and grinding tyrannies of the recreant middle-classes whom municipal honours have drawn off from their hot-blooded radicalism, and converted into cold, unfeeling wielders of magisterial or other local power.

Of the old Lincoln corporation,

generosity, and justice, no less, must confess, that after the most searching inquiry and exposure, they were neither individually nor collectively stained with the acts of peculation, and embezzlement, nor application of public funds to political party purposes, which were so heavily, and, no doubt, truly charged on some of the old guilds in other parts of the country.[2]

[1] L.P.L. U.P. 1481.
[2] The town clerk declared publicly that the city funds and charities had never been prostituted to city electioneering contests, and that none of their enemies had either dared, or dreamed of being able, to make an accusation against them. Even the *Stamford Mercury*, 27 June 1834, said that Lincoln was among the best of the bad.

Cooper thought nostalgically of the noble-hearted old surgeon, Alderman Hett, whose ambition was to achieve note as an ornithologist, and who was so generous to the poor that he was often the victim of designing knaves; of Alderman Cotton who from some oddity was known as 'Alderman Lob', and who gave weekly relief to many at his door; and Charles Hayward, town clerk, who, though nominally servant, was actually the master of the old corporation, and who was held in high honour though for lack of sympathy with popular progress he was not likely to be a favourite with a people so strongly political as the Lincoln citizens had become. The only radical alderman of the old corporation, Wrigglesworth, had become a councillor, and later mayor, of the new: in spite of his slenderness of intellect he was loved for his honesty and benevolence. Like Cooper he was disillusioned by the results of reform, and especially of the New Poor Law. 'I cannot understand,' he would exclaim, in the hearing of the numerous participants in his English hospitality, 'I never thought that Reform was to make the poor more miserable, and the poorest of the poor most miserable: it is a mystery to me! Surely it is a mistake in Lord Grey and Lord Brougham.'

In his bitterness Cooper no doubt looked at the past through rose-tinted spectacles, but he does well to recall that the members of the old corporation were human beings similar to those of all ages, and were not personally to be blamed for an anachronistic system they had inherited and were powerless to change; and not to be judged too harshly for not being more virtuous than their fellows.[1]

Edward Peacock, *laudator temporis acti*, wrote a generation after 1835:

Those who remember the old Corporations, before the restless desire for change had swept them away and given us democratic uniformity in their place, will not require to be told that Corporation dignities were valued by the most highly educated and intelligent people in our towns; not only for the direct influence they gave, but also as a mark of social distinction. The time when civic rank

---

[1] See Thomas Cooper's *Wise Saws and Modern Instances* (1845), II, 'The Old Corporation'. When his tales were republished in *Old Fashioned Stories* (1874), the names of members of the old corporation, which had been previously omitted, were inserted. In 1853 Cooper published *Alderman Ralph, or the History of the Borough and Corporation of the Borough of Willowacre, by Adam Hornbrook*. It is a tale of incompetent villainy defeated. It is placed in the town of Willowacre on the Slowflow, a river port with a tollbridge, which suggests Gainsborough; but the latter is not a borough, and the accounts of the corporation and the Guildhall point to Lincoln. It is significant that the title-role is that of the senior alderman of an unreformed corporation, an upright man, in contrast to the baronet who, having been elected to parliament as a true-blue, becomes a reformer, and to the rascally lawyer, who was an overseer of the poor. There are many recognisable touches: the select company that met in the Wheatsheaf (see above, p. 243); the talk of improvement in street paving and lighting, the gas works, and domestic water supply; the vagrant Irish; the empty prettiness of election speeches.

carried with it some of the respect that aristocratic privilege had done in former days had become so entirely a matter of history that our younger readers will find it difficult to believe that it existed in the lifetime of their fathers.[1]

No doubt with the great gain brought by municipal reform there was also some loss.[2]

[1] *Ralf Skirlaugh the Lincolnshire Squire* (1870), III, 103.

[2] Mr and Mrs Webb's description in *Manor and Borough* (1924), II, 730–3, of the old corporations as associations of producers, to be contrasted with the new as associations of consumers, does not fit the old Lincoln corporation in its latter days. It had long ceased to consist of companies of craftsmen with monopoly rights, and distinction between freeman and non-freeman had become arbitrary. Conditions in many other corporations were so similar that it may be doubted whether the facts generally, in latter days, could be made to fit into any neat economic categories.

CHAPTER XI

LATER GEORGIAN SOCIETY: HIGH TOWN

THE squires no longer kept houses in Lincoln; they could generally make the journey from home along the turnpike roads, though the risks of flood remained. It was easier, however, to travel on horseback than by carriage, a form of transport which still required a considerable undertaking. Charles Anderson remembered the difficulties presented by a journey on the low road from Lea along the Fossdyke:

We used in going to Lincoln to have horses from Lincoln to meet us at Drinsey Nook, otherwise we should never have got there. We generally had four horses, and the road used frequently to be under water between Marton and Fenton and between Fenton and Kettlethorpe Lane: at Drinsey Nook it was hardly passable...my grandmother kept no horses, but had an old coach in which she travelled, never without four horses. It was a most comfortable vehicle—short sided—had arm rests, inside within were cases for wine bottles and sandwiches, and would hold six at a pinch, and one dicky in front.[1]

As the population grew, and with it problems of poverty, crime and traffic, the amount of public business increased that had to be transacted by the justices in quarter and special sessions. In addition to the usual business they were confronted also with the need for new buildings for the courts and the gaol at Lincoln Castle. The county hall which had been built in the castle yard in 1776[2] began to subside, and it was found to have been built upon a subterranean quarry: a fact it was embarrassing to admit. An Act was obtained for its rebuilding in 1822, and by 1826 the new hall could be used for business, though it was not completed for another two years. The architect was Robert Smirke, whom Mr Colvin describes as 'probably the most successful architect of the early nineteenth century, though not the most gifted'.[3] The building is in a thin Regency Gothic style, being built of brick and faced with Ancaster stone.[4]

The enterprise was marked by extraordinary wrangles. E. J. Willson wrote to Subdean Bayley:

22 September 1822. The new County Hall seems to commence with some strange circumstances. The contracts are proposed to be taken under such unusual restrictions, and so entirely under the control of Mr Smirke, that Mr Fisher,

---

[1] L.A.O. Anderson, 5/2/2, p. 19b.
[2] Above, p. 20.
[3] *Biographical Dictionary of English Architects 1660–1840* (1954), p. 545.
[4] An account of the building, compiled from the papers of the County Committee, was written by J. Mordaunt Crook in *L.A.S.R.* IX (1962), 151.

Mr Hayward, my father, and the other Lincoln builders, do not think it prudent to subject themselves to such bondage. There is some hidden intention in these terms.

He goes on to suggest that their purpose was to secure the architect a commission on all goods supplied.

The whole history of it would afford one of the most inconceivable instances of perverted evidence that ever was brought to light. The effrontery of the *governor* quite overpowers all he meets with. Mr Smirke was egregiously deceived in his first survey, as he acknowledged to me in my house, and then denied it positively before the magistrates.[1]

The governor was John Merryweather, who had been acquitted of charges of brutality brought against him on behalf of a female prisoner in 1812. He was evidently assertive and quarrelsome; and as he took part in the affairs of other local institutions he naturally clashed with Dr Charlesworth, who wrote:

23 September 1822. Are you aware that all Merryweather's hothouses have been paid for by the county; and that he is now keeping his two illicit daughters in the Castle? Also that the magistracy of the county at this time would be ruled by Tuxford the Turnkey (who rules Merryweather) had he intellect and tact to know how to wield his weapon.... Smirke will turn out to be a tremendous sharper: Merryweather will wet his feet in the same water with the architect.... By what strange fatality is it that this large and proud county intrusts its purse and its noblest public works to such a felon's management? I wish I could be a Lindsey magistrate for one year! How mild and gentle would I be, but how surely would I rescue the county from this disgraceful thraldom!

On the provision of beds for the debtors, Charlesworth wrote:

10 January 1825. The chaplain and surgeon would be worse than the gaoler: being both his creatures, and therefore they would be a cover for his actions, for which he would then cease to be responsible.

He thought there should be a clerk accountable to the magistrates.[2]

At about the same time the watchtower was added to the keep. The Judges' Lodgings were built in white brick in 1812, across the castle ditch to the north of the entrance from Castle Hill. At the conclusion of this considerable programme the justices obtained an Act to enable them to purchase the castle from the duchy of Lancaster, and they completed the purchase in 1831: the price was £2,000.[3]

The economic and therefore the social position of the gentry had been strengthened by the high rents that accompanied the high prices of the

---

[1] *Lincs. N. & Q.* x (1908–9), 19.   [2] Bromhead MSS.
[3] *M.L.* pp. 100–2.

war period. Furthermore the gentry, or some of them, had become more serious-minded than their forebears half a century earlier.[1] Banks had done in Lincolnshire what Coke of Holkham and the duke of Bedford had done elsewhere, and made agricultural topics fashionable. As landlord and tenant prospered, the city of Lincoln, which had no independent industry of its own, prospered in dependence on them; and the squires formed a link between the two societies above- and belowhill. They belonged to the society abovehill—in a sense they were themselves 'the county', and they spoke and acted for it; and they were the patrons of the citizens belowhill in their political, social and charitable affairs. They were the leading figures in the markets and fairs. Tennyson was drawing on his early memories of Lincolnshire markets when he drew a picture of Sir Walter Vivian in *The Princess*:

> No little lily-handed Baronet he,
> A great broad-shouldered genial Englishman,
> A lord of fat prize oxen and of sheep,
> A raiser of huge melons and of pine,
> A patron of some thirty charities,
> A pamphleteer on guano and on grain,
> A quarter sessions chairman, abler none;
> Fair-haired and redder than a windy morn;
> Now shaking hands with him, now him, of those
> That stood the nearest—now addressed to speech—
> Who spoke few words and pithy.

And in his *Sixty Years After* Tennyson wrote of the squire who

Served the poor, and built the cottage, raised the school, and drain'd the fen.

On the whole the rule of the squire seems to have been benevolent, though benevolence was conditional on submission, usually given without question.[2] There were, of course, the indifferent and bad specimens. Thomas Miller, a Gainsborough man writing of a Trentside family, depicts in *Gideon Giles the Roper*, published in 1841, the justice who was a vulgar roystering blackguard, taking delight only in drinking, foxhunting, and committing poor devils to prison; who wanted the new poor-house to have only a single brick wall, and if it blew down, so much the better. His son was beloved, and it was for his sake that when the fires of the incendiary flashed redly in the dark wintry sky, the hated father's property escaped.

---

[1] Above, p. 109.
[2] As Tennyson's *Northern Farmer: Old Style* said, 'God Almighty little knows what he's about a-taking me, And Squire will be so mad an' all'.

But Miller's favourite was Justice Bellwood, a worthy old magistrate, who was a hater of oppression:

if there was a loophole in the law through which he could allow the weak and injured party to escape, he did it....He was a strong compound of all that is thoroughly English, brimful of fiery passion and kindheartedness, and stuffed with prejudices to the very throat, but they were his own dear hobbies, and never indulged in for a moment if they injured a worthy man.[1]

The Lincolnshire justices received a striking testimonial from Samuel Bamford, who was a political prisoner in Lincoln Castle after the 'Peterloo massacre', when a Manchester reform meeting was broken up by the military. He testified to the courtesy and consideration he and his fellow prisoners had received from the justices, and their good treatment; and he added that in their own county they would probably have been put in the worst dungeon to be found.[2] Dr Tennyson of Somersby, who was a magistrate, said the Manchester magistrates should be indicted for murder; if they were hanged it would be of great use to the magistrates generally, but especially to the clergy.[3]

Henry Dalton of Knaith told Dr Tennyson's father that he was advertising a warning against poachers at Walesby:

I mean to write a few words to Lord Yarborough. I know very well that if I had mentioned to him a desire of preserving the game in the wood he would have proposed that we should conjointly present our compliments to all the poachers in the country, begging them from &c. &c. but the method I have taken is most suitable to the occasion.[4]

But he was not so fierce himself. Suspecting his own keeper of an alliance with poachers, he took to watching, surprised the poachers at the keeper's house dividing the game they had taken, and stealing upon them unawares in the midst of their parley as to who should have this share and who that, put in his claim by saying, 'And which is mine?'. He did not punish them, being content with his success and the amusement it gave him.[5]

---

[1] Pp. 135–6, 203. The original of Gideon Giles is supposed to have been Dunstan the roper of Torksey Bridge, and of the humorous character Ben Brust, Ben Whittaker the ferryman of Littleborough, who used to keep the Ferryboat inn at Laneham (C. Bonnell, *Thomas Miller, Poet-Naturalist* (1904)).

[2] *Passages in the Life of a Radical* (ed. Dunckley), p. 316, and see p. 322.

[3] L.A.O. Tennyson d'Eyncourt (2 Sept. 1819).

[4] *Ibid.* (31 Aug. 1809). Henry Dalton presented the Rev. T. R. Malthus to the living of Walesby. In his *Essays in Biography* (paperback edn 1961), p. 96, J. M. Keynes surmises that they were relatives, and this is probable (see J. O. Payne, *Collections for a History of the Family of Malthus* (1890), p. 88 and pedigree).

[5] L.P.L. Anderson's notes in *L.D.B.* sub 1802.

Sir Charles Anderson, who records this story, has another pleasant incident about George Uppleby, the squire of Barrow on Humber,

of the Lincoln coach being stopped near Grantham by highwaymen when he was travelling with a country neighbour to London. One highwayman put a pistol at Uppleby's head, whereupon the other said 'Why, that's Squire Uppleby, you may'nt shoot our Squire Uppleby.'[1]

The relation of the lord of the manor with farmer and peasant was still feudal. It was idealised half a century later by Edward Peacock, himself a good specimen of the class, in his *Ralf Skirlaugh The Lincolnshire Squire*, when he says of his hero that

it really gave the possessor of Skirlaugh manor no little delight to be addressed by the title of 'Squire', a half-affectionate, half-courteous term, that our poor never use to any but those for whom they entertain a sincere respect.

Here was feudalism in its aspect of privilege: on the side of obligation it is illustrated by Skirlaugh's assertion that 'I am in the habit of maintaining, and, if need be, of seeing justice done to my own poor'.[2] Of course few squires attained to the ideal, but so long as their inferiors were submissive, they and the country clergy would generally help them, especially against other tyranny, such as that of poor law officials.

The proper social sphere of a tenant farmer had been defined by Banks. A landlord, like a patriarch or a father of his tenants, ought to live among them, delighted at their happiness, and meeting their benedictions whenever he saw them. His care must be, first, not to distress them by exorbitant demands of rent; and secondly, not to suffer them to grow rich enough to make their sons into consumers of the produce of the earth, as lawyers, parsons and doctors were. These latter classes should be taken from the younger branches of gentlemen's families, and farmers suffered to save enough out of their farms to make their sons farmers and their daughters farmers' wives, happy and cheerful.[3]

His memorandum was probably written in the middle years of the war. Later, some landlords were saying that in the piping times of war the tenant farmers had got above themselves. Lord Scarbrough complained in 1818 that in spite of the high price of wool his tenants in Lincolnshire were not paying their rents, and in 1821 that

had they not been lifted out of their sphere by the great agricultural meetings, at the Duke of ——, and Mr —— (which has totally in many instances destroyed the most useful member of society, the *industrious*, *working* farmer), had they not

[1] L.P.L. Anderson's notes in *L.D.B.* sub 1816.
[2] I, 164, 168.
[3] Hill, Banks, 3/12. Perhaps he had forgotten that his great grandfather was an attorney.

given dinners with different sorts of wine, drove their gigs, and sent their daughters to boarding schools at 40 and 50 guineas a year, instead of teaching them to be good housewives at home, they would have had something to spare for worse times, and not endeavour to make the whole burden fall on the landlord.[1]

He would have been horrified, a few years later, to find tenant farmers riding to hounds and dining at Brocklesby; when Anderson had been there he referred to 'the usual complement of graziers and great tenants of My Lord's, who, though very amusing for a day or two, are abominable bores if you stay longer'.[2]

Such treatment of tenants meant that they were not afraid to criticise their betters, at least collectively. A Brocklesby farmer witness told a parliamentary committee in 1836 that farmers and occupiers thought the county rates were not fair.

They are laid by the magistrates at quarter sessions, an irresponsible body, and generally speaking paying but little towards the rate; they also are of opinion that they are a body of gentlemen not conversant with the management of matters upon which they are called upon to decide, such as the erection of county bridges &c.[3]

Good relations between the gentry and their non-feudal inferiors were dependent, as they were with their own vassals, upon a due acceptance of the established social order. Familiarity from below could usually be repelled by a combination of starch within and frost without. Sometimes, however, there were complications, as in the agreeable and well-documented comedy of the duke and duchess of St Albans, when they proposed to visit Redbourne Hall near Brigg, which the duke's father had acquired through his first wife. The ninth duke, a youth of 27, reputed to be gentle and weak of wit, had lately married a spouse old enough to be his mother. She was Harriet Mellon, an actress and the daughter of a strolling player,

[1] Lord Scarbrough MSS, EMC 22/16, 24/18. Each winter he sent money to the poor, acknowledging that the price of corn told against them. His view of farmers was widely held, as witness the following rhyme.

Farmers in

1722	1822
Man to the plough;	Man tally-ho;
Wife to the cow;	Miss piano;
Girl to the sow;	Wife silk and satin;
Boy to the mow;	Boy Greek and Latin;
And your rents will be netted.	And you'll all be gazetted.
	(Hone's *Table Talk*, III, 463.)

[2] Wilberforce MSS, 21 March 1824.
[3] *State of Agriculture: Second Report* (1836), p. 76.

who had first married Thomas Coutts the banker,[1] and at his death inherited his vast fortune. She was abused by many for her vulgarity and her humble origin, but she had a doughty champion in Sir Walter Scott, who wrote of her:

I have always found her a kind, friendly woman, without either affectation or insolence in the display of her wealth, and most willing to do good if the means be shown to her. She can be very entertaining too, as she speaks without scruple of her stage life.[2]

Charles Anderson confirmed this last point, for he recalls her saying at Redbourne to his mother when tea was brought on a tray, 'Ah, I never taste such good tea as when my poor mother used to make it out of a kettle under a hedge'.[3]

It can be imagined therefore that the news of the impending arrival of Their Graces caused a tremendous flutter both above- and belowhill. The duke attended the mayor's banquet at the Reindeer, and invited the company to Redbourne to a hawking: he was hereditary Grand Falconer of England. There was a great gathering at Redbourne. He had German falconers attired in trousers of green and orange velvet, wearing long white gauntlets and steeple-crowned hats with bands of gold on them, and adorned with black plumes.[4] A fair proportion of fashionable folk attended, and there were champagne, Punch à la Romane, fireworks, dancing, coffee, ices, supper on the sideboards, and endless speeches. Charlesworth reported to Bromhead, who had been invited but did not go:

Mrs Roe is surprised. She understood the Duchess was to be put down. I laughed and asked her who could put down a duchess, wife to the fourth man in the kingdom, received at Court, and respected in a respected family, of which she formed a part, possessed of nearly £100,000 per annum, and a heart as hospitable as her fortune was large. The poor woman cried for mercy, and her daughter lamented aloud their ill-fortune in not being invited.

There was later a display of falconry on Lincoln race course, and the city was thrilled; and the common council admitted the duke a freeman of the city. Her Grace was at once invited to be patroness of the Dispensary Ball, and she accepted; though the managers thought they must restrain her lavishness and persuade her not to provide negus, as the costly precedent might deter others from accepting the office in future years. The ball was of course a great success.

---

[1] On her death the duchess left her huge fortune to her first husband's granddaughter, who later became the Baroness Burdett-Coutts.

[2] Diary, 25 May 1825.

[3] L.P.L. Notes in *L.D.B.*, sub 1828.   [4] By 1837 the sport had ceased to exist.

But Charlesworth was wrong about the surrender of the county: they had not surrendered. Lord Brownlow went straight to the point with Bromhead:

20 October 1828. ...this is with regard to the mode of proceeding you would think it right to adopt at the ensuing Stuff Ball, of which you are one of the Stewards, under the probable contingency of the appearance of the Duke and Duchess of St Albans at that meeting: I have understood that the Lady Patronness Mrs Boucherett intends to nominate Lady Brownlow as her successor for next year, but as it is Lady Brownlow's *positive determination* not to be brought into contact in any way with the Duchess of St Albans it will be essential to avoid proposing the Duke as one of the Stewards for next year, otherwise Lady Brownlow must decline the office of Patronness; moreover as this Ball is altogether a meeting for *Society* and not for any object of charity, it is peculiarly necessary that the Ladies of the County should vindicate the honor of their sex from any unworthy commixture, and I trust they will rally round a lady of high birth and unblemished reputation, leaving of course the Duchess (if she comes) to enjoy the highest seat in the Assembly, but otherwise without notice or regard.

Bromhead wrote that the high sheriff had publicly taken his sister to visit the duchess, but there could be no nomination for a stewardship of the ball, as the duke was already engaged as steward of the races.[1]

Presently Charles Anderson could write to his friend Samuel Wilberforce that the duke and duchess had left the county:

10 November 1828. I never saw either the whole time they were here. My Mother called to satisfy my Father and the old Lady at Lincoln, but her Grace tho' she talked much never returned the visit. I fancy she thought they would not mix as well as her brandy and water (a favourite beverage of her Grace). They flew the hawks on Lincoln racecourse, and as you would see, two birds flew away, one of which was retaken in a haystack, whither he had fled for refuge to avoid the crows and magpies. I do think it a glory to Lincolnshire to think she was so well cut, not probably that the people did it from proper motives, but mainly on account of her former low birth and her present forward manners, but my aristocratic feelings are quite comforted with the idea that Coutts' money bags could not buy the popularity of the Lincolnshire gentry. We are above such things, Sir, as Boyle would say.[2]

Her Grace must have adulation, and she was not the first or the last to find Lincoln people undemonstrative. In 1830 Charlesworth reported on a further visit by her:

I hear the Duchess is disgusted with the city: no shout when she placed the Falconer's cup upon the stand before the populace, with her own hands, her health not drank at the Mayor's dinner, nor her contribution to the races mentioned in any of the speeches.[3]

The novelty was over and the entertainment value gone.

---

[1] Bromhead MSS.   [2] Wilberforce MSS.   [3] Bromhead MSS.

More ordinary people found it difficult to enter the ranks of the gentry. Alfred Tennyson's grandfather, an attorney who had made money during the war by buying land, settled at Tealby and became a magistrate and a deputy lieutenant. Yet he was never really accepted as one of the county; and his younger son Charles's desire to establish himself as a country gentleman and to found a family prompted him to take the name of d'Eyncourt, derive his descent from a baron of that ilk, and build the Gothick pile of Bayons Manor around the modest Tealby Lodge. His nephew Alfred did not think much of his uncle Charles's pretensions to Norman blood,[1] but, looking at county society from his family angle, used to denounce the old aristocracy of his boyhood, their pride, prejudice, narrowness and bitter partisanship. He wrote:

At a public ball at Lincoln the whig families would sit by themselves on one side of the room, tory on the other, noticing each other as little as possible. But the youth of each sometimes danced together in the middle. Two ladies of opposite politics found themselves on the same sofa, and avoided each other mutually as much as they might without turning their backs. But the curiosity of one lady induced her to take up a piece of the gorgeous flowing dress of her neighbour to look at it more closely when she thought the owner's head was turned away. Round comes the rival lady's face with a sneering smile upon it: 'Madam, if you'll allow me, I'll send you my mantua-maker's bill to look at....' We are certainly better off in manners nowadays.[2]

Sometimes the proudest of the local gentry became aware that others from a larger and more fashionable world looked down upon them. Anderson once found with his aunt two ladies who had lived all their lives apparently in Brighton, which they imagined the quintessence of perfection; and they were quite horrified with Lincolnshire, the inhabitants of which they seemed to consider as partly frogs and partly geese or eels.[3]

A new and picturesque figure entered the circle when, after the death of the fourth Lord Monson, the Burton hounds were bought by George Osbaldeston, a Yorkshire squire whom Arthur Bryant describes as a 'shrivelled up, bantam cock of a man with short legs, a limp, a gorilla-chest and a face like a fox-cub', but who excelled at every sport he touched.[4] He and his mother took up residence at the Bishop's palace, and he showed fine sport for about four years, saying that it was the best country he ever hunted in

---

[1] Although Alfred may not have known it, his uncle Charles was constantly seeking a coronet.

[2] *William Allingham: a Diary* (1907), p. 340. As an old man, Tennyson studied the clusters in Hercules through Norman Lockyer's telescope at Hampstead, saying 'I can't think much of the county families after this'. (Joanna Richardson, *The Pre-Eminent Victorian* (1962), p. 183). Thomas Miller commented on the bitter blood at the Stuff Ball.

[3] Wilberforce MSS, 8 April 1831.

[4] *Age of Elegance* (Penguin edn), p. 284. He gave £1,000 for the pack.

his life; and he lent colour to the society in the upper city. At a dinner party before a county ball he heard Miss Cracroft twit Miss Burton on the inferiority of her bouquet. He left the dinner party, got on horseback just as he was, and rode 25 miles to get an even finer flower. After four hours' riding he was able to give Miss Burton her triumph at the ball supper. It was pranks such as this which provided topics of conversation during the long dull intervals between the balls that punctuated the season.[1]

From 1816 the country was hunted for eight years by another famous figure, Thomas Assheton Smith, who had been introduced by Napoleon to his officers with the words: 'Voici, Messieurs, le premier chasseur de l'Angleterre.' He was a rich man, and hunted six days a week without receiving a subscription. He courted popularity belowhill by attending all the card parties and other social functions that he could in the city. In 1818 he had a ball at the county Assembly Rooms with a view to promoting the union of high town and low town societies, and it was attended by most of the gentry and a considerable part of the trading families; and he planned to have fortnightly assemblies above- and belowhill. But 'his project of bringing the Minster to the Buttermarket and the Buttermarket to the Minster does not take.... Smith went home early in high dudgeon'. At the hunt ball in 1819, wrote Charlesworth, 'Smith was very drunk, and his troop were half seas over. Mrs and Miss Hett and Fanny Jepson (alias Mount AEtna) were the only high town ladies.'[2] Smith grew sick of friendly society dinners, and his successors did not repeat his attempts at social harmony.

Smith had been discouraged from another quarter; having transferred his stable and kennel establishment from Burton to Lincoln, Lady Warwick (formerly Lady Monson) feared that the hunt would no longer be considered as belonging to Burton, and wrote to Smith asking for some good security that the whole would revert at the proper time to the Monson family. Smith did not like this doubt of his good faith, and appealed for the support of the country.[3]

He was followed for a short time by Francis Foljambe of Osberton near Worksop, but in spite of his incredible energy the arrangement was only a makeshift. Anderson wrote:

9 February 1828. Before next winter I hope there will be something decisive fixed about the country, and that there will be a regular pack established at Lincoln or Burton. Foljambe hunts this country now as well as part of Notts, and it is more than anyone without two bodies can well stand. He manages however to do a

[1] Osbaldeston wished to marry the widowed Lady Monson, but after meeting encouragement found himself jilted in favour of Lord Warwick (see E. D. Cuming, *Squire Osbaldeston: his Autobiography* (1926), pp. xviii, 17–18, 31, 192).

[2] Bromhead MSS, 2 and 23 Dec. 1819.

[3] L.A.O. Tennyson d'Eyncourt, 10 Nov. 1818.

great deal, and as he returns to Osberton every day after hunting, and almost always rides, I daresay he sometimes travels above 100 miles in a day, and is out hunting the next morning as if nothing had happened.

8 April 1828. They had an extraordinary run of 30 miles yesterday, and on Monday killed in Lincoln, the fox taking down the street thro' the Minster Yard and down what they call the Grecian Stairs, a flight of steps I daresay you remember coming up the hill. Had the Cathedral gates been open he would probably have attended divine service as Boyle would say....[1]

Thereafter Sir Richard Sutton (who married Miss Burton) took the mastership of the hounds, holding it until 1842.

The social tide ebbed and flowed in the high town, and as the gentry ceased to keep houses there the cathedral clergy succeeded to their leadership. George Pretyman became bishop in 1787. He owed his preferment entirely to William Pitt, having been his tutor at Cambridge, and becoming his adviser and literary executor. He was learned, prim and pedantic, giving an impression of 'half-amused, half-bored, wonderment'.[2] Pitt secured for him the deanery of St Paul's whilst he was still bishop, in the face of George III's opposition; and he was translated to Winchester in 1820. In 1803 he inherited Riby near Grimsby from the eccentric Marmaduke Tomline, to whom he was not related, and with whom, indeed, his acquaintance was slight, and he took the name of Tomline.[3] He did not visit Lincoln much, and figures in its history chiefly in the patronage he conferred on members of his family. The last of them lingered on the Lincoln scene until 1866.[4]

Pretyman did however give to Lincoln the only famous member of the cathedral body in this period. He collated William Paley, author of the *Evidences of Christianity* and other works, to the office of subdean in 1795. For

[1] Wilberforce MSS.

[2] J. Holland Rose, *William Pitt and National Revival* (1911), pp. 52–3.

[3] '22 June 1803. Marmaduke Tomline of Riby Esq. died. In the evening it was communicated to the Bishop on his arrival at Caistor, previous to his holding a Visitation and Confirmation there the next day, that Mr Tomline had left his estate at Riby to his Lordship, requiring him to take the name of Tomline. This noble bequest appeared the more remarkable as there had scarcely existed any acquaintance between the Testator and the Bishop' ('Extracts from the Diary of a Lincolnshire Clergyman' in *Lincs. N. & Q.* ix (1906–7), 185). Anderson recorded that the bishop nearly lost the estate through meanness in giving Tomline stale tea when he called at Buckden. Subdean Bayley told the story that when the bishop died at Farnham, Bayley, who was one of the executors, went down with his colleagues; in the morning when they came down to breakfast they found the tea chest locked. Ringing the bell, and asking the servant for the key, the latter solemnly replied, 'Sir, the key is in his Lordship's pocket' (L.P.L. Notes in *L.D.B.*, sub 1787).

[4] The late Miss Swan used to tell the story, which had no doubt come down in her family, that the bishop's wife one day came to the bishop saying, 'I hear the poor chancellor cannot last long', to which the bishop briskly replied, 'Then we must get George out of the navy'.

the remaining ten years of his life Paley spent his three months' residence in Lincoln save when prevented by ill-health. He loved his spring residence in the city, when the numerous gardens and orchards were in full blossom. Henry Best has preserved stories of his conversation, uttered in his broad northern dialect, and full of robust common sense. One related to the book club.[1]

There was a book club at Lincoln, the members of which assembled once a week, at tea-time, and after tea each one took of books what he wished to read during the week following. The secretary said, 'Mr Subdean, what books do you choose?' He, casting a look as of doubt and dismay on the table covered with pamphlets and new publications, said 'I will try not to take more than I can read; but one's eye is always bigger than one's belly on these occasions'.

Whist followed the choice of books, and thereafter talk.

Some one, speaking of a very worthy man, a clergyman in the city, said that he was a jacobite. One of the company cried out 'What! a jacobin?' 'No', said Paley, '*bite* not *bin*; who ever thought Mr D. a *jacobin*?'

Best, who had joined the Roman Church, defended the jacobite position, and Paley addressed him.

'Sir, you are a jacobite?' 'Yes.' 'And Mr D. is another?' 'He is so reported.' 'Then there are two of you. Well, I did not think the Pretender had been so strong.'[2]

Dean Kaye died in 1809, after having been confined to his room for four years by a paralytic stroke. He was succeeded by George Gordon, the son of the former precentor. He had several livings in the county, and he bought the freedom of the city. He had been tutor to Lord Bath, and perhaps by his influence became dean of Exeter; it is said that he had gained the affections of his patron's daughter Lady Isabella Thynne, and that the deanery of Lincoln was procured for him in order to remove him to a safe distance.[3] Gordon was a kind and liberal man, without distinction or

---

[1] The club was established in 1792. In Anderson's time the members had their own cellar of wine, and dined once a month at the White Hart, after which the books were sold and the evening ended with whist (L.A.O. Anderson, 5/2/2, p. 28).

[2] *Personal and Literary Memorials* (1829), pp. 174–6. On one occasion at dinner at Burton, Paley listened to some officers discussing their days hunting until his patience was exhausted, and he interrupted them to say: 'Gentlemen, I think you have talked enough about hunting now. I'll tell you what hunting really is—a parcel of men with vacant minds meet at the covert side. The dogs smell a stink, they run, and the men gallop after them. That's hunting' (E. D. Cuming, *op. cit.* p. 24). Anderson relates that when Paley's daughter put on a newly fashionable poke-bonnet, the doctor disapproved, and said, 'I say, Sall' (or whatever her name was), 'when one sees a long avenue one expects to see a good hoose at the end on't'.

[3] The Lady Isabella never married: the dean called his only daughter Isabella (L.A.O. Anderson, 5/2/2, p. 28). A like version was told to me by the dean's great grandson, the Rev. George Staunton of Staunton near Newark.

pretension. From his several preferments he was believed to have an income of £20,000 a year, and he became an obvious target for reformers. He stood stoutly upon the rights of the Church and the old ways generally, and later he was always to have the honour of proposing Colonel Sibthorp for election as member for the city.

In these years, and under the influence of Kaye, the Minster was being cleared of many puerilities. The gravestone of Tom Thumb was no longer to be found, and little monuments were removed or rearranged.[1] Greater matters also called for notice. The outer Chequer Gate, probably in disrepair, was taken down about 1799. The Great Tom, the bell which had been cast in 1611, was found to be shaking the central tower too much when it tolled: it weighed 4½ tons. In 1802 it was therefore fastened, and only the clapper moved. In 1827 the bell was found to be cracked, and was sent to London to be recast. It was said that the new bell lacked the grandeur of its predecessor.[2]

The spires upon the western towers, whose threatened removal had caused a commotion in 1727,[3] were reported on in 1807, and the dean and chapter laconically resolved that, it having been deemed advisable to remove them, the residentiaries had given their consent and order thereto. The only person who seems to have expressed himself strongly on the subject was Banks. He proposed an association of inhabitants of the diocese to compel the chapter to replace them, and, if funds permitted, also the spire which had been blown from the central tower in 1547; and he applied to Sir William Scott, the future Lord Stowell, for legal advice, remarking in reply to a request for further information by him that

the whole business of the Church is with us carried in a manner so secret, and all enquiries of the laity met with so marked a caution, that in the case of a culprit would arouse suspicion: no wonder therefore that I am unable to answer this and many other necessary questions.

Counsel advised that the chapter could not be called to account, and the spires were not restored.[4]

William Cobbett commented in 1830 that he thought the cathedral the finest building in the whole world, though its neglected state made him

---

[1] *Lincoln and Lincolnshire Cabinet* (1827), pp. 4, 16.

[2] William Gardiner, *Music and Friends* (1838), II, 715. A great procession accompanied the new bell through the city, with bells ringing and a band of music. It was wheeled on a truck into the Minster and down the nave, with a little boy chimney sweep perched on top.

[3] Above, pp. 39–40.

[4] Banks Corr. XVII, 52, 69–71, 157; *Banks Letters* (ed. Warren Dawson), pp. 22, 524, 554, 744; Edward Smith, *Life of Sir Joseph Banks* (1911), p. 314. A cartoon depicting the ghost of the spires appearing to the dean is amongst the Banks papers in my possession.

melancholy; and of course he was indignant against those who enjoyed its revenues.[1]

The cathedral dignitaries were despotic in their regulation of Minster Yard society; nor, said, Edward Peacock,

is there any appeal from their decisions in point of eligibility. The Color Ball is the test; and although some individuals may procure admission there who would not be welcome at a chancellor's dinner, yet their presence would be considered an intrusion by the elite of the county, and they would undoubtedly be exposed to the mortification of neglect.[2]

Among the residents there were generally a few people of independent means, and one or two doctors and lawyers. The Swan dynasty of lawyers, of whom the first was the nephew of Mrs Gordon, had arrived. For a short time George Tennyson lived in part of Deloraine Court, though he soon left for Grimsby, having inherited property likely to benefit by the Grimsby haven project. His daughter Elizabeth was glad to leave; she told her grandmother:

22 September 1797. We none of us regret leaving Lincoln. Everybody agreeable seems tired of the place and talks of leaving. Mr Field is not at home, but when he returns and is informed of this resolution of my father's I think he will be sorry. Indeed, we shall be as much hurt to leave them, for no one who is thoroughly acquainted with Mr or Mrs Field but must respect and esteem them. Miss Swan is another friend we shall be sorry to part with. She is a friendly neighbour, and possessed of an excellent heart and understanding, but we must own that the generality of Lincoln people are not pleasant.[3]

They were probably disappointed at the reception they met with in Minster Yard; he was just an attorney who had prospered.

Many of the houses were occupied by the widows and unmarried daughters of gentry and clergy. There were twice as many women as men in St Mary Magdalene's parish, and they largely predominated in St Peter in Eastgate and St Margaret. In the *Gazetteer* of 1826, apart from the clergy and a verger, only four male residents in Minster Yard are named, whilst there were fourteen women. The men were so few that women had to take their turns as parish officers, and St Margaret's vestry declared in 1813 that for many years past one-third of the houses in the parish had been inhabited by females only. A perpetual deputy overseer was therefore appointed.

[1] *Rural Rides* (ed. Cole), II, 658–9. Miss Hatfield, *Terra Incognita* (1816), p. 7, found the performance of the choir much below mediocrity.

[2] From a MS entitled 'Sayings and Doings of Lincoln Worthies in the olden time; or Lincoln as it was, and Lincoln as it is, being a faithful picture of the City in the 13th and 19th Centuries' in my possession (p. 150). It was compiled in the middle years of the nineteenth century, and is of value for conditions of that time.

[3] L.A.O. Tennyson d'Eyncourt.

Charles Anderson has preserved some memories of the extraordinary old ladies who lived in Minster Yard. Mrs Sedgwick, who talked the broadest Lincolnshire, used to say that she had three gowns, 'Hightum, Tightum and Scrub' (pronounced *Scroob*) for high days, dress days and common days. Miss Nancy Bennett, a curious old spinster whose love was said to have been killed at the battle of Bunker's Hill, lived in a Number house: at an oyster party at Mrs Palmer's where some of the prim ladies were shocked at Mr Williams the under-sheriff kissing a young lady behind the door, Miss Nancy gave her opinion thus (she always put an *h* to her *ss's*): 'Sich a fussh about a kissh behind the door, indeed! In my young days we always exhpected such things.' Old Miss Ellison, sister of Colonel Ellison, had been very handsome, and was a fine figure, but as stiff as a poker and very prim: a fat Miss Penrose lived with her.[1]

The character of the upper city was changing relatively to the lower. It did not participate in the modest improvements being effected there. After a period of housebreaking the inhabitants of the Bail and Close subscribed for a watch, but voluntary effort was not enough; and it was soon abandoned. The Bail had no public street lights, and there were only a few lamps in Minster Yard, maintained by the dean and chapter. A few square lanterns were occasionally lit near the Assembly Rooms, and a parish vestry, prompted by an accident, might light a few for a short time, but nothing could be more dreary than the Bail and Newport on a winter evening, when there was no gleam of light to help a stumbling passenger on the irregular, broken and dirty pavements.[2] Until 1810 there was no postbox uphill, and the inhabitants had to go downhill to post their letters. Thomas Frognal Dibdin testified that about 1813 there was no inn in the neighbourhood of the cathedral at which a civilised traveller could tarry: he had to stay belowhill. Twenty years later a decent and comfortable inn, the White Hart, afforded all that a reasonable visitor could wish.[3]

When Nathaniel Hawthorne visited Lincoln, coming by railway, he noted the stately and queer old houses and many mean hovels on 'the broad back of the hill', and commented: 'I suspect that all or most of the life of the present day has subsided into the lower town, and that old priests, poor people, and prisoners dwell in these upper regions.' He thought the houses in the Close were in too neglected and dilapidated a state for so splendid an establishment as the cathedral.[4] Thomas Cooper knew the

---

[1] L.A.O. Anderson, 5/2/2, pp. 27–8. Sir Joseph Banks's sister gave the same names to her three gowns, which were all made of the wool grown by her brother. No doubt she was wearing one of these in Gillray's caricature of her in *The Old Maid on a Journey*.

[2] Willson, VI, 60 *b*.

[3] *Bibliographical Antiquarian and Picturesque Tour in the Northern Counties of England and in Scotland* (1838), I, 89. [4] *Our Old Home* (1890 edn), I, 241, 251.

place better; he wrote that the humble bee seemed almost afraid to disturb the solitude by a hum; and that venerable maiden ladies had no vicissitude of existence, save an occasional scold at their servants, or a grumbling complaint of 'short measure' to the coalman as he made his weekly call.[1]

Changing times had brought a new emphasis on respectability. Secular activities were no longer thought suitable for Minster Yard. The exercising of soldiers on the green at the east end of the cathedral was declared a nuisance and stopped in 1799. Workshops and inns were becoming offensive and out of place. The western Exchequer Gate had housed an inn, the Duke of Marlborough, which vanished with the gate; the surviving arch had another drinking house, the Great Tom, the large chamber of which was frequently used for dancing and merriment, the excesses of which at last induced the chapter to have the sign taken down.[2] In 1810 the chapter virtually issued a charter to the inhabitants by declaring that in any future lease of a house in Minster Yard or the Close a clause should forbid its use as a public house, inn, butcher's shop or any other shop, bakehouse, auction room, brewery, school, military hospital: in short in any other way than as a private dwellinghouse.

It was this abovehill society which the young Edward Bulwer studied when he was member for Lincoln in the 1830's, and in his *A Strange Story* he described it under the thinnest of disguises. There was the old Abbey Church in the town of L——, round which were the genteel and gloomy dwellings of the Areopagites of the Hill, the few privileged families living aloof from the wealthy merchants and traders in the marts of commerce.

These superb Areopagites exercised over the wives and daughters of the inferior citizens to whom all of L——, except the Abbey Hill, owed its prosperity, the same kind of mysterious influence which the fine ladies of Mayfair and Belgravia are reported to hold over the female denizens of Bloomsbury and Marylebone.

Although Abbey Hill was not opulent, a concentration of its resources in all matters of patronage made it powerful. As to its shops:

Abbey Hill had its own milliner and its own draper, its own confectioner, butcher, baker, and tea-dealer; and the patronage of Abbey Hill was like the patronage of royalty, less lucrative in itself than as a solemn certificate of general merit. The shops on which Abbey Hill conferred its custom were certainly not the cheapest, possibly not the best. But they were undeniably the most imposing. The proprietors were decorously pompous—the shopmen superciliously polite. They could not be more so if they had belonged to the State, and been paid by a public which they benefited and despised. The ladies of Low Town (as the city subjacent to the Hill had been styled from a date remote in the feudal ages) entered those shops with a certain awe, and left them with a certain pride. There

[1] 'Nicholas Nixon', in *Wise Saws and Modern Instances* (1845), II, 111.
[2] Willson, XIII, 55.

they had learned what the Hill approved. There they had bought what the Hill had purchased. It is much in this life to be quite sure that we are in the right, whatever that conviction may cost us.

And he makes Mrs Poyntz, one of the Areopagites, sum up the whole matter:

The principle that suits best with the Hill is respect for the Proprieties. We have not much money; *entre nous*, we have no great rank. Our policy is, then, to set up the Proprieties as an influence which money must court and rank is afraid of. I had learned just before Mr Vigors called on me that Lady Sarah Bellasis entertained the idea of hiring Abbot's House. London has set its face against her; a provincial town would be more charitable. An earl's daughter, with a good income and an awfully bad name, of the best manners and of the worst morals, would have made sad havoc among the Proprieties. How many of our primmest old maids would have deserted tea and Mrs Poyntz for champagne and her Ladyship? The Hill was never in so imminent a danger. Rather than Lady Sarah Bellasis should have had that house, I would have taken it myself, and stocked it with owls.[1]

[1] (1875 edn), pp. 12, 39, 98. The reference is clearly to Lady Warwick, formerly Lady Monson, and daughter of the second earl of Mexborough. She was one of the 'Brighton Click' (*Journal of Mrs Arbuthnot*, I, 88). Her reputation is indicated in *Catalogue of Political and Personal Satires* (B.M.), x, nos. 14074, 14075. Henry Dalton of Knaith wrote to George Tennyson that Lord Monson's family was no doubt highly respectable, but it was not of a description from which he would choose a servant for his purpose (L.A.O. Tennyson d'Eyncourt (28 Sept. 1810)).

CHAPTER XII

LATER GEORGIAN SOCIETY: LOW TOWN

THE ladies who climbed the hill to learn what the Hill approved no doubt applied their knowledge when they attended the assemblies in the city Assembly Rooms over the Buttermarket. There were six or seven such assemblies during the year when they might shine, besides the charitable assemblies. Of these latter Adam Stark wrote that

When any inhabitant, of good character, is overtaken by sudden misfortune, any respectable widow burthened with a number of children, or aged man incapable of providing for his own support; some leading lady or gentleman steps forward, and solicits, by public invitation, the company of the charitable at an assembly for the benefit of the sufferer; every respectable individual thinks himself bound in honour to attend; and on entering the room gives what he pleases to the *patroness* or *patron* of the meeting, who collects the subscriptions.... The subscription is always sufficiently large to relieve the distressed object.

Eight or nine of them might be held in a year, averaging almost £400 per annum for their beneficiaries, who must either have starved or been supported by their parishes. So they might be saved from the debasing situation of a pauper.[1]

It required some assurance of the necessary social standing to assume the office of a patron or patroness, and the co-operation of the Hill was desirable. One of the Swan family wrote to George Tennyson:

13 January 1802. ...you will be surprised when I tell you that I assumed sufficient consequence to make a charitable card assembly last Monday with Mr Henry Hutton, and a very good collection we had. Lady Webster has been very kind to the object the assembly was made for. The Risum family do a great deal of good in charities in this place.[2]

Patronage played a very large part in all social and charitable activity. It is fortunate that leaders were forthcoming. During the eclipse of the Monson interest the function of patronage at Lincoln was chiefly filled by Frederick John Robinson, a member of a Yorkshire family of Newby who by his marriage in 1814 to Lady Sarah Hobart, daughter of the fourth earl of Buckinghamshire, had become a county magnate and acquired a seat at Nocton. As Lord Goderich he had the misfortune to become prime minister on the death of Canning in 1827, a post for which he was unfitted, and which he held for only a few months. Nevertheless he was a capable

---

[1] *History of Lincoln* (1810), pp. 269–72.
[2] L.A.O. Tennyson d'Eyncourt. The Riseholme family were the Frank Chaplins.

administrator; he had held office under Lord Liverpool, and was yet to serve under Lord Grey and Peel. His influence and his good nature made him a useful local figure.[1]

Every beneficent public activity in the city and district found a guiding hand in Edward French Bromhead, whose father, General Sir Gonville Bromhead of Thurlby near Lincoln, was created a baronet for his services in quelling the Irish rebellion. He was educated at Glasgow University and at Gonville and Caius College, Cambridge, where he was of founder's kin through his great grandfather William Gonville. He was called to the Bar, but practised little; as a mathematician he was sufficiently distinguished to correspond with Whewell and Babbage; and he was a botanist and antiquary. It was probably because of his poor health that he never took the position in life for which his great ability fitted him: he eventually became blind. His friend Dr Charlesworth paid him a well-deserved tribute:

6 September 1827. Nearly all the institutions of Lincoln have already the stamp of your mind and hand: several have been entirely formed by you, and others totally remodelled, while *all* would eventually have felt your influence. Lincoln itself would in a course of years have been remodelled under your eye. The whole population would in some degree have partaken of the tone of your mind....[2]

The ill-health that limited and cut short his public activities had one advantage for posterity, for it meant that his friend Dr Edward Parker Charlesworth of Lincoln kept him informed by letter of the events that interested him. Charlesworth, whose father was a Fellow of Trinity, Cambridge, and subsequently rector of Ossington, Nottinghamshire, had been a pupil of Dr Harrison of Horncastle, and graduated M.D. at Edinburgh, and when he settled in practice in Lincoln took part in almost every public activity. He became physician to the County Hospital in 1808.[3] He was able and a hard worker, and the influence which these qualities earned for him was used in a most dictatorial way. Sometimes he drove his associates to feel that it was better to be wrong and against him than right and with him. The doctors were constantly quarrelling among themselves, and he was in his element.[4] The editor of the *Lincoln Herald* wrote to Bromhead in 1829 of an offer by Charlesworth to write for him: his mind was under the influence of considerable irritation about the

[1] He later became earl of Ripon; his son, the first marquis of Ripon, was viceroy of India.

[2] See his obituary notice in *Gentleman's Magazine*, 1 (1855), 523. Evidence of his contributions on all manner of subjects to the *Philosophical Magazine, Monthly Magazine* and *Technical Repository* is contained in L.A.O. Misc. Don. 161.

[3] *Short Account of the Old and New Lincoln County Hospitals* (1878), p. 52.

[4] Mrs Massingberd wrote in 1830 of the quarrels of the Cooksons and Swans and other doctors in Lincoln (L.A.O. Massingberd, 1/80).

Asylum: could Bromhead draw his attention to some new interest? A long and elaborate lampoon upon him was found during building work in the Bail in 1929. It begins:

The celebrated Dr Charles Worthnothing, with gratitude for past favours, begs leave to inform his friends, and the public in general, that he has at very considerable expense, refitted the old shop near the Minster, where he will continue to take them in as usual, upon the readiest and most simple method. Dr C. W. gives his advice, gratis, upon all cases, and is to be consulted as usual, by letter, post paid, enclosing the compliment of a One Pound Note.

N.B. A back door and lamp in the passage have recently been added, for the greater accommodation of the Doctor's more private patients.[1]

The work for which he became famous was done in the reform of the treatment of insanity. He became a governor of the Lincoln Lunatic Asylum (now called The Lawn Hospital), and was constantly doing battle with the anti-reformers, being sometimes in power and sometimes out. In 1828 he published his *Remarks on the Treatment of the Insane*, and having the support of Gardiner Hill, the resident physician, was able to write in 1835 that, having a willing board and willing agents, he was simplifying the lock and key system and knocking off restraints. After his death in 1853 a statue of him was unveiled by Dr Conolly, who paid tribute to his long fight for humane treatment of the insane.[2]

One of his enemies was Colonel Sibthorp, and a quarrel, thought to have arisen out of an asylum affair, arose in 1824 and led to a duel. The seconds urged mutual apologies. According to his own account Charlesworth refused, saying 'that if my coffin stood on one side of me, and riches, friends and honour on the other, so circumstanced I would turn to my coffin rather than make a concession the breadth of a hair'. They met, and shots were exchanged; the seconds intervened and declared themselves satisfied. 'Something was said about shaking hands: we turned round and parted. I should not have liked to refuse his proffered hand, but am better pleased as it is.' Mr Swan attended as doctor. There is no surviving account by Sibthorp, who did not write much, though he talked incessantly.[3]

[1] *Lincolnshire Echo*, 30 Sept. 1929, by courtesy of Mr G. F. Morton.

[2] Sir James Clark, *Memoir of Dr Conolly* (1869), pp. 36–9, and see pp. 49–50; *D.N.B.* and references there cited. The statue stands in the grounds of The Lawn, and can be seen at the junction of Drury Lane and Carline Road: the sculptor was Thomas Milnes (R. Gunnis, *Dictionary of British Sculptors 1660–1851*, p. 261).

[3] The lampoonist above quoted refers to Charlesworth's subservience to Bromhead and his duel with Sibthorp:'...this unrivalled performer will swallow a large toad by desire of a person of distinction; and if further desired by the same person will stand upon his head, dance a Fandango or Bolero, and endeavour to make himself amusing and useful. It is found that the latter feat must be occasionally dispensed with, as the Doctor has not yet recovered the effects of an attempt to swallow a Kernel of peculiar construction; it stuck in his throat for a long time, and is still very sore and troublesome.'

Charlesworth was the first president and evidently the prime mover in the formation by subscription in 1814 of the Lincoln Library. There had been earlier literary societies: one, which was numerous, met at the Reindeer, the other, Willson thought, at the Spread Eagle.[1] Presumably one of these was the City Book Club, which later was dissolved and its stock transferred to the Lincoln Library, on condition that they made the Rev. John Carter, who had served the club for nearly thirty years, a shareholder for life.

By 1827 there were 270 proprietors of the Lincoln Library, among them gentry, clergy, merchants, farmers and tradesmen, and the library acquired 6,000 volumes. Dissension arose early, and in 1816 Charlesworth appealed to Bromhead to serve on the committee, and succeeded in preventing him from resigning in the next year. On the one hand were the clergy and gentry of tory colour; on the other a mixture of whig or mildly tory gentry, professional men, a few moderate clergy, citizens and dissenters. In 1827 four of the clergy were displaced from the committee by four laymen, who were more likely, said Mr Hett, the clerical champion, to become the tools of a party, meaning Charlesworth. The latter wrote to Bromhead that 'Hett's speech grows by the yard. A week since it was by measure three times the length of his arm, and occupied 24 quarto folios. The burden of his song is "that the parsons were turned out...".' Two years later clerical wrath exploded when a sermon by Dr Copleston, an eminent Oxford divine, priced at 2s., was rejected and the New Newgate Calendar, at a cost of £1. 16s., admitted. Charlesworth boasted privately that in spite of the outburst the 'dynasty' (meaning himself and his party) was impregnable; he had been inclined to admit to the committee a couple of carefully chosen clergy, but 'to let in large bales of black cloth without first refuting him (Hett) may look as if *he* had brought us to it'. Peace presently returned, and Charlesworth wrote:

14 January 1821. ...poor Billy Hett is absolutely obliged to content himself with groaning. The Subdean[2] says nothing, but looks blue and shy—his wife cuts me— and the Institution is daily rising higher in public estimation. The irritation of party feeling (save with about 8 or 10) has intirely subsided and gone to rest. The clergy no longer affect to feel insulted. I am on very friendly terms with most of them, and they only smile when they hear how completely the old influence still prevails. In a word the Dynasty is become legitimatized and acknowledged by the neighbouring Courts.

But Hett was soon able to complain that the Bible had been rejected and a work on foreign architecture bought: it seems it was the commentary upon the biblical text to which objection was taken. Hett was joined by

[1] Willson, v, 59. [2] H. V. Bayley.

Precentor Pretyman, who became one of the 'Ashantees' of the Library. Charlesworth commented:

20 October 1827. What the Devil is to the Parsons the Parsons are to me. As the Devil would devour us all without mercy but for the above gentleman's protection, so would the Parsons devour the Library but for mine.

Bromhead was trying to improve matters by changing the rules, and Charlesworth, who always accepted his lead, offered 'to train both speakers and applauders for the occasion'.

The inevitable general reaction against Charlesworth and his methods in the city prompted him to write to Bromhead in 1835 that the Library was the last fortress of the rational party in Lincoln. He complained that religious controversy and party virulence were creeping in through the medium of novels, the *Autobiography of a Dissenter* especially. He thought his own party and the neutrals were on the decline, and the country was gaining at the expense of the town. Earlier, in 1827, he had said 'the cry against me has always been, since the Library explosion, that wherever I plant my foot my body follows, that nothing short of absolute rule will satisfy me'. He was ousted in 1831, but with all his faults he had done good work, and there was nobody who could take his place. He could still support Bromhead there, and in 1838 could still make a party to maintain the Library as 'the last remaining stronghold of Conservatism'.[1]

The Lincoln Library served the middle class, both old and new; in 1822 the New Permanent Library was formed to serve a lower social class—tradesmen, mechanics, apprentices and inhabitants of the villages—with Bromhead as president. The admission fee was 2s. 6d. and the subscription 1s. 6d. a quarter; it soon had 100 members and 400 volumes. It was forerunner of the Mechanics Institution, which was formed in 1833, and in which it was merged.

There had been an outbreak of typhus in Lincoln in November 1825, and no doubt it was under this impetus that Alderman Hett proposed an institution for the medical relief of the poor. When it was founded in January 1826 it consisted mostly of citizens and a few of the gentry. F. J. Robinson was patron. It became the dispensary for the sick poor of the city, Bail and Close, and a house was bought for it on the Cornhill. Most of the parishes subscribed to its funds. To raise more money it was agreed to hold an annual charitable assembly about the time of the Stuff Ball. Many of the doctors, including of course Charlesworth, joined in,

---

[1] The minutes of the Library are now in L.P.L. See also *Lincs. N. & Q.* XII (1912–13), 97.

and in spite of their many quarrels and rivalries a vast deal of good work was done.[1] Charlesworth reported:

13 April 1828. I told Gardiner yesterday that he would live to see nearly every respectable person in Lincoln a subscriber to it (he assented), that it was the pet Institution of Lincoln, that any anxiety went to the preservation of its popularity (so he perceived), that no increase of Governors would increase the number of patients, who were now, and I hoped always would be, all the sick poor of Lincoln (he added 'very poor'—you will mark that new hitch). I told him I regarded the Institution as an outlet for all the good and charitable feeling of the town which the other institutions did not embrace: and that the effects would be beneficial, in a political point of view, to those assisting, as to those assisted.

The dispensary relieved the County Hospital very largely of town patients. The Hospital was, however, firmly in the hands of the clergy and gentry, and did not quickly respond to new movements. The dispenser needed a power to remove instantly to the hospital any case of infectious fever. But there was no fever ward, and no action was taken to provide one. Charlesworth was in the forefront of the battle:

29 October 1826. Nothing will touch the Hospitalites but public opinion, if that: but in this instance I think they might be forced to yield, or the subscriptions would be withdrawn. This point carried would lead to a venereal ward—next in utility to a fever ward—by stopping infection.

At present the Hospital is a mere 'House of Idleness', or a receptacle for scrofula, consumption and old sores. I am convinced there is not another hospital in England at once so rich and so inadequately employed in the service of surgery, sickness and science.

He continued to press for a separate fever building, which he said the hospital could afford. 'It would make the institutions of Lincoln more complete and respectable.' Perhaps he was the only man with a clear vision of a whole range of institutions for the improvement of the life of the city. He founded the Medical Library, and he had visions of public gardens and baths, and a coffee room for small tradesmen.

Vigour or change was hardly to be expected at the grammar school, which was under the joint control of the dean and chapter and the common council. It had declined under a master, Mr Hewthwaite, who had held with the school various country livings until he died in 1802 at the age of 73. The usher, the Rev. John Carter, was appointed master, and was presently advertising for a young man to teach writing and accounts for $1\frac{1}{2}$ hours in the morning and 2 hours in the afternoon, at a salary in the first year of £40: he must be unmarried and a member of the Church of

---

[1] The minutes of the dispensary were kindly produced for me by Messrs Danby, Eptons and Griffith.

England. A house in Broadgate was bought for the master, and the usher's salary was raised from £30 to £50. A speech day, or potation day, was instituted, and the old boys dined together annually at the Reindeer.

Willson told Subdean Bayley that the master of the school was very praiseworthy for indefatigable industry, but laboured under a grievous lack of polish and good taste.[1] Both he and the usher were thought competent, but there were few boys in the school, and inquiry showed that the usher had treated the boys with great severity, and the master had condoned his conduct. Both were censured and brought to resign. The chapter appointed Mr Garvey master: he advertised for boarders at 30 guineas a year, promising to treat them with the greatest tenderness. The school recovered, but only for a time, and soon the usher was admonished for neglect and the master departed. The evidence given to the Municipal Commissioners about the school was scathing, and it did not recover until more deep-seated difficulties were tackled by the reformed corporation.

By way of contrast the commissioners pointed out that a school kept by a dissenting preacher had 80 scholars—the grammar school (intended for 100 boys) having 30 or 40 only, though for the most part the school was free—whose parents paid considerable fees.[2] In these years there had been a marked growth of private schools. They have left little trace, but White's *Gazetteer* of 1826 names seventeen day schools and six day and boarding schools. They varied from groups meeting in private houses to larger establishments of some social pretension. The census of 1841 shows that the Misses Atkinson of 'The Priory' in Minster Yard had fourteen boarders and four assistants and three female servants; Mr George Boole in Pottergate had ten boys and one assistant; Thomas Bainbridge in Michaelgate had twenty-seven boarders and two assistants at his Classical and Commercial Academy; and Mrs Cappe of 5 Cornhill had thirty-three girls and four teachers. The master and the usher at the grammar school both took boarders; and Mr Hett took a few carefully chosen pupils into his house.

National movements for religious education were under way both in the Church of England and the dissenting bodies, and Bishop Tomline, though innocent of reforming zeal or enthusiasm, approved of the participation of his diocese. The formation of the Bible Society had roused the much older Society for the Promotion of Christian Knowledge into activity, and at a meeting in the cathedral vestry in 1811 a Lincoln committee was formed. It resolved to establish a depot of books and to collect subscriptions, and

---

[1] *Lincs. N. & Q.* x (1908–9), 20. Banks refused to allow Carter to use his manuscript collections (*Lincs. Archivists Report*, VIII, 35).

[2] *Report of Municipal Commissioners*, p. 2357; *L.R. & S.M.* 4 Oct. 1833.

some hundreds of Bibles and prayer books were distributed. The branch did not flourish, however, for the first annual report was not issued until 1829 (following its re-establishment in the previous year), but thereafter its annual distribution of books and tracts ran into thousands.[1]

Another educational movement was more successful. At a county meeting called by the bishop and the lord lieutenant in 1812 to promote the education of the poor, it was decided to establish a first school in Lincoln, and a subscription was entered into.[2] Sir Robert Heron, who was something of a radical, moved that the plan of education should not exclude Christian dissenters' children, even though they continued to attend their own place of worship. This proposal was defeated as being against the fundamental object of the National Society, but it was later announced that dissenters' children would be admitted, conforming to the London rule whatever it might be. They might accompany their parents to their respective places of worship at other times of the day. The Church catechism should be taught and church attendance strictly enforced. Land was leased from the city corporation and a school built.[3] In 1813 the school committee were allowed by the vestry of St Peter at Arches to take down public seats on each side of the western entrance of the parish church and put up seats for scholars and teachers. By 1825 there were 307 boys and 202 girls in the school: the original numbers had doubled.

Dr Charlesworth, who was impartial in his dislike of clergy and dissenters, commented in 1833 that many dissenters gave small sums to the school, and many of their children attended it.

Are they picking our bones, and desirous of *as much* as they can get; or do they want the 'established church' younkers to be prepared for discontent and dissent by setting themselves above labor?

He also complained of the blind and contracted government of the school by the clergy and their adherents, although they disliked the school, and left laymen to do most of the collecting of money for it. He noted in 1837 that the bigger boys who used to apply to be masters were going to the grammar school and the Banks school, and that the labour of the masters was quadrupled.

The growth of this large school had the effect of closing a number of Sunday and daily charity schools and throwing their teachers out of work; and a charitable assembly for their benefit was held in 1813. The dissenting communities did not succeed in establishing a British and Foreign School,

---

[1] L.P.L. U.P. 989, 1489, 501, 502.
[2] The National Society was formed in London in 1811, and Tomline was one of the first bishops to move in his diocese for the purpose.
[3] It is now the Corporation Offices in Silver Street.

the rival of the National School, until after the passing of the Reform Bill, which had a tremendous effect on the morale and standing of the dissenters generally.

Like the grammar school, the Bluecoat School had difficulty in changing with changing times. Joseph Fowler wrote of it in 1812 that

the Bluecoat School, which is an excellent establishment where upwards of 30 boys are boarded and educated until able to take care of themselves if fit for service, and the most industrious and attentive are put to respectable trades. There is now one apprentice to the first surgeon in Lincoln, and another to a respectable ironmonger that I know of.[1]

The Ordinances made in 1611[2] had provided that those boys who were apt for further learning might be sent to the grammar school, and it was later to be one of the complaints against the school that so far as the records showed this had never been done. (In fact there was one boy in 1681 who being a Burghersh chanter was allowed to go to the grammar school with the other cathedral choir boys.) Apprenticeship for seven years on leaving school having been part of the original scheme of things, the governors had latterly felt bound to put boys only to those occupations where apprenticeship was the custom. In a period of 27 years (1802–28) in which the trades of the selected masters happened to be always recorded, there were 110 boys bound, of whom twenty-three went to cordwainers (besides two to curriers and one to a leatherdresser), nineteen to joiners, fifteen to blacksmiths, eight to wheelwrights, six to tailors and five to stonemasons. The remainder were divided amongst a large number of trades.[3]

By the turn of the century the apprenticeship system was breaking up. Boys left their masters with recriminations on both sides. The governors found that the boys were often discharged without their knowledge, and they asked the justices not to discharge any more without their concurrence. Parents sought to put their boys to trades which the governors disapproved as not coming within the statutes: the letters patent of James I specified 'sciences, mysteries, manufacture or agriculture'. Difficulties arose in finding masters to take apprentices, and were not overcome by increasing the premium to be given with a boy from £8 to £16. Boys were sometimes allowed to leave school without being apprenticed, this being put down to bad health. At one time boys had been expelled as a matter of course if they refused to be bound to a mechanical trade. In 1822 changing conditions caused a definite departure from the statutes: boys were to be discharged at 14 instead of 16, so that they could complete their time at 21. The

---

[1] *Correspondence of William Fowler* (1907), p. 265.   [2] *T. & S.L.* p. 135.
[3] A handful of weavers carried on in Welton and Potterhanworth into the nineteenth century. The records of Christ's Hospital are now in L.P.L.

governors had such a respect for the statutes that they would not have departed from them without some clamant reason.

In 1837 the Charity Commissioners reported on the hospital. The school itself they found good. A boy rarely left it without a thorough knowledge of reading, writing and arithmetic. The diet was excellent—though a little earlier the visiting governors often complained of the poor quality of the boys' beer—and the clothing good; and on leaving each boy was given a complete suit of clothes, a Bible and Prayer Book. The management of the charity was found satisfactory.

But when the commissioners turned to consider how the boys fared after leaving, they found that not a few conducted themselves ill. A special meeting was held for inquiries: taking Lincoln boys only, apprenticed from 1830, half had behaved themselves ill, a quarter well, and of the remaining quarter there was no information. Those only were put in the first class who had either run away from their masters, or who had been imprisoned for one or more petty offences. The record of the Potterhanworth boys was worse: the rector said that with scarcely one exception the boys in after life turned out the most idle and dissolute in the parish. The commissioners had their explanation. They said that the boys were taken at the age of 7 from amongst the poorest and most indigent. They soon forgot their hardships, and were well fed, clothed, lodged, treated and educated. At 14 their condition changed for the worse. They were apprenticed to some mechanical trade, and met with hard work and harder fare; and they were subjected to a master perhaps ignorant of even the rudiments of that education in which the apprentice was skilled. It was not surprising, held the commissioners, that a boy should become dissatisfied and run away. This generally happened in the first year, and there was then little chance of the boy continuing steady and industrious. Some boys got posts as clerks or bookkeepers, and in these cases the boys behaved well. The commissioners made it plain that in their opinion the fault did not lie in the boys themselves, but in the circumstances to which they were subjected.[1]

The need for agencies of improvement is eloquently testified by such evidence as there is of the manners and customs of the poorest classes. An observer in 1827 commented on the absence of institutions for improving the intellects of mechanics such as were to be found in other towns: and he wondered whether something could be done to humanise the city. He said that in 1801 he had found them rude and uncultivated, and 25 years later they remained the same.[2]

[1] *Report of Charity Commission* (1839), Lincolnshire, pp. 355–8.
[2] *Lincoln and Lincolnshire Cabinet* (1827), pp. 11, 23.

Nevertheless a growing public opinion was having some effect. The barbarous sport of bull-baiting, periodically denounced by the *Mercury*, became intermittent and gradually died out. Guy Fawkes day had once been preceded by several nights of fires and riots, with banditti infesting the streets. Every parish had its bonfire and its guy; on one occasion an obnoxious constable was the guy; on another a man whose wife was a wanton. A magistrate's order to remove the effigies was defied; an unpopular alderman's window was broken and a burning squib put through the keyhole. Another time a tradesman was guyed and beheaded. There were complaints of much drunkenness accompanied by daring breaches of the peace. A form of social gathering which turned a landlady's house into a brothel was said in 1810 to be dying out.[1] Tea and supper parties were taking their place.

At the races in 1831 it was said that there were upwards of 500 thimble-riggers and pick-pockets on the course; riots broke out, the gamblers defended themselves against outraged rustics and townsmen by drawing out the legs of their thimble-tables and using them as weapons, and they might have won the day had not about fifty gentlemen and fox-hunting farmers joined in the attack. The gamblers' booths were destroyed and carriages burnt.

At the mayor's feast in 1827 Richard Mason, the town clerk, said he hoped that the mayor would quell those disgraceful tumults and dangerous disorders which transpired at particular periods of the year and which placed the ancient city of Lincoln half a century behind other cities in point of good order and civilisation. Help was looked for from the new police, and a conviction for keeping a disorderly house would set off all parish officers to diminish a terrible nuisance, which was carried on with impunity and bravado and outrageous indecency.

Such disorders were aggravated, and other troubles caused, by drunkenness. The parish constables were ill equipped to deal with it, but the new police were better able to do so, and they were found to be efficient by the Municipal Commissioners. The latter complained, however, of laxity in the magistrates' control of licensed houses. The number of these houses was not accurately known, but it was believed to be about sixty-two.[2] At least nine of the houses belonged to members of the corporation, and two to a magistrate. The licences of both these houses had been obtained by deception; the tenant of one of them had often been convicted of keeping a disorderly house frequented by thieves, and fined. Nevertheless his licence was renewed. The other house was occupied by the magistrate

---

[1] Stark, *op. cit.* p. 273.

[2] White's *Gazetteer* of 1826 gives 66 hotels and taverns, and that of 1842 gives 73.

himself. It had been complained of as a nuisance because of the disorderly conduct of women of bad character who frequented it. This licence also was renewed.[1] The undue tenderness of the bench of justices to one of their own number cannot fail to have undermined the authority of the bench in dealing with other licensees.

Matters were suddenly worsened in 1830. Dislike of control in general and of magistrates' control in particular led parliament to pass the Sale of Beer Act, which established free trade in beer-shops and beer. Support came from various other arguments deployed by different sections of the community: it would promote the sale of malt and hops, it would cheapen the poor man's beer, it would lessen the sale of spirits. The result was disastrous. Sibthorp, who opposed the bill, said that there were nearly 200 public houses in Lincoln, though this must have been an exaggeration. By 1842, apart from licensed houses, there were thirty-nine beer-houses in Lincoln. Ingilby was soon to denounce beer-houses in the Commons as sources of incendiarism and acts of violence, referring to them as Tom-and-Jerry shops, and pointing to the evils of tiddly-winks, the game played in them—no doubt for gambling purposes.[2]

In an attempt to stem the growing evil, moves were made for formation of a temperance society, and approaches were made to Bromhead in 1833 by the Rev. Mr Quilter of Canwick and Mr Bergne the Independent minister; it is a conjunction of names which points unmistakably to the evangelical movement. They were successful, and Bromhead had constructive suggestions for the substitution of coffee, cider and ginger-beer, for the old 'let me treat you to a glass'. The attempt was hailed as one of the most important moral movements of the time, to cope with one of the greatest evils. The society had a long hard struggle; and it had to accommodate the weaker brethren by ruling that brandy in puddings was eating and not drinking, and therefore not under ban.

Though the Savings Bank[3] was providing a means of thrift, the friendly societies, some of which had existed for a long time,[4] had proved a failure.[5] Their members paraded and went together to church once a year, but one of them could write to the *Mercury* in 1828 to say that the societies had done more harm than good. They met in alehouses: the alehouse-keeper was Father of the Club, and sold beer to the members. One landlord had said that he would not be troubled by a society unless the members

[1] *Report of Municipal Commissioners*, pp. 2356–7.
[2] Sibthorp opposed on the ground of injury to vested interests, presumably of existing licence holders (*Parliamentary Debates*, N.S. xxv, 866). For Ingilby see 3rd series, xxi, 876.
[3] Above, p. 194. [4] Above, p. 59.
[5] Only one society was registered at quarter sessions under an Act of 1819: it was held at the Green Dragon, and its amendments to rules were allowed at sessions in 1822.

spent two guineas a month. Decent members paid their money on club night and left, but the soakers remained. The subscriptions were not enough, and the societies were bankrupt before the younger members could benefit. One club transferred to a private house, but further suggestions to that end met with a storm of abuse. Fortunately the female societies, founded about 1808 and later reconstituted, were more successful; they were controlled by gentle-women, and had honorary members whose subscriptions helped the finances.

A select committee of the House of Commons reported in 1825 on the defects of friendly societies, including the lack of evidence about average sickness and mortality, and the expense of convivial practices; and in these years efforts were being made by magistrates and clergy to found societies in which they could ensure good management and a moral purpose. The Rev. Thomas Becher of Southwell was one of the pioneers. Subdean Bayley wrote to Bromhead that Lord Brownlow was disposed to lay before the grand jury at the assizes the project of a county superintending society:

29 February 1828. I hope the formation of a general society will be gradually followed by a dissolution of the existing local ones. They are all made on wrong calculations (not excepting the last of them, that at Lincoln). They are all liable to bankruptcy, and if examined by you (and who else in the county can examine them?) would probably be found already bankrupt. The female one at Lincoln, being of recent institution, may yet be prosperous: the individual members of these should get out of the scrape as soon as may be, and divide what there may be of stock....Mr Nicholson, a young architect here, has been much with Mr Becher, and knows a good deal of the detail.

Brownlow was doubtful of success if large contributions were needed from honorary members, and the grand jury proved unwilling to move in advance of a new Act. In a city a committee was formed to start a new society; the Rev. John Penrose and William Brooke the printer were active, and Bromhead drafted the rules. Charlesworth of course took a hand. He studied the scheme laid down by Becher.

20 August 1828. It may do for ten miles round Southwell Cathedral, but will not do here. The rules are drawn with great ability, but the thing is too complex and *too provident*: Lincoln freemen will not be drilled at their own expense. It is altogether aristocratic in the management, as such an engine must be: it places men in harness and keeps them there. This also is necessary if you will force upon them habits of economy, regularity and subordination: it is in fact of the order 'Harmony', class 'Becher', genus 'Southwell'. I think it will not take here—I do not like any of the stocks from which it springs.

He thought Bromhead's draft rules simpler and better. That November the rules of the new society were ready for enrolment; Bromhead had corresponded with Becher, and his subscription tables were examined by George Boole the mathematician. They were higher than Becher's.

The new Act was passed in 1828, and enrolment followed. It was confidently predicted that when new societies were conducted by competent persons on safe principles, they would be a great improvement upon the scrambling, vague and often fraudulent system of the old clubs. Thereafter the Oddfellows and the other friendly societies did increasingly valuable work for their members in sickness and distress.

The gradual quickening of life found expression in the issue of local books and journals. Enterprise was on a modest scale, and its finance was precarious. In 1802 John Drury printed and sold *An Historical Account of Lincoln and the Cathedral*, which was no more than Wood's pamphlet[1] with the charter of Charles I to the city in English translation, the Mayor's Cry[2] and a list of mayors and sheriffs thrown in. The first man to produce a printed history of Lincoln was a Scotsman, Adam Stark, the son of an architect who had advised Sir Walter Scott about the remodelling of Abbotsford. Stark married in Lincoln, where he had a bookshop; later he moved to Gainsborough. He wrote and himself printed *The History of Lincoln* in 1810, dedicating it to the admirers of antiquity in general and the inhabitants of Lincoln in particular.[3] He drew largely on Gough's edition of Camden's *Britannia* for his material. Like a later writer, he remarks on the dumb compotations of the common people of Lincoln: and he notes the absence of a public library, condemning the cathedral library as a repository of mildewed paper. He refers to a weekly newspaper just established in Lincoln: it was his own *Lincoln and Hull Chronicle*, started in 1809, and unfortunately dying within the year.

Stark remarked that the abovehill city was the general residence of the gentry and clergy, and that belowhill inhabited by merchants and tradesmen, the court and the mercantile parts of the city respectively. He was an upholder of the established social order. But reform was in the air, and subversive ideas abroad. Another *History of Lincoln* was printed by and for Drury and Sons in 1816. It was dedicated to Lady Monson, who was representative of the whig interest (it refers oddly to 'a character established on the practice of every domestic and public virtue'). It distinguished the more opulent and genteel portion of the community abovehill from those below, 'merchants and tradespeople, a class of persons certainly not less respectable or less valuable than those who live upon the fortunes bequeathed by their ancestors without contributing anything to the general stock of industry and wealth' (p. 146).

---

[1] Above, p. 61.

[2] A code of traditional by-laws which was proclaimed from time to time; it is printed in *T. & S.L.* p. 216.

[3] For his other works, and notes of his life, see an article by his great grandson Henry G. Gamble in *Lincs. Magazine*, II, 87.

Meanwhile more serious inquiries into local history were being made, especially by Banks. His curiosity began to embrace the history of the county in 1782 when Grosseteste's tomb was opened.[1] In 1788, when the river Witham was being cleaned, he advertised in the *Mercury* for news of weapons or utensils found in its bed, and he was always on the spot quickly if any discoveries were made. After frequent exchanges of letters with the antiquary Richard Gough he wrote in 1799 of his collection of maps, prints and engraved portraits: 'It is now become a valuable mass of materials, which will be of use if either myself or any other person should undertake a history of the county'.[2] At his death in 1820 his Lincolnshire collections were by his direction assembled at his home at Revesby Abbey, whence unhappily they were sold and dispersed in 1919 and 1920.[3]

Others were assembling historical material, and among them John Cragg of Threekingham, a land valuer and inclosure commissioner. In 1800 he advertised a *Villare Lincolniense*, to include an account of all the towns and villages in the county, and asked for information. His proposed publication did not appear.[4]

William Marrat of Boston was the first to attempt a printed history of the county, to be written, printed, bound and published by himself. It began to appear in parts in 1814, in paper wrappers. He acknowledged the help of Banks, Cragg and others, but complained later that Banks had denied all knowledge of him and objected to the use of his name. On this refusal of help it was thought that the work could not be carried on, and it was abandoned.[5] Something of the man is told to William Brooke, the Lincoln printer, by his brother-in-law, and passed on to John Ross:

(From) what I know of the man I should have thought him the last man to have undertaken such a work. He was writing master at Banks' when I was at school, and was afterwards schoolmaster at Sibsey. He published a mathematical work on mechanics, which I fancy had merit in it, and while fixed here (at Boston) as a bookseller with a Mr Jackson, was a member of our Bread and Cheese...he was an idle man and too fond of ale. He went to Liverpool....I fear he ended his days in poverty. I think by the bye he had an escapade to America, but was soon tired of Jonathan, but let me not disparage the poor man, and keep my observations *entre nous*.

[1] Above, p. 47.
[2] John Nichols, *Illustrations of the Literary History of the Eighteenth Century* (1822), IV, 693–8.
[3] See Warren R. Dawson, *The Banks Letters* (1958), p. xviii. His larger collections on scientific subjects have also been scattered: Mr Dawson has assembled the evidence.
[4] Some part of his collection of Lincolnshire books and manuscripts is now in L.A.O.; the rest has been dispersed.
[5] The first three volumes appeared, and parts of volumes IV and VI (*Lincs. N. & Q.* XIX, 70–4). Volume V was to have been devoted to the city of Lincoln.

He adds elsewhere that 'his imprudence always spoilt any favourable project that opened for him'. It is not difficult to divine Banks's reasons for disowning him.[1]

The younger Drurys, printers in Lincoln, had more ambitious ideas of an annual publication. Edward Drury started upon the project, but according to Charlesworth was deterred by idleness and ill-health, and furthermore he was absorbed in politics on the side of reform. He handed over all his papers to his brother John, who issued a prospectus for a *Lincoln and Lincolnshire Cabinet and Annual Intelligencer*. It appeared in 1827, and contained a spirited description of the city, the new county hall, the races, the charities, and a topical review of the history of the Witham and Fossdyke, then a very live subject. In planning a second annual John Drury applied to Bromhead, and submitted a list of contents. The book, he said, had originated with a Mr Jewett; he was anxious to improve upon the first number, which contained many errors. He had a memoir of Colonel Ellison, who had just died, and he wanted an account of Lord Goderich, and how he got into the Ministry. He hoped Bromhead would be his pilot, as Drury, who also kept the post office, had not enough time to spare. When the second number appeared it had a full account of the lunatic asylum, no doubt provided by Charlesworth, and of other institutions. It referred to a Burton hunt suggestion that the ordnance survey should be induced to produce a map of the county; and to the topographical library being built up in the Lincoln Library which might make possible a county history; and to a county Debrett. These were projects entertained by Bromhead and Charlesworth, both of them collectors of local material. A much smaller annual appeared in 1829, without articles, and so the hopeful series ended.

Dependence for local news on the *Lincoln Rutland and Stamford Mercury* was widely felt to be unsatisfactory. Richard Newcomb, who had long been proprietor, was then an old man, and his son Richard the younger was in effective control. A Stamford reformer wrote to Charles Tennyson about the difficulty of coaxing him to go quietly in harness:

The reasons are obvious enough to me: he has not taken that leading station which his ambitious spirit instructs him he ought to have done. He is Milton's Devil who would rather 'reign in Hell than serve in Heaven'....My friend Richard is a most accomplished good hater when he takes to it.[2]

Charles Seely had mooted the idea of a newspaper for Lincoln in 1827,[3] and Charlesworth thought that the want of impartiality in the *Mercury*

---

[1] Ross Corr. IV, 12 Oct. 1859 and 7 Oct. 1860. The first of the Brookes had bought the stock of the bookseller Simmons in 1788.

[2] L.A.O. Tennyson d'Eyncourt (16 Feb. 1831).

[3] And see White's *Gazetteer* for 1826, p. 43: several unsuccessful attempts had been made to establish a newspaper.

would induce many to patronise it; he thought Edward Drury would have undertaken a paper but for his friendship for Newcomb, whose Lincoln correspondent he was. It was James Amphlett, apparently a newcomer, who started the *Lincoln Herald* in 1828; he remarked two years later that his paper divided Boston with *Bee* or *Stamford Herald*. Amphlett was not a reformer; and James Hitchens, who had been election agent against the duke of Newcastle at Newark, and had started the *Newark Times*, was casting his eyes towards Lincoln. The growing enthusiasm provided a larger public; and Richard Mason, speaking freely after dinner, remarked of the *Herald* that nothing but a reform paper would do for Lincoln, and that Hitchens would make a different thing of the business. Charlesworth shrewdly observed that so long as there was only one paper in Lincoln Amphlett would be neutral, but if another started he would immediately take the opposite side: he heard that Hitchens had taken a house in Lincoln, and added 'he will make sad havoc with honest people during his short reign'. By the end of 1830 £700 had been subscribed for Hitchens's new paper, the *Lincoln Times*, and, wrote Amphlett,

in the present feverish excitement of public opinion he will be able to take great credit for directing the current of popular prejudice against the Aristocracy and the Church: his chief leading view (29 Nov. 1830).

Amphlett therefore veered towards the tories; if they failed him, he would have welcomed a merger with the *Mercury*.

The political battle was at its height, and Edward Drury, who was trying to form a political union in support of reform, tried to undermine Amphlett by organising his workmen. In May 1831 Amphlett reported to Bromhead on these developments:

The radicalism of Lincoln has received a strange momentum within the last few months: some are already becoming quite intolerant. Drury is busy organising the Electoral Club, and is secretly promoting the interests of Hitchens...his man has been secretly forming the journeymen printers of Lincoln into a society, who are endeavouring to prevent any man working in my office, except in some arbitrary relation of the number of apprentices as proportioned to the number of men. Fine *Liberty* men these!

Charlesworth thought poorly of Amphlett, remarking that his paper could not be at par when he was lost in dirt, indolence and guzzle. But at least it kept alive, while Hitchens's failed, for reasons which Charlesworth explained to Bromhead:

25 May 1831. I forward the farewell paper of Hitchens. A paper that pays the proprietor for publishing requires to have a sale of 500 copies, and to have 30 advertisements weekly. *The Times* had very nearly the required sale, but got no advertisements. It was worked by 4 men and 2 boys—deemed by the working part of the trade a most liberal and princely establishment, to be expected only for a paper in great demand, or for one published for a particular purpose by a wealthy party or by an amateur....

Amphlett's paper is worked by one man and several boys at about a fourth part of the expense of the other paper: this is deemed by the working part of the trade very mean and bad: they have combined under a code of rules (which I will send you) and do not admit Amphlett's man into their Society. E. Drury has had serious thoughts of taking up *The Times*, but is deterred by the pains, penalties, expenses &c. (The penalties were for non-payment of stamp duties. Charlesworth said the circulation of the *Times* was 400 weekly).

Hitchens returned to Newark. Efforts were made to keep his paper afloat, and Amphlett on his part was struggling to maintain his *Herald*. He appealed to

those persons, who may not be prepared to see the city's authorities run down by clamour, and publicly derided, by a press exclusively in the hands of the lower classes, without any local counteractive organ—as is the case at Boston, now placed out of the pale of the law by the supreme controul of a rabble and a revolutionary journal.

He gave warning that Lincoln would be in the same plight in six months' time unless he was supported. The argument was a persuasive one, and he received some help from tories; but the paper did not last long, and may have succumbed to the new tory *Lincoln Chronicle* which began in 1832.

Presently the *Lincoln Times* reappeared with Peter Wilkins as editor, containing, as Charlesworth said, nothing except a squeak for Hitchens against his late friends. The new editor was soon dismissed by his subscribers. Hitchens too was quickly out of his *Newark Times*, and trying to start another paper, to be printed by Leary or Brumby, and *The Lincolnshire Independent Whig and Notts Intelligencer*, conducted by James Hitchens, late editor of the *Newark Times*, was announced: a reference to his 'sleepless eye' drew the marginal gloss 'gin and water' at Thurlby. But he was in trouble with a government prosecution for not paying stamp duty on his paper, and had to struggle with the costs, although the fine imposed on him had been remitted at the instance of Serjeant Wilde, by, according to Charlesworth, 'a most partial and base concession of the government'. His goods were sold, and realised £38. After municipal reform he was rewarded for his party services by appointment first as city coroner at Lincoln, and then as county coroner, but at the Newark election of 1840 he was involved in the smuggling away of some tory voters and sentenced to six months' imprisonment.

W. S. Northhouse started the *Lincoln Gazette* about 1835, with the support

of Yarborough—Ingilby called it the *Brocklesby Gazette*—but he did not
last long. He was succeeded by Edward Drury, on whose behalf Charles
Anderson Pelham wrote to Charles Tennyson asking for support: it had to
compete with a new tory newspaper, the *Lincoln Standard*, which began in
February 1836.

The circulation and influence of these local newspapers was very
small. Edward Drury told Tennyson in 1834 that only one in twenty
people saw a newspaper, and that often only once a week. When Northhouse left the *Gazette* it had a circulation of about 400; by November
1836, under Drury, it reached 800. The *Standard* was selling 150 copies
in 1838.[1]

Dissension, both between the upper and lower city and the parties within
each, became sharper as the real public issues behind the battles of the
Reform Bill and Catholic Emancipation and the removal of dissenters'
disabilities superseded the faction fights of the reds and the pinks, the
Monsons and Sibthorps. In particular the growth of Protestant dissent was
bringing out the clash between Church and Chapel which was to loom
large in the life of the city throughout the century. On the one side were
ranged the tories and high-and-dry churchmen; on the other the radicals
and dissenters supporting the whigs as the party most likely to help them.
The whigs were in a difficult position: they needed the votes of the dissenters.
Lord Yarborough and Ingilby subscribed to their building funds, and
Sir Culling Eardley Smith presented the Independents of Lincoln with a
tent to assist their camp meetings. For the most part the whigs did not
like their allies, and did as little for them as possible.

It is not easy now to enter into the intensity of feeling aroused by the
politico-religious quarrel. The idea that every Englishman was born into
the Church of England was shattered, and in the Establishment there was a
deep resentment against those who shattered it, coupled with a contempt
for those of a lower social class who presumed to withstand their betters.
The dissenters were constantly aware of their inferiority in all points:
marriages in the parish church, registration of the births of their children,
burials in the churchyards, the rating of their chapels, and their payment
of church rates to the parish church. They were excluded from many
public offices by law, and from many other posts by prejudice. They were
mostly of the lower middle class or the poor, and their ministers were
drawn from lower ranks of society than the clergy. The pressure of the
black cloth, felt everywhere, was all the greater in a cathedral city, where
the higher clergy had much greater weight than their brethren in the

---

[1] Most of this account of the newspapers is taken from the Bromhead MSS: a few
facts come from the Tennyson d'Eyncourt papers.

parishes. Dissenting bitterness found expression in an outburst of Benjamin Byron, the first minister of a new Independent body in Lincoln. When he resigned after ten years in Lincoln he wrote of

the goading, the harrassing, the insults, the indignity and the thorough-faced brutality with which I was treated in the earlier years of my ministry here, by those old professors of religion who were born out of due time, flung into the world as it were, by a strange slip of nature, at least a thousand years too late; and, alas! whose ideas respecting religion are only fit for that state of moral darkness which covered Europe during the middle Ages.

Though there were thirteen Anglican churches in the city including the cathedral, he thought it no breach of Christian charity to record that there was not one decidedly pious and evangelical minister.

The early progress of Methodism, which had revivified the older dissenting communities, had coincided with the French war, when the slightest deviation from established ways provoked the most bitter hostility. William Bedford, a leading dissenter, recalled in 1830 that when he came to Lincoln fifty years before there was but one dissenting congregation. Forty years before, the bitterness was such that he had determined to leave the city, and he remembered three leading citizens being summoned to the Guildhall on the outbreak of war to take the oath of allegiance. About 1802 a man threw a squib or gunpowder serpent into the Wesleyan meeting-house during a service, and when the minister and others charged an individual before one of the justices, Alderman Parsons, the latter refused to commit him on the ground that the evidence was insufficient. The Methodists then applied in the King's Bench for a criminal information against Parsons, on which Lord Kenyon ruled that the subject should go to a county grand jury: the jury threw out the bill. Parsons may have been right about the evidence, but his motives were suspect, and the hostility of a county grand jury was a matter of course; and party feeling ran high, especially after the common council commended Parsons for behaving so creditably. In 1812 the city quarter sessions refused licences to Methodist preachers on the ground that they had no special congregations to which they were required to be licensed. This matter too went to the King's Bench.

A priest vicar, the Rev. William Hett, published pamphlets attacking Methodists, alleging that it was no uncommon thing for a boy of 16 to apply for a licence to preach, take the oath, and pay his shilling fee: and he might only be doing so in order to escape the risk of serving as a militiaman. Hett also made virulent attacks upon dissenting teachers.[1]

In spite of all attacks the movement grew. In 1812 a new Toleration Act gave partial relief to dissenters. A first Methodist Sunday school in Lincoln

[1] L.P.L. U.P. 569, 570, 571, 574.

was opened in 1806; it taught reading and writing, and was held for five hours on Sundays. Two other schools followed. A large chapel was opened in 1815, which by 1820 had a congregation of about 700, and by 1836 their Wesley Chapel, built to hold 1,400 people, was in use. They were the principal supporters of the Benevolent Society, formed in 1803, for the relief of the poor. The Calvinistic Methodists, followers of Whitefield, having first used the Presbyterian meeting-house, built their Zion Chapel in 1802, and drew a congregation of 100; a body of Calvinistic Baptists bought a site in Mint Lane in 1818 and built a chapel; a new community of Independents was formed in 1819 in the old Baptist meeting-house and soon built in Tanners Lane; and the Ranters, or Primitive Methodists, a breakaway body, opened a chapel in 1819, with a congregation of 150, with a display of hysteria which struck the beholder as akin to a brawl. There were 100 Unitarians and a few Quakers, and there was a small Roman Catholic chapel.[1]

All this activity evidenced a degree of fervour which seemed all the greater because of the contrast with the somnolence of the Church of England, which could hardly have presented a broader target to its critics; and among them not only the dissenters but the political reformers, whose campaign against the Church played a leading part in the fight for the Reform Bill. The *Black Book* selected some choice examples of Lincolnshire abuses, beginning with Bishop Tomline, who was also dean of St Pauls. John, his brother, was archdeacon and precentor when he died in 1817. George, a son, was chancellor of Lincoln, prebendary of Winchester, and rector of three livings; Richard, a son, was precentor, with four livings. Their father had procured for Richard the wardenship of the Mere Hospital, which owned 630 acres of land within five miles of Lincoln: it was left to maintain six poor men and a warden. The whole estate was let for £32, out of which £24 was paid to the poor brethren: how much was pocketed by the warden in fines on renewal of the leases was not known. His brother George was master of the Spital, to the north of the city, the income of which was over £600 a year, of which £27. 4s. was paid to four or five pensioners.[2]

Pluralism among the incumbents of city parishes became more of a scandal as the population grew. The perpetual curate of St Mark, the Rev. John Nelson, was also a vicar choral of the cathedral, and held four country livings; whilst the vicar of St Martin, the Rev. George Davies Kent, was a canon of Lincoln and held three other Lincolnshire livings and

---

[1] These figures are taken from the first church book of the Tanners Lane (later Newland) Independent Chapel.

[2] The office of registrar to most of the archdeacons was also granted to the bishop's sons and grandsons.

one in Kent.[1] Mr Hett, the hammer of the Methodists, was a prebendary and vicar choral of Lincoln, vicar of Dunholme, rector of Mavis Enderby, vicar of St John's and rector of St Paul's in Lincoln, minister of Greetwell and Nettleham chapelries, and rector of Thorpe on the Hill; he was also chaplain to the marquis of Stafford.[2]

In 1817 a writer in the *Stamford Mercury* could say that the rector of St Peter at Arches had an income of not less than £2,000 a year, but was too selfish to pay a curate; that out of eight churches belowhill, only one, St Martin, had morning service on both the last Sunday and a fortnight before. On the other hand there were four dissenting churches; in three of them there was public service three times every Sunday, though the ministers' average income probably did not exceed £60. It was being said that if the parishes could be reduced in number, the clergy stipends might be improved, divine service could be performed twice on a Sunday, and congregations would not be driven to the chapels.

The districts of growing population were the worst served, and among them Newport, north of the Bail. In 1822 E. J. Willson wrote to the subdean, Bayley:

Newport, it seems to me, is in more need of civilisation than any other part of the city. There is no church, no school, no person of the least influence, no checking the grossest rudeness and insubordination; the two parishes have each a constable; one, an elderly man, of no more use in his office than an old woman; the other, a Methodist, who is out at his meetings the whole Sunday, the day of all others the most liable to disorder. We see parties of twenty or thirty lads wrestling or playing at chuckpenny in the high road, and I was quite blamed for imprudence in dispersing an assembly of this sort about a month ago. I lately heard that Mr Grey had thirty pounds from the sale of trees etc. in St Nicholas churchyard; if that is true, I think it would be well employed in assisting the erection of a low tower, or a sort of chapel, to serve for funerals and parish meetings. Both parishes now go to the public-house to settle their affairs, a very indecent practice at best.[3]

[1] *Extraordinary Black Book* (1831 edn), pp. 24, 524. Dr Goddard, archdeacon of Lincoln, was chaplain to the king, vicar of Bexley, vicar of Louth, and rector of St James Garlick-hithe, London; and the Hon. H. L. Hobart, vicar of Nocton, was dean of Windsor and Wolverhampton, rector of Hesley and vicar of Wantage (pp. 513, 517).

[2] P. 516. Many of the country clergy lived in Lincoln and other towns in what came to be called rookeries; the reason sometimes being lack of a vicarage house. One of them, the Rev. Tillotson Laycock, vicar of Hackthorn, Cammeringham, Ingham and Owersby for upwards of 40 years, had a notion that Newport Arch, being very old, was likely to fall, and whenever he rode into Lincoln, on reaching Newport he put in his spurs and rode full gallop as if riding for his life. This was so regularly done, both in entering and leaving Lincoln, that boys used to stop and see the operation (Sir C. Anderson in *L.D.B.* sub 1815).

[3] *Lincs. N. & Q.* x (1908–9), 19. One of the incumbents of St Nicholas read himself in in a room at the Turk's Head inn.

When the worst days were over Thomas Cooper, the young radical who had become Lincoln correspondent of the *Mercury*, waxed eloquent:

The neglect of the people's spiritual state by the Lincoln clergy was never more notorious than at present. St Mark's church is a mere scene for mockery every Sabbath, as the service takes place at a time when a congregation cannot be found, and the reverend ministrant is becoming superannuated. St Benedict's is another of the once-a-day Sabbath resorts; while the whole of the large population of Newport is entirely without a *canonical* spiritual teacher. O No! we crave pardon. The Rev. Mr Garvey, a vicar of the cathedral, reads a form once a year to the tombstones of St Nicholas churchyard (for there is no church!) and pockets a few score pounds for his immense labour.[1]

His sarcasms were only just in time: he knew a movement was afoot to build a new parish church of St Nicholas.

It would however be wrong to suppose that there was no life in any of the parish churches. St Peter at Arches was active; the body of the church would seat over 400 plus those who might sit in the aisles, and over 200 in the gallery. The churchyard, narrowed by street widening, was increased by the removal of houses, and an organ was put in. Rents were charged for pews, and if those to whom they were let did not occupy them they were forfeited. In 1821 the living was augmented, so that two sermons might be preached every Sunday. St Swithin had not been rebuilt since the Civil War, and as the population of the parish was growing fast a new church, a 'neat plain building', was built in 1801, and a vestry added later. The application for a brief declared that the parishioners were mostly labouring people, and the parish heavily burdened with poor. St Martin, the church of the other growing parish, was enlarged in 1809, being paid for by the sale of pews. At St Mary le Wigford the corporation seats were divided and more pews provided.

The influence of the evangelical movement was beginning to be felt, and like later religious movements it cut across social divisions. Perhaps the first clear expression of it is to be found in the formation of a Lincoln auxiliary of the British and Foreign Bible Society in 1816, which provided the only platform on which Anglicans and dissenters were likely to meet. Mrs Waldo Sibthorp supported it, her son Richard became one of its secretaries, and her son Coningsby, M.P., was counted as a supporter; Mr Cropper, a Lincoln gentleman of means, was another; and its treasurer was Mr George Moore, the cashier of Smith Ellison's Bank. The Smiths themselves, who were closely connected with William Wilberforce, were strong supporters. The movement was in the hands of pious laymen, dissenting ministers, and a few country clergy, among them Mr Quilter of Canwick, and under the patronage of the whig gentry. Most of the clergy,

[1] 27 Oct. 1837.

and in particular the cathedral clergy, kept aloof. There followed movements in support of Anglican and dissenting missionary societies, and a branch of the Religious Tract Society, for the distribution of tracts tending to the improvement of the poor in religion and morality. The Dorcas Society, with Mrs Sibthorp as patron, was formed in 1816 to provide the poor with clothing.

The first quickening of life in the parishes came from Richard Sibthorp, who preached for some months in St Peter in Eastgate church. He was an evangelical preacher, and was followed chiefly by the low churchmen. Anderson wrote of him to Samuel Wilberforce:

21 January 1828. He is by far the best preacher I ever heard, and with Mr Stewart...the only extempore preacher I ever liked. All the Lincolners flock to hear him. He is brother to the Member who is such a raff.[1]

Another tribute came from Abel Smith, the evangelical banker, who was looking for a house for his brother-in-law Alexander Leslie Melville, then about to become the Lincoln resident partner in the bank; he wrote:

2 March 1830. Mr Cropper...I am sure a genuine devoted Christian...gives a poor account of spiritual things; even Mr Moore (vicar of St Peter in Eastgate) the best minister, does not either preach nor go to Bible meetings, but he has got, he believes, a pious curate, Mr Pridmain. Mr Cropper knows Mr Sibthorp very well and likes him much.

Like other evangelicals, he thought better of the dissenters than of the high-and-dry churchmen:

Mr Cropper is like me, for he seems, when he cannot get fed in the Church, to see what the dissenters are doing—but he is not a dissenter nor does he give a preference to them.

Melville, he said, would find a complete lack of spiritual society in his own class.[2]

Sibthorp would have liked to become incumbent of St Peter, but he was not approved; Charlesworth said that the chancellor had given the living to 'some poor devil of whom he knows nothing except that the Corporation of Lincoln or the parish of St Peter had not recommended him'. But Charlesworth equally disapproved when a move was made to enlarge the church to hold Sibthorp's congregation:

19 May 1831. ...we took the alarm only just in time to save ourselves from the play of a (masked) battery upon our parish purse. The dissimulation of the saints is odious and frightful....

[1] Wilberforce MSS; and see J. Fowler, *Richard Waldo Sibthorp* (1880), p. 47.

[2] National Provincial Bank, Smith Ellison papers. Abel Smith finished a letter about finding a house and servants by saying that he thought of James iv. 13, 14 for Melville; for himself he had been breaking the tenth commandment: 'may your heart be kept alive in this inanimate town.'

Into this world of high-and-dry-churchmen, absentees and pluralists, there came in 1827 John Kaye as bishop. He had been regius professor of divinity at Cambridge, and although a whig had been first promoted to the bench as bishop of Bristol by Lord Liverpool. He supported the repeal of the Test and Corporation Acts (for the relief of dissenters), though he opposed Catholic emancipation and defended church rates. He did not belong to any ecclesiastical party, but he became a member of the Ecclesiastical Commission, whose reforming activities sent many a shiver down clerical spines. In his attack upon abuses he increased the spiritual effectiveness of the Church, and he prepared the way for revival. As he said long afterwards, non-residence of the clergy had been almost the rule, and residence the exception. He attacked pluralities and the absence of parsonage houses, and called for two services on Sundays in parish churches. For the sake of getting a government grant for church schools he was willing to acquiesce in like grants for dissenters' schools.

No bishop had lived in or near Lincoln since the Civil War. The principal episcopal residence had been at Buckden, but when Huntingdonshire was transferred from the see of Lincoln to the see of Ely in 1836 Kaye moved to Riseholme, a country house bought for him by the Ecclesiastical Commissioners two miles north of Lincoln.[1]

The young Charles Anderson approved of Kaye:

31 July 1828. We have had our new Bishop (Kaye) here for two or three days, and were much pleased with him. He is a very agreeable man and seems to know *everything*. His knowledge of his Diocese is wonderful considering the short time he has been in it. He intends to force residence and not allow a curate to hold more than 2 churches on any plea, and also to enforce double duty. For the evening service he recommends instead of a sermon a running comment on a chapter in the Bible, and recommends the clergyman to use as much scripture language as possible for the sake of the common people. His Charge was beautifully clear. Indeed, he seems quite a godsend to this extensive diocese, and we rejoice he had not been raised to London or the Primacy.

Later, writing as a tractarian, Anderson found the bishop wanting. He had preached at the consecration of Trinity Church at Gainsborough:

29 June 1843. His sermon was very like the man, the first part excellently orthodox, and taking a high view of Church Doctrine, and then came the 'but' at the top of the ladder, and then step by step down again till one didn't know whether he was a Dissenter or a Churchman.[2]

---

[1] There was at once an outcry about Riseholme, both because of the cost (£52,000) and because the old palace could have been used; part of it was occupied by one of the bishop's officials (see Samuel Wilberforce, *Essays contributed to the Quarterly Review* (1874), i, 306).

[2] Wilberforce MSS: L.A.O. Anderson, 5/2/2, p. 321. He wrote scathingly of the Rev. C. S. Bird, the vicar of Trinity, Gainsborough: 'Old Bird the vicar, a weak

The new high church party to which Anderson belonged had of course nothing in common with the old high-and-dry churchmen; and at this early date it had few friends in the diocese of Lincoln. Certainly he could not expect to find any help at the Minster in a project for establishing a depot for the Oxford *Tracts for The Times*.

6 June 1830. I went to the Minster on Whitsun Eve, and except myself, the officiating Vicar and 10 singing boys there was not a soul. It really quite affected me in that vast and noble pile....It seemed as if the Cathedral was chaunting her own dirge, but I hope for brighter days.[1]

28 October 1836. The residentiaries of the Minster are of that stamp of High Church which ought to be called Low, for their affection to it only extends to it in a temporal point of view. The Dean,[2] who is far the best, is old and inactive, the Pretymans most worthy scions of their most noble stock, Sutton[3] one who like most of that name loves the loaves and fishes in the literal sense, who devour a jowl of salmon with their eyes before it is cut, yet a *goodnatured* fellow. The minor clergy lackeys to the Minster, except one or two who I suspect are *toute au contraire*, and would think nothing but a rag of the old woman in scarlet can come from Oxford, so that I see little prospect of success.[4]

Evangelical put in by Bishop Kaye, was so afraid of anything like Churchmanship. He was very near giving in to having the church finished without even a cross on the east gable, but I got one put on by using the argument that the Independent meeting house at Lincoln had one, and therefore the English Church being Christian ought to follow their example. I also got one of two hideous stone pulpits which were to be placed on each side of Church removed by telling the Committee they would be if erected like two ambones in Milan Cathedral! Such was the utter ignorance and prejudice and folly which were then prevalent in Gainsboro' and encouraged both by Vicar and Bishop' (L.A.O. Anderson, 5/2/2, p. 289). Another view will be found in the Rev. C. S. Bird's *Sketches* of his own life (1864), chapters XVI and XVII.

[1] In 1905 Richard Hall recalled his memories as a cathedral choirboy more than 70 years before. The bishop was rarely present at services, and it was no uncommon thing to begin a quarter of an hour late, or for the organist to leave during the service to assist at St Martin's. The boys had few holidays, but were set to work in the organist's garden. There were fine apple trees, a mulberry tree, and some gooseberry bushes, and no boy ever left the garden without a stain on his character. Only the vestry was heated (*Critch's Annual*, 1906, p. 13).

[2] Gordon.

[3] Rev. Thomas Manners Sutton, the subdean.

[4] Wilberforce MSS. Welby Pugin wrote in 1834 that 'in my travels I am daily witnessing fresh instances of the disgraceful conduct of the greater portion of the established clergy. At a place in Lincolnshire called the ——, the Rev. —— goes to perform the service in *top boots* and *white cord breeches*. Then I have seen the —— of Lincoln Cathedral, the Rev. Mr ——, son of the late Bishop —— (who refused to subscribe to the erection of his throne in —— Cathedral) lost £7,000 at the last Lincoln races...! (B. Ferrey, *Recollections of A. N. Welby Pugin and his father Augustus Pugin; with Notices of their Works* (1861), p. 88). Precentor Pretyman was clearly the second of these characters, and he was probably also the first. He was said to hurry from a cathedral service to Doncaster, where he would appear on the course with book and pencil.

A whole generation was to pass before the Oxford Movement reached the Minster. Meanwhile the view taken of the chapter from belowhill was not markedly different from that of Anderson. The dissenters, some of their civil disabilities removed by the repeal of the Test and Corporation Acts, by the Reform Bill and the Municipal Corporations Act, were emerging into public life, building their schools and waging war in the parish vestries against church rates; and entering upon the great struggle, religious, political and social, between Church and Chapel, which was to be a central feature of local life for the remainder of the century.

THE PLATES

1   South-west prospect of the City of Lincoln by Samuel and Nathaniel Buck, 1743

2 Lincoln, from a painting by Augustus Charles Pugin (1762?–1832)

3　Cathedral High Altar (*c.* 1784), from a drawing by S. H. Grimm

4*a* Cathedral and Castle, *c.* 1784

4*b* Cathedral and St Paul's, *c.* 1784. Both (*a*) and (*b*) are from drawings
by S. H. Grimm, *c.* 1784–6

5*a*   St Paul, built 1786

5*b*   St Botolph, built 1723. Both (*a*) and (*b*) are from drawings
by S. H. Grimm, *c.* 1784–6

6*a*   St Peter in East Gate, built 1781

6*b*   St Mark, built 1740. Both (*a*) and (*b*) are from drawings
by S. H. Grimm, *c.* 1784–6

7 a   St Peter at Gowts, and St Mary's Hall, from a drawing by S. H. Grimm, *c.* 1784–6

7 b   St Peter at Arches (1724) and Butter Market (1757)

8   Brayford Head, 1790, from a drawing by W. Nutter

9   Lincoln from Gowts Bridges, 1790, from a drawing by W. Nutter

10*a* High Street looking south to the Stonebow, 1818

10*b* Steep Hill looking north, 1818. Both (*a*) and (*b*) are from drawings
by William Henry Brooke

11 *a*　High Street from St Peter at Gowts parish, looking north, 1818

11 *b*　High Street looking north to the Stonebow, 1818. Both (*a*) and (*b*) are from
drawings by William Henry Brooke

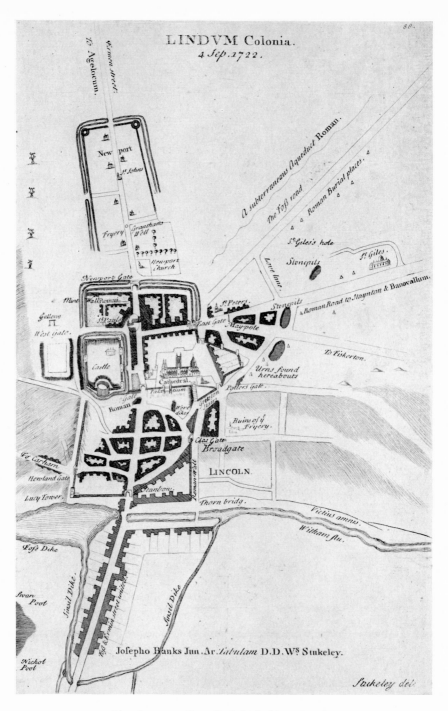

12   Lincoln, 1722, from Stukeley's *Itinerarium Curiosum*

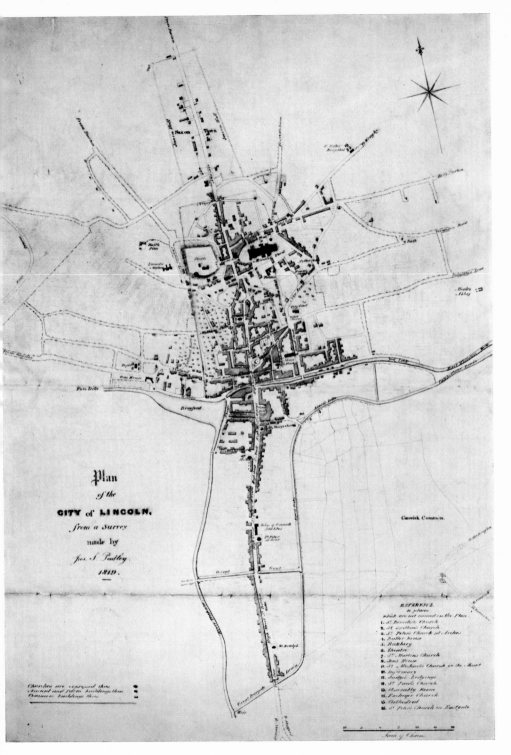

13 Plan of the City of Lincoln, from a survey made by J. S. Padley, 1819

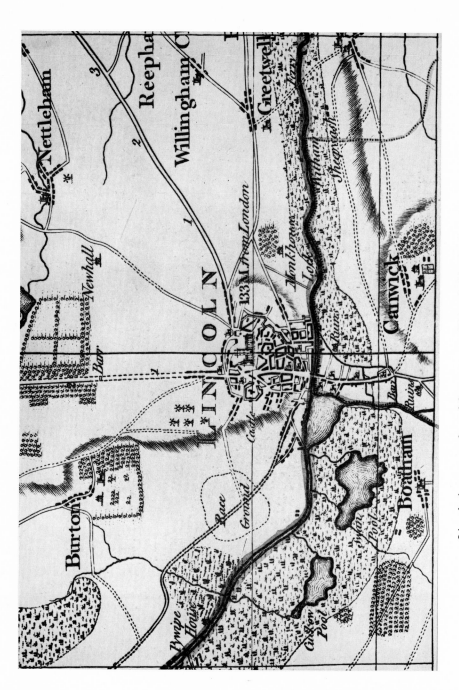

14 Lincoln in 1779; enlarged from a map of Lincolnshire by Andrew Armstrong

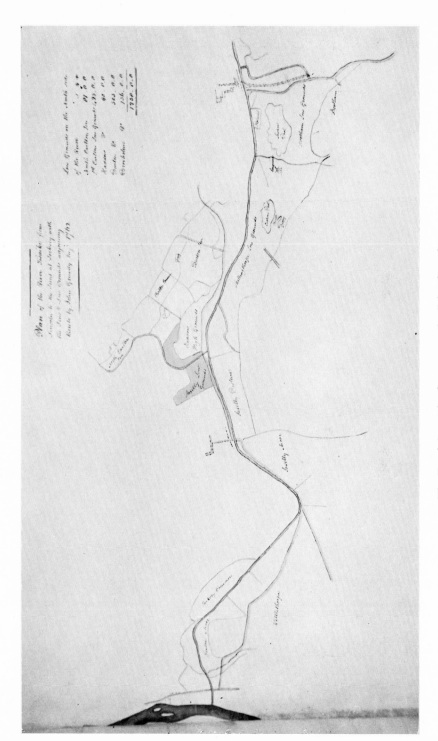

15   The Fossdyke, 1762, from a map by John Grundy

16 Sir John Monson, first Lord Monson, from a portrait by Sir Godfrey Kneller

17   Sir Richard Kaye, Dean of Lincoln

Colonel Coningsby Sibthorp. L.L.D.
Born 1706.
Died 1779.

18   Colonel Coningsby Sibthorp, from a portrait by Charpentier

19   Richard Ellison (died 1792)

20   Sir Joseph Banks, from a portrait by T. Phillips

APPENDIX I

CORN PRICES RETURNED BY LEET JURIES, 1722–1834 (PRICES IN SHILLINGS)

[Recorded in the Common Council Minutes.]

	Wheat Per strike	Rye	Barley	Oats	Beans	Peas
1722	Old 4 / New 3½	2½	2¼	Old 1½ / New 1¼	2½	—
1723	Old 26 / New 28	Old 16 / New 18	15⅔–16	9½–10	21–22	—
1724	28–30	20–23	18–20	8–8½	20–23	—
1725	34	24	16	10	14	—
1726	40	28	18	10	22	—
1727	45	36	24	13	20	—
1728	44	38	26	13	20	—
1729	24	18	16	11	24	—
1730	32	24	15	9	18	—
1731			No entry			
1732	20	16	12	9	16	—
1733			No entry			
1734	32	24	16	12	20 (horse beans)	—
1735	38	28	16	11	18 (horse beans)	—
1736	32	28	19	10	20	—
1737	26	20	20	12	24	—
1738	24	20	14	12	21	—
1739	30	21	16	10	18	—
1740	40	30	20	16	30	—
1741	28	20	16	14	—	New peas 25
1742	23	16	18	12	22	—
1743	20	14	12	10	16	—
1744	21	14	17	11	20	—
1745	32	21	14	11	21	—
1746	25	17	12	10	17	16
1747	22	16	12	9	17	—
1748	30	20	18	12	20	—
1749	27	20	17	13	24	—
1750	26	16	15	13	22	—
1751	32	21	18	14	24	—
1752	31	21	16	10½	23	—
1753	35	21	21	12	25	22
1754	29	20	17	14	24	20
1755	30	18	14	12	19	—
1756	40	30	20	13	24	—
1757	40	28	22	14	30	—
1758	34–36	22–24	16–18	12–14	20–22	—

	Wheat Per strike	Rye	Barley	Oats	Beans	Peas
1759	24–26	14–16	15–17	8–10	16–18	—
1760	23–24	16	15–15½	11–12	22–24	—
1761	20–23	16–18	11–13	9–11	—	15–16
1762	34–38	28–29	25–25½	13–16	28–30	—
1763	35–38	24–27	22–24	15–17	32	—
1764	44–50	30–34	23–24	11–13	28–30	—
1765	40–43	30–32	23–25	12–14	22–24	—
1766	40–47	30–34	21–24	14–16	New 22–24 Old beans 28–32	—
1767	44–48	30–32	26–27	13–15	Old 25–28	—
1768	40–42	26–28	18–20	12–14	24–25	—
1769	37–39	29–31	14–16	13–15	32–34	—
1770			No entry			
1771	50–52	38–40	26–28	14–15	30–32	—
1772	52–54	38–40	25–26	14–15	32–34	—
1773	50–52	30–32	28–30	15–17	20–22	—
1774	53–56	38–40	30–32	15–16	36	—
1775	40	32	25	15	28	—
1776	36–40	25–27	16–18	14–16	28–30	—
1777	40–42	28–30	19–20	12–14	30–32	—
1778	33	20	18½	12	24	24
1779	28–30	18–20	17–19	10–12	24–25	24–25
1780	30–33	20–23	15–17	10–13	20–22	—
1781	33–38	26–28	15–16	11–13	24–25	—
1782	50–54	30–36	28–30	12–14	—	—
1783	40–52	28–33	27–31	15–18	34–40	—
1784	46–50	32–34	24–28	15–18	28–32	—
1785	45–48	30–34	28–30	14–16	36–40	—
1786	38	28	21		40	—
1787	42–46	28–30	21–23	15–18	—	—
1788	38–42	24–26	20–22	16–18	—	—
1789	50–52	28–29	24–25	14–15	24–25	—
1790	48–50	30–32	24–26	18–20	30–32	—
1791	44	33	30	18	33	—
1792	48½	—	28½	17–18½	—	—
1793	40	—	38	18–22	—	—
1794	52	42	37	22	44	—
1795	80	45	33	24	50	—
1796	66	36	38	20	—	—
1797	63	32	31½	18	—	—
1798	46	32	31	18	32	—
1799	84	—	34	26	46	—
1800	103	63	70	31	—	—
1801	95	63	54	27	64	—
1802	65	28	35	18	33	—
1803	62	26	34	21	40	—
1804	65	32	36	23	—	—
1805	84	42	60	26	—	—
1806	76	45	48	23	47	44
1807	73	43	48	28	60	—
1808	90	44	60	32	70	60

	Wheat Per strike	Rye	Barley	Oats	Beans	Peas
1809	110	56	68	34	63	—
1810	—	—		—	—	—
1811	84	38	44	22	48	46
1812	103	66	80	43	—	—
1813	92	51	—	30	—	—
1814	80	40	—	22	—	—
1815	57	31	36	18	34	—
1816	76	37	34	25	40	—
1817	76	44	40	25	42	40
1818	86	67	65	35	80	80
1819	64	37	40	23	54	48
1820	63	33	40	24	44	42
1821	60	35	35	20	42	—
1822	46	26	21	18	27	24
1823	47	27	30	22	35	32
1824	58	40	30	20	40	36
1825	68	45	44	26	50	48
1826	57	40	46	29	54	50
1827	50	34	35	26	60	40
1828	73	40	36	26	46	44
1829	55	35	38	24	44	36
1830	68	38	38	25	42	40
1831	58	38	37	20	42	36
1832	54	35	34	21	40	33
1833	52	32	32	19	43	—
1834	40	31	31	22	40	36

APPENDIX II

FOSSDYKE NAVIGATION ACCOUNTS

The accounts for 1714–24 and 1732–7 are contained in L.A.O. Lincoln Corporation MSS, Birch's *Catalogue*, XII, and summarised in L.A.O., B.S. 12/3/1/3/78, 'Attorney General *v*. Ellison'. Those for 1746–1832 are in B.S. 12/3/1/3/149.

Shillings and pence have been omitted.

	Gross receipts (£)	Net receipts (£)
1714–15	101	77
1715–16	242	159
1716–17	141	59
1717–18	112	39
1718–19	91	40
1719–20	144	104
1720–1	162	33
1721–2	136	47
1722–3	63	−123
1723–4	110	61
1732–3	109	78
1733–4	66	31
1734–5	121	56
1735–6	136	53
1736–7	112	50

	Gross receipts (£)	Incidents and repairs (£)	City rent and salaries (£)	Net receipts (£)
1746	595	—	—	—
1747	432	—	—	—
1748	581	—	—	—
1749	572	—	—	—
1750	528	—	—	—
1751	779	—	—	—
1752	674	—	—	—
1753	636	—	—	—
1754	744	111	95	537
1755	932	92	95	744
1756	989	160	95	733
1757	1,086	1,007	95	—
1758	862	23	95	744
1759	944	12	95	836
1760	860	385	95	727
1761	999	104	95	799

	Gross receipts (£)	Incidents and repairs (£)	City rent and salaries (£)	Net receipts (£)
1762	937	32	95	810
1763	1,254	18	95	1,140
1764	1,370	232	95	1,043
1765	1,084	41	95	948
1766	1,323	68	95	1,159
1767	1,007	247	95	888
1768	1,367	45	95	1,226
1769	1,207	846	95	265
1770	1,122	110	95	917
1771	1,269	219	95	955
1772	1,441	186	95	1,159
1773	1,193	89	95	1,108
1774	1,499	66	105	1,327
1775	1,188	740	105	343
1776	1,481	171	105	1,204
1777	1,538	22	105	1,410
1778	1,438	44	105	1,289
1779	1,303	26	105	1,172
1780	1,656	64	105	1,487
1781	1,521	41	105	1,375
1782	1,675	54	105	1,515
1783	1,420	84	105	1,241
1784	1,885	41	105	1,738
1785	1,844	122	105	1,616
1786	1,963	59	105	1,798
1787	1,935	99	105	1,731
1788	1,707	50	105	1,542
1789	2,367	50	105	2,212
1790	1,911	90	105	1,715
1791	1,985	54	105	1,825
1792	2,197	83	105	2,009
1793	2,225	110	105	2,010
1794	1,523	117	22	1,383
1795	2,337	151	57	2,128
1796	2,200	90	123	1,987
1797	2,545	45	123	2,376
1798	2,372	87	123	2,161
1799	2,670	239	123	2,307
1800	2,756	788	123	1,845
1801	2,560	355	123	2,082
1802	2,739	332	123	2,283
1803	2,745	135	123	2,487
1804	3,830	193	123	3,513
1805	3,092	571	225	2,295
1806	4,121	444	225	3,451
1807	3,498	253	225	3,018
1808	4,158	312	233	3,612
1809	4,302	1,211	257	2,833
1810	4,718	223	257	4,237
1811	5,159	487	257	4,414

	Gross receipts (£)	Incidents and repairs (£)	City rent and salaries (£)	Net receipts (£)
1812	4,815	630	257	3,927
1813	5,527	367	257	4,902
1814	5,908	668	257	4,982
1815	4,615	1,551	307	2,756
1816	5,695	688	307	4,698
1817	5,701	257	307	5,136
1818	6,173	573	307	5,292
1819	5,494	2,055	307	3,132
1820	6,897	2,305	307	4,283
1821	5,655	522	311	4,831
1822	6,904	365	307	6,231
1823	7,424	1,127	332	5,964
1824	7,657	920	341	6,395
1825	8,624	837	335	7,451
1826	7,466	2,126	335	5,005
1827	7,308	3,613	335	3,359
1828	7,861	865	335	6,661
1829	7,657	626	335	6,696
1830	8,481	611	335	7,535
1831	7,588	738	347	6,502
1832	6,934	521	347	6,066

POPULATION STATISTICS

A. Returns of Population by Parishes.

B. Parish Register Entries. (1) Baptisms; (2) Burials; (3) Marriages.

For the returns of 1705 and 1721 see Cole, *Speculum Dioceseos Lincolniensis* (L.R.S.), pp. 80–3; and for the population returns of 1801–31, the census abstracts of those years. Parishes in the Bail and Close will be found under the Wapentake of Lawress in the Parts of Lindsey. The 'four towns' of Bracebridge, Branston, Canwick and Waddington were part of the county of the city of Lincoln until 1835, and their population was treated as belonging to the city.

Records of baptisms and burials in the parish registers, supplemented by the bishops' transcripts in L.A.O., are fairly complete. The marriage records are defective.

A. *Returns of Population by Parishes*

	1705 Families	1721 Families	1801 Families	1801 Persons	1811 Persons	1821 Persons	1831 Persons
St Benedict	60	69	115	547	550	628	654
St Botolph	26	50	87	354	455	585	614
St John	—	—	23	101	133	159	216
St Margaret	32	32	53	303	311	403	359
St Mark	30	24	61	262	322	430	450
St Martin	80	160	270	1,187	1,487	1,768	1,942
St Mary Magdalene	100	107	153	659	708	701	646
St Mary le Wigford	40	48	111	503	599	590	702
St Michael	25	80	107	468	509	716	843
St Nicholas	16	21	34	147	228	223	442
St Paul	30	60	85	316	387	423	447
St Peter at Arches	60	60	78	413	420	498	534
St Peter in Eastgate	26	42	95	336	343	333	404
St Peter at Gowts	60	60	95	413	481	549	661
St Swithin	150	168	236	940	1,553	1,869	2,202
Total	735	981	1,603	6,949	8,486	9,875	11,116
House of Industry (not included above)	—	—	—	248	113	120	101

B1. Baptisms

	1701–10	1711–20	1721–30	1731–40	1741–50	1751–60	1761–70	1771–80	1781–90	1791–1800	1801–10	1811–20	1821–30	Total
St Benedict	97	108	120	141	108	97	92	94	109	176	176	178	164	1,160
St Botolph	71	66	72	94	54	46	63	85	113	132	141	184	202	1,323
St John	4	3	11	21	17	57	39	54	36	41	40	68	78	469
St Margaret	67	57	72	48	47	48	47	60	46	46	49	34	35	656
St Mark	28	33	56	57	54	38	42	58	55	71	98	156	94	840
St Martin	244	265	292	355	319	305	354	350	363	431	400	527	556	4,761
St Mary Magdalene	146	132	182	167	162	142	117	109	127	136	169	146	146	1,881
St Mary le Wigford	79	62	55	93	62	82	110	165	172	178	175	145	146	1,524
St Michael	78	83	99	109	107	98	156	178	113	129	80	100	115	1,445
St Nicholas	—	19	22	31	29	52	46	37	55	64	67	72	93	587
St Paul	86	87	103	105	93	107	90	102	108	167	177	222	197	1,644
St Peter at Arches	126	134	137	112	95	91	83	102	104	94	99	134	127	1,438
St Peter in Eastgate	64	45	64	99	72	77	83	61	101	111	96	88	41	1,002
St Peter at Gowts	103	84	90	98	61	57	76	117	77	129	124	163	183	1,362
St Swithin	259	248	265	365	312	273	371	303	326	348	498	602	622	4,792
Total	1,452	1,426	1,640	1,895	1,592	1,570	1,769	1,875	1,905	2,253	2,389	2,819	2,799	25,384

B2. *Burials*

	1701–10	1711–20	1721–30	1731–40	1741–50	1751–60	1761–70	1771–80	1781–90	1791–1800	1801–10	1811–20	1821–30	Total
St Benedict	86	123	146	112	129	91	96	96	104	106	104	99	148	1,440
St Botolph	63	63	94	90	70	48	80	74	97	80	65	99	128	1,051
St John	—	—	—	—	10	5	4	13	—	—	2	—	—	34
St Margaret	79	56	65	66	49	41	57	53	26	22	27	27	28	596
St Mark	32	29	65	66	55	42	46	40	49	63	58	114	106	765
St Martin	267	298	315	346	299	257	229	341	328	302	340	316	324	3,962
St Mary Magdalene	122	128	166	184	178	149	137	149	116	96	109	99	116	1,749
St Mary le Wigford	91	81	85	92	80	78	86	92	127	135	115	108	139	1,309
St Michael	70	97	110	114	95	90	91	130	168	164	121	98	78	1,426
St Nicholas	—	19	53	58	34	49	75	69	68	79	93	82	117	796
St Paul	78	97	116	121	101	89	82	96	98	203	94	129	167	1,471
St Peter at Arches	134	131	141	106	89	85	103	98	94	81	100	71	101	1,334
St Peter in Eastgate	73	3	35	78	67	52	55	52	102	81	80	95	56	829
St Peter at Gowts	77	100	111	95	68	63	94	90	62	81	75	93	124	1,133
St Swithin	238	271	302	326	268	265	236	384	339	337	385	386	524	4,261
Total	1,410	1,496	1,804	1,854	1,592	1,404	1,471	1,777	1,778	1,830	1,768	1,816	2,156	22,156

B3. Marriages

	1701–10	1711–20	1721–30	1731–40	1741–50	1751–60	1761–70	1771–80	1781–90	1791–1800	1801–10	1811–20	1821–30	Total
St Benedict[1]	22	26	37	26	22	3	—	—	—	—	—	14	50	100
St Botolph	1	—	28	39	33	39	60	70	59	71	72	77	72	621
St John[2]	—	—	—	—	—	1	—	—	—	—	—	—	—	1
St Margaret[3]	199	87	169	208	165	8	—	—	—	—	—	—	10	846
St Mark[4]	22	16	10	23	15	7	—	—	—	—	—	—	4	97
St Martin	120	84	117	95	71	188	169	241	208	182	184	142	146	1,947
St Mary Magdalene	21	32	73	79	73	81	136	136	134	54	85	41	35	980
St Mary le Wigford	22	16	37	40	40	47	114	109	111	79	142	81	79	917
St Michael[5]	—	—	—	—	14	—	—	—	—	—	—	69	47	130
St Nicholas[6]	—	4	—	—	5	—	—	—	—	—	—	—	—	9
St Paul[7]	94	122	138	98	98	46	—	—	—	30	28	29	36	719
St Peter at Arches	34	31	39	41	47	59	91	114	137	145	43	52	34	967
St Peter in Eastgate[8]	—	—	—	—	3	—	—	48	79	43	106	54	26	359
St Peter at Gowts[9]	11	19	13	18	17	—	—	—	—	—	—	—	34	112
St Swithin[10]	37	66	102	96	49	—	—	—	—	—	132	171	164	817
Total	583	503	763	763	652	479	570	718	728	604	792	730	737	8,622

NOTES

1. St Benedict. None recorded between 1752 and 1819.
2. St John. Only one marriage recorded for the period.
3. St Margaret. No marriage register has survived for the period 1754–c.1820.
4. St Mark. No marriage register has survived for the period 1754–c.1820.
5. St Michael. Only fourteen marriages recorded between 1701 and 1750, and these are in the decade 1741–50.
6. St Nicholas. Only nine marriages recorded during the period 1701–1830.
7. St Paul. No marriage register has survived for the period 1754–90.
8. St Peter in Eastgate. No marriages recorded in registers 1683–1747; then only four until the decade 1771–80.
9. St Peter at Gowts. No marriage registers have survived for the period 1754–1826.
10. St Swithin. There were no marriages in this church 1754–1803; they were celebrated at St Peter at Arches.

APPENDIX IV

Abstract of Instructions for executing the Office of Town Clerk of the City of Lincoln beginning with Holyrood Day.

September

On the 14th September, being Holyrood Day, the new Mayor and Sheriffs are elected and sworn.

In the interval between the 14th September and the 29th the goalers' and bailiffs' bonds are engrossed, after first receiving from each of them the names of their sureties.

On the 29th September, being Michaelmas Day, the Mayor and Sheriffs enter upon the execution of their offices, the Mayor first undergoing the ceremony of his investiture.

September or October

As soon after Michaelmas as is possible the goalers' and bailiffs' bonds are executed, and if there are any prisoners in the goal an assignment is made of them from the old Sheriffs to the new.

On the Monday next after Michaelmas Day a general Court Leet is held, when the four Chamberlains enter upon the execution of their offices and other business is transacted.

After the Court Leet a new list of the Common Council is made out.

At or about the same time warrants are issued for holding a special Sessions in the week after the general Quarter Sessions for appointing Surveyors of the Highways.

About the same time a Rental called the old Mayor's Quit Rent Bill is made out and delivered.

October

On the Saturday in the week next after the week in which Michaelmas Day happens to fall the first general Quarter Sessions is held.

In the week after the general Quarter Sessions a special Sessions is held before two Justices for appointment of Surveyors of the Highways, agreeable to the warrants issued for that purpose.

About this time the Mayor is sworn in Master of Christs Hospital,[1] and generally on the Saturday after the general Quarter Sessions, but always within a month after Michaelmas Day a Court Leet is held at Potterhanworth.

In the month of October estreats of all fines &c. imposed at the four several Quarter Sessions of the Peace held previous to Michaelmas Day are to be made out, and a Commission must be issued to swear the Clerk of the Peace to the truth of them.

October or November

At the latter end of October or very early in November the Chamberlains' Rentals are made out and delivered.

November and December

In the month of November an adjourned Quarter Sessions is held for administering the oaths to the new Mayor Sheriffs and Chamberlains.

About this time or at all events before Hilary Term the Crown Processes must be

---

[1] The Mayor was Master of Christ's Hospital, or Bluecoat School, whose principal endowment was the manor of Potterhanworth.

returned and delivered over, with proper instructions to the County Under-sheriff in order that he may be apposed thereon and pass their final account.

In the latter end of November or beginning of December preparation must be made for passing the old Mayor's Accounts, and in order thereto the Low Layton account must be made out and settled.[1] And about the middle of December his accounts are passed accordingly, vizt. for the poor on the Saturday and the general account on the Tuesday before St Thomas.

January

On the Saturday in the week next after the week in which the Epiphany happens to fall the second Quarter Sessions is held.

February or March

Preparatory to the general Assizes and about three weeks or a month before the day a panel must be made out of a Nisi Prius Jury and sent up to the Agent.

March

The Assizes will be appointed in this month and precepts delivered for returning jurys &c. which must be returned accordingly. A balloting box must be in readiness, and if there are any causes, panels of the Nisi Prius jury must be ingrossed upon parchment to annex to the returns of any writs of Habeas Corpora &c.

The Michaelmas Court Leet is generally adjourned to some day in this month and then held for receiving the jurys presentments.

March or April

On the Saturday in Easter week a special Sessions is held before two justices for granting licences to the publicans, previous to which a sufficient number of printed licences and recognizances must be got and filled up.

On the Monday after Easter week another Court Leet is held and adjourned over.

On the Saturday after Easter week the third Quarter Sessions is held.

April

Towards the latter end of April the first meeting is held for the affairs of taxes, when the commissioners qualify. Then warrants are issued for bringing in the names of assessors. Then warrants with abstracts annexed are issued for returning assessments; which being brought in, other warrants are issued for appointing collectors and appeal days. The appeal day for the Land Tax is generally the latter end of June or beginning of July. The first appeal day for the Window (tax) is between the (   ) August and (   ) September and the second between the (   ) January and (   ) February in the following year.

April or May

In Easter or Trinity term the County Under-sheriff goes to London to be apposed upon the Crown Processes; previous to which the City Processes must be returned and a Deputation obtained from the City Sheriffs empowering the County Under-sheriff to be apposed thereon.

May and June

Meetings will be held in these months for the affairs of taxes.

[1] John Smith of London, merchant, by will dated 20 October 1653, devised property at Low Layton in Essex, and at Braytoft and Algarkirk in Lincolnshire, for the benefit of the poor of specified parishes in Lincoln.

July

Early in July, vizt. on Saturday in the week next after the week in which the feast of St John the Baptist happens to fall the fourth Quarter Sessions is held.

When an order is made at any of the four sessions for a County Rate warrants are immediately issued for collecting it.

August

The adjourned Court Leet is held for receiving the Jurys Presentments and these are immediately afterwards affeered and copied into two books with the Steward's warrant annexed to each book for collecting them.

September

Very early in September the Hospital accounts are made out and fairly copied, and on the 12th of this month the general yearly audit is held. Other meetings are held as occasion requires.

N.B. The above is the regular stated duty of the Town Clerk, set down in the order in which it arrives. But there are many other casual businesses which must be attended to besides, vizt., common councils, apprentice indentures, inrollments and infranchisements, entering the latter upon stamps, making out examinations, warrants, orders, proceedings in the Foreign Court and Court of Requests, &c. &c.

INDEX

Hobart, Rev. H. L., 297 n.
  Robert, Lord Hobart, fourth earl of
    Buckinghamshire, 96–9, 218, 220–
    1 n., 224, 276
Holkham, co. Norfolk, 120–1
Holland, Edward, 72
Holton Beckering, co. Lincs, 105
Holton le Moor, co. Lincs, 182
Hood, Lord, 32
Hooke, Mr, Minister of Haxey, 25
Hooton, John, 72
Horncastle, co. Lincs, 23, 27 n., 98, 122 n.,
    161, 168, 198
  Navigation, 134–6, 137, 200
Horse racing, 17, 54, 250, 286
Hospital, County, 70–1, 171, 210, 277,
    281
  Lawn (formerly Lincoln Lunatic
    Asylum), 278, 291
Howard, John, 20–1, 187, 247
Hull, 84, 117, 122 n., 137, 139, 197–8
Hull Banking Company, 204–5
Humber, 51, 117, 126
  Ferry at Barton, 139
Humberston, James, 128
Hume, Joseph, 255
Hunnings, Butter, 187
Hunt, Leigh, 229 n.
Huntingdon, countess of, 69
Hussey, Rebecca, 20 n.
  Sir Thomas, 18
Hutton family, 182
  Henry, 57, 276
    his wife Judith, 57
  Thomas, 182
Hykeham, North and South, co. Lincs,
    52

Inclosures of land, 112, 113, 174–5,
    181
Independents, 68, 287, 294–6
India Bill, Fox's, 32–3
Indulgence, Declaration of, 66, 68
Industry, House of, 183–7, 192, 206–9, 213,
    247
Ingelows of Boston, bankers, 191
Ingham, co. Lincs, 297 n.
Ingilby, Sir William Amcotts, 197 n.,
    229 n., 230, 235, 254, 287, 293,
    294
Ireland, labourers from, 170, 178, 190,
    192–3
  wool imports from, 192

Jacobites, 24 n., 25–7, 66
  rebellion of 1715, 23, 76
  rebellion of 1745, 5, 29, 83–5
James, John, 38, 40
Jepson, Fanny, 268
Jersey School, 158–61, 249
Jessop, William, 134–5
Jewett, Mr, 291
Jews Bill, 88
Johnson, Dr Samuel, 24, 45 n.
  William, 158–9

Kaye, John, bishop of Lincoln, 300–1
  Sir Richard, dean of Lincoln, 46, 47, 50,
    71, 160, 270–1
Kelsey (*rectius* Kelsall) Edward, vicar of
    Boston, 23
Kent, Rev. George Davies, 296–7
  aldermen, 96
  George, mayor, 40
Kenyon, Lord, 295
Kettlethorpe, co. Lincs, 77, 259
Keyworth family, 203
  John, 203
  Thomas Michael, 204
Kilnwick, co. Yorks, 107 n.
King's Lynn, 117, 142, 241 n.
Kingston, duke of, his estates, 104
Kirkstead, co. Lincs, 69
Kirton in Holland, co. Lincs, 25
  in Lindsey, co. Lincs, 104
Knaith, co. Lincs, 111, 180, 190–1, 262
Knight, Rev. Mr, priest, 67
Knight, John, 61
Kyme, South, co. Lincs, 102

Lamb, Charles (quoted), 56
  John, 65 n.
Lancashire, 203, 209
Lancaster, duchy of, 3, 260
Land bank proposed, 204
Langhorne, Rev. John, 7 n.
Langton, Bennet, 45
Langton by Spilsby, co. Lincs, 45 n.
Langworth, co. Lincs, 61 n., 104, 122
Laud, William, archbishop of Canterbury,
    47
Laycock, Rev. Tillotson, 297 n.
Lea, Co. Lincs, 26, 259
Leadenham, co. Lincs, 124 n.
Leary, printer, 293
Le Despenser, *see* Dashwood
Leeds, 101, 108, 119, 128, 134